PENGUIN BOOKS

MYTHS, ILLUSIONS, AND PEACE

Dennis Ross advised Barack Obama on the Middle East during the 2008 presidential campaign and is now a top State Department official handling the region that includes Iran and Iraq. Ross served as the chief peace negotiator for the Israeli-Palestinian conflict under presidents George H. W. Bush and Bill Clinton, and he is the author of the bestselling book *The Missing Peace*. Analyst and former journalist David Makovsky is a fellow at the Washington Institute for Near East Policy and an adjunct lecturer at Johns Hopkins University. He is the author of *Making Peace with the PLO*. The authors live in the Washington, D.C., area.

MYTHS, ILLUSIONS, and PEACE

Finding a New Direction for America in the Middle East

Dennis Ross

and

David Makovsky

PENGUIN BOOKS

PENGUIN BOOKS

Published by the Penguin Group
Penguin Group (USA) Inc., 375 Hudson Street, New York, New York 10014, U.S.A.
Penguin Group (Canada), 90 Eglinton Avenue East, Suite 700, Toronto,
Ontario, Canada M4P 2Y3 (a division of Pearson Penguin Canada Inc.)
Penguin Books Ltd, 80 Strand, London WC2R 0RL, England
Penguin Ireland, 25 St Stephen's Green, Dublin 2, Ireland (a division of Penguin Books Ltd)
Penguin Group (Australia), 250 Camberwell Road, Camberwell,
Victoria 3124, Australia (a division of Pearson Australia Group Pty Ltd)
Penguin Books India Pvt Ltd, 11 Community Centre, Panchsheel Park, New Delhi – 110 017, India
Penguin Group (NZ), 67 Apollo Drive, Rosedale, North Shore 0632,
New Zealand (a division of Pearson New Zealand Ltd)
Penguin Books (South Africa) (Pty) Ltd, 24 Sturdee Avenue,
Rosebank, Johannesburg 2196, South Africa

Penguin Books Ltd, Registered Offices:
80 Strand, London WC2R 0RL, England

First published in the United States of America by Viking Penguin,
a member of Penguin Group (USA) Inc. 2009
This edition with a new afterword published in Penguin Books 2010

1 3 5 7 9 10 8 6 4 2

THE LIBRARY OF CONGRESS HAS CATALOGED THE HARDCOVER EDITION AS FOLLOWS:
Ross, Dennis.
Myths, illusions, and peace : finding a new direction for America
in the Middle East / Dennis Ross and David Makovsky.
p.   cm.
Includes bibliographical references and index.
ISBN 978-0-670-02089-8 (hc.)
ISBN 978-0-14-311769-8 (pbk.)
1. United States—Foreign relations—Middle East.   2. Middle East—Foreign relations—
United States.   I. Makovsky, David.   II. Title.
DS63.2.U5R66 2009
327.73056—dc22   2008055899

Printed in the United States of America
Set in Dante MT Std
Designed by Daniel Lagin

For Debbie, Gabe, Rachel, and Ilana
Dennis Ross

For Varda, Jonathan, Joshua, and Elliana
David Makovsky

Contents

Preface

There can be little doubt that America's standing in the world declined dramatically during the administration of George W. Bush. Questions about its national security policy in general, and particularly about its approach to the Middle East, became commonplace. While there was much to criticize and to question about Bush policies in the Middle East—and the two of us were deeply troubled by the administration's tendency to disengage and to miss possible opportunities—we also came to be increasingly troubled by how some of the president's critics perceived and portrayed the region. The tendency to fly metaphorically at fifty thousand feet and to miss the complexities of the region was, unfortunately, not limited to the Bush administration. Too many of its critics, especially on the Middle East, offered an equally simplistic view of the region, and those views would have produced similarly misguided policies—even if they proceeded from a different starting place.

If disengagement outside of Iraq tended to guide the administration and its neoconservative ideological base, engagement with little thought has often guided its critics—critics who see and often describe themselves as realists. But is it realistic to engage diplomatically with groups like Hamas if it means we undercut Palestinians who believe in coexistence and a secular future for their people? We doubt it, and yet so-called realists advocate such an approach. What would be the consequence of following their advice? We would lose moderate, secular Palestinians, we would elevate Islamists throughout the region, and we would undercut any possibility of achieving peace between Israel and its neighbors. Much as with the mistaken Bush administration policies in the Middle East, we would pay a steep price and prove once again how ineffectual we are in the region.

More simple-minded policies are not what America needs in the Middle East today. On the contrary, it is time to base policy toward the Middle East on the complex realities that America confronts there. For too long, ideological blinders or theoretical views of the region have guided those who shaped and made U.S. policy. It is time that changed. And that is why we decided to write a book that explores the myths and the illusions that too often have driven American approaches to the region. We are not content only with exposing why certain key assumptions have been wrong and have produced mistaken policies. We want to outline and explain the key assumptions that ought to be driving what America does and how it does it in the region.

If the Middle East did not matter, we could be more cavalier in looking at wrong-headed assumptions about it. But with American interests and well-being increasingly riveted on what happens in the Middle East, we no longer have that luxury. With 9/11, we learned the hard way that the Las Vegas rule doesn't apply to the Middle East: what happens there does not stay there. Pathologies in the Middle East will not remain isolated. They can and will affect us and our security. Whether we are dealing with an ascendant Iran determined to pursue nuclear weapons, or Islamists who seek greater leverage in the region and beyond, or trying to see whether peace between Arabs and Israelis remains in the cards, we had better understand what is possible and which choices and options provide us the best possible leverage to change the behaviors of those whose behavior must be changed.

And that, ultimately, is what we set out to do in this book. We are not just seeking to debunk mythologies. We are trying to explain the path we ought to be taking in the Middle East while also illuminating the core set of principles and assumptions that should underpin that path.

Why might the two of us be well suited to providing a new guide to the Middle East?

We bring over twenty-five years of observation, questioning, and acting in the area. We have confronted the realities of the region not theoretically but practically. Dennis has dealt with the leaders of the Middle East and officials (and relevant nonofficials, including reformers and dissidents) in intensive periods leading to war and during efforts to make peace. He helped in the formation of the Gulf War coalition in 1990–91 and also was an architect of the Madrid conference launching Arab-Israeli negotiations after the conflict. He subsequently served as the Clinton administration's point person and lead negotiator on the Arab-Israeli conflict, playing a role in every track of the negotiations (Israeli-Palestinian, Israeli-Syrian, and Israeli-Jordanian) and brokering several agreements that emerged even as he also endured failed summits at Geneva and Camp David.

David has been a journalist for American and Israeli publications. As a journalist, he did not just cover stories in the region; he actively interviewed leaders and those in and outside political circles. He observed the Middle East from the ground up and saw the interplay of the different forces—social, economic, and political—that shape the dynamics of the region.

We joined forces at the Washington Institute for Near East Policy as colleagues since 2001, often visiting the Middle East together. We continue dealing with the region from the top down in terms of talking to leaders, but also from the bottom up as we work with NGOs and others in the area.

Our perspective is grounded in the region. While we may both look for larger trends, we understand that U.S. policy toward the Middle East cannot be shaped by abstractions. Those who seek to impose grand theories on this part of the world—whether of the right or the left—miss the context from which policy must emerge. We will offer what amounts to a centrist view of what to do in the Middle East. Unlike the Bush administration, we favor active diplomatic engagement. We understand the importance of power in an area characterized by conflict and coercion. But just as the military option should never be taken off the table, neither should the diplomatic tool of statecraft ever be dismissed. Similarly, unlike many of the Bush administration's critics—those who portray themselves as realists but who seem to reflect little understanding of Middle East reality—we don't favor indiscriminate engagement with any and all actors, including nonstate actors such as Hamas and Hizbollah.

Our mantra, which will come through in the following pages, is *engagement without illusion*. We must pursue peace without illusion while understanding the difficulty of achieving it but recognizing the consequences of not making the effort. We must compete with the radical Islamists by using force where necessary while realizing that only other Muslims will discredit the radicals and that any strategy for competition must rely on social, economic, political, and diplomatic tools. Engagement cannot be a panacea for peace or for preventing Iran from going nuclear, but it creates possibilities for success and produces a context for tougher policies should it fail.

In the end, we offer a guide for a new realism—one shaped by understanding the factors that actually govern behavior in the region; one guided by always understanding the context in which our policy must proceed; and one inspired by the need to preserve hope and possibility in a region too often characterized by neither.

Chapter One

INTRODUCTION AND OVERVIEW

Why write a book about myths in the Middle East? Mythologies in the Middle East are not new. Past American presidents have often thought they could reshape the region, believing that our preoccupations and fears were shared by those in the area.

President Eisenhower thought that Arab leaders shared the fear of godless Communism, and he assumed they would join us in containing the Soviet threat and creating an anti-Soviet alliance in the Middle East. But Eisenhower failed to realize that internal rivalries and the conflict with Israel mattered more to Arab leaders, and his policies were costly and ineffectual as a result.

President Kennedy had a better grasp of emerging realities in the developing world, realizing that in much of the "third world," leaders tended to be driven by nationalism and were not about to submerge their goals to a United States–led anticommunist crusade. But his administration, too, somehow believed that it could identify with the needs of the nonaligned and wean a nationalist leader like Gamal Abdel Nasser of Egypt away from the Soviet Union without his seeking to play us off against the Soviets for Egypt's (really his own) benefit.

For its part, the Johnson administration badly misread the events leading to the 1967 war by failing to understand Nasser's need for a victory and what it would take to prevent him from expelling the United Nations Emergency Forces from the Sinai desert.

Similarly, the Nixon administration was very slow to pick up on the significance of Anwar Sadat's expulsion of the Soviet military from Egypt in 1972. Had his administration understood and responded, there might not have been the 1973 war, which cost the Israelis dearly and risked a superpower confrontation, with the Soviets reportedly moving nuclear weapons toward the Suez Canal. However, for the Nixon administration at the time, habits and perceptions of Middle Eastern reality were shaped by the belief that Sadat could not be very different from Nasser.

Even the Carter administration was slow and grudging in its initial response to Sadat's announcement of his readiness to go to Jerusalem and address the Israeli Knesset. The president and his advisers had a fixed image of the Middle East and were convinced that only a comprehensive approach to peace could work. Sadat seemed to be spoiling their plans and undermining the logic of an approach in which all the Arab states and the Soviet Union would go to Geneva to launch a peace conference. They failed to see that for Sadat, this meant creating a lowest common denominator path in which Syria had a veto over what Egypt could do; indeed, that Syrian rejectionism could prevent Egypt from recovering the Sinai desert. President Carter and his advisers were operating on fixed assumptions of how the Middle East worked and couldn't believe, therefore, that Sadat would actually go his own way, separate himself from the weight of the Arab consensus, and produce something meaningful. They failed to see that he could transform the landscape of the region by staking out a separate posture. Somehow they were so locked in to the myth of Arab unity that they could not, at least initially, grasp that Egypt, the largest Arab state, could break through the isolation of Israel and crack the taboo on dealing with it—and that this would produce an electric reaction within Israel and create a historic moment for peacemaking in the Middle East. Fortunately, Walter Cronkite and the other leaders of the American media at the time saw the essence of the moment and rushed to cover it, bringing along the Carter administration in their wake.

In all these cases, and others, a basic misreading of the region misled and produced misguided policies. Assumptions about the region were typically wrong and cost us. In the past, we certainly paid a price for not understanding the region. But today the potential costs of being wrong are far higher.

Historically, the Middle East has not been central to our national security concerns. True, ensuring that no hostile power gained control or leverage over oil's free flow may have been a vital interest, but we still tended to look at the area through a certain prism: once the Cold War began, our main preoccupation was the Soviet Union. All concerns were derivative of the conflict with the Soviets.

We might have paid a price for mistaken assumptions about the region, but the price, like the region itself, was secondary. Developments in the region mattered in the first instance because of how they might affect the competition with the Soviets. The Soviets could not be allowed to gain leverage over the oil supply or improve their position in a geo-strategically significant crossroads like the Middle East. The USSR posed an existential threat to the United States. But the Soviet Union no longer exists, and the threats that preoccupy us today are centered in the Middle East.

Today, the greater Middle East is the locus of our main national security concerns. In fact, while the free flow of oil remains important to us and others internationally, we have an array of other preoccupations and dangers that drive our foreign policy and that will confront President Obama—and they are nearly all in the Middle East: the war in Iraq; the growing threat of revolutionary Iran and the danger of its possessing nuclear weapons; the increased risk of proliferation generally, and the danger of the worst weapons falling into the worst hands; the emergence of apocalyptic terror groups and the radical Islamist ideology that drives them; the Arab-Israeli conflict; and the widespread hostility toward the United States that is far more acute in the Middle East than anywhere else.

There is no doubt that the preeminent threat of our time is that radical Islamists—most of whom emanate from the Middle East—may get their hands on a nuclear weapon. All agree about the cataclysmic nature of nuclear weapons. During the Cold War, there was a sense that both the United States and Soviet Union made similar calculations about not using such weapons, and therefore deterrence was successful. Yet it remains unlikely that Islamist religious extremists who embrace suicide bombing are deterrable. They may look at the use of such weapons as a means to reach some form of religious imperative against others, critical to achieve what they consider the legitimate objective of creating an Islamist caliphate or faciliating the return of the Hidden Imam (more on this later) while securing their own benefits in another world. It is precisely the ascendance of such a school of thought that should lead us to oppose the Islamists, even as we seek to partner with those non-Islamist forces in Arab societies who are uniquely positioned to discredit them in a way that we are not. This obviously does not mean taking force off the table to deal with such threats, but we are better positioned to use force if we are seen as having first exhausted all other options.

What makes this Islamist threat so severe is that it is not limited to states, which may be more prone to accept the rules of deterrence. The international system has traditionally been based on states, but the power of nonstate actors such as al-Qaeda is profound, whether it is to acquire weapons or to launch wars. Of course, fighting jihadi terrorism is a given that should be sustained, but it may not be enough to deal with this threat. This is a brand-new challenge that affects American interests on proliferation, potentially destabilizes Arab regimes inside the region that many Islamist groups view as heretical, threatens Israel, and even endangers countries with high Muslim populations as far away as India.

To be sure, the Obama administration will have to address other foreign policy challenges. However, even many of these connect in one way or another to the Middle East. The rise of China will be a major challenge, but China's energy needs will give it far greater interests in the Middle East than ever before. Will China be a help or a hindrance in coping with or trying to counter some of the main threats in the area? Getting North Korea to fulfill its promise to denuclearize certainly has value in its own right, but perhaps the main reason for being concerned about its nuclear developments is that the DPRK has never developed a weapons system that it has not sold, and its main customers are in the Middle East. (The fact that North Korea was helping Syria to build a nuclear reactor—which Israel preemptively bombed—is a not-so-subtle reminder of our stake in getting the DPRK to give up its nuclear weapons program.) Even on climate change, likely to be an overriding priority for President Obama, there will be an important connection to what happens in the Middle East. Not only are Middle Eastern countries among the worst offenders of energy usage and inefficiency, and likely to become much bigger consumers of energy and emitters of greenhouse gases as their economies grow, but oil producers could play a major role in affecting pricing policies that determine whether energy alternatives to oil become financially viable. Should, for example, the main oil producers fear that alternatives to oil will become more attractive, they could choose, at a certain point, to produce more in order to reduce the price and prolong our dependency on their oil. (With the global recession and reduced demand as a result, the price of oil has declined, and the incentive to create alternatives to fossil fuels may unfortunately also diminish.)

No matter how one slices it, what goes on in the Middle East will be of profound importance to our national security and our well-being. More than ever before, it is important for us to understand the Middle East as it is. Mythologies that mislead us will result in costly mistakes with lasting legacies. We need look no further than Iraq to see how costly such misguided policies can be.

In no small part because of its basic misreading of the area, the Bush administration committed many mistakes. It wrongly thought that our military power could be used to create a new reality there that others would simply accept. To be fair, it is unlikely that the Bush administration would have invaded Iraq unless it had genuinely believed at that time that Saddam Hussein possessed weapons of mass destruction. Others have dissected that war and its aftermath; that is not our purpose here. What is relevant for our purposes is how the Bush administration envisioned the regional consequences of its action: it thought regime change in Iraq would transform the region. It thought we could set in motion, much like a falling row of dominoes, the creation of a new Middle East. Replace a totalitarian despot like Saddam Hussein in the heart of the area, and the true democrats would be free to emerge—or so President Bush and his chief advisers assumed.

They were convinced that forced regime change, not diplomacy designed to produce changed regime behavior, would transform the Middle East and reduce the threat of terror. They were similarly convinced that democracy could be the natural order of the region, and that sectarian or tribal differences counted for very little. As an article of faith, they thought elections would be self-correcting mechanisms, and it rarely occurred to them that elections might actually empower antidemocratic Islamists. Such an eventuality was inconceivable to an administration that was consumed by its own mythologies about democracy promotion, and its belief that those in the Middle East would inevitably share our view of it and accept (or simply adjust to) our way of producing it.

No doubt the Obama administration will reject many of the assumptions that guided President Bush and those around him. But the appropriate response to the mistakes of the Bush administration is not an opposite view that is equally flawed and equally simplistic.

If the myth of Bush and the neoconservatives was to believe in our capacity to impose our form of democracy and our image of what the region should be, the myth of many on the left and self-described "realists" like Zbigniew Brzezinski may be that we can impose peace between Israelis and Palestinians and transform the Middle East in the process.

Yet in seeking to advance their political philosophies, neither neoconservatives nor self-described realists have rooted their views in Middle East regional realities. By imposing their respective templates, they obscure reality, and in so doing, they often create unrealistic policies for the United States. Just as Bush and the right dismissed the profound differences in identity—sectarian and tribal—so those on the left also tend to dismiss ideological opposition to Israel's existence. Yet this cannot be wished away, because it is real. The main opponents of Arab-Israeli peace (primarily the Islamists) reject it not for tactical reversible reasons but because their belief systems and ethos and self-definition see peace with Israel as a negation of who they are. These opponents must be overcome or discredited from within, and those in the region who favor or believe in peace must be prepared to fight for it and not continue to be passive or so easily put on the defensive. For that reason, peace, like democracy, must grow and be nurtured from within; it cannot be imposed from without.

We are not arguing here that it is impossible to change or transform the region; we are saying that it is a dangerous illusion to try to do so or to believe that the United States can fashion policy toward the Middle East without taking account of the complex realities of the region.

The mythologies of the right and the left have one thing in common: though coming from opposite sides of the spectrum of belief, they each endorse the primacy of U.S. action while ignoring the basic need for local responsibility and local investment psychologically and politically. Without recognizing or acknowledging it, both the right and the left have assumed that outsiders—in this case the United States and those who join with us—have the capacity to do for the locals what they are unwilling to do for themselves.

For the neoconservatives, America would rid the region of Saddam Hussein, and everything would fall into place. We would defeat Hussein and the Ba'athists; this would serve as an object lesson for the Iranians and others who back terror, reject democracy, and threaten U.S. interests.

The Iranians and the Islamists would be intimidated, and the natural democrats in the area would be emboldened. Elections could then be engineered, and the democrats would emerge naturally, without need for institutions or a culture of tolerance and accountability. From this viewpoint, it is not important or necessary to develop pathways for overcoming sectarian animosities and distrust, or to build bridges toward forging national identities.

On the other hand, listen to the left or some of the self-declared realists, and their main proponents will say that peace is too hard for Israelis and Palestinians to make on their own; the concessions that are required for peacemaking are too difficult politically for them, so America needs to do it for them and simply impose peace. Since the mainstreams want it, once peace is imposed, it will be sustainable. But what about the opponents of peace? Will they simply melt away? And if the local parties haven't conditioned their publics for peace and invested in it, will they have the stake or commitment to take on those who will resist it—or will they continue to expect us to do for them what they have not been willing to do for themselves?

The Bush administration too often erred by seeing the world as it wanted it to be. Too often faith-based or ideologically driven assessments guided its objectives and its policies. Yet the corrective to the Bush administration's failures should not be ideologically driven policies from a different starting point. We need reality-based assessments; we need to see the Middle East as it is, warts and all. Our stakes in making this a region that does not threaten our well-being have never been higher.

That is why we have written a book designed to identify the key myths about the region on both sides of the political spectrum. We aim to debunk them not for the sake of criticism but for the sake of fostering a corrective. This book offers a set of assumptions that present a more accurate picture of the region so that policymakers will shape an approach to the Middle East that responds to reality, not mythology.

One point worth noting at the very outset is that Arabs, Israelis, and Iranians have developed their own mythologies about one another and the United States. Each sees the others—and America—through a particular lens of history and experience. Those mythologies have taken on a life of their own and certainly shape the perceptions of all the parties. Arabs and

Israelis, in particular, tend to believe the worst about each other, and each suspects the United States of being driven by its concerns about its relations with the other side. The Arabs generally are convinced that the Israeli lobby drives U.S. behavior—why else, they ask, wouldn't America follow its "real" interests and respond to what the Arabs want in terms of "international legitimacy" and "justice"?

Similarly, Israelis worry that the United States at some point will seek to accommodate the Arabs—given oil interests—at Israel's expense. Even during the Bush administration, which seemed aware of Israel's concerns, Israeli leaders from Ariel Sharon to Ehud Olmert worried whether after 9/11 or in the efforts to counter Iran's nuclear program, Israel's interests would be sacrificed to bring Arabs and Europeans into a broader coalition.

These mythologies often find their echoes in the perspectives of those who debate Middle East policy in this country. Too often the debates here provide more heat than light. Too rarely are the real assumptions that lie behind the differing positions revealed, considered, and validated—or invalidated. That is what we seek to do. We look at some of the core assumptions that have led to what we call mythologies.

We use the term "myths" because these assumptions don't reflect reality but are taken as givens. They may be untrue or invalid, but for those who embrace them, they are unquestioned. We take a closer look at these myths, exploring their roots and explaining why they fail to fit the reality of the Middle East. In the course of doing so, we offer a truer picture of what drives behaviors in the Middle East and what should drive our policies. We don't just distill our interests; we present the dos and don'ts of how best to pursue them.

Ultimately, our aim is to crystallize the essential assumptions that should guide America in the Middle East. These assumptions will emerge from our discussion of the myths and the appropriate answers to them.

We have divided the book into three sections. In the first, we deal with the core mythology of "linkage." In essence, every issue or conflict in the Middle East has been seen as "linked" to the Israeli-Palestinian conflict; solve it, and every other conflict will be resolved or transformed. No myth has been more enduring. It certainly reflects a "realist" mind-set, and yet it acquired such legitimacy that in many ways it became a template for understanding the region. We discuss why it emerged and why Arab leaders had an incentive to promote it externally and internally. We then explore how it affected the behavior of different American administrations dating back to Franklin Delano Roosevelt's. We also, of course, explain why it is so misleading and so important to debunk. But debunking linkage does not mean foregoing a pursuit of Arab-Israeli peace and the resolution of the Palestinian conflict. A discussion of the mythologies about how best to deal (or not deal) with the Arab-Israeli conflict, and our view of the right path, fills out the remainder of section one.

The second part of the book deals with mythologies related to the larger themes of engagement versus nonengagement and regime change versus the change of regime behavior. Our major focus in this section is on Iran. The challenge of Iran looms as one of the most formidable ones the Obama administration will face. Iran is competing with the United States throughout the Middle East—from Iraq, to Lebanon, to the Israeli-Palestinian arena. In every instance, Iran is trying to build its leverage and influence and undermine the existing political order—often using militias that are also political movements, such as Hizbollah, Hamas, and the Mahdi Army. Its acquisition of nuclear weapons would be certain to add to its coercive capability and transform the Middle East as we know it—not to mention the effect it could have on nuclear nonproliferation internationally. No one questions that the stakes involved in affecting Iranian behavior, particularly on the nuclear issue, are extremely high. But not surprisingly, the self-described realists and the neoconservatives take very different positions on what to do about Iran and the threat it poses.

To be a realist ought to be a good thing, but as we will see, today's self-described realists are anything but realistic. In international relations, the school of realism is defined principally by a core set of beliefs:

- states are guided by tangible interests and by the desire for power;
- values and ideology are more artificial than real, designed principally as devices to justify the pursuit of power;
- balance-of-power principles shape how states interact—if a state confronts others with comparable or greater power, it will retreat.

For the self-described realists of today, Iran may be a challenge, but ultimately it is perceived to be like any other state, and thus nuclear weapons in its hands need not cause hysteria. Deterrence can and will work just as it did in the past with the Soviet Union and China. For the realists, engagement without conditions is required.

Neoconservatives, as the name implies, are not conservatives in any traditional sense. Though of more recent vintage than realists, and certainly prominent in the Bush administration, the neoconservatives are transformationalists at heart. Like most Americans, they are believers in American exceptionalism and the idea that we have a unique mission to extend U.S. values internationally and thus change the world. But America, in their eyes, should use the military as the primary tool to defeat those whose ideology is a threat to us. For the neoconservatives, the Iranian regime is revolutionary, has declared war against us, and cannot be appeased, and negotiations with it represent an exercise in self-delusion. Engagement is a trap, and nothing short of regime change or the use of force can be accepted.

We explore the core of realist and neoconservative assumptions, explaining their basic fallacies and why the policies that flow from them would be quite dangerous, and then we propose a third way for dealing with the challenge of Iran. As a corollary to our discussion of Iran and the arguments surrounding policy toward it, we also offer a chapter on the myths surrounding both engagement and nonengagement, with an eye toward explaining the difference between states and nonstate actors and the consequences of engaging with groups such as Hamas and Hizbollah without conditions.

The final section of the book consists of two chapters on American values, interests, and democracy promotion. Here we once again challenge the conflicting mythologies on whether, or how, we should try to transform the region, whether what goes on within states matters to us, and whether the Middle East presents a clash of civilizations or a clash within a civilization (namely, Islam). Any discussion of American values and their importance to the pursuit of our interests in the Middle East should also take on the so-called realist view that Israel is a strategic liability, not an asset. This book would not be complete without debunking that myth, which is designed to justify a wholesale change in our policy toward Israel. Why does such a discussion fit in a section on interests and values? Because when it comes to Israel, America's policy has always been driven by a mix of our interests and values. We share values with Israel and are connected to it as a like-minded democracy. It is also a committed friend in a region where friends may not always be reliable. Differences are a given with any ally, and Israel is no exception. But America's stakes in Israel—both tangible and intangible—will not and should not change any time soon.

The notion of interests and values is a good way to tie together the main threads of the book. American foreign policy almost by definition must inevitably be guided by an amalgam of interests and values. Our place in the world and the purpose of our foreign policy can never be strictly based on some abstract concept of power and interest. No policy is sustainable if it is not also seen by the American public and its representatives as serving some higher purpose. That is part of the American ethos. At the same time, our foreign policy requires making choices between near-term tactical needs and longer-term strategic values. No U.S. president is going to ignore the importance of preserving stability in a place like Saudi Arabia even if he or she truly wants to see it liberalize and become more democratic.

We conclude that the mythologies on one side or the other have reflected the tendency to lose sight of the need to preserve a balance between our interests and our values. This book is about trying to identify the right balance in the assumptions we make about the Middle East. This book is about setting the record straight and debunking the myths that have misled American policy so that we may chart the right course in the region. It has never been more important to do so.

Chapter Two

LINKAGE: THE MOTHER
OF ALL MYTHS

Of all the policy myths that have kept us from making real progress in the Middle East, one stands out for its impact and longevity: the idea that if only the Palestinian conflict were solved, all other Middle East conflicts would melt away. This is the argument of "linkage." Neoconservatives have always rejected it, given their skepticism about Arab intentions and their related belief that the Israeli-Palestinian conflict cannot be resolved. While realists have been its most determined purveyors, this myth transcends all others and has had amazing staying power here, internationally, and in the Middle East. In fact, few ideas have been as consistently and forcefully promoted—by laymen, policymakers, and leaders alike.

One need not look too far for examples of linkage's pervasiveness. Note the words of Egyptian president Hosni Mubarak in early 2008 when, standing next to President George W. Bush at a joint press conference following their talks in the Sinai resort town of Sharm al-Sheikh, he recounted their conversation: "I emphasized that the Palestinian question, of course, is the core of problems and conflict in the Middle East, and it is the entry to contain the crisis and tension in the region, and the best means to face what's going on in the world, and our region—I mean by that, the escalation of violence, extremism and terrorism."[1]

King Abdullah of Jordan made much the same argument during an interview with an American television network in 2006: "I keep saying Palestine is the core. It is linked to the extent of what's going on in Iraq. It is linked to what's going on in Lebanon."[2]

Not only Middle Eastern leaders see the Palestinian issue at the heart of all other regional problems. Brent Scowcroft, former national security advisor to Presidents Gerald Ford and George H. W. Bush, echoed this basic point of view in an essay published in early 2007:

A vigorously renewed effort to resolve the Arab-Israeli conflict could fundamentally change both the dynamics in the region and the strategic calculus of key leaders. Real progress would push Iran into a more defensive posture. Hezbollah and Hamas would lose their rallying principle. American allies like Egypt, Saudi Arabia, and the Gulf states would be liberated to assist in stabilizing Iraq. And Iraq would finally be seen by all as a key country that had to be set right in the pursuit of regional security.[3]

Similarly, the Iraq Study Group, cochaired by James Baker and Lee Hamilton, placed special emphasis on the idea of linkage: "To put it simply, all key issues in the Middle East—the Arab-Israeli conflict, Iraq, Iran, the need for political and economic reforms, and extremism and terrorism—are inextricably linked."[4]

Such bold statements are rarely qualified. In effect, they are guided by a central premise: that ending the Arab-Israeli conflict is prerequisite to addressing the maladies of the Middle East. Solve it, and in doing so conclude all other conflicts. Fail, and instability—even war—will engulf the entire region.

The major problem with this premise is that it is not true. There have been dozens of conflicts and countless coups in the Middle East since Israel's birth in 1948, and most were completely unrelated to the Arab-Israeli conflict. For example, the Iraqi coup of 1958, the Lebanon crisis of 1958, the Yemeni civil war of 1962–68 (including subsequent civil wars in the 1980s and '90s), the Iraqi Kurdish revolt of 1974, the Egyptian-Libyan Border War of 1977, the Iran-Iraq War of 1980–88, the Persian Gulf War of 1990–91 (including Iraqi Kurdish and Iraqi Shiite revolts of the same year), the Yemeni-Eritrean and Saudi-Yemeni border conflicts of the mid-1990s, and the U.S.-Iraq War, begun in 2003.

Many of these conflicts were long, bloody, and very costly. The Iran-Iraq War alone lasted eight and a half years, cost in the hundreds of billions of dollars, and took between six hundred thousand and one million lives.[5] Yet this conflict, like the others listed above, would have taken place even if the Arab-Israeli conflict had been resolved.

Since the origins of so many regional tensions and rivalries are not connected to the Arab-Israeli conflict, it is hard to see how resolving it would unlock other regional stalemates or sources of instability. Iran, for example, is not pursuing its nuclear ambitions because there is an Arab-Israeli conflict. Sectarian groups in Iraq would not suddenly put aside their internal struggles if the Palestinian issue were resolved. Like so many conflicts in the region, these struggles have their own dynamic.

In addition, as tragic as the conflict between Israelis and Palestinians has become, it has not spilled over to destabilize the Middle East. There have been two Palestinian intifadas, or uprisings, including one that lasted from 2000 to 2005 and claimed the lives of 4,000 Palestinians and 1,100 Israelis—but not a single Arab leader has been toppled or a single regime destabilized as a result. It has remained a local conflict, contained in a small geographical area. Yet the argument of linkage endures to this day, and with powerful promoters. Why does it persist? And why has it been accepted among top policymakers if it is factually incorrect?

In this chapter we take a closer look at the argument of linkage. We discuss its more subtle undercurrents, and why Arab leaders have historically sought to use it less for conflict resolution than to influence U.S. policy in the Middle East. Specifically, they have created a powerful narrative around the concept—one that has over time indelibly shaped U.S. assumptions of regional behavior.

Initially, the narrative of linkage was used to try to get the United States to disassociate from Zionist Israel. Over time, and as the narrative developed, the responsibility for resolving the Arab-Israeli conflict was put on the United States. Not only was the United States asked to act in place of Arab nations, but it was impelled to do so lest its relations and influence in the Arab world suffer—or so the narrative went.

In this chapter we review how Arab leaders sought to convince U.S. policymakers of what was at stake for the Americans' interests in the region, and how these policymakers were increasingly influenced by the developing narrative.

We show that at historical junctures dating back to the middle of the twentieth century, Arab rhetoric on linkage has not been followed by action. In other words, though Arab leaders made specific statements about how they might proceed based upon progress in the Israeli-Palestinian conflict, their subsequent actions rarely made good upon these statements. The irony is that Arab regimes—with few notable exceptions—have largely shaped their foreign policy around their own priorities, independent of both U.S. ties to Israel and the Arab-Israeli conflict. Even when the United States allied with Israel, the Arab states maintained close relations with Washington. With few exceptions, Arab regimes have pursued their national interests instead of developing policy based on the Palestinian conflict.

The subsequent gap between rhetoric and action is wide. It has historically misled America, creating unfulfilled expectations on both sides. U.S. action has often been predicated upon expected Arab responses to favorable U.S. policy. But when the United States has adopted a linkage-based approach, as purportedly favored by Arabs, the results have rarely been what the United States expected.

As we illustrate, there were times when the United States responded to Arab rhetoric by pushing Israel to make concessions—often for reasons external to the dynamics of Arab-Israeli peacemaking—without favorable Arab response. The impact of such policy failure was significant. U.S. interests were not met, nor were prospects for peace improved. Moreover, when Israel believed that U.S. actions were motivated by giving in to Arab demands, it became less willing to respond to entreaties for concessions. Still, Arab leaders continued to issue dire warnings about the consequences of U.S. ties to Israel, threatening negative retaliatory steps against the United States. But these too have rarely come to pass. Too often, the United States neither won favorable Arab reciprocity when it did as the Arabs suggested, nor suffered a disaster when it did not heed Arab warnings.

In short, the argument of linkage has profoundly misled U.S. policymakers who embraced its logic and the assumptions that underpinned it. As we will see, it has influenced a U.S. policy approach to the Middle East that has often been erroneous, even counterproductive. Time and again, American administrations misread the facts, affected by the arguments of Arab leaders and the apparent logic of linkage. An active peace process is key to building the foundation of coexistence between Arabs and Israelis, and to marginalizing radical forces in the region. Yet one can be very supportive of the peace process, as we both are, without accepting the argument of linkage. The belief that the Arabs have leverage over the U.S., stemming from the misguided concept of linkage, has and will continue to frustrate U.S. efforts in the Middle East. It is therefore imperative to explore the origins of this mistaken view and its evolution over time. To find out, we need to start by discussing the Arab use of linkage—and the conflict with Israel—before turning to examine how American policymakers have viewed the region through the prism of linkage over time, and the problems this has created.

THE ARAB VIEW OF LINKAGE

By focusing on the Israeli-Palestinian issue, Arab regimes have sought to shape U.S. policy options in the Middle East. Since, in the mind of many Arab leaders, Israel is the victimizer and not the victim, they have felt it only right to have the United States view the conflict through the eyes of the Arabs.

In the earlier years of the conflict, Arab states wanted the United States to view the situation as a zero-sum game in which it was obligated to take sides. When this did not occur, they sought to convince America that every step toward Israel was a step away from the Arabs. When this too did not work, and nations such as Egypt and Jordan came to view war as a drain on their finite resources (making peace with Israel in 1979 and 1994, respectively), the new idea was to emphasize the need for the United States to act to end the conflict, but on terms acceptable to the Arabs. Arab leaders realized the best way to hook the Americans into an active role was to portray the conflict as one with the potential to resolve all other issues—or, alternatively, to exacerbate all regional problems if not addressed.

Still, Arab enmity toward Israel has been genuine, not contrived. Attitudes toward Israel's existence in the region reflect old Arab grievances against Western powers—grievances exploited by Arab leaders of all stripes. Over time, Arabs who came to accept coexistence with Israel focused principally on Israel's control over lands captured in 1967. Yet even those who are prepared to accept Israel's existence—such as Egypt and Jordan— deny the Zionist enterprise any moral legitimacy. For them, Israel exists as a fact, not a right. In contrast, rejectionist Arabs focus on Israel's very existence as the problem, but emphasize that Israel's control of the West Bank is particularly egregious.

Arab enmity toward Israel has existed since its inception in 1948—long before the occupation of the West Bank and Gaza began in 1967. Arab regimes believed the United Nations was wrong to agree to partition Palestine into two states in 1947, and so five Arab armies plus contingents from two others attacked Israel on May 15, 1948—the day it came into being. The fact that Israel withstood the Arab assault added insult to injury, and the humiliation was compounded by Israel's stunning 1967 victory, which left it with territory that effectively tripled its pre-1967 size.

Israel's post-1967 holdings became a central issue for Arab leaders advancing the merits of linkage. In 1990, Saddam Hussein claimed that he had invaded Kuwait to help the Palestinians, saying he would consider withdrawing his forces if Israel withdrew from the land it had occupied since 1967. His goal was to garner Arab support. Saddam understood that he was isolated and needed to link his invasion to a cause that would appear legitimate. While his claim was patently contrived, the administration of George H. W. Bush had to fight the linkage argument as it put together its coalition against Iraq in 1990. The oil-rich Persian Gulf states, including Saudi Arabia, were all well aware that Saddam's effort to eradicate the nation of Kuwait was a threat to them as well and could not be linked to any other issue. Egypt saw Iraq as a threat to Cairo's regional leadership, and Syria has always viewed Iraq as a rival. However, these leaders of nondemocratic regimes were not immune to the deep public sentiment that sympathized with Saddam Hussein's defiance of the United States and the existing regional order. Therefore, some allies argued that if Arab states were to join the coalition against Iraq, the United States needed to organize an international conference to settle the Arab-Israeli conflict. The first Palestinian intifada (1987–93) had created enormous tension in the region, and many complained that the United States—as Israel's main ally and benefactor—was perpetuating Israeli occupation. The first Bush administration wisely refused to link the two issues. It did not want to link reversing Saddam Hussein's invasion of Kuwait with solving the Arab-Israel conflict. Apart from the urgency of addressing the former and the sheer complexity of the latter, the United States did not want Saddam to get any credit that would enable him to claim to the Arab world that his aggression in Kuwait had yielded diplomatic dividends for the Palestinians. That would only burnish his credentials instead of diminishing them.

Saddam won support in the Arab world from those who asserted that U.S. policy applied a double standard. They asked why Israel was permitted to effectively ignore UN Security Council resolutions when Iraq was forced to comply. With regard to Israel, Palestinians and Arabs generally focused on UN Security Council Resolutions 242 and 338, adopted after the 1967 and 1973 wars. These provided guidelines for negotiations between Arabs and Israelis. The terms of a final peace settlement were not established in the resolutions themselves, but negotiations and mutual compromise between the parties were required. Many in the Arab world did not see any difference between these resolutions and those pertaining to Iraq. But the 1990 UN resolutions against Iraq were passed in response to Saddam's invasion of Kuwait; they required his compliance, not his acceptance. Noncompliance triggered sanctions, and led to the use of force against Iraq's absorption of Kuwait.

These differences were pointed out, but drawing such distinctions between the Security Council resolutions involving Iraqis and Israelis was not convincing to many in the Arab world, who asked why Iraq had to implement resolutions while Israel did not. Seeing all UN resolutions as having the force of international law, many Arab leaders argued for equal treatment.

For the Arab world in general, this view of the UN resolutions was a face-saver. Arabs would resolve the conflict with Israel, but only on the basis of international law—"international legitimacy," as they called it. Their justification for furthering the conflict was that if Iraq had to follow international legitimacy, Israel must too. Messy, difficult negotiations made it look as if the Israelis were trying to avoid their UN-mandated responsibilities. Land for peace—what resolutions 242 and 338 came to represent—was simple. If the Israelis would simply withdraw, there would be no need for complicated negotiations—and no longer any reason for conflict, for war. But the Arab/Palestinian concept of peace was simply the absence of conflict; it was not acceptance, reconciliation, or cooperation, and certainly not warm relations. Arabs might grudgingly acknowledge Israel's existence and end the conflict, but minimize relations with it.[6]

The United States did not remain indifferent to the resonance of this issue in the aftermath of the Persian Gulf War of 1991. President George H. W. Bush put forward four principles for a new regional order: security, arms control, economic development, and the resolution of the Arab-Israeli conflict. Of these, the United States focused its initial and greatest attention on the Arab-Israeli conflict. It worked intensively to organize the 1991 Madrid international peace conference—and did so not as a form of delayed linkage, but because the conference had two elements to it. The first was to launch bilateral negotiations, and the other was subsequently to initiate multilateral talks on arms control, economic development, and the environment, a process designed in part to integrate Israel into the region by having Israel sitting with its Arab neighbors to discuss these issues. Here was an effort to keep the Arab states from sitting back and waiting for the Palestinian issue to be solved, and instead to induce them to play a more active role in settling with Israel and taking on some of the other sources of regional instability.

LINKAGE: TERRORISM AND THE PURSUIT OF POWER

The linkage idea has not always been formulated as a policy prescription. It has also been used as an explanation for terrorism. By anchoring political violence to a grievance, terrorist perpetrators sought not only to justify their actions, but to neutralize those who would oppose them.

In the early 1970s, Middle East airline hijackings occurred frequently, sometimes in the name of liberating Palestine. Extremist groups perpetrated violence in Europe. Also in the 1970s, debates about the definition of terrorism became prominent at the UN, and Arab delegates, as well as others, began referring to the "root cause of terrorism." If the singular conflict between Israelis and Arabs could be called the root cause of all other conflicts, it must be a legitimate—indeed, a very important—grievance. The regional consequences of the festering conflict would thus gain significance, and egregious actions taken in its name would gain acceptability and also attract new recruits for the cause.

For people like Osama bin Laden, violence is driven by a desire to reshape the Mideast and the greater Muslim world without U.S. interference, and invoking linkage has been a significant tactic in achieving this aim. Prior to 9/11, Bin Laden had either ignored the Palestinian cause or mentioned it only in passing. In his two well-known fatwas, or religious edicts (the 1996 "Declaration of War against the Americans Occupying the Land of the Two Holy Places" and the 1998 "Declaration of the World Islamic Front for Jihad against the Jews and the Crusaders"), bin Laden stated that the presence of U.S. soldiers in Saudi Arabia, the home of Islam's two holiest places, was the greatest affront ever perpetrated by the United States against the Muslim people.[7]

His 1998 fatwa went on to state, "The Arabian Peninsula has never—since God made it flat, created its desert, and encircled it with seas—been stormed by any forces like the [American] crusader armies spreading in it like locusts, eating its riches and wiping out its plantations."[8] During those years, bin Laden's priority was the removal of pro-U.S. Arab regimes and the restoration of a central governing Islamic body, or caliphate; it was not addressing the needs of the Palestinians.

But after 9/11, bin Laden discovered the utility of the Palestinian issue. Suddenly he began more openly trying to tie his actions to the cause of the Palestinians. In one videotaped message after 9/11, he declared, "Neither America nor the people who live in it will dream of security before we live it in Palestine."[9] Much like Saddam Hussein, bin Laden was trying to gain legitimacy by implying that his attack on America was entwined with the plight of the Palestinians.

Yet these claims cannot help but seem transparent in light of bin Laden's actions. The al-Qaeda network did not attack America because of the absence of peace in the Middle East. It had obviously begun planning its terrorist attack even as peace talks were progressing. Arab-Israeli peace would not dismantle the terror networks, nor would it affect their determination to attack Western civilization and modernity itself.

Does all of this imply that pursuing Middle East peace is not important now? Of course not, and it is clearly in U.S. interests to try to resolve the conflict; it unquestionably does resonate throughout the region. But terrorism and its perpetrators will continue to be threats whether or not peace between Palestinians and Israelis is established. Today, Arab countries support current U.S. efforts against terror, at least tacitly, because they understand that bin Laden's al-Qaeda network is capable of committing atrocities against them on the scale of those committed against the United States. Arab leaders are just as much of a target in al-Qaeda's desire to remake the political framework of the Middle East. Their support is not a favor; rather, it is an act of self-defense. It should be said, however, that if

Palestinian nationalism fails to win the goal of statehood, one cannot preclude the possibility that al-Qaeda will gain supporters among Palestinians. Already, there have been small signs of such groups in Gaza.

Osama bin Laden is not the only rejectionist who finds the perpetuation of the conflict useful. As one gets closer to Israel's borders, other nonstate actors in the Middle East—namely, Hizbollah and Hamas—have a twin approach to the conflict and to Israel that goes beyond a sense of grievance on behalf of the Palestinians. They have a desire to perpetuate the conflict, as it is a convenient cloak for their more radical reach for power. For these rejectionist groups, opposition runs even deeper. Their adherents see peace with Israel as antithetical to their ethos and self-definition. In other words, Israel's existence is a negation of who they are.

For example, Hizbollah, the Shiite militant group in Lebanon, has insisted that it is a "resistance" movement, not just a political party. It says it holds weapons because it must "expel the Zionists" from Lebanon. But Israel left Lebanon in 2000, and the border, known as the "blue line," was demarcated by the UN. Hizbollah won political plaudits at home for purging Israel from the land at that time. Hizbollah now says it needs weapons because, on behalf of Lebanon, it wishes to "liberate" a tiny area called Shebaa Farms from Israel, equal to 0.2 percent of the area of Lebanon. Syria has insisted the area is not even Lebanese. Walid Jumblat, head of the Progressive Socialist Party and a leading figure in Lebanon's Druze community, has said the issue is just an excuse for Hizbollah to hold weapons. Hizbollah, which views itself as an ascendant Shiite group, intends to use these weapons to exert power over the other sectarian groups in Lebanon, which, unlike Hizbollah, disarmed following the Lebanese civil war. It would be foolish to believe that left to its own devices, Hizbollah will disarm. Hizbollah leader Hassan Nasrallah has publicly stated that he would not do so even if this Shebaa border grievance against Israel is resolved to Hizbollah's satisfaction. Once again, the conflict with Israel is being manipulated as part of an inter-Arab quest for power—even, in the case of Hizbollah, as it also reflects a genuine ideological enmity.[10]

Confrontation with Israel has also been convenient for a rejectionist country—Iran. Iranian president Mahmoud Ahmadinejad routinely calls for "wiping Israel off the map" and has denied the Holocaust. By doing so, he may seek to win Arab support for his ideas, but it is very doubtful that if Israel no longer existed, Iran would not seek greater control over Gulf oil. Iran sees itself as a regional power, but hides its ambitions by portraying itself as an Islamist country leading the battle against Israel. It is convenient for Iran to exploit the Palestinian issue as a means of cloaking regional ambitions. This will be discussed further later in the book.

A STRATEGY OF DEFLECTION

While Arab enmity for Israel has been genuine among many, some Arab states have taken an instrumentalist approach to the conflict, viewing its perpetuation as useful and even necessary in maintaining their legitimacy. According to Hala Mustafa, Egyptian intellectual and editor in chief of al-Dimuqratiya (Democracy), defiance of Israel has defined many Arab regimes since their inception, replacing previous Arab defiance against colonial rule. This defiance is a central pillar of Arab legitimacy, Mustafa writes.[11] Arab state-run media, textbooks, sermons, and essays express the idea that Israel is morally illegitimate. By casting Israel as an expansionist power that lacks legitimacy because of its poor treatment of Palestinians, Arabs have historically discredited efforts to make peace with it as neither feasible nor desirable. In light of this view, Arabs have no responsibility to resolve the conflict, and no Arab leader need explain why he has failed to do so.

Antipathy toward Israel has given authoritarian Arab regimes a patina of legitimacy and brought them closer—at least on this issue—to their mortal enemies the radical Islamists, who reject any non-Muslim sovereignty in the Middle East. It has also garnered popular support. Egypt's charismatic president from 1954 to 1970, Gamal Abdel Nasser, swayed throngs of followers with his pledge to eliminate Israel.

Many Arab leaders have used the conflict with Israel not only as a means to build their popular support but also as a device to deflect criticism away from their failings on domestic issues—failings that could potentially threaten their own grasp on power. With the state apparatus mobilized over the decades ostensibly to defeat the "Zionist entity," the regime can be excused for not being able to fulfill its responsibilities to its own people. If there is a lack of political reform, or if the economy declines, both can be justified in the name of conflict. (Even in those states like Egypt and Jordan where peace agreements have been made, there remains a public impulse to blame continuing problems on Israel and the continuing denial of Palestinian rights). As Barry Rubin has written, Arab regimes have created an all-embracing "ideological system" to justify everything in the name of the conflict:

> Each element in it provides a trump idea that can be used to block, delegitimize, and destroy any truly alternative view. If someone demands democracy, the response is that the Arab-Israeli conflict (or the Islamist threat) doesn't permit this luxury. When anyone criticizes the government's human rights record, people often attack the critic for not complaining about Israel instead. When anyone raises questions about economic mismanagement, he is insulted for covering up the fact that it is really the fault of the United States. To demand the rule of law passed by a freely elected parliament would mean being branded a threat to Islam and its legislation, which is made only by God.[12]

During the sixties, Nasser avoided political reform by arguing that the country needed to be on a war footing, insisting that no cry must be heard over the din of liberation. This became a central proposition of Arab leaders: namely, that they could not be expected to make favorable changes as long as they were confronting Israel. As it turned out, Nasser failed in his confrontation with Israel and was crushed during the 1967 war. Even following Nasser's decline and the demise of pan-Arabism after 1967, many Arab intellectuals remained in a state of denial regarding Israel's future. One famous Moroccan historian, Abdullah Larqoui, made it clear that compromises were not to be made with an entity that was doomed to disappear. He declared that a day would come when "everything would be obliterated and instantaneously reconstructed and the new inhabitants would leave, as if by magic, the land they had despoiled; in this way, justice shall be dispensed to the victims, on the day when the presence of God shall make itself felt."[13]

But this strategy of deflection has become more obvious to Arab publics in the aftermath of September 11, 2001, and the Arab voices questioning the manipulative "deflection strategy" have grown louder. According to Nabil Khatib, executive director of the satellite television network al-Arabiya, the Arab regimes have no interest in resolving the

Palestinian issue, preferring to blame others than to deal with it.[14] The lack of Arab accountability has led to two realities: first, regimes—including those that America supports, such as Egypt—that promote hostility toward America in order to deflect criticism and anger; and second, a culture of victimhood, not accountability, that has permeated much of the Arab and Islamic world. Problems are never the fault of the Arabs or Muslims, and it is always up to others to fix them. Under such circumstances, it is easy to blame the United States—and both radical Islamists and America's putative friends do so. The idea of linkage is convenient for Arab leaders, as it enables them to avoid dealing with domestic problems and to demand that others, such as the United States, provide the immediate solutions.

The Egyptian writer Hassan Hafez has stated that such denial weakens Arab states' accountability to their own people. In the Egyptian opposition newspaper *al-Wafd*, Hafez writes, "I wonder why we blamed Israel for every fault in [our] society. This is the logic of the weak, who seek a peg on which to hang all their mistakes in order to evade a true confrontation with reality." Instead, he states, "We have to grab those responsible for our failures by the collar instead of blaming Israel for all our problems like cowards. [Blaming Israel] causes us to look ridiculous before the world and it makes the small Israeli state look great. We have to be honest with ourselves before we blame others! When we blame others, we are being untrue, we mock common sense, and we scorn our own people."[15] Or, as Khatib put it, "For fifty years, Arab regimes have used Palestine as an excuse to avoid dealing with all issues—poverty, education, economy."[16] While it is popular for Arab leaders to say publicly that they are committed to reforms, genuine economic reform can be wrenching. It means creating transparent rules that could disadvantage groups that are used to economic privilege. Moreover, a potent private sector is seen by some as diluting the centralized political authority of the state to distribute largesse at its discretion.

Dozens of Arab intellectuals authored a landmark study, the United Nations Development Program (UNDP) *Arab Human Development Report*, which in 2002 cited a substantial lag between Arab countries and other regions in the areas of governance, education, and the economy. The study decries the Israeli-Palestinian conflict as having a genuine deleterious impact on Arab policy and spending priorities, but also explains that it has been used as a pretext by Arab states. The UNDP report states:

> By symbolizing a felt and constant external threat, occupation has damaging side effects: it provides both a cause and an excuse for distorting the development agenda, disrupting national priorities, and retarding political development. At certain junctures it can serve to solidify the public against an outside aggressor and justify curbing dissent at a time when democratic transition requires greater pluralism in society and more public debate on national development policies. In all these ways, occupation freezes growth, prosperity, and freedom in the Arab world.[17]

PEACE BETWEEN REGIMES, NOT PEOPLES

Several Arab countries remained on a war footing against Israel for many years. Egypt and Syria were the frontline states, fighting in the wars of 1948, 1967, and 1973. Jordan and Iraq were involved in the first two wars. Lebanon also fought in 1948, while Saudi Arabia and Yemen were nominally involved. Even those Arab countries not involved in actual fighting still rejected Israel and its right to exist. From 1948 until the 1990s, a majority of the twenty-one Arab states took no steps to suggest they might deal with Israel. It was not until 2002 that all the Arab states said they were willing to have normal ties with Israel, but only after Israel actually withdraws from all lands won in the 1967 war.

While perpetuating the conflict burnished the legitimacy of Arab regimes and deflected criticism of their domestic problems, it posed a problem as well. Some Arab leaders recognized that continuing war exacted a high economic cost on Arab countries. But for these countries to recognize that there should be a homeland for Jews in the Middle East would undermine the anti-Zionist diet being fed to the very political class that served their regimes. The solution was found in negotiating peace treaties between governments (Egypt and Israel, and Jordan and Israel) that ended the conflicts but did not produce peace between populaces and societies. The underlying enmity remained strong, and little attempt was made to dissipate it.

War was costly, especially given the Arab defeats in 1948 and 1967. Mubarak explained the futility of wars, stating:

> We fought for many years, but where did we get? We also spent 100 billions on wars, apart from thousands of martyrs until we reached the present situation for which we are now suffering. I am therefore not ready to take more risks. . . . Wars have generally not solved any problem. Regardless of the difficulties or obstacles surrounding the peace process, our real effort focuses on removing these obstacles and bringing viewpoints closer.[18]

Indeed, Mubarak's view has been that war is self-defeating for Egypt, which has sacrificed a great deal for the Palestinian cause. For adopting this pragmatic cost-benefit approach, Mubarak's regime has been rewarded with over $2 billion in U.S. assistance per year since the early 1980s. Foreign aid has greatly helped stabilize the Egyptian regime.

Perpetuating war simply did not make financial sense for states like Egypt and Jordan. But it had a political cost as well. For them, the conflict has become a cudgel in the hands of their Islamist rivals to punish what the latter would term "implicit compliance" with Israeli actions. The more scenes of Israeli occupation are shown on al-Jazeera television, the more Arab impotence in preventing such actions is highlighted. For Jordan, there is an added fear that despairing Palestinians might give up on the West Bank and create demographic pressure on the East Bank of Jordan. Therefore, these regimes probably *do* want to see the conflict resolved. But they do not want to be associated with the messy task of compromise, which could call into question their Arab nationalist credentials. This is where the linkage argument becomes more important. If resolving this conflict holds the promise of resolving all conflicts in the Middle East, or if, conversely, failure to do so means that the conflict will metastasize across the region, the United States may find it necessary to use its leverage with Israel to force concessions and therefore absolve the Arab states from twisting the arms of the Palestinians. Such a solution has the benefit for Arab leaders of producing feasible economic and political results without sacrificing credibility in the region.

Until then, the Arab states try to have it both ways by avoiding the consequences of war while also maintaining a public position advantageous to their regimes. Thus, the peace between Israel and Egypt is a "cold peace." President Mubarak, who came to power in 1981 in the aftermath of Anwar Sadat's assassination, has not visited Israel except to attend the funeral of Prime Minister Yitzhak Rabin in 1995. (He told a radio interviewer at the time that the visit did not count because it was for a funeral). Egypt and Jordan insist that the peace would be warmer were it not for the conflict with the Palestinians. This claim is questionable. In the best case, Arab publics would not be satisfied unless Israel cedes the Golan Heights to Syria. Furthermore, the lack of friendliness between countries that do have peace treaties reinforces doubts among the Israeli people regarding the desirability of a treaty with either the Palestinians or Syria. Israelis wonder if peace with Cairo and Amman is cold, why wouldn't it be freezing with Damascus and Ramallah?

Quietly, Israel and Jordan enjoyed covert diplomatic relations long before they signed a peace treaty. Since the treaty, security ties have become more extensive. The Jordan-Israel border has been calm, as both sides cooperate to avert infiltration by Islamist-oriented Palestinian extremists. But this cooperation is often hidden from the Jordanian public. Take the example of the qualified industrial zones (QIZs); they were conceived by the Clinton administration and supported by the U.S. Congress in the aftermath of the Israel-Jordan peace treaty. The QIZs permit textile and other products made in Jordan that have at least some Israeli content to be exported to the United States without tariffs. The hope was to promote economic cooperation between Israel and Jordan and to provide a peace dividend for the Jordanian economy and workforce.

In fact, the QIZs have succeeded beyond their planners' wildest expectations. Jordan's exports to the United States grew from $5 million in 1998 to over $1.5 billion in 2006, in an economy that has a gross national product no larger than $10 billion. It is estimated that more than thirty thousand new jobs have been created, largely for Jordanian women. Sadly, this major success story is almost never publicly attributed to the peace process with Israel, and so the Jordanian populace does not make the connection.

Other Arab states prefer not to be engaged in war with Israel, but neither do they actively seek to promote peace. An Arab peace initiative was adopted by the Arab League at the Beirut summit in 2002; Arab leaders agreed that if Israel ended the conflict on terms deemed acceptable, they would normalize relations with Israel. While this is certainly progress, once again it is up to Israel to concede first, granting East Jerusalem and the West Bank to the Palestinians and the Golan Heights to the Syrians, before the Arabs would to take any steps toward Israel. In essence, Israel would have to solve everything before anything was required of the Arabs. In other words, the onus for peacemaking remained squarely on Israel.

Not only did the onus remain on Israel, nothing was done to prepare the publics for peace. Although it would have involved some effort, there are many things the Arab states could have said and done. They could have acknowledged that although they have legitimate demands of Israel, Israel has legitimate demands of them as well. They could have offered to integrate Israel into the region if it complied with Arab requests. In other words, the Arab states could have made clear that Israel has rights, not just obligations. They could have dealt with the moral legitimacy of Israel as a permanent fixture in the region. They could also have said that no side would get everything it wanted, but that everyone must compromise. This would have been helpful before the fateful Camp David summit in 2000. Because Palestinian leader Yasir Arafat did not say this, he raised expectations, rather than lowering them, and then became trapped by this approach.

On the contrary, Arab state-run media continued to maintain a steady diet of anti-America, anti-Israel diatribes, even during the peacemaking years of the 1990s. Middle East historian Fouad Ajami described Arab leaders in a *Foreign Affairs* article, saying:

> . . . sly and cunning men, the rulers knew and understood the game. There would be no open embrace of America, and no public defense of it. They would stay a step ahead of the crowd and give the public the safety valve it needed. The more pro-American the regime, the more anti-American the political class. The United States could grant generous aid to the Egyptian state, but there would be no dampening of the anti-American fury of the Egyptian political class. Its leading state-backed dailies crackled with the wildest theories of U.S.-Israeli conspiracies against their country.

Later in the article he continues:

Egyptians have long been dissatisfied with their country's economic and military performance, a pain born of the gap between Egypt's exalted idea of itself and the poverty and foreign dependence that have marked its modern history. The rage against Israel and the United States stems from that history of lament and frustration. So much of Egypt's life lies beyond the scrutiny and the reach of its newspapers and pundits—the ruler's ways, the authoritarian state, the matter of succession to Mubarak, the joint military exercises with U.S. and Egyptian forces, and so on. The animus toward America and Israel gives away the frustration of a polity raging against the hard, disillusioning limits of its political life.[19]

What stands out is the durability of Arab regimes, and their ability to use a variety of techniques, including the linkage argument, to ensure that they are not blamed. The fear that failure to resolve the Palestinian issue could lead to regime collapse is also promoted for this purpose, though there is no evidence that this is true. Indeed, notwithstanding the fact that the second intifada was the first conflict with Israel that truly entered people's living rooms, thanks to satellite television networks such as al-Jazeera, it is remarkable that it did not destabilize any of the Arab regimes. Remarkable because even though there was outrage among Arab publics and demonstrations at the beginning of the intifada (particularly over the tragic and unresolved killing of a twelve-year-old boy named Mohammad Dura, which was shown on television), and even though no Arab regimes intervened on behalf of the Palestinians against the Israelis, no Arab leaders fell from power. Egypt and Jordan recalled their ambassadors but did nothing more. Rather than seeing linkage threaten regimes, we have instead seen Arab leaders largely insulated from the Palestinian conflict—so much so that they could resist all calls to go to war against Israel on behalf of the Palestinians (even at times when al-Jazeera was trying to highlight the worst possible images of Israeli abuse of Palestinians) without paying a political price.

At an Arab League summit in Cairo in October 2000, President Mubarak responded to the call of the Yemeni president to go to war by saying publicly:

I'm telling the one who said that he won't participate in the summit unless war is declared against Israel, that war is not that easy. These statements only win the applause of the peoples. The matter is serious. It needs logic. It is time for wisdom. We don't need applause. We need solutions to the situation. They don't realize the meaning of war and its subsequent destruction. The Arabs as well as Israelis understand the true meaning of war. The decision of war is not that easy. No Arab leader would take such a decision on his own. The situation needs sound realistic evaluation. . . . War will not put an end to the problem. There are many other ways to address it. Whoever wants to launch a war, it is OK. Go ahead. The Arab countries are free, independent, and sovereign. We are not preventing any of them from launching war.[20]

The Egyptian people knew that the Arabs fought for the Palestinian cause from 1948 to 1973, and there was no appetite for more war. If war was not desirable, domestic upheaval was not feasible. Nervous about the advent of the Iranian Islamist revolution in 1979, Arab regimes feared that the Iranian experience could spark revolutions in their own countries. So they spent more money bolstering their domestic intelligence services. Today it is common for the heads of the intelligence services to be linchpins for leaders. Their tactics have sometimes been brutal, but no Middle Eastern leader has been overthrown by Islamists since the 1979 Iranian revolution. Things are more complex today than they were decades ago, when coup plotters needed only to seize a television and radio station to be successful. Today's Arab regimes are resilient and will not be easily toppled (the implications of authoritarian rule will be discussed in another chapter). In short, deflection has been a useful technique for preserving power, and whatever the claims, the conflict itself has not threatened the hold on power of any regime.

While the Arab use of linkage and the Palestinian issue may have had multiple purposes—from deflection and legitimization to affecting America's behavior—there can be little doubt that different U.S. administrations believed deeply in the concept and were influenced by it. We turn now to a discussion of the concept of linkage and the way American officials saw it and were shaped by it.

Chapter Three

THE U.S. APPROACH
TO LINKAGE

The Arab emphasis on linkage has certainly influenced American policy over the last half century. In this chapter we survey how the idea of linkage evolved over various U.S. administrations, and how the United States responded to Arab demands. We will also look at how reality differed from rhetoric and how an embrace of linkage misled generations of American policymakers, starting with the Roosevelt administration.

THE ROOSEVELT ADMINISTRATION

In many ways, the linkage argument can be traced back even before the actual founding of Israel, back to the 1930s when Arabs were concerned about the growing influence of the Zionist enterprise. In these years, the Arabs wanted the United States to dissociate itself from the Zionists. Arab leaders contended that the potential Zionist nation was illegitimate, so there was no need for Arab accommodation. They asked the United States to decide where its interests lay: with the Zionists or the Arab world. If the United States moved toward the Zionists, the Arab world would, they said, alter its relationship with the United States accordingly. In other words, the Arab nations would shape their relationship to the United States based on the latter's choice. The onus was on America, not the Arabs—and if America chose wrong, Washington would be responsible not only for its poor standing in the region, but for all the festering problems of the Middle East.

These arguments are spelled out in an extraordinary set of letters from Saudi king Abdul Aziz al-Saud (Ibn Saud) to President Franklin Delano Roosevelt beginning in the late 1930s. At this time, the oil-based relationship between the United States and Saudi Arabia was in its early stages of development.

Ibn Saud declared in a November 1938 letter that, historically, the Jewish presence in the Middle East was brief, beset by tragedy and massacres, and that the Jews had eventually been driven out. In a 1943 letter, Ibn Saud mentioned "the religious animosity between Muslims and Jews which dates back to the time when Islam appeared and which is due to the treacherous behavior of the Jews towards Muslims and their Prophet." He added:

> For if—God Forbid!—the Jews were to be granted their desire, Palestine would forever remain a hotbed of troubles and disturbances as in the past. This will bring great difficulties for the Allies in general and for our friend Great Britain in particular. In view of their financial power and learning, the Jews can stir up enmity between the Arabs and Allies at any moment. They have been the cause of many troubles in the past.[1]

He reiterated in yet another letter to FDR that he viewed Zionism as a threat to all Arabs: "All we ask is that the Allies should fully realize the rights of the Arabs and, for the present, prevent the Jews from going ahead in any new matter which may be considered a threat to the Arabs and to the future of every Arab nation."[2] Ibn Saud concluded by saying he hoped that injustice would not be done and relations between the Allied powers and the Arabs would be "best and strongest."[3] In February 1945, Ibn Saud told American diplomats, "If America should choose in favor of the Jews, who are accursed in the Koran as enemies of the Muslims until the end of the world, it will indicate to us that America has repudiated her friendship with us and this we should regret."[4]

It was a sign of Saudi Arabia's growing importance for the United States that FDR agreed to a summit meeting with Ibn Saud as the U.S. president returned from the fateful Yalta summit near the end of World War II. FDR arrived from Yalta on the U.S. battleship *Quincy*. As the ship anchored in the Great Bitter Lake (Buhayra al-Murrah al-Kubra), FDR met Ibn Saud on February 14, 1945. During the meeting, and notwithstanding

Ibn Saud's letters, FDR sought his support for Zionism, citing the destruction of millions of European Jews during World War II. But the Saudi leader was adamant. He insisted that the Germans should pay by giving the Jews parts of their land as a homeland, rather than taking land from the Arabs.

By the end of the meeting, FDR had pledged that he would not support the Jews at the expense of the Arabs. (Ibn Saud's defiance became legendary; according to Abdul Rahman Azzam, who headed the nascent Arab League, Ibn Saud claimed that he declared to FDR during their meeting: "I will never rest until I and all my sons have been killed in the defense of Palestine. . . . [S]wear that you will never support the Zionists."[5]) FDR clearly feared that U.S.-Saudi relations and access to oil would be jeopardized as a consequence of U.S. support for Zionism. According to people who talked to FDR after the meeting, he was taken aback by the depth of Ibn Saud's animosity toward a Jewish state, and feared future bloodshed. David Niles, one of only two White House political advisers to FDR who were asked to remain in the Truman administration (and who played a role in Truman's support of Zionism), later declared that he had "serious doubts that Israel would have come into being, if Roosevelt had lived."[6]

THE TRUMAN ADMINISTRATION

The idea that U.S. ties with the Arabs would be irreparably hurt by U.S. recognition of Israel in 1948 weighed heavily on many senior State Department officials during the administrations of FDR and his successor, Harry Truman. One of these men, Loy Henderson, was considered among the elite of the Foreign Service officers in the State Department. Having served in Moscow during World War II and in Iraq, he was a believer that U.S. foreign policy goals should all be directed toward containing the Soviet Union. In that context, he saw the establishment of Israel as alienating U.S.-Arab relations at a time when much hung in the balance. In the postwar period, Henderson was appointed director of the department's Near Eastern, African, and South Asian Affairs bureau. In September 1947, he wrote to Secretary of State George Marshall and declared that the "partitioning of Palestine and the setting up of a Jewish State [is opposed] by practically every member of the Foreign Service and of the

Department who has been engaged . . . with the Near and Middle East."[7] Many in the State Department, including the head of the Policy Planning Staff at the time, George Kennan, argued strenuously against recognizing a Jewish state, lest it encourage Moscow to exploit the unrest it would cause by coming into the eastern Mediterranean and confronting American interests at Suez and east of it.

One of Henderson's successors, Peter Hart, saw U.S. recognition of Israel as a defeat for U.S. government experts on the Middle East. He stated, "The area experts to a man were scandalized by what happened in 1948. We had made a tremendous effort to lay the ground for good relations with the Arabs, and all of a sudden, when we were in a good position, all of our hopes were dashed."[8]

Many of these government experts on the Middle East had a romance with the Arab world and saw Israel as a colonizing enterprise rather than a legitimate nation-state whose ethos was self-reliance. Francis Fukuyama, the public intellectual and a former State Department policy planning staff member, would later decry these early Arabists and their successors in the U.S. government as embodying a "sociological phenomenon, an elite within an elite, who have been more systematically wrong than any other area specialists in the diplomatic corps. This is because Arabists not only take on the cause of the Arabs, but also the Arabs' tendency for self-delusion."[9]

Truman observed that these experts and State Department diplomats were hostile. He blamed them for seeking to sabotage his policy of recognizing Israel: "The Department of State's specialists on the Near East were almost without exception unfriendly to the idea of a Jewish state. . . . Some thought the Arabs, on account of their number and because of the fact that they controlled such immense oil resources, should be appeased. . . . Some among them were also inclined to be anti-Semitic."[10]

The issue would come to a head as Britain announced it was ending its post–World War I mandate for Palestine, and brought the issue to the United Nations for a decision.

In 1917, Britain had committed itself to the establishment of a Jewish homeland in Palestine. The Arabs cite a British commitment at around the same time during World War I to taking Middle East territory from Ottoman Turkey and giving it to them. Rival Jewish and Palestinian Arab nationalisms would compete for this land. Over time, Britain backed away from its commitment to a Jewish homeland through such measures as the White Paper. After World War II, Britain wanted to divest itself of the problematic parts of its empire.

It was a UN vote in 1947 that called for the partition of the land for two states, one for Jews and one for the Palestinians. While the mainstream, pragmatic wing of the Zionist movement supported partition, the Palestinians did not. All the Arab and Muslim states voted against it. This vote would prove to be ironic because Arab polemicists would subsequently list the establishment of Israel as a crime, never mentioning that its establishment was rooted in a United Nations decision.

The matter was not yet settled. In the United States, the diplomatic and security establishment believed that the nascent Jewish state would be overwhelmed militarily.[11] On February 12, 1948, Secretary of State Marshall said at a meeting of the National Security Council that it was possible that any serious attempt to implement a partition in Palestine would set in motion events that would result in at least a partial mobilization of the U.S. armed forces.[12]

Marshall, Secretary of Defense James Forrestal, and others feared that U.S. support for a Jewish state would jeopardize access to Mideast oil. Forrestal famously explained U.S. dependency on Arab oil as follows: "Unless we have access to Middle East oil, American motorcar companies [will] have to design a four-cylinder motorcar sometime within the next five years."[13] The Joint Chiefs of Staff issued a memorandum entitled "The Problem of Palestine," in which they, too, argued that the partition of Palestine into Jewish and Arab states would endanger U.S. access to Middle East oil.

A notable dissenter from this approach was Truman aide Clark Clifford, who argued that the Arab oil threats were empty. In a memo to Truman, Clifford wrote that "the fact of the matter is that the Arab states must have oil royalties or go broke. . . . [Their] need of the United States is greater than our need of them." Clifford added that the United States needed to stand up to the Arab states and not rescind its November 1947 UN vote in favor of partition. He declared, "The United States appears in the ridiculous role of trembling before threats of a few nomadic desert tribes. This has done us irreparable damage. Why should Russia, or Yugoslavia, or any other nation treat us with anything but contempt in light of our shilly-shallying appeasement of the Arabs?"[14]

These same issues would be discussed at different levels of the Truman administration during the first part of 1948, including a major meeting with the president on May 12, 1948. By many accounts, the meeting was very tense. Marshall took offense that Clifford, a political adviser, was even in the room when the discussion focused on foreign policy. Truman, seeking to ease his advisers' tension surrounding the issue of whether to recognize Israel, quipped to Marshall that it sounded as if the secretary of state would vote against him in the 1948 election. A somber Marshall replied, "Yes, Mr. President, if I were to vote at all, I might do just that."[15] Marshall expressed his belief that domestic political factors—i.e., garnering the American Jewish vote in a few key states—might affect Truman's decision making, given that he faced a tough election campaign in 1948. In contrast, Clifford argued that the state would be born regardless, and a strong U.S.-Israel relationship could be essential in preventing the Soviets from exploiting any ensuing regional chaos.

Truman said he would not make a decision on the spot; he spurned his advisers and recognized Israel two days later, within minutes of its declaration.[16] Many have written about his decision. Critics sought to contend that he was driven by domestic political considerations as he faced an uphill battle in the 1948 presidential election. However, this analysis ignores several other points. Truman saw that the Zionists were holding their own in the internecine fighting that had gone on since the November 1947 partition vote. No U.S. assistance had been required up to that point. Moreover, he had an instinctive sympathy for Zionism. He wrote Eleanor Roosevelt about all the emotions surrounding his decision, saying, "I regret this situation very much because my sympathy has always been on their [Zionist] side."[17] He was horrified by the Holocaust and the loss of six million Jews at the hands of the Nazis. Moreover, he viewed himself as a person who had a deep love for the Bible and history, and viewed his decision as restoring the Jewish people to their land. Not long after Israel was established, Truman was very proud to compare himself to the ancient Persian monarch who had enabled the ancient Jews to return from Babylon to Jerusalem.[18] Moreover, the U.S. support for the establishment of Israel goes back to the U.S. support of the Balfour Declaration in 1917 and quiet support as far back as Woodrow Wilson.

Despite the fears of the Joint Chiefs and Marshall, the United States did not find itself embroiled in the Arab-Israeli war of 1948. Because of these fears, however, it imposed an arms embargo on both sides of the conflict. In fact, what appeared to be an evenhanded embargo really negatively affected only the Zionist side, since the existing Arab states already had regular armies. Some small weaponry was smuggled to Israel by private individuals, but such shipments were illegal at the time. The day Israel was established, Arab armies attacked, yet Israel won the war despite the arms embargo.[19] Contrary to the fears of the Joint Chiefs of Staff, there was no need to mobilize any part of the U.S. armed forces to secure Israel.

Furthermore, and critically, the U.S.-Saudi oil relationship was not imperiled by Israel's existence. Saudi Arabia provided an uninterrupted oil supply to the United States, despite Ibn Saud's threats that the United States had to choose between the Jews and the Arabs. Not only was the U.S.-Saudi relationship not damaged, but it greatly improved over time, even during Ibn Saud's reign.

Ibn Saud kept his focus on the bilateral relationship between the United States and Saudi Arabia. Notwithstanding his claims and threats, Ibn Saud had a wider-angle view of his country's interests than some American policymakers. They took his arguments at face value and feared being cut off from Saudi oil as a result of U.S. support of Israel. But Ibn Saud understood that the United States was going to be the dominant power in the postwar period, and, as a country run by one family, Saudi Arabia needed U.S. support to ensure the existence of the regime—and such support was forthcoming. Here it is worth noting a letter President Truman wrote to Ibn Saud in October 1950, in which Truman says, apparently alluding to any potential threats from the Soviet Union, "I wish to renew to Your Majesty the assurances which have been made to you several times in the past, that the United States is interested in the preservation of the independence and territorial integrity of Saudi Arabia. No threat to your Kingdom could occur which would not be a matter of immediate concern to the United States."[20]

Additionally, Ibn Saud was attracted to the power of the United States and sought its support as a check on the British. He feared that London supported the rival Hashemites in Jordan and Iraq more than it did the House of Saud. As would occur many times, an inter-Arab rivalry trumped other considerations. In line with his interest in good relations with the United States, Ibn Saud was very supportive of the Arabian-American Oil Company (ARAMCO), formed a few years earlier. When ARAMCO wanted to expand the number of American oil companies in the consortium, Ibn Saud blessed the move, after being guaranteed that the new American oil companies would not be "British controlled."[21]

Over time, the U.S.-Saudi oil relationship flourished amid skyrocketing demand and more equitable revenue sharing. Between 1949 and 1951 alone, Saudi oil revenues from ARAMCO nearly tripled.[22] American oil production became a primary source of wealth for Ibn Saud's country.

Ibn Saud's threat that America must choose between the Arabs and Israel or face the consequences—the biggest fear of the American policymakers of 1947 and 1948—did not materialize. The United States could support the existence of Israel without an oil cutoff from the main Arab oil supplier, Saudi Arabia. American policymakers who opposed Truman, and who had bought the linkage argument, proved to be wrong. Their fears were unfounded: the United States was able to both recognize the existence of Israel and maintain access to Saudi oil. In practice, the Saudi regime did not pursue a region-based confrontation with America, but pursued its own interests, which required close ties with the United States to survive and prosper.

THE EISENHOWER ADMINISTRATION

A key event in Middle East policy during the Eisenhower administration was the 1956 Suez Crisis. During the crisis, the United States came out on the side of the Arabs more clearly than ever before or after. However, this failed to win over any leaders or to strengthen pro-Western moderates in the Arab world. To the contrary, it led to an increase of Soviet influence in the region, and helped Arab radicals. Nasserism flourished over the next decade, and the seeds were planted for the next major war in 1967.

The Eisenhower administration, like several of its successors, saw the Middle East through the prism of U.S.-Soviet Cold War relations. Dwight Eisenhower's main interest was to keep the Arab states away from Soviet influence. In a curious way, this drove the United States to view nascent Arab nationalism as a more credible force than aging monarchies to counter the potential appeal of Soviet Communism in the region. Secular nationalists, many of them young Arab military officers, might be strong enough to ward off Moscow. And the United States was a good ally in this regard. After all, it was not associated with European colonialism in the region, which had helped shape the defiance that came to define Arab nationalism.

Therefore, Egypt's charismatic nationalist leader Gamal Abdel Nasser seemed someone the United States needed to court in hopes of keeping him outside the Soviet orbit. Early in Eisenhower's tenure, Secretary of State John Foster Dulles stated, "Our basic problem in this vitally important region is to improve the attitude of the Muslim States toward the Western democracies, including the United States."[23] Even in September 1955, after Nasser turned to the Soviets for an arms deal—much to the consternation of the Eisenhower administration—the United States did not shun him. It was telling when Kermit Roosevelt of the Central Intelligence Agency wrote from Cairo to CIA director Allen Dulles that "Nasser remains our best, if not our only, hope here."[24]

The United States thought it could forestall the implementation of Soviet weapons deals by providing financing for Egypt's massive Aswan High Dam in 1955. If it could help Nasser provide electricity for his own people, and thus strengthen his domestic importance, he might be more amenable to the United States—and to establishing ties with Israel. At the time, Eisenhower's former deputy secretary of defense, Robert Anderson, was making secret trips to mediate between Egypt and Israel, and there was anticipation that U.S. efforts would inspire Egypt to make corresponding steps toward Israel. However, Nasser did not deliver on this anticipated result. Rather, he rejected the entire financing idea, claiming that it would limit his room to maneuver in arms acquisition deals with the Soviets.

As Anderson's effort proved fruitless, U.S. wariness increased. In early 1956, following one of Anderson's trips, Eisenhower wrote in his diary, "Nasser proved to be a complete stumbling block. He is apparently seeking to be acknowledged as the political leader of the Arab world."[25] The U.S. attitude became tougher in May 1956, when Nasser recognized Communist China and began to engage in barter trade. In response, the United States decided to cancel its financing of the Aswan Dam.

Yet the Eisenhower administration did not want to give up on Nasser—even after he took the dramatic step of nationalizing the Suez Canal. The British and French were livid, stating that the move undermined oil shipping from the Persian Gulf. Britain declared it a violation of the international status of the Canal as ratified by the 1888 Constantinople

Convention. While Britain no longer had troops along the Canal, it did claim to have key rights in the Suez Canal Company, which ran the Canal. But Eisenhower was a firm believer in international law, and he believed the law was on Egypt's side. He was upset by British prime minister Anthony Eden's suggestion that military force be used to retake the Canal. Eden wrote, "There is no doubt in our minds that Nasser, whether he likes it or not, is now effectively in Russia's hands, just as Mussolini was in Hitler's. It would be as ineffective to show weakness to Nasser now in order to placate him as it was to show weakness to Mussolini. The only result was and would be to bring the two together."[26]

Eisenhower thought military action against Egypt would be disastrous. He declared, "[T]he people of the Near East and of North Africa and, to some extent, of all of Asia and all of Africa, would be consolidated against the West to a degree which, I fear, could not be overcome in a generation and perhaps not even in a century, particularly having in mind the capacity of the Russians to make mischief."[27]

Eisenhower's relations with Britain and France cooled, and a drift in U.S.-Israel relations was also evident. Israel thought the United States cared little for its security problems amid ongoing Palestinian fedayeen (guerrilla) raids from the Gaza Strip into Israel and bellicose statements from Nasser calling for Israel's destruction. In October 1956, Nasser blocked Israeli shipping through the Straits of Tiran, vital to Israel's access to the Red Sea and its southern port of Eilat. (The Straits would later be Israel's energy lifeline when it quietly purchased oil from the shah of Iran.) Believing its links to the United States were unlikely to significantly improve, Israel strengthened its relations with France and Britain. Britain had been the majority shareholder in the Suez Canal before it was nationalized by Nasser. France wanted to punish Nasser for training rebels in its colony of Algeria. This tripartite relationship gave birth to the Suez Crisis.

Israel, France, and Britain formulated a plan: Israel would lash out against the terror attacks by moving across the Sinai toward the Canal. Once they were there, Britain and France would say they were taking over the Canal—for the interim—in order to separate the protagonists. Israel launched its strike on October 29, 1956, and was shortly joined by British and French forces. Meanwhile, Eisenhower was furious that the operation had been coordinated without the approval of the United States. He demanded that the military action end and that the British, French, and Israelis withdraw from the Suez Canal and the Sinai.

Eisenhower's response reflected both genuine outrage and calculation. First, he believed the operation ran contrary to international law. Second, he thought it would alienate Arab nationalists from Western countries, including the United States, thereby bolstering the Soviet position in the region and dealing a blow to the newly formed United Nations. By making its opposition to the military actions public, the United States demonstrated anticolonialist bona fides to the Arab world—and to the third world in general. (While Eisenhower was taking a stand on the Suez, the Soviets were invading Hungary to stamp out a rebellion, but Eisenhower believed Hungary was a lost cause.) On October 31, before the British and French militaries had even arrived at the Canal, Eisenhower authorized a UN General Assembly resolution calling for a cease-fire, for Israel to return to its original borders, and for the imposition of an embargo against Israel until it had withdrawn. It also called on all UN members to avoid the use of force.

An ecstatic U.S. ambassador to the United Nations, Henry Cabot Lodge, called Eisenhower. He declared, "Never has there been such a tremendous acclaim for the President's policy. Absolutely spectacular."[28] Four days later, Vice President Richard Nixon also spoke of the windfall that the United States could reap by separating itself from Europe in the third world. In a campaign speech on November 2, Nixon declared, "For the first time in history, we have shown independence of Anglo-French policies toward Asia and Africa which seemed to us to reflect the colonial tradition. That declaration of independence has had an electrifying effect throughout the world."[29]

The United States had taken the side of a third-world Arab country against old U.S. allies Britain and France, and against Israel. Lodge said that following Suez, Arab states developed an "increased respect" for the United States, and "referred several times to indications that Egypt would make concessions once Israeli withdrawal had been accomplished."[30]

Under heavy pressure from Eisenhower, Britain and France withdrew. In addition, Israel withdrew from most of the Sinai, but wanted its pullback from Gaza and the southern edge of the Sinai to be contingent upon a UN decision to take up positions in these locations in order to prevent terrorist raids by Palestinian fedayeen and a second Egyptian attempt to close Israeli shipping. Eisenhower was adamant. He demanded that Israel withdraw completely and unconditionally. He gave a nationally televised and broadcast address on February 20, 1957, to press his case. While it was true that the threat of UN sanctions was not being applied to the Soviet Union in relation to Hungary, Eisenhower said, "two wrongs do not make a right." Thereafter, a United Nations Emergency Force (UNEF) would be set up on the Gaza-Israel border, but it would not take over administration inside Gaza, nor would the UN guarantee shipping. Eisenhower stated with assurance that Israel's withdrawal would lead to peace. He declared, "Equally serious efforts have been made to bring about conditions designed to assure that if Israel will withdraw in response to the repeated requests of the United Nations, there will then be achieved a greater security and tranquility for that nation. This means that the United Nations would assert a determination to see that in the Middle East there will be a greater degree of justice and compliance with international law than was the case prior to the events of last October-November."[31]

Eisenhower's speech is often viewed as a high-water mark in U.S.-Arab relations, since the United States demonstrated that it could both publicly reprimand Israel and demand that Israel's military actions be reversed. The Eisenhower approach was deemed successful because Israel subsequently withdrew. This approach became the Arab template for how the United States should deal with Israel. Over the decades, the resonance of Eisenhower's action meant that there was no need for the Arabs to negotiate with Israel, as it was easier to press the United States to act on their behalf. As the Arabs put it, the U.S. needs to "deliver" Israel.

Despite Eisenhower's prediction that Israel's unconditional withdrawal from Gaza and the remaining part of Sinai would lead to "greater security and tranquility," this rosy picture did not materialize. The United States had acted in favor of Egypt, with the failed expectation of a corresponding move. (Moreover, the United States also suggested to Israel that it did not think Egypt would reoccupy the Gaza Strip, but this prediction also did not come to pass.) Almost exactly ten years later, in 1967, Israel would go to war over the same issues. While visiting Jerusalem in 1957, Secretary of State Dulles pledged to his Israeli counterpart, Golda Meir, that the United States would fight to keep Egypt from again closing the strategic Straits of Tiran to Israeli passage. Israel was keen on an agreement that if the Straits were closed, it would have the right to defend itself against such a flagrant action. Yet as we will see in the discussion of Johnson administration policy, in the month leading up to the 1967 war, Nasser closed the Straits after he expelled UN peacekeepers stationed in the Sinai desert, and the United States did not act to reverse either move but did pressure Israel not to use force.

Leaving the Israeli issues aside, however, the central point is that the United States did not receive an ounce of credit from Nasser for taking on Britain, France, and Israel. One can argue that Eisenhower was correct to take the position that he did for a variety of reasons, but there should have been reciprocal steps from Nasser. Acknowledgment and action on Egypt's part would have been significant for the United States' relations with Egypt. Relations between the United States and Egypt had cooled in 1955 when Egypt began buying weapons from the Soviets. But after Suez there was no quid pro quo, and America's goodwill gesture was met by Nasser with defiance and determination to play an even more anti-Western role in the Middle East. While the United States did the heavy lifting in reversing the Suez Crisis, Nasser rose to iconic status and became the indisputable leader of Arab nationalism.[32] He used the victory to destabilize a variety of Arab regimes in the aftermath of the crisis. As analyst Peter Rodman wrote, "Instead of the last roar of colonialism, the issues posed by Suez [were] the first roar of a new era—the first case of a Third World radical taking Soviet arms and playing the anti-Western card."[33] The other key beneficiary was the Soviet Union, which belatedly offered a nonstarting proposal to send troops to the Canal, but saw the improvement of Soviet-Egyptian relations in the aftermath.

The United States suffered as a result of Suez, but so did the Europeans and more moderate Arab regimes. The United States did not seem to realize how the aftermath would affect pro- and anti-Nasserist forces. Rodman assessed the situation as follows: "Instead of helping Arab moderates, we had undermined or weakened them. Instead of restoring stability to the Middle East, we had unbalanced it, against us."[34] Indeed, there was a bevy of negative consequences for Arab politics in the wake of the Suez Crisis, inspired by the strength of Nasser. His appeal was such that Syria joined a union with Egypt in 1958. In the same year, a civil war broke out in Lebanon, and pro-Western forces lost. The same thing happened in Iraq, as the pro-Western Hashemite king, Faisal II, was deposed and hanged from a lamppost. Another pro-Nasser coup occurred in Sudan, and in Yemen a few years later. It is interesting that the only time that Eisenhower dispatched U.S. military forces to a conflict during his presidency was to Lebanon in 1958 for a four-month period. Ironically, the move was prodded by the Saudis as a belated message to Nasser. Eisenhower told members of Congress that the United States had to act, as the Saudis told him that "if we do not come in, we are finished in the Middle East."[35] Eisenhower later recalled that U.S. action was needed since Nasser "seemed to believe that the United States government was scarcely able, by reason of the nation's democratic system, to use our recognized strength to protect our vital interest."[36] It seems the message was sent too late.

It should also be pointed out that the Suez Crisis was a turning point in European involvement in the Middle East. After Eisenhower humiliated France and Britain, the two countries drew different conclusions. France parted ways with the United States by immediately developing its own nuclear deterrent and later withdrawing from the NATO command.[37] Britain, on the other hand, began coordinating more closely with the United States to avoid another Suez; but over the ensuing years it accelerated its drawdown of forces in the Middle East, leading to a situation in which regional security would fall squarely on the shoulders of America.

Eisenhower ultimately regretted the policy he pursued in the Suez Crisis. A decade later, in a meeting with Richard Nixon in Gettysburg, Pennsylvania, he said his action had prevented Britain and France from playing a constructive role in the Middle East. Nixon recalled, "[Eisenhower] gritted his teeth as he remarked 'why couldn't the British and the French have done it more quickly.'" Eisenhower went on to observe that U.S. actions to reverse the crisis for Nasser's benefit "didn't help as far as the Middle East was concerned. Nasser became even more anti-West and anti-U.S. We agreed that the worst fallout from Suez was that it weakened the will of our best allies, Britain and France, [from playing] a major role in the Middle East or in other areas outside of Europe."[38] Ironically, the same Nixon who at the time was thrilled that the United States had thus distanced itself from the Europeans and Israel would later describe American policy during the Suez Crisis as "the greatest foreign policy blunder the United States has made since the end of World War II."[39] And at the center of it lay the misleading notion of linkage.

THE JOHNSON ADMINISTRATION

The 1956 Suez Crisis set the context for the 1967 war, and the Eisenhower administration shaped the challenges that Lyndon B. Johnson's administration faced in the run-up to that war. The Johnson administration vacillated when confronting these challenges for a variety of reasons. Among these reasons was Johnson's preoccupation with the Vietnam War, but also the fear of offending the Arab states. It was this uncertainty that, in the end, guaranteed a war. Could the United States have prevented war with a viable policy? It is unknowable. However, it is clear that linkage brought war closer. The Arabists in the State Department asked America to allow aggression, especially as Nasser threatened to cut off shipping to Israel and moved his army into the Sinai to attack Israel. During the course of U.S. vacillation, Nasser openly gave speeches about his desire to liquidate Israel, and he reached a defense pact with Jordan. Due to Nasserism's popularity, Jordan's King Hussein was afraid to not mobilize. U.S. indecisiveness led the surrounding Arab armies to believe there would be no political consequence for their action. Israel's remarkable victory in the 1967 war created both problems and opportunities. The disposition of the territories Israel won remains a key focus of diplomacy. However, it also gave the United States leverage, as the Arabs would ultimately seek out Washington due to its enhanced relationship with Israel.

Historians debate whether Nasser desired war with Israel or whether a series of events created such a dynamic in May 1967. Whatever his motivation, Nasser called for the removal of the UNEF forces that were deployed after the Suez Crisis. He then closed the Straits of Tiran. In 1957, the Eisenhower administration had pledged to Israel that the United States would keep the Straits of Tiran open if Egypt ever closed them again. The Straits were the conduit for Israel's oil supply from Iran, as no Arab states would provide Israel with oil. Therefore, keeping the Straits open was vital to Israel. This was the price Israel had insisted upon in exchange for its withdrawal from the Sinai in 1957. In 1967, the Johnson administration would be tested on whether it would adhere to that pledge.

In May 1967, Israeli prime minister Levi Eshkol sent his foreign minister, Abba Eban, on a trip to Paris, London, and Washington in a bid to reopen the straits and stave off war. Eshkol held back his own generals, who feared that any hesitation would give Nasser time to build up Egyptian troops in the Sinai and launch a war. Moreover, the generals believed Israel could not keep a citizen's army of reserves mobilized indefinitely without crippling the economy.

Eban's first stop in Paris was emblematic that key capitals viewed the crisis and commitments of a decade past through the prism of their current relationships with the Arab world. France feared that any step toward Israel would undermine its relationship with the Arabs. When Eban faced France's famed leader Charles de Gaulle, the latter did not deny that his country had also pledged to keep the Straits open in 1957. But much had changed for France during the interim.

In the 1950s, France had felt isolated from the Arab world because of its unwelcome control of Algeria.[40] At the same time, France's relationship with Israel flourished. France was not only Israel's partner in 1956, but it provided Israel with its nuclear reactor in Dimona. In the early 1960s, however, France ended its debilitating presence in North Africa, and its relations with the Arabs were restored. De Gaulle believed he could not have close ties with both the Arabs and Israel, so, for him, it was preferable to walk away from the commitment to protect Israel's passage through the straits. De Gaulle summed up the change in France's Middle East policy when speaking to Eban, saying, "That was 1957, now is 1967."[41] De Gaulle added that Israel was not "sufficiently established to solve all her problems herself."[42]

De Gaulle saw the Soviets more as part of the solution than as part of the problem. In fact, the Soviets were part of the problem. Moscow was fomenting verbal attacks on Israel while giving Nasser utterly erroneous information during the month that Israel amassed troops and stood poised to attack Syria; this contributed to Nasser's moving troops into the Sinai. De Gaulle told Eban that the Soviets might be able to help resolve the situation, but he gave him no reason to believe that Moscow would play a constructive role. Eban left de Gaulle's office crestfallen. He told waiting journalists at the Elysée Palace, "I have told President de Gaulle that the blockade of the Gulf of Aqaba is an act of aggression. Israel is in a position of preparedness but not of alarm. Her forces are capable of defending the vital interests and the territory of the State. The blockade is a piratical act. A world which resigned itself to such acts would be a jungle."[43] Eban's meeting in London also did not produce a breakthrough.

The last stop on his whirlwind trip was Washington. While the United States had not faced an experience like that of France in Algeria, Johnson also hesitated to honor past commitments. First, there was ignorance as to what the commitments actually were. In fact, Johnson's aides did not even have the necessary records to inform themselves. Before President Johnson met Eban at the White House, his top foreign policy adviser, Walt Rostow, was forced to visit Eisenhower's home in Gettysburg, Pennsylvania. Eisenhower issued Rostow an affidavit stating that in 1957 the United States had indeed pledged to open the waterway if Egypt closed it again.[44]

The problem extended beyond a lack of historical knowledge, however. Johnson had a major problem in the present: America's deepening military involvement in the Vietnam War. Johnson sensed there was no American congressional or public appetite to back up the commitment to Israel, and he wanted to avoid confrontation with Egypt.

Reaction to Nasser's earlier decision to expel the UNEF was also tepid at best. One idea, put forward by British minister of state for commonwealth affairs George Thompson, called for maritime countries to declare free passage through the Straits of Tiran. If this was not honored, an international flotilla—or, as it became known, the Red Sea regatta—led by the U.S. Sixth Fleet, would sail through the Straits of Tiran. The British view was that Nasser would find it hard to keep the waterway closed amid multilateral unity.

Yet in discussion with top aides before meeting Eban, Johnson admitted that the regatta response was woefully insufficient. He asked his advisers, "If you were in Eban's place and we told you we were relying on the UN and a group of maritime powers, would that be enough to satisfy you? Will I regret on Monday not giving Eban more today?"[45] At a preliminary meeting with Israeli diplomat Ephraim Evon, Johnson had called the UN a "zero." During his meeting with Eban, Johnson said, "You are the victims of aggression." Despite these private remarks, he urged Israel not to act, asking them to give the regatta a chance. Johnson gave Eban a handwritten note from Secretary of State Dean Rusk that stated, "I must emphasize the necessity for Israel not to make itself responsible for the initiation of hostilities."[46] The Rusk note also included a cryptic statement that could be read both as a pledge of support and threat. It said: "Israel will not be alone unless it decides to go alone." At that point, Israel decided to view this vaguely worded statement as an assurance. That meeting led the Israeli cabinet, by the narrowest of margins, to delay a preemptive strike. Israel was warned by the United States not to publicly mention a regatta. It was even denied a liaison with the U.S. Army.[47]

Yet even the regatta idea was opposed within the U.S. bureaucracy. The regatta episode epitomized the view of State Department Arabist diplomats about the value of U.S.-Israel relations during a time of crisis. According to their view, Israel was a burden to the United States, and commitments to it need not be fulfilled. In contrast, it was appropriate to take fears of threatened U.S. interests in the Arab world at face value. Arabs had rights, while Israel had only needs—which, unlike rights, are debatable. So, while it was understood that the United States had made a commitment to Israel, the advice of America's leading Arabists was to ignore this commitment and the implications it would have for Israel's security.

The Arabists' differing views of the Arab states was rooted in a mix of factors. One element was calculus—a belief that Israel was a strategic liability while the U.S. needed to court the Arabs, who had oil and who they feared might partner with the Soviets if they felt estranged from the United States. Another element was personal experience. Arabist diplomats had served in the Arab world, and some were descendants of missionaries who had developed a certain romance of the Arab world.[48] In contrast, few Arabists served in Israel. They saw it as hurtful to their career as regional specialists. Their only experience with Israel was for it to be the object of complaints they heard expressed by Arab leaders. Israel thus caused them problems on a daily basis with the host governments— and their own approach, internalized over the years, became one of being anti-Israel, cloaked in the language of what was good for U.S. interests in the Middle East.

The tone was set by Secretary of State Dean Rusk, who feared that even participating in a regatta could harm U.S.-Arab relations. As Rusk told Belgian foreign minister Pierre Harmel, "To commit ourselves in this way now would not only reduce our flexibility in seeking a peaceful solution but could bring us into direct military confrontation with Nasser."[49] American diplomats in the Middle East were even more direct and cabled Washington, urging that the United States not keep its commitments to Israel. Ambassador Dwight Porter cabled from Beirut that the Arabs would not believe the issue of the waterway was so important, saying, "Would the United States be as concerned over the issue if it were Jordan's port of Aqaba?" Ambassador Hugh Smythe cabled from Damascus, "On the scales, we have Israel, an unviable client state whose value to the United States is primarily emotional, balanced with [the] full range [of] vital strategic, political, commercial/economic interests represented by Arab states." The top U.S. diplomat in Amman, Findley Burns, urged the United States not to keep its commitments to Israel. If Israel did go to war, Burns warned, "We will never be able to convince the Arabs we have not encouraged her to do so. This will wreck every interest we have in North Africa and the Middle East . . . for years to come."[50] Blatantly ignoring the UN resolution that called for partition in 1947, U.S. ambassador in Egypt Richard Nolte said the United States had no obligation to a country "established by force." He feared the regatta, stating, "It is inconceivable to us that [the] UAR [United Arab Republic, i.e. Egypt] with full Soviet backing would not, repeat not, militarily confront any naval or other force which attempts to enforce 'free passage.' "[51] Charles Yost, a retired U.S. Middle East diplomat who was called back by Johnson during the crisis, flew to Cairo to meet with Egyptian foreign minister Mahmoud Riad. Emerging from the meeting, he cabled Washington that Israel should accept the new status quo and forget about access to its southern port of Eilat.[52]

Two men dissented from the majority view among U.S. Middle East diplomats in the run-up to the 1967 war. They were Hermann Eilts, ambassador to Saudi Arabia, and David Newsom, ambassador to Libya. Both called for U.S. destroyers to go to the Straits of Tiran. Eilts later stated, "The other Arabists were all against it. They were afraid of the Egyptian reaction. It was the same old localitis again." He added, "But Nasser's best troops were bogged down in [war with] Yemen, so the Egyptians wouldn't have fired on our ships. And the Israelis, seeing that we were serious about protecting them, might not have felt the need to launch a preemptive attack on Egypt, as they soon did."[53] (Eilts later said that Secretary of State Henry Kissinger cited this recommendation when offering him the top Cairo post in 1973.)

However, it was not just the State Department that was opposed to the regatta. The Pentagon also saw this idea as leading to potential confrontation with Egypt. Asked by top U.S. Mideast official Luke Battle, who had been an ambassador to Cairo, what would happen if a U.S. ship in the regatta were fired upon, the chairman of the Joint Chiefs of Staff, General Charles Wheeler, slammed his fist on the table: "Luke, it means war."[54]

The United States was adamant about avoiding conflict for a number of reasons, not least its absorption and growing involvement in the Vietnam War. Some in the Pentagon might have been concerned that action would trigger Soviet intervention and lead to a wider conflagration, while others felt that Israel could defeat Nasser on its own and that the United States should not hold Israel back. The Johnson administration feared that if the regatta were attacked by Egypt, this would lead to something similar to the Gulf of Tonkin resolution that initiated the Vietnam War. Therefore, the United States did not stand behind it. Moreover, the world was not supportive. The idea of the regatta began to fizzle out, as only two of the eighteen countries asked—Australia and the Netherlands—signed up to join. Even Britain, which initiated the idea, did not stand behind it. Worse, the British were prepared to accept a new status quo in the region, with the cabinet stating, "The military disposition by the Arab countries and particularly by the UAR [Egypt] represented a permanent change in the balance of power in the Middle East to the disadvantage of Israel, which both she and the Western Powers would have to accept."[55] Only six countries agreed to a draft resolution at the United Nations in support of Israel's right of passage through the Straits of Tiran. The United States had no blueprint for defusing the crisis. It seemed to matter little that a defiant Nasser would declare, "Our basic objective will be the destruction of Israel. The Arab people want to fight."[56] The U.S. approach remained unchanged and ineffectual.

Up to the last moment, Rusk continued to rebuff any Israeli request for assurances, while also calling on Israel to avoid preemption. A bitterly disappointed Israeli ambassador to the United States, Avraham (Abe) Harman, could not believe the United States would allow the Egyptians to block the Straits. Harman wondered, "Does Israel have to tolerate 10,000 casualties before the United States concede[s] that aggression occurred?"[57]

In a broader sense, Israel viewed U.S. inaction as part of an essentially amoral policy, in keeping with the regional U.S. arms embargo that lasted from 1948 to 1963. The United States knew that the embargo hurt the nascent state of Israel more than it hurt the Arab states, with their conventional armies and alternative sources of weaponry. The lack of international consequences to Nasser's closing of the Straits further reinforced the Zionist ethos of self-reliance. Critically, the expulsion of UNEF, and U.S. and European failure to adhere to past commitments to open the Straits, led Israel to sour—for decades—on the idea of international assurances as a foundation of peacemaking to fill the vacuum of Israeli territorial withdrawal.

The lack of any consequences for Nasser's closing of the Straits was significant in the eyes of Israeli security officials, who saw there was nothing to gain by waiting. Egyptian forces were amassed near Eilat in the Gaza Strip, and—because of the defense treaty with Jordan—in the West Bank. The Jordanian military was in East Jerusalem, the Syrians in the Golan Heights. There was no reason for Israel not to head to war.

The war catalyzed a political earthquake that shook the Middle East. Despite a U.S. arms embargo during the war and its aftermath, Israel's size tripled from the land it won in 1967, and Nasser's pan-Arabism was eclipsed. The Six Day War became the open wound from which the Arab world would never recover. In the aftermath of the 1967 war, the Arab leaders refused to take any steps toward Israel. At the same time, Nasser actually led the other Arab leaders to reject calls by some radical elements to maintain a very short-lived suspension in oil supplies during the war. Nasser said it was self-defeating for the Arabs. Diplomatic measures by some Arabs again did occur. Yet contrary to the fears of the advocates of linkage, the war and its aftermath did not lead to a material loss for the United States. There would be no looming confrontation between America and the Arab world.

Johnson's policy shifted in the aftermath of the war, apparently as a reaction to Eisenhower's pressure on Israel after the Suez Crisis. Eisenhower had forced Israel to relinquish the Sinai in 1957, but this did not prevent the next war in 1967. In the wake of the 1967 war, Johnson now emphasized that Israeli withdrawal would not come without reciprocal actions, unlike 1957. Rather, the Arabs and Israel would have to reach a negotiated peace. And so, toward the end of 1967, UN Security Council Resolution 242 was born. Land became a bargaining chip in peace negotiations—known as "land for peace," meaning the bargain was that

Israel would retain the new land until the Arab states were willing to offer peace in return. The efficacy of this approach would be at least partially proved with the peace negotiated between Israel and Egypt over
the next ten to twelve years.[58] The value of UN Security Council Resolution 242 would not be felt immediately after its passage. Indeed, there
would be continued clashes between Egyptian and Israeli forces along
the Suez Canal in 1969–1970, dubbed the War of Attrition, and then the
1973 war. Yet by the end of that war, the value of UN Resolution 242,
which was reaffirmed and embodied in UNSC 338, became even more
clear. Egypt would want to recover its Sinai Desert land, and the price
would ultimately be peace. With Egypt out of the coalition against Israel,
the period of interstate wars between Israel and the Arab countries ended
in 1973. In this context, Egypt viewed its ties with the United States as in-
dispensable. Only America had influence over Israel, a key lever to reclaim land lost in the 1967 war. The hope of restoring Egyptian land
would create a rapprochement between Washington and Cairo, since
Moscow had no such influence over Israel. Once again the linkage argument and the expectations associated with it proved to be wrong.

The concept of linkage underwent a change beginning in 1967. Before the 1967 war, it took the form of calling for the United States to break
its commitments to Israel and to side with the Arabs instead, even when
doing so produced no meaningful reciprocal actions. However, Israel's
stunning victory on three fronts introduced a new variable to the situation. The Arab states could act reciprocally by making peace with Israel
in return for Israeli land withdrawal. But this idea was not accepted by
the Arab world. In the 1967 postwar conference in Khartoum, the Arab
League issued its infamous resolution declaring "three no's"—no negotiations, no peace, no recognition of Israel.

But the more basic question of linkage remained. There were two
views in the United States regarding Arab goals. One view was that the
Arabs were focused on comprehensive steps in order to maximize their
leverage to force Israeli concessions with minimal, if any, reciprocal
moves. The other was that they were more focused on their own national
interests and willing to engage in reciprocity. The Arabists in the United
States almost always assumed the former, when the reality became increasingly clear that key players in the Arab world focused more on the
latter at key junctures in the 1970s. Moreover, in the 1970s a new dimen-

sion emerged. A localized struggle between Israelis and Palestinians became a key pressure point as Arab countries tried to leverage U.S. action in their favor.

THE NIXON ADMINISTRATION

There was broad agreement within Richard Nixon's administration that the Middle East should be viewed in the context of overall relations with the Soviet Union. At the outset of his administration, Nixon offered his own version of linkage, but as part of his strategy for affecting Soviet behavior. As he later explained: "Since U.S.-Soviet interests as the world's two competing superpowers were so widespread and overlapping, it was unrealistic to separate or compartmentalize areas of concern. Therefore we decided to link progress in such areas of Soviet concern as strategic arms limitation and increased trade with progress in areas that were important to us—Vietnam, the Mideast, and Berlin. This concept became known as linkage."[59]

In other words, U.S.-Soviet cooperation in the Middle East would be a litmus test for achieving broader ties. But the question remained—how should U.S.-Soviet ties be measured? Should the United States work with the Soviets to ease regional tensions, or was Soviet involvement in regional disputes dangerous? According to the first argument, the United States should work with the Soviets because Middle East conflict resolution would limit Soviet mischief-making. The second approach was to halt the Soviets from supporting Syria and Egypt, among others. At the start of his presidency, Nixon seemed to lean toward the first approach, which was favored by Secretary of State William Rogers. When that approach hit a dead end by the start of Nixon's second year in office, he shifted to the second approach, favored by Henry Kissinger.

Rogers began his job as secretary of state without experience in foreign policy, let alone the Middle East. (He had served as attorney general during the Eisenhower administration.) At the start of Nixon's first term, the president gave Rogers permission to try a comprehensive approach to the Middle East. The term "comprehensive" would come to mean resolving all the different fronts of the 1967 war, including resolution with Egypt, Syria, and, until 1974, Jordan. (In 1974, Arab states insisted that Jordan yield its authority for negotiations to the Palestinians themselves. The division of authority between Jordan and the Palestinians would remain controversial even after Jordan's King Hussein severed his relationship to the West Bank in 1988.) The two absent parties were the Arabs and the Israelis—a fact that raised suspicion in the region. Predictably, the Soviets wanted to know how the United States viewed a final settlement between the parties, and Rogers relayed that it involved returning to the prewar 1967 borders with minor territorial changes or adjustments. This would form the basis of the Rogers Plan—a standstill cease-fire—put forward on December 9, 1969. There were no direct talks between the Arabs and Israelis, no Arab normalization with Israel, no peace treaty, and no detailed focus on security.

William Quandt, who was in the Nixon White House and subsequently became a Middle East diplomatic historian, described the Rogers Plan as implying that "the quality of the peace agreement, the standards to be applied to Arab commitments were not too rigorous."[60]

Rogers's entire approach failed, however, amid opposition from the Soviet Union, Israel, and Egypt—essentially all the major players it was meant to satisfy. On December 22, 1969, Israel rejected the Rogers Plan in the sharpest terms imaginable: "Israel will not be sacrificed by any power or inter-power policy and will reject any attempt to impose a forced solution on her. . . . The proposal submitted by the United States cannot but be interpreted by the Arab rulers as an attempt to appease them at the expense of Israel."[61] Ironically, the Soviets would reject the Rogers Plan a day later, even though cooperation with the big powers—especially the Soviets—was the premise of U.S. diplomacy in 1969.

Reflecting on the defeat of the Rogers Plan, Nixon suggested that the plan was not driven by the desire for peace, but rather to form the basis of U.S.-Arab relations. Nixon wrote:

> I knew that the Rogers Plan could never be implemented, but I believed that it was important to let the Arab world know that the United States did not automatically dismiss its case regarding the occupied territories or rule out a compromise settlement of the conflicting claims. With the Rogers Plan on record, I thought it would be easier for the Arab leaders to propose reopening relations with the United States without coming under attack from the hawks and pro-Soviet elements in their own countries.[62]

Here was an approach based on the traditional concept of linkage applied to the Middle East, in which concerns about Arab reactions defined what the United States should do, including pressuring Israel. Kissinger's postmortem of this approach was extremely critical. According to Quandt, "Kissinger also found it misguided and possibly dangerous for the United States to improve its relations with adversaries—the Soviet Union and Egypt—by pressuring its own friend, Israel. While such things might be done in the interest of achieving a genuine peace agreement, they should not become part of the standard American negotiating repertoire. The Soviets and Arabs should instead learn that U.S. influence was conditional on their restraint and moderation."[63] Or, as Kissinger himself wrote, "I believed that a steady stream of American concessions would increase Soviet temptations to act as the lawyer for Arab radicals. Proponents of an active policy wanted to win the radicals to our side by making generous offers. I argued that the radical regimes could not be won over; their moderation was more likely if we insisted on a change of course as a precondition of major American involvement."[64]

In truth, Rogers's approach had been guided by the traditional logic of squeezing Israel to try to force it to make the needed concessions; to this end, the administration twice held up arms shipments to Israel during this period. This arms delay was distressing to Israel since it happened during the War of Attrition. Arab leaders, on the other hand, were not pressed to take difficult steps that might prove controversial in their own domestic environments. All this was supposed to produce moves toward peace. Yet in the end, despite how little the Rogers Plan demanded of Egypt and Arab radicals, Nasser did not embrace it. Once again, U.S. action was predicated upon the expectation of certain Arab responses to favorable U.S. policy, and such responses simply did not emerge.

From Nasser to Sadat and from Rogers to Kissinger.

But realities in the region were about to change. Nasser died in 1970 and was replaced by his vice president, Anwar Sadat. Some ridiculed Sadat as a lightweight who could not possibly fill Nasser's shoes. But the new Egyptian leader made it clear from the outset that he differed from other Arab leaders in at least three distinct ways. First, he would not count on others to put forward diplomatic ideas, but would initiate them as well.

Second, if he wanted Israel to take a step, he would reciprocate with tangible measures. Finally, he realized that linking diplomacy to a comprehensive peace would create a lowest-common-denominator effect and encourage regional spoilers, such as Syria. Over time, Sadat would give more primacy to the interests of Egypt than to the PLO or the long and winding road to comprehensive peace. This would prove to be an earthquake for the Arab world, even if it was not immediately apparent. In retrospect, Nasser's death marked the end of pan-Arab nationalism. There had been cracks in the movement beforehand, but it died with Nasser. Afterward, Arab states would still pay lip service to the importance of this idea, but in practice, each country would prioritize its own national agenda.

In February 1971, Sadat delivered a speech to the Egyptian parliament that seemed to pick up on an idea being floated by Israeli Defense Minister Moshe Dayan. As a first step toward breaking the military deadlock, Israel would move its troops away from the Suez Canal. Sadat made clear he was not offering peace in return. However, his proposal introduced two new ideas: gradualism, and nonbelligerency following Israel's withdrawal from all territories won in 1967. For the first time, an Arab leader broke with the rejectionism of the Khartoum Conference. It is possible that energetic diplomacy in 1971 could have prevented the outbreak of the 1973 War. Yet it is also possible that Sadat's move was only a chimera. Kissinger wrote years later that he was skeptical of the proposal, since there was no guarantee that the ten thousand Soviet technicians based along the Canal during the War of Attrition would actually leave. He thinks Israel may have rejected the idea, fearing the Soviets would exploit the vacuum left by Israel.[65]

By the spring of 1973, Anwar Sadat planned to go to war with Israel. Given the failure of his 1971 Canal initiative, he saw this as the only way to break the deadlock. Sadat tested American intentions. His national security advisor returned from secret meetings with Henry Kissinger only to learn the United States would not urge Israel to withdraw from the Sinai. The status quo was unacceptable to Sadat.[66] Later in the spring, he held secret talks with Syrian president Hafez al-Asad to decide the dates for the war. At the same time, he made public speeches, calling 1973 the "year of decision." In his speeches, he called for oil to be brandished as a weapon. Since he had also said the two previous years were each the year of decision, his threats were ignored. Kissinger would later admit publicly, "I must say, we did not take Sadat very seriously," adding this was so because the Egyptian leader "was [always] making terrible threats, which he never implemented."[67]

U.S. and Israeli intelligence had missed all the signals that war was on the way. Jordan's King Hussein even tipped off Prime Minister Meir in advance. Both the United States and Israel thought Egypt would fight only if it thought it could achieve a military victory. Instead, Egypt fought to break a political deadlock.

On October 6 the war began with a joint surprise attack by Egypt and Syria. Some would call it Israel's Pearl Harbor because it was a surprise attack that triggered a major war. It broke out on Yom Kippur, the holiest day of the Jewish calendar. Sadat had already mobilized Egyptian troops twice that year as part of his deception, forcing Israel to make the expensive move of mobilizing its own, reserves-based army. On the third time, Israel dismissed the move—but this time it was for real. At the start of the war, the United States expected an Israeli rout, given their lightning victory in 1967. Instead, it was Egypt that crossed the Suez Canal. Israeli planes were shot down by Soviet surface-to-air missiles. For four long days, the Israeli military suffered losses. It begged the United States for an airlift. Israeli Prime Minister Golda Meir wanted to make an emergency trip to Washington.

Why was the U.S. airlift of weaponry to Israel delayed four key days during the first week of fighting? This is one of the lasting enigmas of the 1973 war. Some have sought to explain away the traumatic moment in U.S.-Israel relations by attributing it to either American bureaucratic infighting or low-level U.S. logistical bungling. Others seek to paint a picture of a struggle inside the U.S. government with President Nixon, Secretary of State Kissinger, and Defense Secretary James Schlesinger playing the roles of heroes and villains.

After extensive examination of U.S. decision-making during that period—including a look at transcripts of conversations, interviews and memoirs of U.S., Egyptian, and Israeli policymakers—it is clear that the airlift's delay and its subsequent takeoff were deliberate and calculated moves by three key characters: Nixon, Kissinger, and Schlesinger. (Central in understanding the broader picture is a book of transcripts published by

Kissinger thirty years after the war, based on his secretaries' transcriptions of his telephone conversations. These records were declassified in 2001 by the National Security Council.)[68] The airlift episode must be seen as part of broader U.S. foreign policy. Examining it requires an understanding of how U.S. strategy evolved during the first week of the war. The delay was not the result of bureaucratic bottlenecks or the freelancing of a single official.

It is clear that, at the start of the war, the U.S. favored a neutral stand that would not risk the gains of détente that remained central to American foreign policy interests. Expecting an Israeli rout of the Arabs along the lines of 1967, Kissinger urgently sought a U.N. Security Council resolution that would call on the parties to return to the prewar lines, to the status quo ante. Kissinger felt a simple cease-fire that would freeze the existing situation on the battlefield would be a mistake. He told U.S. ambassador to the UN John Scali on the first day of the war, "If we call only for a cease fire, we would be using the UN to sanctify aggression—[an aggressor] can grab territory, ask the UN to call a cease-fire and then if the victim—creates a dangerous precedent [sic]."[69]

That said, Kissinger viewed a joint U.S.-Soviet resolution calling for a return to the status quo ante as key for both demonstrating the value of détente and for avoiding friction between the two superpowers. It could also cause the Arabs to question the value of friendship with Moscow. Conversely, freezing the situation on the battlefield while Israel was losing would hurt America's ability to influence Israel in the postwar period. As Kissinger told White House Chief of Staff Alexander Haig on October 7, "My profound conviction is that if we play this the hard way, it's the last time they [the Israelis] are going to listen. If we kick them in the teeth, they have nothing lose."[70] Furthermore, Kissinger thought an Arab victory would make the Arabs intractable. He added, "I think if the Arabs win, they will be impossible and there will be no negotiations."[71]

The Soviets, however, rejected the idea of a joint resolution to halt the fighting, and the idea of returning to the status quo ante seemed to fade. Yet Kissinger saw time on his side. He was convinced that, as soon as Israel reversed the tide of Egyptian advances across the Suez Canal, the Arab states and Egypt's patron in Moscow would be clamoring for the very UNSC resolution that they had just spurned. As Kissinger had told Haig and many diplomats, the United States would not stop Israel from reversing the tide. To the contrary, he even favored giving them small things such as ammunition and spare parts to obtain their return to the prewar line. The anticipation of Israeli success was so high that the challenge would be in getting Israel to not exceed the prewar lines. Kissinger determined that the U.S. was up to the challenge. He told Haig, "My view is if the Israelis make territorial acquisitions we have to come down hard on them to force them to give them up."[72]

On October 7, Israel had already requested forty Phantoms, but Kissinger and Schlesinger were unsympathetic since they were convinced that an Israeli victory was certain anyway. On October 8, Israel's ambassador to the United States, Simcha Dinitz, relayed a personal request from Golda Meir to Kissinger urging that he approve the Phantoms. Kissinger suggested this was being discussed with Nixon, but made no promises. In consultations between Nixon and Kissinger, both saw an Israeli victory as imminent and therefore kept their focus on invigorating postwar diplomacy.

This strategy collapsed on October 9, as the U.S. was notified that the Israelis were suffering high casualties and were unable to repel the Egyptian attack. The Israeli counterattack was sputtering, and, more critically, there were unusually high losses of soldiers and equipment. In the first few days of the war, Israel lost forty-nine airplanes (including fourteen Phantoms downed by Soviet surface-to-air missiles, known as SAM-6's) and a stunning 500 tanks, 400 of which were lost along the Egyptian front. As Kissinger would subsequently write, "Our strategy had been based on the assumption of an overwhelming and rapid Israeli victory—an assumption at every point supported by intelligence sources and Israeli communications. This caused our diplomacy without urgency, since time, we thought, was improving our negotiating position. That assumption was exploded by a telephone call from Dinitz." Kissinger added, "What Dinitz was reporting would require a fundamental reassessment of our strategy."[73]

These calls grew more insistent, including a request from Golda Meir to make an emergency visit to see Nixon, which the United States rejected as a sign of desperation. At a key meeting of senior U.S. officials on October 9 to discuss the new situation, CIA director William Colby believed that Israel was exaggerating the direness of the new situation. Schlesinger saw no problem with sending auxiliary equipment not requiring American technicians. But he was opposed to meeting Israel's requests for planes and other heavy equipment. In Kissinger words, Schlesinger's opposition was based on the concern that "turning around a battle that the Arabs were winning might blight our relations with the Arabs for a long time. Schlesinger stressed the distinction between defending Israel's survival within its pre-1967 borders and helping Israel maintain its conquests from the 1967 war. Other participants concurred."

Kissinger insisted that he himself had demurred. He would subsequently recall, "My own view was that events had gone beyond such fine-tuning. There was agreement that a defeat of Israel with Soviet arms would skewer the political as well as the strategic equilibrium in the Middle East. Avoidance of an Israeli defeat was therefore in America's strategic interest. It was at that point, not during the war, that we could appeal to the Arab nations by the way we conducted the postwar diplomacy."[74]

However, there is no evidence that Kissinger thought providing airplanes and heavy equipment was a good idea. He would have supported the provision of ammunition and assorted electronics in principle, even though this was held up by a desultory approach at the Pentagon. But he felt differently about an airlift of heavy equipment, such as planes. First, he supported Schlesinger's approach in a conversation with Nixon. Second, he rejected personal calls over the next four days by leading U.S. senators Frank Church, Hubert Humphrey, and Henry Jackson for the United States to send Phantoms for the Israelis to fly. Kissinger was willing to send Phantoms, provided not more than two per day would be sent. This was notwithstanding the fact that he had been notified by his aide, Brent Scowcroft, that "a third of the [Israeli] air force is out of action."[75] Third, Kissinger saw avoiding a major airlift as securing détente and believed he could end the war before a massive Soviet airlift already en route had landed. As Kissinger told the Soviet ambassador to the United States as late as October 13, "Until this minute, not one American airplane has landed in Israel. Not one—my whole strategy has been based on reliance on you."[76]

At this stage, Kissinger's view had evolved, and he now thought he could count on the Soviets to press Egypt to end the war with a cease-fire in place. This would provide Egypt with a limited victory, but Kissinger felt this would be acceptable if Israel made advances on the Golan Heights. Based on back-channel messages to the White House at the beginning of the war from the Egyptian national security advisor, Hafez Ismail, Kissinger believed that Egypt would be content to remain under a missile-defense umbrella across the Suez Canal without advancing, and that Israel's existence was not in peril. Exactly thirty-five years after the start of the war, Kissinger publicly alluded to the U.S. view of the war as an opportunity to pry the Egyptians away from the Soviets, so long as Egyptian successes would not accrue to Moscow. Kissinger declared, "So when the war started, we decided that that was in a way the opportunity we had been looking for. We were absolutely determined to prevent any victory to be achieved by Soviet arms. But we also thought that having achieved this, we could use that demonstration to begin a peace process with the Arab side. And we sent a message to Sadat on the first day of the war saying, you are now making war with Soviet arms. But keep in mind that you have to make peace with American diplomacy."[77]

Withholding massive arms shipments would force Israel to accept a simple cease-fire in place, even if it was losing on the Egyptian front. The U.S. strategy at this time has been explained by William Quandt, who was senior director of the National Security Council for the Middle East at the time. As he has written, "The resupply of arms to Israel had been deliberately delayed as a form of pressure on Israel and in order not to reduce the chances of Sadat's acceptance of the cease-fire proposal."[78] Quandt's point is reinforced in the memoirs of Egyptian Foreign Minister Ismail Fahmy. In his first meeting with Kissinger on October 29, 1973, in Washington, Fahmy said that Kissinger admitted the tactic. According to Fahmy, Kissinger "stressed that the United States had refused to send any assistance to Israel during the first seven days of the war" in order to get a UN Security Council ceasefire to Egypt's liking.[79]

A conversation between Nixon and Kissinger on the morning of October 12 clearly indicates that Nixon and Kissinger were in sync with their post-October 9 strategy. They wanted the war to end immediately, before people could say it was the Soviet airlift en route that made the difference in victory. And as can be seen from the transcript of their conversation, they drew a clear distinction between flying in relatively small items and a massive resupply operation, which they favored only after the war:

K: Right now, there's a sort of a balance in the sense that the Israelis gained in Syria and lost in Egypt.

N: Although they haven't gained in Syria quite as much as we'd hoped apparently.

K: I can't get a clear report of that.

N: Now what about our own activities with regard to resupply, etc. Has anything gone forward in that respect?

K: Well, last night we finally told Schlesinger just to charter some of these civilian airlines, airplanes from civilian airlines for the Defense Department and then turn them over to the Israelis.

N: Good.

K: We've tried everything else and these civilian airlines just wouldn't charter to the Israelis directly.

N: That's all right.

K: So that's going to start moving later today.

N: But they have not yet actually run short of equipment?

K: No. And of course, the most important assurance you gave them was that you'd replace the equipment.

N: The planes and tanks, right?

K: Right. So that they can expend what they've got, knowing they'll get more.

N: The lines that be, it seems to me, if you're—simply that we're not going to discuss what's going to be done, but the President has always said that it is essential to maintain the balance of power in the area.

K: I'm giving a press conference today.

N: But maintaining the balance of power, do you think that's too provocative?

K: No, we've always said that we—

N: That's what I mean. That's a signal to the Israelis, etc.

K: I'm giving a press conference today. I've got to navigate that one.

N: Yeah. Well, there's no more to be done. Of course, I don't know anybody has got a better idea as to what we're doing.

K: There's nothing else to be done, Mr. President. After all—

N: In terms of intervention, that's out of the question.

K: Impossible.

N: In terms of massive open support for Israel, that will just bring massive open support by the Russians.

K: And it wouldn't change the situation in the next two or three days, which is what we're talking about.

N: —The Israelis are not looking at two or three days. That's our problem, isn't it? They may be looking at two or three weeks before they can really start clobbering these people.

K: In two or three weeks the international pressures will become unmanageable.

N: I see. Well, then, if it's two or three days then, the Israelis have just got to win something on the Syrian front. Right?

K: That's right.[80]

The decision was a joint one of Nixon and Kissinger together. In subsequent memoirs, Nixon wrote:

Despite the great skepticism of the Israeli hawks, I believed that only a battlefield stalemate would provide the foundation, on which fruitful negotiations might begin. Any equilibrium—even if only an equilibrium of mutual exhaustion—would make it easier to reach an enforceable settlement. . . . I was also concerned that if the Arabs were actually to start losing the war, the Soviet leaders would feel that they could not just stand by and watch their allies suffer another humiliating defeat, as they had done in 1967.

Nixon and Kissinger wanted to end the war with a limited Egyptian victory. They thought such an outcome would be favorable to the United States, believing it would obviate the need for a Soviet airlift and would break the post-1967 diplomatic stalemate. It would give the Israelis an incentive to negotiate, while allowing Sadat to feel that his country had regained its pride. Egypt would then feel freer to take steps toward the United States, preserving U.S. relations with the Arab world. Overall, it was the anticipation of Soviet action that shaped U.S. behavior, and not concern for mounting Israeli fatalities (Israel sustained close to three thousand deaths during the war). Permitting the airlift, U.S. policy makers reasoned, would prolong the war and raise Soviet stakes to match those of the United States. The United States did not want a total Israeli victory because, in its view, this would cement Israel's resolve not to make any territorial concessions in the Sinai.

Moreover, the linkage mindset, at least in part, also affected U.S. strategy. There was a concern within the administration that a major Israeli victory—even without U.S. assistance—would jeopardize U.S. relations with moderate Arabs, and perhaps even lead to radical coups against pro-Western regimes in the region.

The administration was seeking a new balance in the Middle East and believed it could achieve it if, by war's end, Egypt held part of Sinai. In this way, Israel's very existence would not be threatened; America could bring the most populous Arab country into the Western orbit; and détente with the Soviets would not be undermined. Clearly, there was an unstated divergence of interests between Israel and the United States. Nixon later wrote, "I was convinced that we must not use our influence to bring about a cease-fire that would leave the parties in such an imbalance that negotiations for a permanent settlement would never begin." A massive Soviet airlift, however, could produce an imbalance in favor of the Arabs that needed to be prevented. For that reason, Nixon and Kissinger wanted a "cease-fire in place" resolution at the UN. The United States hoped Britain would introduce the resolution on Saturday, October 13.

On the same day, October 12, the sixth day of the war, with still no American airlift in sight, with the Egyptians having dug in along the Canal, and with the Golan advance of the IDF having stalled, Israel was forced into a diplomatic corner. Meir sent instructions to Foreign Minister Eban, then in New York, saying Israel would indeed agree to accept the unfavorable UN "cease-fire in place" idea, knowing that agreeing to end the war out of weakness would impair Israel's postwar bargaining position. Eban recalls the shock upon receiving her instructions in New York. There were subsequent reports that the message was so sensitive that it was never formally entered in the archives of the government. America's "delivery" of Israel meant that the hard part was done; all that remained was the easy part—that is, for the Egyptians to agree to end the war as a victor. The Soviets took the Egyptian position for granted, and the superpowers began planning for Britain to introduce the resolution at the UN for the next day, Saturday, October 13. Until then, the strategy of forcing Israel to accept the cease-fire by withholding the airlift appeared to be working.

Yet, the seeds for the destruction of the strategy were also manifestly evident. Indeed, on October 12, Kissinger seems appalled that Israel's offensive in the Sinai stalled due to the lack of weapons. In other words, the U.S. sought to calibrate the denial of heavy weaponry to get Israel to support an unfavorable cease-fire, but realized there were risks if

Egypt and Syria reached the wrong conclusion. The conversation between Kissinger and Schlesinger close to midnight on Friday, October 12, is very instructive, as it suggests that even the nondelivery of ammunition, not just the nondelivery of planes and tanks, had serious consequences for the war.

Kissinger told Schlesinger, "The whole diplomacy is going to come apart if they look impotent. It can only work if they look as if they were gaining, not if they look as if they were losing." Schlesinger was incredulous that the Israelis were truly running short of ammunition. Kissinger, declared, "They are out now. They have stopped their offensive. And they are now in deep trouble in the Sinai."

Kissinger added to Schlesinger, "We told them every day that this stuff was coming. There wasn't a day that we didn't tell them that they would have twenty aircraft in the morning and then they didn't have them in the evening."[81]

In fact, on the morning of Saturday, October 13, the U.S. strategy unraveled. Sadat rejected the resolution, saying he would accept it only if Israel would pledge to withdraw from all territories captured in 1967. Sadat seemed to be intoxicated by Egypt's early success; he may have wanted to maximize Israeli casualties; and he felt strong knowing that another Soviet airlift was on its way. Fahmy, Sadat's foreign minister, recalled being with Sadat at that time; he did not hide his displeasure with Sadat's decision to reject the cease-fire. Fahmy, who believed that his published remarks in *al-Ahram* in 1972 on why war was needed to break the diplomatic logjam created the seed for Sadat's decision to go to war and led to his appointment as foreign minister, now believed Egypt needed to cash in its chips. He later wrote:

> Sadat, however, made overly confident by his army's victory and Assad's assurances that Syria had no problem, refused to accept the cease fire in place. This was a mistake. Although under normal circumstances a prolonged war would have been in Egypt's interests, the US decision to send arms to Israel changed the situation and made an early cease fire preferable.
>
> Sadat personally informed me that he had conveyed the Egyptian refusal to accept the cease fire to the British ambassador in Egypt, who was pressing him to accept it. I was very upset by this

decision and could not hide my distress. "But what can I do?" he replied, "The Israelis normally accept a cease fire and never respect it, but continue to violate." I answered: "It is true that they have always behaved in that way in the past and will probably do so now. But it is still better that they violate the ceasefire now, when they are still on the East Bank of the Suez Canal, than later, because they might succeed in crossing it." Sadat just kept silent, trying to digest the implications of what I had told him.

My prediction was unfortunately correct. A few days later the American arms shipments had reached the point where the Israelis were able to cross the Suez Canal. This created a situation of near panic within both the military and the political leadership of Egypt.[82]

In short, Sadat rejected the winning terms in favor of holding out for maximalist demands. It is hard to escape the view that it was lack of military progress by Israel that emboldened Sadat, and this lack of progress was tied to the lack of U.S. support. The Egyptians reached the wrong conclusion. Kissinger later recalled in cryptic terms and with use of uncharacteristic understatement, "the seeming inability to synchronize diplomatic and military means provided the impetus for the airlift."

As Fahmy confirmed, Sadat's blunder was his unwillingness to end the war with his gains ratified by the UN Security Council. He would correctly view this blunder as the political turning point of the war. Kissinger heard from British Foreign Minister Alec Douglas-Home on Saturday morning that it did not look as though Sadat was ready for a cease-fire in place. Kissinger said, "If this goes on, we will have to send a massive airlift in there."[83]

Indeed, once Sadat balked, and the United States saw it had nothing to gain from pressuring Israel further and withholding arms, Nixon and Kissinger immediately switched gears. As Quandt subsequently wrote: "Now everything was coming unstuck. Kissinger was angry at Sadat, at the British, and at the Soviets. . . . A new strategy had to be devised, and quickly."[84] With Soviet weaponry continuing to flood the Arab states on October 13 (Nixon claimed that the Soviets were now supplying seven hundred tons of weaponry and matériel daily to Syria and Egypt), any further U.S. passivity would bring a most unwelcome result. The United

States no longer viewed any form of Egyptian victory as favorable. To the contrary, in the wake of a Soviet airlift, any Egyptian victory would have been seen as a disaster, since the political credit would accrue to the Soviet Union and not Washington. This would firmly entrench the Soviets in Egypt after the war, and thereby reverse one of America's main gains. Moreover, the Soviets would be in a position to set the diplomatic tempo.

For the United States, it became imperative to shift gears and help Israel, believing this would humble the intransigent duo of the Soviet Union and Egypt. Kissinger's reaction was swift. Reflecting on what occurred in 1973, the secretary of state wrote:

> The die was now cast; matters had reached a point where maneuvering would be suicidal and hesitation, disastrous. The parties could not yet be brought to end the war—or the Soviets to support this course—by a calculation of their interests. All that was left was to force a change in the perception of their interests. We would pour in supplies. We would risk a confrontation. We would not talk again (with the Soviets) until there was no longer any doubt that no settlement could be imposed. . . . Conciliation is meaningful only if one is thought to have an alternative. . . . But we had no alternative, anyway.[85]

Nixon and Kissinger met to review the course of the most recent developments. There was no going back, and there would be no more manufactured bureaucratic excuses. By all accounts Nixon, who had previously been preoccupied by the morass of Watergate, became animated and forceful on this occasion and agreed to take on the responsibility of managing the superpower confrontation that arose as a result of the massive airlift. The United States sent a $2.2 billion emergency-aid package of loans and grants for Israel through Congress. The airlift followed, and was considered the biggest U.S. weapons supply since the Berlin blockade of 1948. The United States sent a thousand tons of weapons and matériel using C-5A and C-141 aircraft, as well as C-130's, in a matter of days. Over the next weeks, there were a total of 550 U.S. military flights to Israel. By the end of the first few days, the U.S. effort had surpassed the Soviet airlift to all three Arab states.

The airlift clearly marked a new stage for the United States in the war. Once the airlift was in full swing, Kissinger conceded that his earlier strategy of going for the "cease-fire in place" was "too much with mirrors."[86] Indeed, the mirrors were obvious, reflecting the past logic and pattern of linkage. When the United States made a major move toward the Arabs and no corresponding step toward Israel, the result proved counterproductive, just as it had in the past. U.S. actions convinced the Arabs that their own actions were irrelevant, since the United States functioned on their behalf in dealing with Israel. As it turned out, when the United States made a major move toward the Arabs without a reciprocal move, its interests were not enhanced, nor were prospects of peace improved. As with the other cases of linkage outlined above, the United States' arm-twisting tactics in dealing with Israel in 1973 succeeded in getting Israel's acquiescence but did not achieve their objective, given Sadat's opposition. America's failure was compounded by its inability to use its back channel with Ismail to get a better reading of the Egyptian intentions. Ultimately, Kissinger relied on the Soviets and the British for this purpose. In a furious phone call to the Soviet ambassador in Washington, Anatoly Dobrynin, on October 13, Kissinger suggested that he had been double-crossed by the Soviets, who, the secretary of state insinuated, were leading the United States on in the belief that such a cease-fire was obtainable. Kissinger fumed. "Why do we have to deal with you [on matters] that depend on Sadat, why not deal with Sadat directly?"[87] Given the failure of the entire episode culminating on October 13, Kissinger would now deal directly with Egypt. The United States needed to engage without illusions.

Postwar Diplomacy: Linkage Returns, and the Oil Weapon Is Used

Yet if the political tide of the war turned after Sadat's refusal to accept a limited victory on October 12, U.S. wartime pledges on postwar diplomacy would soon take shape.

On October 17, Nixon pledged to four visiting Arab foreign ministers, led by Saudi foreign minister Omar Saqqaf, that Kissinger would seek to mediate peace. Kissinger, who had soured on prospects of peace since the Rogers Plan failed, would now be personally enlisted in the cause.[88] Moreover, it was the first time that Nixon made such a postwar commitment. It was probably not coincidental that Nixon made the commitment the very same day that oil ministers met in Kuwait City to discuss raising oil prices. In other words, U.S. peace mediation would be the lubricant to deal with potential wayward pulls of U.S. policy between support for Israel and dependence upon foreign oil. This rationale for peace mediation would repeat itself in the future. Bluntly, the United States would be trading peace diplomacy for favorable oil prices.

On October 18, Nixon was optimistic that the worst was behind him. He told his cabinet, "[In] meeting with the Arab foreign ministers yesterday, I made the point that we favored a cease-fire and movement towards a peace settlement based on UN Resolution 242. Arab reaction, thus far, to any resupply effort [benefiting Israel] has been restrained and we hope to continue in a manner which avoids confrontation with them."[89]

But this was merely the calm before the storm. The Arab states were not content with Nixon's commitment to peace mediation. On October 20, they slapped on an Arab embargo that involved a cut in oil production. According to a top oil historian and analyst, Daniel Yergin, the Saudis did not want to support the embargo, but were forced into it due to inter-Arab dynamics, including a strident role played by Iraq.[90] Kissinger would call the Arab move "political blackmail."

The Arabs had made halfhearted efforts toward an embargo in 1967, but these had gone nowhere. What had changed over the ensuing six years? The oil market looked different in 1973, creating a perfect storm. The ingredients were all there, including rising consumption, lack of U.S. spare capacity, and new rules in Arab ownership of oil revenues. Taken together, these conditions gave Arab states the ability to unilaterally set prices and agree to cuts in oil production in a way that was bound to have more of an effect than previously.

By contrast, back in 1947, the United States imported about 8 percent of its oil. By 1973, the figure had skyrocketed to 36 percent.[91] In 1967 the United States still had spare oil capacity, but not by 1973. In 1967 the Arabs did not have the economic leverage to push prices higher and therefore use the excess revenue to offset production cuts. In contrast, by 1973 both these factors had changed, and the oil embargo sharply affected the world economy, leading to a sustained recession, which ended only in 1975.

The issue was not just a rise in world consumption of oil between 1967 and 1973; a key factor was that the Arab states engaged in gradual nationalization of oil pumped from their countries. Until 1973 the American oil companies made most of the profits. However, the Arab oil states decided to change the rules, insisting that they reap a majority of the profits. The first to make the switch was Libya. The world watched as a radical Moammar Gadhafi staged a coup in 1969, and in the next year, decided to demand more oil revenues from oil companies operating there. Once those companies agreed, other Arab countries followed suit. By 1973, the Saudis succeeded in obtaining no less than a 25 percent share of the operating oil company ARAMCO.[92] Moreover, due to a variety of factors, including a free-market ideology, the United States decided at the time that it could not interfere in decisions relating to the private sector. The United States was convinced that an oil cartel could not sustain itself, as individual states would seek to undercut their competitors and sell more. This did not happen. Everyone ignored the writing on the wall, but suddenly the Organization of the Petroleum Exporting Countries (OPEC) seemed to be in an unassailable position and could unilaterally set prices and production levels. As Kissinger would subsequently state, "[N]o longer able to dampen the world price by spurring our own production further or even to protect ourselves against supply cutoffs, we rapidly lost leverage. The balance of power on energy was shifting from the Texas Gulf to the Persian Gulf. The OPEC producers were moving into the driver's seat. It was only a matter of time before they took advantage of it."[93] All these factors together created the economic context for the Arabs to use linkage in a way that they hadn't before. Suddenly there was an oil weapon.

Fahmy insists that his speech at the *al-Ahram* think tank in 1972 led to Sadat's call to brandish the oil weapon. This call would soon be echoed in Saudi Arabia as the Saudis demanded that U.S. oil producers use their advertising to call for a new U.S. policy in the Middle East. On August 23, 1973, Sadat made an unannounced visit to Saudi Arabia's King Faisal in Riyadh. He notified the Saudi monarch of his decision to go to war. Faisal promised Sadat to use oil as a weapon.[94]

The theme of linkage began to echo in the United States at the highest levels even before the war. First, Joseph Sisco, head of the State Department's Bureau of Near Eastern Affairs (NEA), told Israel Television on September 8, "While our interests in many respects are parallel to the interests of Israel, they are not synonymous with the state of Israel. The interest of the United States goes beyond any one nation in the area. . . . There is an increasing concern in our country, for example, over the energy question, and I think it is foolhardy to believe that this is not a factor in the situation."[95]

President Nixon picked up the theme in a press conference on September 21. He declared, "Israel simply can't wait for the dust to settle and the Arabs can't wait for the dust to settle in the Mid-East. Both sides are at fault. Both sides need to start negotiating. That is our position. . . . One of the dividends of having a successful negotiation will be to reduce the oil pressure."[96]

After the 1973 war began and Arab fortunes began to turn, the decisions by the oil producers came in rapid succession. On October 16, OPEC raised the price of oil. The following day, a decision was made to reduce production. By October 20, the oil embargo was declared against the United States. (The Netherlands would also be targeted, given its policy of support for the United States and Israel.) Taken together, these steps seemed to be an earthquake that would change the world economy. Linkage was at its peak. Even a senior U.S. diplomat would get involved, who would subsequently be fired by Kissinger for not following instructions. The newly arrived U.S. ambassador to Saudi Arabia, James Akins, told ARAMCO executives in Saudi Arabia "to use their contacts at the highest levels of U.S.G. to hammer home the point that oil restrictions are not going to be lifted unless political struggle is settled in a manner satisfactory to Arabs."[97]

But in reality, did the oil embargo have much of a political impact? It is worth reflecting on what actually transpired. Arab leaders made no bones about their objectives. They aimed high. They wanted to keep the embargo on until Israel withdrew from all the territories taken in the 1967 war, including East Jerusalem. The fact is that the oil embargo lasted five months. It certainly had an effect on the American willingness to publicly tie its diplomatic activity to the oil issue.[98] And it also influenced our readiness to launch a diplomatic initiative pushing for a first two-part Israel-Egypt disengagement agreement—part of which was concluded in January 1974 and led to Israeli troops pulling back a few miles from the Suez Canal. The embargo also influenced Kissinger's decision to start an Israel-Syria disengagement agreement. None of the specifics of those negotiations had begun when the embargo was lifted on March 16, 1974. The actual negotiations began in earnest with the Kissinger shuttle between Damascus and Jerusalem in early May and continued throughout the month. The more extensive second Israel-Egypt disengagement occurred that August. Both of these agreements were disconnected from the embargo. In contrast, a U.S. package of quid pro quos were key to the second Israel-Egypt disengagement. Of course, Israel would withdraw from the majority of the Sinai only in the wake of Sadat's historic trip to Jerusalem in 1977 and the subsequent Egypt-Israel peace treaty of 1979.[99] In short, the oil embargo had no relationship to the larger peace process issues and negotiations.

Why was the embargo ended? In theory, given its ostensible success, it should have kept going and pushed Israel back to the 1967 lines. What were the motives to end it? As it would turn out, there was a variety of factors that again showed the limits of the linkage logic.

On a purely economic level, an embargo would not be effective over time, given the fungibility of oil. Arabs cut shipments to the United States, but kept providing oil to others. Third parties shipped oil to the United States, thereby mitigating the impact of the embargo. Production cuts could be effective, but this would require discipline of OPEC, which sought to maximize its profits. OPEC members liked higher oil revenues but were often less sanguine about production cuts. Arab production cuts were only 9 percent of overall international production of 50 million barrels per day.[100]

Moreover, oil is a double-edged sword. The world understood that the global economy was economically vulnerable, but the Arab states understood that they were part of the world economy as well, and this limited their actions. The Saudis realized that undermining the U.S. economy could have destabilizing economic implications globally and for them. Indeed, a recession would occur in 1974 and part of 1975 because of the price hikes, and it dampened demand for oil, ultimately driving down Saudi revenues. Saudi oil minister Sheikh Ahmed Zaki Yamani would say to counterparts, "If you went down, we would go down."[101] Some also wondered whether Yamani feared that a fourfold rise in oil prices would lead the United States to vigorously pursue alternative energies, which would be the death knell of the Saudis, in which case it would be preferable to keep prices somewhat lower in order to preserve the U.S. dependency upon foreign oil. Kissinger would later say that oil prices will reflect economic rather than political conditions. Indeed, over the subsequent decades, oil would fluctuate to the point that at times the price was lower in real terms than it was before the embargo.

There was a second set of reasons why the Saudis had little interest in sustaining an embargo strategy. Saudi Arabia always relied on the U.S. military for defense and arms acquisitions. So long as there was an embargo, the United States would not sell weapons or enhance other forms of defense cooperation. The more the American public viewed the oil embargo as political blackmail, the more there might be reaction against Arab oil producers. On January 7, 1974, Defense Secretary James Schlesinger publicly mentioned the prospect of reprisals against those who perpetrated the embargo. The United States would only tighten defense cooperation with Riyadh once the embargo ended—and since the Saudis ultimately counted on the United States as a guarantor of their security, they had an interest in ending the embargo. Once again, an Arab state put its own national interests ahead of linkage concerns.

A third set of limits on the embargo strategy was that the United States held diplomatic cards in the Mideast, not just military ones. Ultimately, the other Arab states wanted Kissinger to pursue not just a first disengagement with Egypt, but also a disengagement agreement with Syria. In principle, Kissinger was keen to do this anyway, because he did not want Sadat exposed as the only Arab leader to sign even a cease-fire with Israel. Having a more radical Syria engaged would provide Sadat with political cover as he moved closer to the United States. However, Syria's insistence that the embargo not be lifted until such a comparable disengagement accord was reached was matched by a U.S. refusal to engage in such diplomacy until the embargo was lifted. A compromise was reached whereby Kissinger began an early round of disengagement talks with Damascus before the lifting of the embargo on March 18, but in fact his Syria shuttling did not begin until April 29, and it was concluded on May 31.

A fourth set of limits was that the embargo could not be precisely fine-tuned to the bilateral specifications of the Saudis. It was relatively easy to start an embargo, but a collection of other states was required to lift it. When a group of Arab states wanted to lift it in February, Damascus insisted it go on a bit longer, until Kissinger started his new diplomatic mission. Moreover, given rivalries inside the Mideast, it became clear that the embargo helped Riyadh's rival, Tehran. Shah Reza Pahlavi headed Shiite Iran, the archrival of Sunni Saudi Arabia. Iran would gain a great deal from the oil turmoil. Saudi Arabia saw that high oil revenues would enable Iran to buy more weapons. Oil revenues would enable the shah to challenge the Arabs and shift the balance of power in the Persian Gulf more toward Iran. Iraq, which was also a Saudi rival, also benefited from the rocketing of prices following production cuts. Moreover, Baghdad could transform wealth into military power better than the Saudis. Iran's oil revenues jumped from $4.1 billion in 1973 to $17.4 billion in 1974, and Iraqi oil revenues grew from $1.5 billion in 1973 to $6.8 billion in 1974.[102]

The final limit on the embargo strategy was that it lost a key supporter, Egypt. Egypt, the biggest Arab country and the one that led the war effort, lost interest when the first disengagement agreement was signed. This was ironic, since it was Sadat who proposed the oil embargo before the war. Yet there was logic to his now reassessing the advisability of the oil embargo. Sadat's views began to change as his relationship with Kissinger and the United States matured, and he wanted to enter the American geopolitical orbit. He became more receptive to U.S. appeals. Nixon insisted that Sadat intercede with Saudi Arabia to have the oil embargo lifted. Kissinger convened the ceremonial opening of the Geneva conference in December 1973 as a cover for U.S.-Egyptian bilateral diplomacy, per Sadat's wishes. Nixon wrote Sadat, "[O]ur nations stand at the threshold of a great turning point in history [but] in order to make it possible for me to move decisively it is necessary that the discrimination against the United States which the oil embargo represents be brought to an end." Nixon added, "[I]t is essential that the oil embargo . . . be ended at once. It cannot await the outcome of the current talks on disengagement."[103] Sadat was not merely responding to U.S. pressure in entering its orbit. He moved toward the United States in no small measure because the Soviets had no leverage with Israel. Only the United States could help him regain the Sinai. At different times, Sadat would say that the United States held "99 percent of the cards" necessary to regain Egyptian land.[104] Egypt did not want the cardholder to weaken and lose the cards in its mediation of the conflict with Israel.

In short, the linkage idea was at its zenith for a few short months in the 1973–74 period. While it had an unmistakable effect during those five months, its impact was limited, short-lived, and not to be repeated. Ultimately, key Arab states such as Egypt and Saudi Arabia would give preference to national interests—political and economic—over a multilateral regional strategy. Linkage advocates saw the Arabs only as Arabs, but the Arabs were divided as individual states by rivalries among themselves and with Iran. Saudi Arabia and Egypt needed both a strong United States and a strong domestic economy, and Riyadh feared that high oil revenues—even if sustainable for only a short time—would disproportionately favor Tehran.

The biggest irony that linkage advocates came up against in 1974 was the fundamental reality that Israel had the land that Egypt wanted. The only one who could obtain that land for Sadat was not the Soviet Union, which had cut ties with Israel in 1967, but the United States. Sadat became disparaging of the Soviet Union's inability to recover Egyptian land[105]— and instead began to focus on America, as he saw that only Washington had a relationship with Jerusalem. This is what Sadat meant when he referred to the United States as holding most of the cards.

Sadat needed U.S. influence to help him recover Egypt's territory in the Sinai. The Arab embargo might put pressure on the United States, but it could also backfire and produce an American reaction against the Arabs. Perhaps that is at least one reason why we have never seen the oil embargo of 1973–74 repeated. Both Egypt and Saudi Arabia over time have demonstrated that the needs of others in the region will always take a backseat to their own national security concerns. As we have seen, Kissinger would launch a new intensive American diplomacy, and U.S.-brokered disengagement agreements with Egypt would lead simultaneously to a partial return of the Sinai, much closer ties with the United States, and a further Egyptian turn away from the Soviet Union. This paved the way for Sadat's historic trip to Jerusalem in 1977, which accelerated his recovery of the rest of Egyptian territory. The Egypt-Israel peace treaty of 1979, the first between Israel and an Arab state—the biggest of them all, no less—finds its origins in the Kissinger diplomacy.

THE CARTER ADMINISTRATION

President Jimmy Carter's administration was also solicitous of the Arab states' agenda, and was the first to deal directly with the Palestinian issue. But Carter's linkage preoccupation was bound to fail once again because it failed to grasp underlying regional dynamics—including inter-Arab rivalries. Once again, Egypt preferred pursuing its own national interests over regional Arab interests. The Carter administration did not see the writing on the wall, and tried to impose a comprehensive approach that failed to take account of national interests, especially Egypt's national interests. The plan did not accommodate Sadat, who would jettison Carter's comprehensive Geneva conference framework and, without consulting Carter, head instead to Jerusalem. It was that trip, highlighted by Sadat's speech in the Knesset, that remains the emotional high-water mark of Israeli-Arab relations. Former Israeli prime minister Golda Meir likened Sadat's arrival to the coming of the Messiah. What is important to understand, however, is that Sadat's arrival came not as a result of Carter's efforts, but despite them. To be fair, President Carter shifted gears the following month both to support Sadat's move and to see if it could be reinforced by engaging other Arab players. And Carter's involvement would prove to be critical in securing the Egypt-Israel peace treaty of March 1979. But this does not excuse the American diplomatic failures through much of 1977, which prompted Sadat to go off on his own. So how did U.S. strategy, again premised on linkage, fail? Why did Carter miss Sadat's signals that he was not happy with the U.S. approach?

President Carter came to power wanting to change many of the features of Henry Kissinger's Middle East diplomacy. He wanted to put aside gradualism and bilateralism, end the marginalization of the Soviet Union, and establish a new focus on the problems of the Palestinians. Instead of following Kissinger's method of establishing a negotiating track with incremental moves such as disengagements, Carter sought to grapple with the core issues immediately in order to make peace.

Second, Carter sought to replace bilateralism with a comprehensive Middle East peace conference. Kissinger had convened a Geneva conference in December 1973. In theory, the conference was convened to demonstrate superpower cooperation. The United States and the Soviet Union were cochairs of the parley. In practice Geneva only convened for one day, and Syria was not in attendance. Kissinger believed Geneva served little function, except to rubber-stamp what he had already agreed upon with the parties separately. In other words, Kissinger saw an international Middle East peace conference in Geneva as a fig leaf for his separate, bilateral, and incremental disengagement agreements between Israel and

Egypt (1974 and 1975) and between Israel and Syria (1974). In contrast, Carter viewed Geneva as the place where Arabs and Israelis would sit together to solve all their problems at once. In theory, this reinvigorated approach to Geneva was more to the liking of Arab states because, to them, it provided collective Arab bargaining. Implicitly, all peace tracks were linked, and subject to the lowest common denominator. No peace agreement with Israel could truly be complete until each individual agreement was concluded. Therefore, all agreements between Israel and its neighbors—Egypt, Jordan, Syria, and the Palestinians—would be subject to the objection of any individual participant.

Third, Carter and Secretary of State Cyrus Vance believed the United States should work closely with the Soviets as part of a broader détente policy between the two countries. If Kissinger wanted to simultaneously maintain the broader rubric of détente while sidelining the Soviets in the Mideast, Carter and Vance viewed détente as a more extensive enterprise of cooperation without regional caveats. The Soviets should not be sidelined, as they were during Kissinger's time. Rather, the United States should coordinate Middle East policy with Moscow, and the Soviets should return to the stage as a key player. Carter wrongly believed that Moscow could deliver Syria and the PLO to negotiations with the Israelis.

Fourth, the Palestinian issue needed to be introduced into the negotiations now that the Arab summit of 1974 had shifted responsibility for this issue from Jordan to the Palestine Liberation Organization (PLO). While Kissinger arranged incremental negotiations with Egypt and Syria, no such agreements occurred with the Palestinians. In contrast, in the spring of 1977, Carter became the first American leader to call for a Palestinian homeland.

These changes were negative from Israel's perspective. The Israelis had become accustomed to Kissinger's approach and had always believed that bilateral diplomacy had a better chance of success, as focused agreements would work better than overly ambitious goals that invariably emphasized collective Arab bargaining to Israel's disadvantage. Moreover, Israel saw the Soviets as a radicalizing force, given that Moscow had cut ties with Israel in 1967 and armed its enemies. The PLO was not just a negative, but an anathema, as the group was seen as committed to Israel's destruction.

Carter's relations with Israel in 1977 were fraught with tension, as the

U.S. president sparred with top Israelis of different moderate and conservative governments. Carter engaged in tough words first with Prime Minister Yitzhak Rabin, then with Prime Minister Menachem Begin and Foreign Minister Moshe Dayan, within his first nine months in office. (Israeli foreign minister Moshe Dayan famously remarked to Carter during a particularly contentious conversation, "Mr. President, I only have one eye, but I am not blind."[106]) Israel took issue with Carter's ideas, but it was Sadat who would go off on his own. While Sadat subsequently and repeatedly paid rhetorical fealty to Geneva and the idea of comprehensive peace, even while he was in Jerusalem, Geneva would never reconvene after the Kissinger era. (But a peace conference that could not impose a solution and was instead a diplomatic opening would reoccur at Madrid at the end of 1991.)

Carter thought he had an excellent relationship with Sadat, whom he viewed as a leader committed to peace, and Carter thought that Sadat would like the idea of a comprehensive peace conference. After all, Arab leaders had told the United States that they sought such a solution. It seems the turning point for Sadat was Carter's October 1, 1977, joint U.S.-Soviet communiqué, which outlined the president's blueprint for a comprehensive Middle East peace conference. The communiqué was not the product of prior give-and-take with Egypt or Israel, and this startled the parties. William Quandt, who worked in the Carter White House, later called the joint statement a "political error, showing considerable amateurishness."[107]

Needless to say, Carter's move had an impact not just on Sadat but also on Israel, which was not consulted in advance. At this point Israel had already been alarmed by Carter's emphasis on a comprehensive approach. The Kissinger path was being jettisoned, and now the joint communiqué indicated that Israel's concerns would be ignored. Israelis read all this in a very ominous light. Yitzhak Rabin, Begin's predecessor, reacted to the joint communiqué by saying it was "the beginning of a process aimed at political solution imposed by the two powers, with the coercion directed primarily against Israel. It is known today that the Soviet and American positions are identical, that is, withdrawal to the lines of 4 June 1967."[108]

Paradoxically, with the joint communiqué and his desire to go to the Geneva conference, Carter was driving Israel's leaders and Sadat together in opposition to his approach. In Sadat's case, he was keen on making rapid progress on the Egyptian-Israeli negotiating track. He had already told Carter privately in their initial meeting in April 1977 that Egypt was ready to sign a peace agreement with Israel.[109] (At U.S. behest over the summer, Egypt also prepared a draft peace treaty.) Remarkably, three days after the U.S.-Soviet October 1 statement, Sadat took the unusual step of sending Carter a personal note saying the United States should not do anything "to prevent Israel and Egypt from negotiating directly."[110] In his October 4 note, Sadat still did not call for walking away from the Geneva conference, but he stated clearly that Geneva would essentially have to be similar to what it was in Kissinger's time. It should merely ratify what the parties achieved on their own.

What scared Sadat? It seems that one theory can be ruled out. Carter's national security advisor, Zbigniew Brzezinski, would subsequently speculate that Sadat veered from Carter after seeing Carter seemingly retreat from the joint communiqué after a tough meeting with Moshe Dayan on October 4. While Brzezinski argues that Sadat now saw Carter as unreliable in the face of Israeli pressure, the theory does not stand up to the facts. Sadat's October 4 letter had already been delivered to Carter before Carter and Dayan sat down to meet in New York that evening. (They were both in New York for the United Nations General Assembly.) Carter would note receipt of the letter in his diary that day, and later record it in his memoir, *Keeping Faith*. Carter noted that the person who delivered the letter, Foreign Minister Ismail Fahmy, did not like the message. (Fahmy resigned when Sadat announced that he would fly to Jerusalem.)

It was not Carter's retreat from the joint communiqué that soured Sadat on Carter's peace initiative; it was three other factors that did. First, a secret Egypt-Israel bilateral negotiating track had started a few weeks earlier, and Sadat apparently worried that Carter's initiative might preempt its prospects. Thanks to the intervention of Morocco's King Hassan, secret talks were launched between Israeli foreign minister Moshe Dayan and Egyptian deputy prime minister Hassan Tuhami in the Moroccan capital of Rabat on September 16. In Dayan's memoirs, he said Tuhami offered to reach an agreement, and viewed Geneva as merely a place to sign their agreement.[111] King Hassan hoped to use the meeting as a prelude to a Sadat-Begin private session. While there is no evidence to suggest that Tuhami and Dayan cut a deal in Rabat—indeed, neither was empowered to do so—it seems that Tuhami's report to Sadat was enough to convince him that a breakthrough was possible. Indeed, Sadat took Tuhami seriously enough to immediately raise the issue of their private talks with Dayan when the two met on the first evening of Sadat's historic visit to Jerusalem (according to Mohamed Heikal, authoritative chronicler and confidant to both Sadat and Nasser).[112]

What is remarkable is that Dayan informed Vance of the secret channel two weeks before the joint communiqué.[113] Yet the United States proceeded with the October 1 communiqué as if this groundbreaking event had not occurred. At best, Carter ignored the back channel that Egypt and Israel had set up for direct communication. While there is little evidence to suggest that Carter offered the comprehensive Geneva framework as a deliberate vehicle to thwart the Egyptian-Israel diplomatic movement, he was subsequently upset that the bilateral breakthrough came at the expense of the comprehensive format.

A second factor that soured Sadat on Carter's new comprehensive approach guided by the joint communiqué was his fear that Syria would gain a de facto veto over what Egypt could do or decide. In Carter's envisioned Geneva summit, Syria could define not only the pace of progress but whether there would be any at all.

Sadat believed al-Asad was not committed to peace, and therefore this new negotiating format was nothing short of disaster for the Egyptian president. In effect, nothing would be agreed upon until everything was agreed upon. The conference would therefore be at the mercy of the most intractable Arab leader, al-Asad of Syria. At the very least, the talks would be paralyzed. But this was the opposite of Sadat's desire for rapid progress. As Nicholas Veliotes, a senior State Department official responsible for Arab-Israel affairs (who subsequently became ambassador to Egypt), would later say, "Sadat possessed the fundamental and unalterable preference to keep control of all negotiating decisions in Cairo's hands, and not let them fall into the Syrian preference for a unified Arab delegation."[114] U.S. Ambassador to Egypt Hermann Eilts later recalled Sadat's displeasure with Syria's procedural procrastination in addressing the Carter administration's preliminary questions about Geneva before October, saying, "To [Sadat's] horror and distress, there was no response from the Syrians. Weeks went by, and Sadat began to say, 'Peace is slipping through my fingers for procedural reasons.' "[115]

The third factor behind Sadat's disquiet with the Carter approach now embodied in the joint communiqué was that Sadat was not keen on enabling the Soviet Union to reenter Middle East diplomacy. In his eyes, Soviet interests would be more aligned with the USSR's client in Damascus and less with its erstwhile proxy in Cairo, which had spurned Moscow. Sadat had just made the transition toward closer ties to the United States and was very skeptical that the Soviet Union had any useful role to play.

Veliotes said, "Sadat had just expelled the Soviets out of Egypt and now Carter was letting the Soviets back in. Sadat surely did not like that."[116] Veliotes also recalled that the other diplomats in NEA were quietly not happy that the Carter administration was bringing the Soviets back to center stage in the Middle East by enabling them to cochair a peace conference after Sadat had sidelined them as part of the Kissinger diplomacy. Carter's move would raise questions in Sadat's mind as to whether he could trust the United States after he threw his lot in with Kissinger. Veliotes's comments reflect the view of Heikal, who claimed that the October 1 statement "angered Sadat, who did not want the Soviet Union to be involved." Heikal quoted Sadat as saying, in the days after the statement was issued, "We kicked the Russians out of the door and now Mr. Carter is bringing them back in through the window."[117] The bottom line is that Sadat wanted to pursue his own national strategy without being barred by a format that would give Syria and the Soviet Union leverage over the decision making.

After Sadat's letter to Carter on October 4, calling on him not to do anything that would preclude the prospects of Egypt and Israel "negotiating directly," Carter still did not give up on Geneva. He wrote to Sadat on October 21 and, in his own handwriting, called upon Sadat to publicly endorse the Geneva conference. President Carter mentioned the current impasse, and then stated: "The time has now come to move forward and your early public endorsement of our approach is extremely important—perhaps vital—*in advancing all parties to Geneva* [emphasis added]."[118] Some have seen this as a plea to Sadat to do something dramatic to break the stalemate, thus providing inspiration for his trip to Jerusalem. But this is not what Carter had in mind. He did not want Sadat to go in a new direction. On the contrary, Carter was not focused on bilateralism. Getting to Geneva was now not only Carter's method, but it became his sole objective.

Carter's letter failed, however. By the end of October, Sadat began thinking about other alternatives. The Egyptian leader went on a whirlwind tour to visit the leaders of Romania and Iran, each of whom had his own ties with the Israelis and encouraged Sadat to negotiate directly with Israel. Heikal recalls the exchange with Romanian leader Nicolae Ceauşescu, when Sadat wanted to know if Begin was willing and strong enough to make peace.[119] Ceauşescu insisted Begin had that strength. On that same trip, Sadat also visited Saudi Arabia. According to Heikal, Sadat "explained to Crown Prince Fahd that he felt American efforts were stuck and that some form of negotiation with Israel would be necessary. Not knowing what Sadat was planning, Fahd could only give general encouragement, wishing the Egyptian president luck in his effort."[120]

Sadat had made his decision. On the day before he announced it in a dramatic address in Egypt's parliament, known as the People's Assembly, Sadat notified Carter on November 8 of his decision to go to Jerusalem. This was the full extent of U.S.-Egyptian consultation between the leaders on the eve of Sadat's historic trip. Instead of being thrilled about such a historic moment, Carter's initial response was hostile. According to Stuart Eizenstat, the top domestic aide to Carter at the time, Carter said that he was "very upset" and wanted to criticize Sadat's move publicly for "ripping apart" the possibility of a comprehensive settlement. Fortunately for Carter, he held his tongue in public. Veliotes insists that the State Department officials were delighted but feared making publicly enthusiastic statements due to the White House's commitment to Geneva.[121]

Kenneth Stein, a diplomatic historian who once worked with Carter and who has researched this period extensively, presents an even bleaker picture of the mood of Carter administration officials—a mood that reflects the president's attitudes and a mood that was guided once again by a misreading of the region and what might be motivating Sadat:

> Carter administration officials were stunned and had difficulty adjusting to the new reality created by Sadat's visit. Washington strongly preferred to pull Sadat back from the bilateral diplomacy in which he was engaged. Not only was the Washington bureaucracy temporarily bypassed as the diplomatic catalyst, but also there was a silence, some incoherence, and resistance to what blatantly appeared to be another Egyptian-Israeli agreement in the making.[122]

President Carter clearly misread Sadat on many levels. He didn't see the mistrust between Egypt and Syria, Egypt's antipathy toward the Soviets, or Sadat's interest in a bilateral channel with Israel. Above all, Carter misread Egypt's sense, after the 1973 war, that it had done its duty for the Palestinian cause and that it was time for Egyptian national interests to take priority over pan-Arabism and for Egypt to reclaim its land. As Heikal explains, food riots had occurred across Egypt earlier that year due to a rise in prices. With the Egyptian military being demobilized in 1977, there were rising economic expectations that Sadat could not meet. Heikal insisted that as a result of these riots and a failed grab at Libyan oil that spring, Sadat felt a need by the middle of 1977 "to negotiate a new relationship with Israel."[123] In that context, Carter also misunderstood that Sadat was a proud Egyptian nationalist above all, who did not feel he needed other Arabs. When asked if he feared isolation by other Arabs, Sadat would reply that the Arabs could only isolate themselves, not Egypt.

Sadat's visit was electrifying. An Arab leader had visited Israel for the first time. Yet the visit occurred not because of Carter, but despite him. Only later would Carter change course and play a critical role in ensuring the Egypt-Israel peace treaty. Sadat's break from the Carter framework was further proof that Egypt, the largest Arab state, was interested in pursuing national, rather than regional, Arab interests. Linkage assumed the reverse, and therefore failed—once again.

Instead, the Arab states would go on to reject what became known as the Egypt-Israel Camp David Accords in 1978 and the Egypt-Israel peace treaty in 1979. Camp David created a framework for Israeli-Arab negotiations over the West Bank. Imagine if the Arab states had used Camp David as a baseline to engage Israel instead of counterproductively spurning Egypt for its involvement at Camp David. In the end, the Arab states isolated Egypt for several years, only to drop the isolation later. However, if they had accepted Sadat's idea of engagement with Israel over the West Bank, the settlement enterprise would have looked like a shell of what it is today. Menachem Begin had just been elected in 1977, and there were only about 5,000 Jewish settlers by the time of Camp David.[124] Begin's settlement strategy was only at its most embryonic stage. The purist approach of the Arabs, who were angry with Sadat, meant there was no lever to influence Israeli policy. Today, there are over 300,000 settlers in the West Bank.

Things could have been different if the Arabs had chosen a more prag-matic course.

Yet the idea of linkage did not die. As noted earlier, Saddam Hussein sought to invoke linkage after he invaded Kuwait in 1990, but he failed for at least two reasons. First, thanks to peace between Egypt and Israel, there was no longer an Arab war option, the biggest Arab state having left the war coalition. Second, with the end of the Cold War, the Arabs could not play on the fear that if the United States would not respond, it would lose in the competition with the Soviets and the USSR would gain in the region at America's expense. Indeed, in this case the Soviets were on the same side, opposing the Iraqi invasion.

Linkage would suffer another blow with the Madrid peace confer-ence in 1991 and the breakthrough in the secret Oslo talks in 1993. More-over, the fact that Israel and the Palestinians would reach their own breakthrough in Norway created its own impact. When Israelis and Pal-estinians were dealing with each other, the context would change. It made it harder for the Arab states to use the Palestinian issue as a pres-sure point, as Arab countries were not well positioned to leverage U.S. action in their favor.

THE GEORGE W. BUSH ADMINISTRATION

The year 2003 saw another version of U.S. policy response to linkage. President George W. Bush was preparing to launch a war against Iraq, amid profound unpopularity in the Arab world and estrangement from a good part of Europe. Bush found himself on the defensive internation-ally. At the same time, the Palestinian intifada had been raging for two and a half years; satellite television showed scenes of suicide bombers in Israeli urban areas and Israeli retaliation against Palestinian militants. As was the case during the first Gulf War, which came at the tail end of the first intifada, Arab officials once again sought to drive home the idea of linkage. Some Arabs raised anew the issue of America pursuing a double standard. At the UN Security Council meeting just before the 2003 Iraq War, Libya's representative, Ahmed A. Own, expressed a view typical of other Arab envoys, charging the world was unfairly focused on Iraq while "turning a blind eye to resolutions concerning Israel."[125] Just as in the first

Gulf War, when they equated UN demands for withdrawal from Kuwait with Resolution 242, which called for negotiations between Israel and its Arab neighbors, the Arabs again asked why Israel was permitted to effectively ignore Security Council resolutions while Saddam was forced to comply.

Unlike in 1991, however, there was a European dimension to the problem. British prime minister Tony Blair was Bush's most faithful European ally in the run-up to the 2003 war. For this loyalty, he was pilloried in the British media and in major antiwar demonstrations. As a million people demonstrated in an antiwar protest in London in February 2003, a *Guardian*/ICM poll revealed that opposition to the war in England had surged to 52 percent and support had plummeted to 29 percent.[126] Blair's popularity rating in February 2003—a month before the war—stood at the astonishingly low figure of approximately 20 percent. Members of his own Labour Party assailed him for being Bush's "poodle," and questioned what Britain was gaining from its close association with Bush and his policies. Within Britain, a chorus of voices emerged calling for reinvigorated U.S. diplomatic involvement in the Israeli-Palestinian conflict. Blair genuinely believed that resolution of the conflict would have the benefit of diluting support for al-Qaeda, and so he was enthusiastic about those efforts.

A senior Bush administration official admitted at the time that Washington was very worried about Blair's public standing, and it believed that demonstrating support for a three-phased "Roadmap" to jump-start negotiations between Israelis and Palestinians would signal that the Palestinian issue was being addressed.[127] This became a central theme of Blair's visit to Camp David shortly after the war began. At a joint press conference on March 28, 2003, at Camp David, Bush declared:

> History requires more of our coalition than the defeat of a terrible danger. I see an opportunity, as does Prime Minister Blair, to bring renewed hope and progress to the entire Middle East. Last June 24th, I outlined a vision of two states, Israel and Palestine, living side by side in peace and security. Soon, we will release the road map that is designed to help turn that vision into reality; and both America and Great Britain are strongly committed to implementing that road map."[128]

On the return home from the United States, a Blair official anonymously told the London *Times*, "Tony Blair is ready to spend all the political capital he has earned in Washington on a desperate attempt to revive the Middle East peace process."[129]

The Roadmap was indeed formally released at the end of April 2003. It was negotiated between the four members of the Quartet—the United States, the European Union, Russia, and the United Nations—and not by or with the Israelis and Palestinians. At different times, Israelis and Palestinians paid homage to it, but it was not implemented. In fact, serious contact between the two parties did not occur until almost two years later, after the death of Yasser Arafat and the election of Palestinian Authority president Mahmoud Abbas. One can debate what should have happened in order to bring the two sides together. Regardless, the Roadmap was a U.S.-led peace proposal driven by the idea of linkage and not by the desire of the parties themselves, and it therefore made the dynamics of the Israeli-Palestinian conflict a function of external considerations. It was bound to fail—and once again a policy initiative driven by the linkage argument went nowhere. It could not be otherwise.

The conflating of the Arab-Israeli issue with the Iraq War did not occur only in 2003. It returned at the end of 2006, immediately after the U.S. midterm elections. At this time, the Iraq Study Group (ISG), cochaired by former secretary of state James Baker and former House Foreign Relations Committee chairman Lee Hamilton, released its findings on how to change course in the Iraq War. As noted at the outset of the last chapter, the report, coauthored by Baker and Hamilton, emphasizes the inextricable linkage of all conflicts in the Middle East.[130] While its Iraq-specific recommendations are quite thoughtful and informed, its calls for a new U.S. mediation between Israel and the Palestinians, and Israel and Syria, were guided by the traditional assumptions associated with many of the linkage arguments we have debunked. Consider, for example, that the ISG report recommended that the United States play a more active role in resolving the Israeli-Palestinian conflict because this would prompt Sunni leaders in Saudi Arabia, Jordan, Kuwait, and Turkey to play a constructive role in Iraq.

Once again we see almost a reflexive argument—based on the traditional mythology—that the Palestinian issue lies at the heart of all matters in the Middle East. The faulty assumption is, once again, that the

Saudis and Iraq's other neighbors are affected more by the Palestinian issue than by the way they define their interests in Iraq or by the internal dynamics there and the perceived weight of Iranian influence on Iraq's Shia leaders.

But that does not reflect reality—and certainly not Saudi behavior. The Saudi agenda in Iraq is driven by its perception of how Iraq's new Shia leadership subordinates Arab interests to the interests of Iran and how it denies Sunnis in Iraq any significant role. Whether true or not, at this stage, this is what the Saudis see. The Saudis were not responsive to what the Bush administration wanted them to do in Iraq not because of the Palestinian conflict but because they have a problem with U.S. policy in Iraq.

The Saudis and other Arab leaders pursue their interests in separate arenas based on what their interests dictate in those arenas—and what the dynamics are in those arenas. Their interests are not derivative of the Palestinian issue unless the Palestinians are directly involved. Arab leaders will support those initiatives that suit their national interests—and not because they fit a presumed regional or overarching interest. The age of Arab nationalism is gone. Yes, Arab leaders are affected by the climate in the region, and the Palestinian issue certainly affects that climate. And yes, the United States should not appear indifferent to something that affects the sense of grievance in the area—and the Palestinian issue surely does. But America should pursue peacemaking because it is the right thing to do, not because we think it is going to transform the region or other regional issues. Those issues, as we have seen, are not derivative of the Palestinian cause and will not suddenly disappear just because the cause has been addressed.

CONCLUSION

Given this history, it is clear that the mythology of linkage has misled policymakers in the past and has endured to this day. For a region with multiple sources of conflict, it should come as no surprise that a concept that seems to offer a "fix" to all problems would be alluring. But, unfortunately, the region is far too complex for that, and there are no simple fixes available.

This chapter does not exhaustively list all the historical examples of how the linkage paradigm has harmed U.S. interests. We have sought to demonstrate the concerted effort by Arab states and by some sympathetic to the Arabist mind-set to suggest that Arab states deal with the U.S. through the prism of the Arab-Israeli conflict, even though the picture is complex and more nuanced. In reality, Arab states tend to pursue their own national interests, and inter-Arab dynamics are their own variable, independent of the Arab-Israel conflict.

This should not be read as a smoke screen not to pursue peace in the Middle East. Rather, as strong believers in peace making, we believe that peace must be pursued for the right reasons, and not because the U.S. owes the Arab world or because it is the "open sesame" magic to solving a myriad of other conflicts. More than anything else, peace should be pursued because it could bring an end to the endless tragedy that has engulfed these two peoples.

We are not blind to the ability of this conflict to ignite the imagination of many in the region. Yet, we see this as distinct from linkage. Specifically, in debunking the mythology of linkage, we have not sought to belittle the importance of dealing with the Arab-Israeli conflict and its most existential element: the conflict between Israelis and Palestinians. We understand very well that the Israeli-Palestinian issue resonates throughout the region and the Muslim world. In other words, while there is no linkage between the Israeli-Arab conflict and other regional conflicts, there is no denying that this conflict is evocative—and in an era of satellite television operating on a 24/7 basis, it is easy to exploit the powerful emotions associated with it. There is also no denying that the conflict triggers deeper sources of anger and grievance that are felt throughout the region.

The Israeli-Palestinian issue is surely not the only source of anger and grievance, but it is one important source that the Islamists exploit in the region—and we have an interest in denying them grievances to exploit. Among Arabs, there is a widespread belief that the Palestinians have suffered a grievous injustice. They have lost a homeland and suffer as a consequence. In the eyes of Arab populaces, this injustice must be undone and the wrong must be righted. So long as it is not addressed and not corrected, the conflict remains a constant reminder of reality that feeds an abiding sense of powerlessness. Radical Islamists prey on this sense of powerlessness and the anger it provokes. The Islamists exploit resentment, both against the United States and against the current regimes in the region. These are grievances that need to be ameliorated. At the same time, we should not be fooled into thinking that this will suddenly make the Islamists melt away. Their frustration is often due to dysfunctional and unaccountable Arab regimes. Only Muslims can discredit Islamists.

Former British prime minister Tony Blair takes this perception a step further and maintains that resolving the conflict would undercut a crucial element of the radical Islamist narrative. In a speech in Los Angeles he declared:

> I want to explain why I think this issue is so utterly fundamental to all we are trying to do. . . . Its significance for the broader issue of the Middle East and for the battle within Islam is this. The real impact of a settlement is more than correcting the plight of the Palestinians. It is that such a settlement would be the living, tangible, visible proof that the region and therefore the world can accommodate different faiths and cultures, even those who have been in vehement opposition to each other. It is, in other words, the total and complete rejection of the cause of Reactionary Islam. It destroys not just their most effective rallying call. It fatally undermines their basic ideology.[131]

We don't believe resolving the conflict will fatally undermine their basic ideology, but it would surely deny them one of the sources of anger they use to recruit or to keep more moderate Arab regimes on the defensive. We believe that for purposes of competing with the radical Islamists and for doing the right thing, U.S. policymakers should be committed to trying to resolve the Arab-Israeli conflict. It has gone on for too long and been used by too many different actors for their own narrow and selfish purposes. It evokes strong emotions in the region and internationally. It draws more attention than most conflicts, perhaps because it seems so rooted in the birthplace of three great religions. It has generated its own mythologies for how to resolve it or whether it is resolvable. The realists who treat linkage as an axiom and an article of faith believe not only that it can be resolved but that the solution is close at hand. Neoconservatives are far more pessimistic; they see the conflict as rooted in the rejection of

Israel and see efforts to resolve it as largely futile until the Arabs have a change of heart. We recognize the difficulties but think the effort to resolve it is necessary and not hopeless.

We next turn our attention to the peace process. While we recognize that resolving the conflict is not a panacea, we see the importance of dealing with it—and that view sets us apart from the neoconservatives. With that in mind, we will start with addressing the neoconservative approach to the conflict and debunking their mythologies before taking on the realists.

Chapter Four

THE NEOCONSERVATIVES
AND THE PEACE PROCESS:
DISENGAGEMENT IS
THE ANSWER

For the neoconservatives, there is a basic myth when it comes to the pursuit of peace between Arabs and Israelis: the Arabs categorically reject Israel, and peace is not possible as a result. The corollary is that if the Arabs prove themselves in terms of accepting Israel, then peace can be possible, but until that point there is no reason for U.S. engagement on peace. Engagement is futile at best and counterproductive at worst, and as a result, disengagement is the right policy prescription.

In this chapter, we will see that the Bush administration instinctively embraced this myth as policy—and we will explore the roots of the myth, its basic flaws, and the unfortunate policy consequences of its pursuit.

DISENGAGEMENT AND THE BUSH ADMINISTRATION

For the first six years of the George W. Bush administration, there was little interest in pursuing the Arab-Israeli peace process. As we saw in the last chapter, the Roadmap to Peace was adopted in 2003 because of Tony Blair's "linkage" concerns, not because the Bush administration was genuinely committed to it. Not surprisingly, the administration did not pursue the Roadmap seriously.

It was not just that being active was unacceptable because it would be seen as repeating the Clinton policy—and at the outset of the Bush administration an "anything but Clinton" instinct appeared to guide its policies; rather, it was the idea that engagement and intensive effort and activity were, in the eyes of President Bush, simply misguided.

In his very first National Security Council meeting, the president opined that the United States should pull out of the Arab-Israeli conflict because "I don't see much we can do over there at this point."[1] When Secretary of State Colin Powell countered that disengagement would reverse thirty years of policy and might destabilize a volatile region, President Bush seemingly dismissed Powell's concerns, saying, "Sometimes a show of force by one side can really clarify things."[2]

The Bush statement reflected a mind-set. The president and some of those around him believed that President Clinton had wanted an agreement too much, pushed too hard for it, and violence was the result. Bush himself, in this same NSC meeting, was quoted as saying, "Clinton overreached and it all fell apart. That's why we are in trouble. If the two sides don't want peace, there's no way we can force them."[3]

Bush's comment was not a one-time spur-of-the-moment response. Ari Fleischer, then the White House press secretary, made a similar point more than a year later in response to a question on whether the Bush administration's reluctance to engage on Israeli-Palestinian peace efforts was contributing to the violence: "Actually, I think if you go back to when the violence began, you can make the case that in an attempt to shoot the moon and get nothing, more violence resulted." He added that "as a result of an attempt to push the parties beyond where they were willing to go, that it led to expectations that were raised to such a high level that it turned to violence."[4]

Fleischer soon disavowed his comments, saying that the parties, not Clinton, were responsible for the violence. But, as Tony Karon of *Time* magazine pointed out, while Fleischer backed off his comment, "the press secretary doesn't make this stuff up on the fly. His comment not only tracks with the Bush Administration's own hands-off approach to the Middle East conflict; it's a sharper reiteration of a point President Bush made on the campaign trail and after—that the US should refrain from forcing the pace or imposing a settlement. . . ."[5]

In its early months, the Bush administration was determined not to force the pace. But the administration was not content simply to avoid pushing the parties. It went well beyond this to make a conscious decision to disengage from making a diplomatic effort on the Arab-Israeli conflict. Instructions were actually given even to stop using the words "peace process."[6]

Neoconservatives had for a long time questioned the value of the peace process. Typically, it would be referred to as the "so-called" peace process, or the term "peace process" would simply be put in quotes to denote its dubious or questionable standing and purpose. Elliott Abrams, who would become a principal architect of Bush administration policy on the Middle East, not only reflected this position in an article he wrote the year before Bush became president and Abrams joined the administration, but also explained that the process itself had little to do with any progress that some associated with it: "As the advances in the 'peace process' since the Cold War and Gulf War have demonstrated, progress on individual issues depends less on the brilliance of our negotiators than on the overall balance of forces in the region."[7]

For Abrams, it was the need "to use American power fully" that mattered. In his eyes, there were "enormous opportunities to advance American interests in the Middle East, but not for the most part through *painstaking negotiations of documents* [emphasis added]."[8] In other words, American interests were not promoted by the intensive diplomacy associated with the peace process; they were promoted by producing a better balance of power. In what would represent core assumptions of the then incoming Bush administration, Abrams said we must stop "subordinating all other political and security goals to the 'success' of the Arab-Israel peace process" and we must draw a "clear distinction between the search for Middle East 'peace' and the search for genuine security for the U.S. and its allies."[9]

Parsing these words, one sees a clear worldview: peace in the Middle East is an illusion; the quest for security, not for peace, must be our goal in the region. No wonder the administration would disengage from the peace process: it was not just a waste of time and effort, it was a costly diversion from the pursuit of our real interests in the Middle East.

Here was the neoconservative credo for the Middle East. It fit well with the basic instincts of the president and the key officials around him. And if President Bush, Vice-President Cheney, and those like Condoleezza Rice were looking for analytical justification for their predispositions, there was a coterie of like-minded thinkers who provided the necessary intellectual sustenance. Norman Podhoretz, Douglas Feith, Richard Perle, and David Wurmser were the main proponents of this thinking, and they offered a well-developed critique of the peace process through the

Clinton years. Podhoretz and Feith were the most prolific in offering their critiques, particularly of the Oslo process, and a review of their many articles reveals a coherent set of assumptions that characterize the neoconservative mind-set—a mind-set that guided Bush administration policies toward Middle East peace and that produced an approach that deeply misjudged the circumstances and unfortunately ensured that real opportunities would be missed.

NEOCONSERVATIVE ASSUMPTIONS ABOUT THE ARAB-ISRAELI CONFLICT, AND THEIR FLAWS

If there is one overriding assumption that shapes the neoconservative mythology about the Arab-Israeli conflict, it is that the Arab world simply does not accept peace with Israel, because it does not accept that Israel has a legitimate place in the region. And for the neoconservatives, it is this "fact" that has ensured that the peace process has been based on an illusion all along. That is why they refer to the "so-called peace process." To discuss it without putting the words "peace process" in quotes is to give legitimacy to a concept that is fundamentally flawed in their eyes.

No one has stated this more clearly than Norman Podhoretz, the influential editor of *Commentary* magazine. At one point, in speaking about the intifada that began in the fall of 2000, he spoke of how at least it had exposed the "main illusions" about the peace process:

> Those illusions went beyond the idea that a compromise with the Palestinians had become possible. They extended to the notion that Israel bore at least as much blame for the Arab war against it as the Arabs did; that if Israel were to reconcile itself to the establishment of a Palestinian state, the Arab world would reconcile itself to a Jewish one; and that it was in Israel's unilateral power to realize this vision of peaceful coexistence. . . . But the dream of wiping Israel off the map was not put into Arab heads by anything Israel did except enter into existence.[10]

The neoconservatives have consistently argued that there have been no revolutionary developments transforming Arab attitudes toward Israel. On the contrary, "Israel's yearning for peace was shared neither by the Arab world in general or by the Palestinians in particular."[11] Elliott Abrams, Podhoretz, and other neoconservatives have pointed to academic Fouad Ajami's words to validate their argument that the Arab world remains hostile to Israel and is not ready to make peace with it. As Ajami stated (and Abrams quoted):

> There has been no discernible change in the Arab attitudes toward Israel. The great refusal persists . . . in the "Arab street" of ordinary men and women, among the intellectuals and the writers, and in the professional syndicates. The force of this refusal can be seen in the press of governments and of the oppositionists, among the secularists and Islamists alike, countries that have concluded diplomatic agreements with Israel and those who haven't.[12]

While Ajami's statement is surely correct, it is also true that Egypt and Jordan have concluded peace agreements with Israel and that those agreements have held even during times that should have threatened them: the wars in Lebanon, intifadas I and II, and periods when Israel has invoked very tough measures against Palestinians in both Gaza and the West Bank. Throughout these times, other Arab states, such as Morocco and some of the smaller Gulf states, have maintained tacit relations with Israel—doing business quietly and from time to time meeting Israeli leaders openly.

Polls throughout the Arab world, and among Palestinians, have consistently shown support for a two-state solution—again, even during times when anger toward Israel over its responses to Palestinian violence has been most acute.[13] Admittedly, those polls tend to reflect a readiness to accept the reality of Israel rather than its moral legitimacy. The Arab world may not particularly like Israel or support reconciliation with it, particularly so long as there is no peace between Israel and the Palestinians, but there does seem to be a desire to end the conflict, at least among the non-Islamists.

The neoconservatives are not convinced. For them, the unwillingness to accept Israel's moral legitimacy is the true indicator of Arab intentions. It is not that the neoconservatives are wrong to focus on the moral legitimacy question; the reluctance to accept Israel's legitimacy certainly helps to explain why those in either the Arab or Palestinian worlds do so little to justify and promote peace with Israel or to actively condemn those who carry out acts of terror against it. Arab condemnations, when they are forthcoming, tend to emphasize that such attacks are counterproductive, not that they are intrinsically wrong.[14]

But by focusing only on the moral legitimacy question, by focusing only on signs of enduring hostility, the neoconservatives tend to dismiss the differences between those in the Arab world who would accept coexistence with Israel and those who will never do so. And yet these differences create the potential both for coexistence—even if it is not perfect—between Israel and its neighbors, and also for open as well as tacit cooperation between Israel and those Arabs and Palestinians who also feel threatened by Islamists.

This potential is a phenomenon that many in Israel have recognized, not only today with the threat that Iran poses to Israelis and Sunni-led Arab regimes alike—note the words of those across the political spectrum from Benjamin Netanyahu to Tzipi Livni and Shimon Peres—but also more than a decade ago, by Yitzhak Rabin. Rabin, even with his doubts about Yasir Arafat, launched the Oslo process in no small part because he believed that if the Palestinian card could be taken out of extremist hands, cooperation with his Arab neighbors against Iran and other fundamentalists would become possible. Shortly after the inception of Oslo, Ephraim Sneh, one of Rabin's allies, made the case for this view, saying, "Most Arab states understand that Islamic radicalism, not Zionism, is the ideology that endangers their stability. This new situation creates an opportunity for a new alliance of sane countries against a common extremist threat."[15]

In an article at the time, Norman Podhoretz took note of Sneh's argument but dismissed it. He argued that the Arab leaders, knowing that they would inflame the radicals and thus threaten their own stability, would not make peace with Israel and join with it even quietly. Moreover, he added, even if some Arab leaders were prepared to reach peace deals with Israel, what about their successors? As Podhoretz asked, even if al-Asad would decide to make peace with Israel, what about his successor—"will he be 'sane' too?"[16]

Here Podhoretz introduces what has been another theme of the neoconservatives when it comes to the Arabs: they are nondemocratic. As such, they cannot be trusted in peacemaking (or much else). Even if there are some Arab leaders who might be willing to make peace with Israel (though they are the exception), their commitments or their agreements cannot be trusted because they are not democrats. Agreements made with nondemocratic states will not survive. That they appear to have done so with both Egypt and Jordan after the assassination of Anwar Sadat and the death of King Hussein does not appear to affect the neoconservative view—perhaps because they would argue that too little time (thirty years in the case of Egypt) has gone by to test their proposition.

The neoconservative distrust of agreements with nondemocratic states is rooted in their view of history and their perception of what happens when democratic and nondemocratic regimes negotiate. Nondemocratic regimes have no intention of living up to their agreements, and the democratic governments, whatever they claim about enforcing such agreements, will live with violations—or so neoconservatives claim. Douglas Feith offers a litany of examples, starting with the Treaty of Versailles and running through the Soviet violation of arms control treaties, to prove that democratic governments are reluctant to provoke confrontations and would rather live with violations that do not simply emasculate the agreements but actually pose great dangers to the democratic signatories. This is what Feith foresaw with the Oslo process.[17]

Feith believed correctly that Oslo was based on the premise of Israeli withdrawal from the West Bank and Gaza, and he and the other neoconservatives perceived any such withdrawal as constituting a grave threat to Israel's survival. It would, Feith argued, "reduce Israel's strategic depth, deprive Israel of control over the Judean and Samarian highlands, reduce Israel's time for mobilization in a crisis [and] increase Israel's chances of being cut in half in a war."[18]

Podhoretz, too, believed that withdrawal posed a profound threat to Israel, but he offered an interesting twist: while acknowledging that there was a rivalry between the Islamist and secular political movements of Hamas and Fatah—for power, not over whether Israel should exist—he thought this rivalry could provide no comfort to Israel. On the contrary, once there was a Palestinian state, there would be a struggle between Fatah and Hamas over control, Syria would intervene, Israel would respond, and then the Arabs would enter in as well—only Israel would be fighting the whole Arab world from a weakened position.[19] (Ironically, more than a decade later, when Israel withdrew from Gaza, it did trigger internecine conflict between Hamas and Fatah, but the Arab world did not unite against Israel or intervene.)

The danger scenarios, which are a staple of neoconservative writings, stem from their basic assumption of Arab and Palestinian rejection of Israel. But the neoconservatives would have had little need to talk about these troubling scenarios if the Arab/Palestinian rejection was so obvious to policymakers and everyone else in the 1990s. With the launching of the Oslo process, in which the PLO renounced terror, recognized Israel, and agreed to negotiate with it, the task of proving that the Palestinians continued to reject Israel and that nothing had really changed became far more acute. For the neoconservatives, it became even more essential and urgent to show (to the Clinton administration at the time) that these negotiations were all about Palestinian duplicity.

Consequently, neoconservatives began to argue more forcefully that the PLO had not given up its "phased plan" to supplant Israel.[20] As Feith put it, the PLO's principles are not "offended by the dismantlement of Israel in stages and through diplomacy, rather than all at once and solely by military means."[21]

The Oslo agreement was, in the neoconservative framework, a new tactic by the PLO. It heralded not a new day but a new approach to the same objective: the destruction of Israel. Podhoretz saw the PLO following the North Vietnamese tactics of "fight and talk" in the service of the same phased plan or "phased goals" to weaken Israel while never giving up Palestinian goals. Abrams spoke of how "Palestinian irredentism would only be nourished by successes."[22] Podhoretz saw, in the creation of a Palestinian state, not an achievement that might furnish steps toward peace but a launching pad for further military operations.[23]

For the neoconservatives, the Oslo process was a variation of the Clausewitzian maxim of pursuing war by other means. The negotiations would be used to get Israel to withdraw back to the June 1967 borders; the Palestinians would continue to nurture grievances; and once ensconced in a state next to Israel, the Palestinians would keep up the struggle in a way that would demoralize Israel and eventually lead to its collapse.

But if the Palestinians, and especially Yasir Arafat, were truly committed to the phased plan that the neoconservatives spoke of throughout the Oslo process, why did Arafat reject the Clinton Parameters proposed in December 2000? Neoconservatives treated the phased approach as the talisman of the Palestinian strategy. They seized on it to explain Arafat's recognition of Israel in the Oslo process. It was not really recognition, they claimed; it was a subterfuge, and represented nothing more than a disguised way of pursuing the phased approach by more subtle means.

And yet the Clinton Parameters should have offered a golden opportunity to accelerate the phased approach. Here was an offer that would have provided the Palestinians with 100 percent of Gaza, 95 percent of the West Bank, and 2 percent of what is currently Israel as part of a territorial swap arrangement; the Arab neighborhoods of East Jerusalem as the capital of the Palestinian state; and international forces to help provide for Palestinian security in a way that would have almost assuredly inhibited the Israeli ability to respond to possible terror threats emanating from the new state of Palestine. But Yasir Arafat rejected the Clinton Parameters even while the Israeli cabinet voted to accept them.

If Arafat was committed to phases, he surely would have accepted the Clinton Parameters. Because Norman Podhoretz is intellectually honest, he did not try to deny the obvious contradiction. He acknowledged that Arafat's rejection showed that his previous understanding of the "phased method" (which Podhoretz had spelled out repeatedly in his writings between 1992 and 2000) was mistaken because the PLO had cast aside a "wonderful opportunity to move into phase two." Podhoretz explained that because Arafat would have had to sign a treaty with Israel, formally renounce the strategic goal of phases, and implicitly accept the Jewish state's moral legitimacy, he could not accept the Clinton proposal—and preferred instead to provoke a large-scale regional war without getting his state first.[24]

Podhoretz's argument is interesting but remarkably removes the edifice on which so much of the neoconservative mythology has been built. Duplicity had always defined the neoconservative views of the Palestinians in general and Arafat in particular. Podhoretz had no problem believing that Arafat signed every Oslo agreement—of which there were five—never intending to fulfill them or his commitments. He had recognized Israel and renounced terror and violence in the previous agreements. Podhoretz did not take those commitments seriously. Yet this time Arafat could not bring himself to be duplicitous? This time Arafat chose to be honest?

To square the circle, Podhoretz fell back on his scenario of regional war. Arafat would use the intifada to provoke a wide Arab war against Israel. Previously he and other neoconservatives assumed that war would come only after there was a Palestinian state, and Israel, having been reduced in size to the pre-1967 borders, would be particularly vulnerable to wider Arab intervention.

Let us leave aside that Israel had not withdrawn in the year 2000 to the position of vulnerability that Podhoretz, Feith, and Abrams had feared. Let us also leave aside that Israel was not in a weakened position—which presumably the phased plan was designed to produce, materially and psychologically. Still, according to Podhoretz, Arafat was prepared to forgo what had been his plan all along, reject the Clinton parameters, which would have facilitated that plan, and count on the Arab states to come in and take care of Israel for the Palestinians.

This, more than other neoconservative assumptions, strains the bounds of credulity for at least two reasons. First, the Arabs have shown no readiness to go to war for the Palestinians. Even in 1948, the war against the newly declared state of Israel was about competition between the neighboring Arab states to see who could grab which part of Palestine—not who could preserve Palestine for the Palestinians. From the beginning of the intifada in the fall of 2000 through its worst moments for the Palestinians, condemnations of Israel have flowed easily out of the Arab world, but no one has rushed to aid the Palestinians. As Hosni Mubarak said early in the intifada, al-Jazeera or other Arabs could fight Israel, but Egypt had suffered enough, and it was not going to do so.

And it is precisely the sentiment that Arab states will prioritize their own interests ahead of the Palestinian cause that explains the second reason why the Podhoretz/neoconservative regional-war scenario lacks credibility. Palestinians have seen Arab leaders, from Nasser to Gadhafi to Saddam Hussein, who consistently championed the Palestinian cause for their own ambitions but never were prepared to fight for the Palestinians. Deeply embedded in the Palestinian belief system is an abiding sense of betrayal—and betrayal by Arab leaders is a fundamental part of the Palestinian worldview. The irony, of course, is that linkage not only misled U.S. policymakers, it led to false expectations among the Palestinians and fed their narrative of betrayal.

While absolving themselves of responsibility for their predicament, Palestinians see the Arabs as consistently letting them down. Throughout the Oslo process, Arafat and those around him were constantly fearful that President al-Asad of Syria would make a peace deal with Israel that would leave the Palestinians with no leverage and Israel with neither the need nor the political capability to respond to them. In early 2000, when the Israeli-Syrian negotiations looked as if they might produce a peace agreement, a leading Palestinian negotiator told one of us, "The Syrians and the Arabs will screw us again."[25]

Arafat was surely duplicitous. He did make commitments and then violate them. But he would never have counted on the Arabs to come and deliver Israel for him. He had become the leader of the PLO in 1969 after the debacle of the 1967 war when it became clear that the Arabs could not produce for the Palestinians—and in the 1973 war they showed they cared about their own territory, not Palestinian rights or needs. Arafat was constantly maneuvering with the Arab leaders for advantage; he would try to build pressure on them by appealing over their heads to the emotions of the "Arab street." But he would rarely count on the Arabs to come to his rescue.

The irony is that we both also believe that Arafat rejected the Clinton Parameters because it meant that he would have to give up grievances and claims. He would have to accept publicly that the conflict was over. If his purpose all along was phases—as the neoconservatives had argued and made a fundamental premise of their critique of the Oslo process— he would not have cared about accepting the Clinton Parameters regardless of what they said. He would have grabbed them, realizing they provided him (and the Palestinian movement) with a historic gain from which he could continue the struggle. But what mattered to Arafat was his image in history, his steadfastness in not giving up the dream that one day after he was gone there might be only one state. He could live with the idea that Israel would continue to exist after he was gone—maybe even for an extended period—but his ideology made it impossible for him to concede openly and for all time that Palestinians did not have claims over what is now the state of Israel.

Maybe Arafat saw the intifada as a tool for leverage against Israel. Maybe he believed that he could get Israel to go along with more concessions without his having to give up all claims. The neoconservatives were not wrong to see Arafat as duplicitous; they were wrong to believe that he had been guided by a "phases" strategy or that he thought the Arabs would fight Israel for the Palestinians.

They were also wrong in other ways. The neoconservatives have typically failed to draw distinctions among Palestinians, seeing them as largely homogeneous. They are not. There are real differences between the Islamists and the non-Islamists—and those differences matter. If nothing else, they create a convergence between the Israelis and the non-Islamist Palestinians, both of whom see the Islamists as a threat: the Israelis because the Islamists seek their eradication, the non-Islamist Palestinians because the Islamists seek to take them back to the Middle Ages. It makes sense to test whether this convergence of interest could produce an agreement. Indeed, the neoconservative mind-set guarantees a self-fulfilling prophecy without ever knowing whether an agreement is possible—worse, it justifies inaction that can only play to the Islamist desire to foster a sense of hopelessness that groups like Hamas seek to exploit.

But the neoconservatives were also wrong to believe that withdrawal (though certainly a risk) was a greater danger than the status quo. For one thing, the status quo in the Middle East is rarely static. In this case, inaction would not only produce radicalization, it would also pose a demographic threat to Israel. If there are 5.7 million Jews in Israel and approximately 1.2 million Israeli Arabs living within Israel and another 3.5 to 4 million Palestinian Arabs in the West Bank and Gaza—and the Arabs have a higher birth rate—the prospect of the Jews becoming a minority in Israel / West Bank / Gaza together is very real.

Almost all Israeli leaders since the early 1990s, including Yitzhak Rabin and later Ariel Sharon, came to understand the demographic danger and to see the occupation of Palestinian lands as threatening the very character of Israel. Given demographic trends, they understood that Israel could be either Jewish or democratic, but not both, if it stayed in the territories. But this was not the neoconservatives' fear. They feared withdrawal more than they feared demographic trends. Feith acknowledged that the "material and moral burdens of occupation" were not to be denied, but for him they did not threaten "Israel's existence."[26] Podhoretz, too, acknowledged that the status quo might be intolerable for Israel, but a "Lebanonized Palestinian state" would unleash calamities and be far worse.[27] For the neoconservatives, Israel's existence would be threatened by withdrawal and the creation of a Palestinian state. It would not be threatened by demographic trends. As Feith said at one point, no one was advocating annexing the territory and granting "citizenship for the Arab inhabitants."[28]

Here again we see irony in the neoconservative position. Peace is not possible because the Arabs are not democratic, but when it comes to the

Palestinians, they cannot be granted full rights within Israel, nor can they have a state that might be democratic, because it is simply too dangerous. Similarly, while the neoconservatives may care deeply about Israel, its values are less important to them than holding territory heavily populated with Palestinians.

To be fair to the neoconservatives, they see the territory in the West Bank as defining the Jewish national identity dating back to the narrative of the Bible. A good portion of the terrain where Abraham, Isaac, and Jacob walked is in the West Bank. For Feith, to trade away the territory is not simply a danger; it is part of surrendering national rights. In his words, "Israel too is an idea," and "There are some things that a nation can never trade away unless it is willing to change its basic character."[29]

For Feith, the land (meaning the West Bank or its biblical name, Judea and Samaria) defined Israel's character. For Israelis like Rabin (and subsequently Ehud Barak, Ariel Sharon, and Ehud Olmert), being Jewish and democratic was essential for preserving Israel, its national identity, its character, and its values as a state. Unlike Feith, they believed that holding on to Gaza and the West Bank threatened to change Israel's character.

To be sure, none of these Israeli leaders saw withdrawal as risk-free, and none was willing to trade away land in a way that he thought would jeopardize Israel's security. None was willing to countenance a Palestinian state that he thought would threaten Israel's survival. While the neoconservatives did not agree with what Rabin (or later Barak or Olmert) was doing, they did not accuse of them betraying Israel. They did not question their motives.

So how did they explain their behavior? Fatigue was one explanation, and the other was American pressure. Israelis were understandably weary from having to endure ongoing terror and wars. They wanted all this to end and chased an illusion in doing so—or so the neoconservatives believed.

But it was not only fatigue and the understandable desire to live in peace; it was also, according to the neoconservatives, American pressure that explained why someone like Yitzhak Rabin, a tough-minded, non-sentimental leader, would be willing not just to deal with Yasir Arafat but also to accept a Palestinian state. Elliott Abrams clearly believed that the need to secure Israel's strategic relationship with the United States—and the Clinton administration's position on Oslo—left Rabin little choice except to follow the path he did. Abrams, in this connection, approvingly quoted Podhoretz's words: "It [Rabin's behavior] had to do with his stress on the overriding importance of Israel's strategic relationship with the U.S. Rabin persuaded himself, I would guess, that unless he endorsed Oslo and went to the White House lawn, he would jeopardize that relationship, and that this would prove more dangerous to Israel than a Palestinian state ruled by Arafat."[30]

It was apparently inconceivable to Abrams and Podhoretz that Rabin would decide, on his own, that creating a process with the PLO might be in Israel's interest. Yet the Israelis launched the Oslo process secretly and directly with the PLO and without the United States. True, Rabin wanted to know how the Clinton administration would respond—seeking Secretary of State Warren Christopher's reaction before finalizing the Declaration of Principles and the document of mutual recognition between Israel and the PLO. But it was an Israeli decision, reflecting Rabin's view that it was possible to reach agreement with the PLO and that it was worth taking the risks associated with doing so, given Israel's strong strategic position at the time. The demographic trends as well as Rabin's view that it made sense to try to create an inner circle of peace with Israel's neighbors led him to try to reach agreement with the Palestinians.

Ariel Sharon in late 2003 came to the conclusion that the demographic trends required Israel to disengage from the Palestinians and to favor the creation of a Palestinian state. It might not be led by Yasir Arafat, but he accepted the idea of an independent Palestinian state next to Israel. Did he do it because of the "pressure" of the Bush administration? Elliott Abrams was in a leading position in the White House, shaping the Bush policy toward the Arab-Israeli issue at this time. Were he and President Bush guilty of applying the same pressure that they claimed the Clinton administration had applied? Or was Sharon, like Yitzhak Rabin before him, deciding that partition of the land into two states—or at least Israeli separation from Palestinians—was necessary to fulfill Israel's vital interest of preserving its Jewish and democratic character?

Strong Israeli leaders like Rabin and Sharon decided what Israel's future required and made decisions accordingly. They acted because of their convictions, not because of American pressures. For Sharon, given the hands-off instinct of the Bush administration, pressures were unlikely to be applied in any case, further demonstrating that he acted because he thought Israel's needs demanded he do so. Unlike the neoconservatives, Rabin and Sharon saw withdrawal and even a Palestinian state as necessary because of Israel's vital interests. For the neoconservatives, withdrawal was a vital threat to Israel. Apart from believing that settling the conflict was impossible, the neoconservatives were also convinced that Arab-Israeli peace was not a vital interest of the United States.

Consider what Elliott Abrams wrote about America's most important interests in the Middle East before assuming his position in the Bush administration: "The United States has two paramount interests in the region today: keeping peace between the Arabs and Israelis, and toppling Saddam Hussein."[31] Note that Abrams was referring to "keeping" Arab-Israeli peace, not "making" it. He was clearly more concerned about regime change in Iraq than in promoting a Palestinian state. Podhoretz at an earlier point was even more blunt in saying that pursuing Arab-Israeli peace was not a vital interest of the United States. In his words, America did not need to be "obsessing" about it; "the notion that settling the Palestinian problem is in the vital interest of the United States never made any sense" because, he argued, it is neither the key to solving the Arab-Israeli conflict—since Arab rejection of Israel lies at the heart of the problem— nor would it bring stability to the region.[32]

It should be noted that Podhoretz did acknowledge that the Arab-Israeli conflict may have been more important to American interests during the Cold War. Then, the fear that any outbreak of hostilities might lead to a confrontation between the United States and the Soviet Union and escalate to nuclear war did give us a reason to be concerned about the conflict. But with the end of the Cold War, that concern, and with it U.S. interest in resolving the Arab-Israeli conflict, largely dissipated—or so Podhoretz argued.[33]

We note this argument because of an interesting parallelism with the self-declared realists on the value of Israel as a strategic asset to the United States. John Mearsheimer and Stephen Walt, who wrote a book on the Israel lobby and see themselves as quintessential realists, suggest that Israel might have had strategic value to the United States during the Cold War, but once that ended, so did our interest in Israel's strategic benefit to America. Ironically, both the neoconservatives and the realists believe that the Cold War gave us a different view of our interests in the Middle East. For the realists, Israel had value, and for the neoconservatives, peacemaking had merit. With the Cold War over, they each have changed their views.

For the neoconservatives, peacemaking is an illusion, a Palestinian state is a danger, and U.S. "engagement" in conflict resolution is misguided. Those assumptions guided the Bush administration policy for most of its tenure. Disengagement was the hallmark of its policy until 2006, and even in the administration's last two years it left its mark.

THE CONSEQUENCES OF DISENGAGEMENT AND ITS LEGACY FOR BUSH-STYLE ENGAGEMENT

Disengagement, the policy born from the myth of absolute Arab rejectionism and the futility of pursuing peace, was supposed to be cost-free for the United States. Given the neoconservatives' cynical views of the peace process, they saw our disengagement as the right move—a policy that would sober the Arabs and not materially change Palestinian behavior or affect America's standing in the region. But their expectations were not fulfilled, and disengagement came with a cost. Whatever the limitations of engagement, there was one profound difference from disengagement: when Israelis and Palestinians are talking, they are less likely to be shooting. There may still be violence, but the scale is vastly different.

Compare the fatalities on each side during the period of the 1990s, when there was an active peace process with intensive U.S. engagement in promoting direct talks between the two sides (and between Israel and the Arabs more generally), to the period from 2001 to 2005 when the United States disengaged and there was no peace process. From 2001 to 2004, roughly 1,100 Israelis and nearly 4,000 Palestinians were killed. By contrast, during the preceding ten-year period of 1990–2000, when there was very active and intensive U.S. engagement, about 250 Israelis and roughly 1,000 Palestinians were killed. In other words, in less than half the time, approximately four times as many were killed on each side.[34]

Engagement and an active peace process did not end the conflict, but they clearly reduced the scope of violence and also preserved a sense of possibility. Disengagement failed on both measures. And its failure deepened the feeling among both Israelis and Palestinians that peace was simply not possible. It fed cynicism and disbelief about peace, and in so doing added to the appeal of Hamas; after all, the greater the frustration and the less the prospect of peace, the better Hamas does—and the more its narrative of "diplomacy can lead nowhere and only violence works" appears to gain validity. And unfortunately, when there is an absence of hope or a sense of possibility, those Palestinians and Arabs who believe in coexistence are undercut. They lose their political space, and they lose an argument on which to make their case.

Among the Arabs more generally, disengagement was also extremely damaging to America's credibility and appeal in the region. It conveyed an image of American indifference on an issue that mattered, from a psychological standpoint, to them. Even if the Arab world talks more about the Palestinian cause than it acts toward it, there is an inescapable reality: the plight of the Palestinians resonates as an enduring grievance and as a perceived injustice. Why, if we cared so little about what mattered to them, should they care about what mattered to us? If nothing else, the U.S. disengagement from the Palestinian issue produced even greater anger toward and dissociation from America and its preferred policies throughout much of the Arab Middle East.

To be sure, engaging after 9/11 and during a time of suicide bombings in the 2001–2004 period was bound to be difficult. Context matters, and the context at this time for peacemaking was terrible. One could even argue that in this period there was little opportunity to engage. And, from this standpoint, the Bush administration had little choice but to *disengage*.

But that ignores that the measure of diplomacy is not always what you achieve but what you prevent or contain or limit. Did the Bush administration do all it could to limit the violence or to create a context for its disengagement?

The answer is, unfortunately, no. The administration made only limited attempts to stop or contain the violence. It failed to follow through on George Tenet's negotiated plan for a cease-fire in the spring of 2001. And though General Anthony Zinni was appointed as a part-time envoy in the fall of 2001, his mandate was very limited. While he was serious, he could deal only with security issues and could not touch political or economic matters—meaning that his capacity to wield pressures and inducements was far too constrained.

Moreover, if the aim was to pressure Arafat and/or justify our disengagement, why wasn't Zinni or someone else in the administration empowered to go to Arab leaders and say if they did not act to get Arafat to do more to stop the terror, we would have no choice but to disengage from all peace-making efforts? That would have had the benefit of possibly affecting Arafat's behavior, putting Arab leaders in a position where they assumed responsibility, and offering a public explanation for disengagement that others could accept internationally.

But the mind-set that favored disengagement precluded such an effort and limited what General Zinni was empowered to try. Similarly, President Bush's speech on June 24, 2002, could have marked a historic watershed—particularly as he called for a Palestinian state, provided it was free of terror and corruption. For the speech to have had true historic significance, there would have had to be follow-through. Unfortunately, there was none. Strong and important words were left hanging as rhetoric. President Bush was right to break with Arafat. Arafat was duplicitous. One cannot call for the martyrs to liberate Jerusalem and yell "jihad" on al-Jazeera and still be a peace partner of the United States and Israel. A lesson of the 1990s is that if a leader cannot tell his public before a fateful summit like Camp David in 2000 that he will compromise, the odds are he will not do so. Arafat may have embodied Palestinian nationalism, but his actions, especially from 2000 to 2004, ensured that he could not be a partner for peace. It was appropriate to break with Arafat. And it was also appropriate for Bush to call for building new institutions for Palestinian statehood. But he and his administration were wrong once again in failing to engage and act on their words. It was as if disengagement had shaped their mind-set and their instinct for involvement.

This legacy, this tendency of thinking, affected the Bush policymakers. Even when the administration in its second term became more willing to engage itself, it limited how it did so. It was hesitant; its involvement remained episodic and was never intensive. It was almost as if the psychology of disengagement still colored its thinking and approach even after President Bush and Secretary of State Condoleezza Rice were proclaiming their seriousness about trying to reach an agreement. The manifestations of this hesitancy during the second term—or at least the inability to take advantage of openings by seizing the moment with an intensive, painstaking effort (the kind Elliott Abrams had derided)—are unfortunately easy to cite.

For starters, though Secretary Rice had spoken of the second term being a "time for diplomacy" and specifically had spoken of the need for heightened U.S. activity on the peace process, the United States basically squandered the opportunity that was created by the confluence of three historic developments: the death of Arafat, the election of Mahmoud Abbas on an unprecedented platform of nonviolence, and Ariel Sharon's decision to disengage from Gaza. With Arafat gone, the United States had an enormous stake in showing that Abbas's way, the way of nonviolence, would pay off for Palestinians and that life would get better. But for this to be the case, the administration needed to create a sense of urgency about delivering for Abbas, who was elected in early January 2005, shortly before President Bush was inaugurated for his second term.

Among other things, to deliver for Abbas required generating significant monies from the Arab oil states and ourselves for immediate investment in housing and infrastructure so Palestinians could go back to work at a time when their per capita income had declined by 40 percent over the years of the intifada; it also required focusing quickly with the Israelis on easing limitations on Palestinian movement. Improvements in each area would have been felt by every Palestinian—and done much to build Abbas's authority and a sense of possibility about the future.

But the moment was lost. There was no significant U.S. effort reflecting any urgency; as a consequence, little changed for Palestinians in terms of their day-to-day lives, and Abbas's authority was eroded, not enhanced. Similarly, when Sharon declared his readiness to withdraw completely from Gaza—both settlements and soldiers—the United States needed to act to make sure that life would get better in Gaza after the withdrawal and that Abbas and the Palestinian Authority would get credit for the Israeli disengagement. Once again, the U.S. effort was very limited; rather than appoint a U.S. envoy to deal with the issue full-time, the administration had James Wolfensohn, the former head of the World Bank, appointed as the representative of the Quartet—the United States, the European Union, the United Nations, and Russia. He represented everyone and no one. Saying no to him carried no consequence. What's more, his appointment was not made until May 2005, just a few months before the Israeli withdrawal. Even then, his authority was limited to the economics of the disengagement, not security. And yet economic improvement in Gaza depended heavily on security arrangements being worked out with Israel to permit access into and out of Gaza, particularly at the crossing points into and out of Israel. Indeed, without security arrangements being worked out and tested in advance, the Israelis were bound to keep the crossing points closed. They would not jeopardize Israeli lives and security, even if it meant shutting down the commerce and related investment necessary for the Palestinian economy to function and develop.

Wolfensohn worked hard over the three months before and after the Israeli withdrawal, and he subsequently blamed his inability to influence the situation on the ambivalence of the administration and its reluctance to take action—effectively, in his eyes, undermining his efforts.[35] Certainly, the administration did not want him to fail. But its instincts inclined it to limit the character of its engagement and his. Instead of Israeli withdrawal from territory—which was not easy and involved Ariel Sharon taking on the settler movement—making a major contribution to peace, today we see Hamas in control in Gaza and unilateral Israeli concessions now discredited in the eyes of the Israeli public.

The Bush administration needed to make sure that the Gaza withdrawal was an achievement for Sharon and Abbas alike. As such, it would have strengthened the center in both Israeli and Palestinian societies. Israel would not look as if it was being chased out of Gaza, the Palestinian Authority would appear to be delivering, and Hamas would be put on the defensive. This crucial opportunity was missed. The Bush administration compounded the damage in 2005 when it ignored the provisions of the Oslo accord that precluded Hamas from taking part in legislative council elections so long as it was committed to Israel's destruction. Believing that elections were always self-correcting mechanisms, the administration insisted on holding the vote—with the result that Hamas won; in many ways, we are living in the shadow of 2005 and the twin mistakes that were made that year.

Limited or episodic involvement also marked the effort made by Secretary Rice before and after the Annapolis conference held at the end of November 2007. In the beginning of 2007, Secretary Rice declared that it was time to resolve the Israeli-Palestinian conflict. She made it clear that she would work to produce a "political horizon" with the parties—an outline of the tradeoffs on the core issues of the conflict that even if presented in general terms would show how the conflict would end. The secretary began making trips once a month to the region, and in July the president announced that before the end of the year we would convene a conference bringing the parties and the international community together. The aim at the time was to have the Israelis and Palestinians present their agreed "political horizon" for how to end the conflict to the conference and have it endorsed by those assembled there.

This sounded good in theory, but once again the level of effort was never intensive enough to produce the desired outcome. Though the secretary did travel frequently to the area, her trips tended to be disconnected. They did not demonstrate any progression and were not shaped by a clear set of objectives that she was working toward achieving. Rather, she would fly in primarily to demonstrate her interest, but she would stay only briefly and would not shuttle back and forth between the sides trying to bridge differences. Finally, only a few weeks before the conference was to be convened at Annapolis, the secretary changed the meeting's objective altogether. At this point, the parties would no longer be presenting their agreed horizon to the conference; instead, the meeting would simply serve as the launching point for permanent status negotiations between the two sides.

There is nothing wrong with changing objectives per se. But imagine if Secretary Rice's seven trips during the year had been tied together with an eye toward preparing an agenda for negotiations, narrowing differences in advance on the parameters of each issue, and shaping what would happen after the negotiations began. None of that was done. Annapolis was convened with no preparation and no day-after strategy.

While nearly fifty countries came, no agreed principles for the conference had been worked out in advance—such as, for example, a statement that all countries were participating based on agreement that a two-state solution should be the outcome, and that negotiations and nonviolence were the only ways to resolve the conflict. There were no Annapolis principles that might have made the conference a milestone. Instead, Annapolis was, in the words of one Israeli participant, the "mother of all photo ops."[36]

Yet even a photo op might have been useful, if it had been prepared with an eye to what would come after it. But it seemed there was also no recognition that, given the cynicism in the region and of the parties, it was essential to show that something would be different after the conference. It was critical to show the Israeli and Palestinian publics that things were changing on the ground as a way of demonstrating that the conference was already producing palpable results—and also as a way of giving the publics a reason to believe that the negotiations could lead somewhere. This does not mean the United States was completely inactive. The Bush administration, with bipartisan Congressional support, recognized that the Palestinian Authority was more financially transparent and provided it with $300 million in budgetary support for 2008, among other actions. But it was not tied to a strategy for bringing about improvements in the daily lives of Palestinians. Such a strategy could have been done with Israel and not at Israel's security expense.

We raise all this not to point to the incompetence of the effort, but rather to say that the style and character of the administration's diplomacy should come as no surprise. The effort reflected a mind-set that had put a premium on disengagement for so long that there simply was no basic understanding of how to engage effectively.

In effect, the neoconservative mind-set—the neoconservative mythology—continued to condition the Bush administration's actions even after the secretary of state convinced the president that engagement—not disengagement—was required. Not surprisingly, it produced an ambivalent approach to engagement. But its real effect was to leave to the new administration a far worse context for peacemaking. By withdrawing from the effort for so long, largely because of neoconservative instincts, the Bush policies had a damaging cumulative impact. They did little to bring an end to the intifada, contributed to disbelief on the part of both the Israeli and Palestinian publics, and ensured that openings that could have truly transformed the environment for building peace were missed.

The damage done has been profound. Reversing the neglect of the last eight years will not be easy. The first task will be to find a way to restore belief in peacemaking and to create a public context that actually empowers leaders to take risks for peace, knowing that their publics will be accepting and supportive.

Here is a reminder that a context for peace must be nurtured and constructed. Whereas the neoconservatives basically rejected that such a context could ever be constructed because of Arab hostility to Israel, the realists believe that it essentially already exists; the only thing needed to produce peace is the will of the United States. For the realists, the conflict can be ended and peace can be made—or, more likely, imposed by the United States. All that is required is that we have the will to do it.

But is it really that simple? Or is this merely another mythology that may be the polar opposite of the neoconservatives' but just as misguided and with assumptions equally flawed? Let us now turn to the realist mythology on the peace process.

Chapter Five

THE REALIST MYTHOLOGY
ABOUT THE PEACE PROCESS

The neoconservative mythology produced the disengagement of the Bush administration from peacemaking efforts between Israel and its Arab neighbors for most of its tenure. The costs of disengagement were high, creating disbelief about the possibility of peace and doing great damage to America's standing in the Middle East. Our recovery from the Bush legacy will not come quickly or easily.

At least that is what we believe when we look at the context for peace diplomacy and the decline of U.S. credibility in the region. But the realists see a different picture. They, too, lament the consequences of Bush disengagement. However, they believe that U.S. engagement can repair things quickly.

Their view stems in part from their belief in linkage. We have explained at great length the durability of linkage as a mythology and why it is so fundamentally misguided and misleading to policymakers. Faith in linkage leads realists to assume that resolving the Palestinian problem will transform the region and our position in it.

And yet we have demonstrated that history tells a very different story—that the picture of the Middle East is more complex; that Arab leaders have used linkage for their own self-serving reasons; and that there may be very good reasons to try to resolve the conflict between Arabs, Israelis, and Palestinians, but the context for peacemaking matters.

Quite apart from their view of linkage, the realists have a view of peacemaking that is based on several other unfortunate and misleading myths. The first is that the Israelis are to blame for the conflict. The second is that the United States is too close to Israel, and this relationship serves only to exacerbate the problem. In response, they produce a third myth: that if America were only willing to offer a blueprint, the conflict could be resolved.

After two terms of the Bush administration's approach to dealing with the Arab-Israeli conflict, it may be tempting to embrace the realist mythology. However, to do so would not just be wrong-headed; it would inevitably set back the steps and the approaches needed to produce real conflict resolution. To know what to do, we need to take a closer look at what not to do and which assumptions will lead us astray.

THE REALIST MYTHS ABOUT THE PEACE PROCESS

While the overarching realist mythology about the peace process is that the United States can settle the conflict—or, as we will see, can apply pressure (primarily on Israel) to do so—there are certainly several critical assumptions that underpin this approach. First and most importantly, realists believe that Israel is primarily responsible for the conflict. Nothing more clearly separates them from the neoconservatives than this assumption. As we saw in the last chapter, Podhoretz, Abrams, Feith, and other neoconservatives all basically saw the conflict as the result of Arab and Palestinian rejection of the Jewish state in their midst. In their view, peace is not possible because the Arabs are simply not prepared to accept Israel's right to be there. For the realists, however, it is not Arab rejection of Israel, but Israel's reluctance to accept its responsibility for the conflict that lies at the heart of the problem.

Realists like John Mearsheimer and Stephen Walt make this an implicit point when they put the onus on Israel and emphasize Israel's obligations to the near exclusion of those of the other side. Reading them, one could only draw the conclusion that Israeli withdrawal is the sine qua non for peace and it is only Israel's reluctance to do it, and our unwillingness to pressure Israel to do it, that explains the conflict. But others go much further and are far more explicit in holding Israel responsible for the conflict. Consider the words of academician Jerome Slater:

> Both because it is so much more powerful than the Palestinians and because it is primarily responsible for the continuing Israeli-Palestinian conflict, Israel has the main responsibility for averting

a catastrophic escalation and finally reaching a fair settlement. Yet Israel has never been willing to acknowledge its role in the origins and dynamics of the Arab-Israeli conflict, has never been willing to acknowledge its moral responsibility for the plight of the Palestinians, and has missed a number of opportunities to settle both the Israeli-Palestinian and larger Arab-Israeli conflict.[1]

Here is a perception of the Middle East conflict that is not only at variance with the neoconservative view; it challenges most of the historical narratives on the subject. Drawing from some of the revisionist histories on the origins of the Palestinian refugee problem, Slater basically ascribes full responsibility to Israel for the root of the conflict. That Arabs and Palestinians simply rejected all possible compromises prior to the establishment of the state of Israel, including the Peel Commission Report of 1937, the Morrison-Grady proposal in 1946, and the UN partition plan in 1947, is basically immaterial to Slater. Similarly, Arab rejection of Israel and calls for its destruction also matter little in his view of the conflict. For him, Palestinians were forced from their lands and Israel has denied its responsibility for this original sin; if there is to be peace, Israel must face up to its responsibility. In his words, "an Israeli willingness to face their history, free of the distortions and the myths that have blinded them, is the psychological prerequisite for the establishment of peace for both the Palestinians and Israelis."[2]

Other academics, like Stephen Zunes, also believe that Israel bears the major responsibility for the continuing conflict. For him the conflict is about basic legality. Enshrined in the UN charter is the principle of nonacquisition of territory by force, and Zunes maintains that Israel must not only withdraw, it is not entitled to any particular reward for doing so: "Even if Israel had agreed to withdraw from occupied parts of the West Bank and Gaza Strip, including East Jerusalem, and recognized the right of return for Palestinian refugees, it could not be fairly presented as a great act of generosity or even an enormous concession, since Israel is required to do so."[3]

For Zunes, conflicts exist in a historical vacuum. Threats and rejection—or real needs and hard political choices—are apparently beside the point. Israel is not entitled to anything; it is obligated by certain legal requirements. Normally, when one speaks about the so-called realists, it is less legalisms and more power and interests that guide them. While that is surely true, it is also clear that when it comes to Israel, the realists weave a story in which Israel is seen as being in the wrong and the Palestinians are the aggrieved party. Israel is the victimizer and the Palestinians are the victim—and the United States is basically on the wrong side.

Similarly, the view of former national security advisor Zbigniew Brzezinski, while perhaps not as extreme, reflects the same basic logic, which tends to see the Palestinians as victims and the Israelis as victimizers, with serious consequences for the United States. Consider his response to the Israeli operation in the West Bank that Mearsheimer and Walt condemned: "[T]here is nearly unanimous global consensus that United States policy has become one-sided and morally hypocritical, with clear displays of sympathy for Israel's victims of terrorist violence and relative indifference to the (much more numerous) Palestinian civilian casualties."[4] For Brzezinski, there is apparently a moral equivalence between those who target noncombatants and those whose response to terror tragically but inadvertently kills civilians—at least when it comes to the Israelis.

Israel, for the realists, is a costly friend to have. In this view, American interests require a separation from Israel, and of course it becomes easier to justify such separation if Israel can be portrayed as being in the wrong. For Brzezinski, there is an imperative in doing so, and sentiment or connections to Israel must not be allowed to interfere with what our interests require: "The United States response [to the Israeli-Palestinian conflict], therefore, has to be guided by a strategic awareness of all interests involved, and not by the claims of any single party."[5] Here Brzezinski, the quintessential realist, is referring to our need not to be bound by Israel's claims—notwithstanding the commitments we might have made to Israel.

For the realists, our mistake is that we have been too close to Israel, and this renders peacemaking difficult. How, the realists ask, can we be an honest broker and take into account both sides' needs when we are guided only by Israeli concerns? The realist claims that recent U.S. administrations—Clinton and Bush 43—have been too close to Israel were lent credence by Aaron David Miller, a former member of the U.S. peace team. Miller, who served as Dennis Ross's deputy during both the Bush 41 and Clinton administrations, wrote after he left government that the United States had functioned far too often as "Israel's lawyer" in negotiations. In other words, we represented Israel in the negotiations, effectively took sides with it, did not push back against its positions, and failed to take Palestinian concerns into account.[6]

One can hardly blame realists like Mearsheimer and Walt for using the Miller description for their own purposes. Their argument, much like Brzezinski's, is that such close identification with Israel isolates the United States in the world and makes peace far less likely. In their words, "backing Israel unconditionally helps make the United States a target for radical extremists and makes America look callous and hypocritical in the eyes of many third parties, including Europeans and Arab allies."[7]

For the realists, it is largely inconceivable that Israel could have a case or that the Arabs and Palestinians might not be living up to their side of the bargain. Israel is the one that holds the key to solving the conflict if it will only change its behavior—and the United States must be the one to get it to do so. But American administrations like those of Clinton and Bush 43 fail to act the way they should either because they are too sensitive to the "Israel lobby" or because their officials are too partial to Israel.

Again, listen to Mearsheimer and Walt: "Although both [Martin] Indyk and [Dennis] Ross supported the Oslo peace process and favored the creation of a Palestinian state . . . they did so only within the limits of what would be acceptable to Israeli leaders . . . [T]he American delegation at Camp David took most of its cues from Israeli Prime Minister Ehud Barak, coordinated negotiating positions with Israel in advance, and did not offer its own independent proposals for settling the conflict."

This has become a conventional wisdom for the realists, with one former official being quoted in a study on the peace process as saying, "Our conceptions were . . . filtered far too much through what Israel needed and wanted and required."[8]

But is this true? Did the United States not make its own independent proposals? Did the Clinton administration act as Israel's lawyer? It is interesting that the Bush 41 administration is often held up as a model for how to operate in Israeli-Palestinian negotiations. Aaron Miller makes the point that Secretary of State James Baker did not act as Israel's lawyer but was tough on both sides. The same study on the peace process noted above also singles out Secretary Baker for praise, observing that "Baker was careful not to allow politics in the region to wield a veto over US policy decisions."[9]

And yet Secretary Baker, who is not seen as being too close to Israel, operated on several premises, including never surprising the Israeli government on peace issues. He felt obligated by the letter from President Gerald Ford to then Prime Minister Yitzhak Rabin in 1975 that committed the United States to never putting a peace proposal on the table without first consulting Israel.[10]

Moreover, if one looks at Secretary Baker's two signature efforts on peace negotiations during the Bush administration—his five-point plan to launch an Israeli-Palestinian dialogue in 1989–90 and his initiative to break the taboo on negotiations that resulted in the Madrid conference in 1991—he worked within the frame of what he felt Israel could accept. The initial efforts to launch an Israeli-Palestinian dialogue proceeded by taking an Israeli proposal made by Prime Minister Yitzhak Shamir and trying to make it acceptable to the Arabs. And Baker's subsequent and successful effort to launch bilateral and multilateral negotiations also operated within the realm of what Israel could accept—no PLO presence at the forum, no Palestinians from Jerusalem on the Palestinian delegation (which meant that Faisal Husseini, who was Baker's main Palestinian interlocutor, would be excluded from the joint Jordanian-Palestinian delegation), no decision-making role for the conference, and a premise that the conference existed only to launch the bilateral negotiations and not to have an ongoing function.[11]

We do not say this to suggest that Secretary Baker put no pressure on Israel. Rather, we make the point to show that the Baker approach started from the premise of how the United States could either take Israeli ideas and make them acceptable to the Arabs or could develop ideas that were basically acceptable to Israel and make them also acceptable to the Arabs and Palestinians. Baker proceeded this way because he came to the conclusion that the Arabs were not prepared to initiate anything and he could use our influence with Israel to push Israel to come up with ideas of its own on peace, or to work with us as we came up with ideas that they could live with if we could also convince the Arabs of their utility.

Was the Clinton approach so different? Perhaps in style, as his public embrace of Israel was far warmer. But again bear in mind that Clinton was working from 1993 to 1996 and 1999 to 2000 with Labor Party–led governments in which the prime ministers (Rabin, Peres, and Barak) were all committed to trying to reach peace agreements. Baker's counterpart was a Likud prime minister—Yitzhak Shamir—who was resistant to moving on the peace process. Given that, is it any wonder that his style was different from Clinton's?

As we noted above, context matters. It matters whom you are dealing with. It also matters how the United States is seen and how it is held. It matters whether it has great standing—and whether it has leverage. Surely it was far easier for Secretary Baker to succeed after the first Gulf War when U.S. power, credibility, and perceived effectiveness were at their apex. It also helped that Yasir Arafat had sided with Saddam Hussein and damaged his credibility in much of the Arab world—and certainly with his main financial benefactors in the Gulf—thus making it easier to exclude the PLO from the Madrid conference.

Finally, it matters what an administration is trying to do. Secretary Baker exhibited great skill in persevering and getting negotiations launched. But initiating negotiations is not the same as concluding them, particularly when the decisions required to settle an existential conflict between Israelis and Palestinians involved taking on history and mythology—indeed, involved making decisions that went to the heart of self-definition and identity.

So the style was different between the Bush 41 and Clinton administrations. But the circumstances were also very different in terms of the leaders to be dealt with, the context for policymaking, and the aims being pursued. Yet Secretary Baker's starting point was very similar to the starting point that characterized Secretaries Warren Christopher and Madeleine Albright's approaches. None of them would surprise Israel. All of them basically sought to produce Israeli ideas to sell to the other side or, as with the Clinton Parameters, started with the premise of gaining a sense of what Israel could live with and then trying to move the Arab or Palestinian position accordingly.

Once again, this was not because of an indifference to the Arabs or Palestinians or an inability to understand them. Rather, it reflected both the commitment to no surprises and also the reality that the Arab world saw the conflict through a certain prism. Arab leaders saw themselves and the Palestinians as the aggrieved party, the weaker party, and felt that the initiative and the first move must always come from the Israelis—or from the United States. Recall the lesson of linkage in the eyes of Arab leaders: the burden for acting on the peace process was ours, not theirs.

In the view of Arab and Palestinian leaders, as in the view of many realists, it is up to Israel to solve the conflict. Their willingness to accept Israel as a fact is the essence of what they are required to do. Accepting Israel's existence is their main compromise and also the card they have to withhold. Accordingly, they would not make the initial move—and given the lack of any conditioning of their publics for concessions to Israel, it was politically costly for regimes that lacked basic legitimacy to look as if they were conceding before getting anything from Israel.

Secretary Baker understood this reality and thus operated on what he needed to get from Israel to begin any meaningful process. It is true that after the Gulf War he began the process by going to the Saudis and others to see if they would accept an approach in which there was both an Israeli-Palestinian negotiation and an Arab state negotiation with Israel in parallel. He did this because we had just fought a war on behalf of the Saudis and others, and he wanted to see if having joined us in a war against Iraq (an Arab brother) they would now join us in a peace effort with Israel. But even this initial effort was soon focused on getting what Israel needed to come to a conference that would launch bilateral negotiations. Getting much from the Arabs was very difficult, and the focus inevitably shifted back to Israel. (While the Arabs were not prepared to initiate much, they did respond to our efforts to join multilateral talks with the Israelis on water, arms control, the environment, and economic development.)

This dynamic tended to guide negotiations in both the Bush 41 and Clinton years. This is not to say that from time to time we did not try to produce concessions from the Arabs, particularly because we understood that this would create both an Israeli incentive and an Israeli need to be seen as responding if there were Arab partners for peace. Indeed, if there is a lesson from the past, it is that the Israeli public will not tolerate Israeli political leaders if there appears to be an Arab partner and those leaders are not up to dealing with it. Such Israeli leaders will not survive in office—note Yitzhak Shamir's election loss to Yitzhak Rabin and Benjamin Netanyahu's defeat at the hands of Ehud Barak. By the same token, when the Israeli public believes there is no Arab partner, it prefers to have leaders who will show the Arabs the consequences of nonresponsiveness;

hence the defeat of Shimon Peres in 1996 by Netanyahu (after four suicide bombs in nine days) and Ariel Sharon's victory over Barak in 2001 after the failure of Camp David, the beginning of the intifada, and the Palestinian rejection of the Clinton Parameters.

And here it is worth calling attention to the Clinton Parameters. They were very far-reaching and were unprecedented in terms of an American bridging proposal to settle the conflict. They came after very extensive discussions and at the request of the parties. Among other things, they would have provided for a Palestinian state with its capital in East Jerusalem, and Israeli withdrawal from 100 percent of Gaza and between 95 and 97 percent of the West Bank. They went substantially beyond what Ehud Barak had been prepared to contemplate at Camp David. Why mention this? Because the Clinton Parameters belie the realist argument that Clinton and his negotiators—including one of us—were never prepared to do anything that the Israelis did not clear, were never prepared to adopt independent positions, and only acted as Israel's lawyers.

These points may fit the realist narrative, but they do not reflect reality. The truth is that during the Clinton administration—much as during that of Bush 41—there was a constant effort to take Israeli ideas and try to refine them, but when that was not sufficient, we inevitably tried to push the Israelis to go further or tried to find ways to bridge the difference between where the Israelis and their putative Arab partners were. The very essence of the negotiating process inevitably meant that as the mediator, our role was to explain the needs of one side to the other as a way of convincing each side that if they wanted to have their needs met, they had to meet the requirements of the other side.

While Aaron Miller may say that we functioned as Israel's lawyer, he neglects to note that Ehud Barak continually accused Dennis Ross of being Arafat's lawyer and Yasir Arafat continually accused Dennis of being Barak's lawyer. Being an active mediator inevitably put Dennis in that position—and Miller, though he was an active participant in the process, was not in the meetings with the leaders when the hard negotiating was taking place. He did not see the persistent effort to explain al-Asad's needs to Rabin or Barak, or their needs to al-Asad, or the countless hours spent explaining Arafat's needs and constraints to the different Israeli leaders or their needs to Arafat.

It may be comforting to believe that the United States did not play this dual role, because it allows the realists to argue that America has not done what it needed to do and if it would only dissociate from Israel everything would fall into place. But this is the myth at the heart of realist attitudes—and because of its persistence in their writings, it is worth looking more closely at the realist argument about the need for the United States to pressure Israel and provide a blueprint for settling the conflict.

THE REALIST CALL FOR A BLUEPRINT FOR PEACE

The realists are convinced that the parties can never solve the conflict on their own—and that the consequences of the continuing conflict are so devastating to American interests in the region that America must present a blueprint for solving the conflict. No one has made this case more fervently or consistently than Zbigniew Brzezinski, who declared, for example, that

> [left] to themselves, the Israelis and Palestinians can only make war, not peace. Neither side is able to take the ultimate steps necessary for a grand, but also painful, historic reconciliation. Given the ominous prospects for the region, for America's interests in it and ultimately for Israel itself, a proposed peace blueprint from the United States could not be more timely. . . .[12]

In effect, Brzezinski's view, like that of other realists, is that the conflict is too important to be left to the parties themselves. Since "they cannot and will not settle on their own," we must do it for them. In his eyes, "this would not be an attempt to impose peace but a case of peace gradually imposing itself."[13]

How it would impose itself, even gradually, is left largely to our imagination. But the reason we must do it, for Brzezinski and others, is that our stakes in the region leave us no choice. It is not moral obligations alone that impel us "to bring about an overall Arab-Israeli peace settlement," in Jerome Slater's words, it is the "responsibility to [our] own self-interests, even to [our] national security in the most literal sense. . . ." He echoes other realists when he says pushing for peace is necessary because "continued American support of Israeli repression of Palestinians will certainly further undermine the U.S. relationship with the Arab world, thereby jeopardizing support for such important American national security interests as containment of Iraq and Iran and continued unfettered access to Arab oil."[14]

Though Slater wrote this in 2001, before the war in Iraq, note how similar its line of argument is to the more recent writings of Mearsheimer and Walt when they state that doing nothing on the peace issue, or "backing Israel so consistently, has not made things better. On the contrary, this policy has almost certainly made things worse for Palestinians and Israelis alike and continues to erode America's reputation in the world and make it more difficult to deal with urgent issues like Iraq and Iran."[15]

As we discussed in the linkage chapters, unfettered access to oil is not tied to the Palestinian issue, and clearly our problems in Iraq and Iran will not suddenly or magically disappear if the Israeli-Palestinian conflict is resolved. Surely the climate will be improved and the ability to exploit this grievance will be undercut—making it harder for Iran to put Arab regimes on the defensive—but the Iranian challenge will remain, and the sectarian tensions in Iraq will not have dissolved.

But for the realists, the relationship between the conflict and our regional stakes is taken as an article of faith. They see us isolating ourselves, they see the challenges from Iran to Iraq to oil becoming more acute, and they see us making ourselves the target of Islamic terror by siding with the Israelis and not resolving the conflict. So we must separate ourselves from the Israelis and push to settle the conflict. And while Brzezinski wrote about peace gradually imposing itself once we present a blueprint, other realists explain that what is really necessary is American pressure tied to an American proposal for peace.

William Quandt, surely one of the more thoughtful realists, has written that the United States has succeeded in moving the parties toward peace in the past only when there has been sustained American leadership at the highest levels and "a willingness to put forward substantive proposals, to cajole, to argue, to persuade, and, yes, to pressure."[16]

Quandt speaks of pressuring the Israelis in their own interest. He cites an episode from the original Camp David when he says that Israel's then foreign minister, Moshe Dayan, told him, at a point when Israeli prime minister Menachem Begin was reluctant to accept an Egyptian proposal, that Israelis counted on "Americans to make us do what we know we have to do. Then we can explain to our public that we have accepted an American proposal. Israelis will understand why we have to say yes to you. We will complain, but just make us do it."[17]

If linkage is an article of faith for the realists, U.S. pressure on Israel is an article of faith for most on the Israeli left. Getting the Israelis to do what they don't want to do on their own but is for their own good is something that Israeli doves from Yossi Beilin to Shlomo Ben Ami have long been convinced is the only way to make peace. They, too, tend to put the onus on Israel for what needs to be done, accepting that the Arabs and Palestinians are too limited or too dysfunctional ever to be able to take the necessary steps toward Israel—and since the Israeli doves cannot convince their own public to take the necessary steps, the United States should simply force Israel to do it.

Is that what Dayan was telling William Quandt at Camp David? Perhaps, but consider the context. Dayan understood the stakes of a failure at Camp David, particularly given the fact that Anwar Sadat had launched the process by coming to Jerusalem and declaring no more war, no more bloodshed. Dayan saw what it took to make an agreement and may have feared that his prime minister was not up to doing what was necessary. Pressuring Israel in circumstances in which it had an unmistakable partner in Sadat was one thing; pressuring Israel in a context in which there is no equivalent of Sadat might be something very different.

This highlights again the issue of context. For the realists, context seems irrelevant. They hold Israel responsible for making the necessary concessions on land—and believe if Israel does not act in its own self-interest, we must act in ours and pressure Israel to do so. This seems to hold true even if Israel is preparing to take painful steps that in the eyes of the realists don't go as far as they need to go. In this connection, it is interesting to note that even as Israel was getting ready to withdraw from Gaza and Prime Minister Sharon was taking on the settler movement, Brzezinski and Quandt drew attention to the need to focus on the push for a final status agreement: "For the next few months, the Israeli-Palestinian agenda is likely to be dominated by the impending Israeli withdrawal from Gaza and by the Palestinian elections. But before the end of the year, the moment of truth for the Bush administration will arrive and the president will have to decide whether to live up to the words he spoke last month by injecting a sense of urgency into the search for final status Israeli-Palestinian peace."[18]

That Israel was taking a difficult step; that Sharon was challenging a powerful constituency; that it was important to make the Gaza withdrawal work so the Israeli public might conclude it could be a model for the West Bank as well; and that it was essential for the Arab world to reach out to Israel to show Israelis that when they took significant steps, it produced acknowledgement and responses from Arab states—again reinforcing for the Israeli public the value of such steps—all seemed to be lost on these realist observers. Ironically, focusing on these kinds of steps might have created the context for being able to move to final status and to succeed at it. But realists tend not to focus on Israeli needs, only on what Israel must do and concede.

And to get the Israelis to make the necessary concessions, the realists think about our leverage on Israel and the importance of our applying it. Jerome Slater argues that in the past, "when the United States has been serious about constraining the Israelis, it has almost always been successful as for example when it used its leverage afforded by American economic and military assistance programs to induce Israeli pullbacks from Egypt, Syria, and Lebanese territory following the 1956, 1967, and 1982 Israeli-Arab conflicts."[19] While his history is somewhat suspect (the only pullback that came shortly after the aforementioned wars took place in 1957, and it came as a result of Eisenhower's threat of sanctions, not inducements), the point is that the realists believe that we have significant economic leverage and should be using it to alter Israel's behavior. Indeed, the realists focus on *our* leverage, not the leverage that Arab initiatives or actions might well create in Israel.

Realists like Mearsheimer and Walt focus on what *we* can do to influence the Israelis and not what those in the region can do. While they seek to create an appearance of balance by suggesting that we should use our enormous leverage on both the Israelis and the Palestinians, it is clear that they seek to apply serious pressure only on Israel. Consider that they suggest that the U.S. government "could threaten to cut off all economic and diplomatic support for Israel. If that were not enough, it would have little difficulty lining up international support to isolate Israel, much the way South Africa was singled out and shunned at the end of last century."[20] In other words, we should treat Israel not as an ally but as the equivalent of an international pariah. By contrast, with the Palestinians, the United States "could hold out the promise of fulfilling their dream of a viable state in the Occupied Territories coupled with massive long-term economic aid."[21] Put simply, the realist view is that the Palestinians need to be induced, not pressured.

Maybe Mearsheimer and Walt are right that the Palestinians do need to be induced, not pressured. Indeed, maybe the Palestinians need much more diplomatic and economic help, not only from us but also from the Arab states that portray such concern for the Palestinian cause and nationhood but provide such little practical or meaningful help.

But a role for the Arabs vis-à-vis the Palestinians and the Israelis is largely absent from the realist discussion. Similarly, the Arab commitment that Israelis and Palestinians need to feel to making and honoring an agreement is also distant from their discussion. To be fair, the realists are convinced that the two sides are incapable of making peace because of internal divisions, politics, weaknesses, and the absence of compelling leaders. Thus, the realists look to the United States to do it for the parties.

The problem with such an approach is that if the parties themselves are not committed to the compromises that must be made to settle the conflict, why will they defend them when they come under attack for making them? Why will they be willing to pay the price and live up to them? Both Arab and Israeli leaders surely will come under attack and be savagely criticized for selling out the national cause or rights when they make such compromises—or when they have to carry them out.

No agreement will ever hold if it looks as if it was made by outsiders—no matter how well-intentioned those outsiders. The great irony is that when there is talk of an American blueprint or imposing an agreement because the two sides cannot make peace, there is a presumption that because the Israeli and Palestinian publics want peace, we simply have to free them of the internal constraints that prevent it. But that presumes that there is an internal consensus on each side for the compromises that are necessary. And unless there is serious conditioning of public attitudes in advance of what is required for peace—including the specifics of the painful concessions on such issues as Jerusalem and refugees—the support for such compromises will not be forthcoming.

The sad reality is that peace may be desired but there is no acceptance of the price that is required to produce it. With the Israeli public, there has at least been some conditioning on the kinds of concessions that would be necessary on borders and Jerusalem, but it is still limited. On the Palestinian side, there has been precious little such public discussion of what is needed—and whenever the Palestinian public is polled on compromising on the refugee issue, the results are not encouraging.[22]

None of this means peace is impossible. But it is a reminder that the realist concept of external blueprints, of pressuring the Israelis while offering inducements to the Palestinians, is once again strangely divorced from reality. Because there tends to be a realist preoccupation with abstractions, they tend to overlook what it actually takes to make peace.

Abstract formulas are unlikely to work if they are disconnected from the day-to-day realities that both the Israeli and Palestinian publics are experiencing. They are unlikely to work if there is not some serious effort to condition publics on what will be required for peace, in terms of giving up the right of return for Palestinian refugees on the Palestinian side or accepting that there will have to be compromise on Jerusalem on the Israeli side. And they are unlikely to work unless the Arab states also play a role in helping Palestinians accept and justify compromise on core issues while also giving Israelis a reason to believe that they really will have a place in the region and relations with their neighbors.

Again, because the realists focus only on abstract slogans or on the Israeli need to make concessions, they tend to be willing to accept very little in terms of obligations on the Arab side. The Saudi initiative in 2002 that was subsequently adopted by the Arab League was in fact a good development. It offered a good counterpoint to the Iranian, Hizbollah, and Hamas narrative that rejects the idea of a two-state outcome to the Israeli-Palestinian conflict. However, it was treated as if it fulfilled what Arab states need to do for the peace process. And yet the day the resolution was initially adopted by the Arab League, there was a Hamas bombing at the Park Hotel in Netanya. The bombing took place on the first day of Passover, and still no Arab League member could find a way to condemn it. The resolution promised Israel eventual diplomatic relations with Arab states if it would first withdraw to the June 4, 1967, lines and accept a just settlement of the refugee issue.

In other words, after the Israelis made all their concessions on both the Palestinian and Syrian fronts, there would be peace at the end of the rainbow; the resolution offered a nice promise for the future. But for the present, no one could or would condemn the Hamas bombing. Was that likely to persuade Israelis? Unlikely, given that Israelis live with the harsh realities of the day and won't accept the promise of the future unless it is tied to something tangible. For the realists, however, the production of the initiative and the resolution was sufficient; the intangible sufficed. It should not have. A creative Arab initiative could be enormously helpful, but it must not be back-loaded. It must be premised on the idea that every step Israel takes toward the Palestinians will be met with an Arab step integrating Israel into the Middle East. It is critical that the incentives be properly sequenced so the Israeli and Palestinian mainstreams see the benefits of peace. A back-loaded initiative looks more like making impossible demands on one side without any reciprocity.

Furthermore, a creative Arab initiative must go beyond generalities. One of the most prominent, forward-leaning Arabs, former Jordanian foreign minister Marwan Muasher, has said that Israeli withdrawal would be met by Arab guarantees should the peace be violated by Hamas or others.[1]

---

*At the Washington Institute's Weinberg Founders Conference, Marwan Muasher stated, "Let me remind everyone, and I was, let me just say it, I was one of the architects of the Arab Peace Initiative. Let me remind us all of what the Arab Initiative offered not Arabs, but Israelis, because for the first time in the history of the conflict, you have an initiative that attempts not just to cover Arab needs, but Israeli needs as well. Four major offerings: one, a collective peace agreement, not between Israel and its neighboring states, but between Israel and every single member of the Arab League, the whole Arab world. The second is collective security guarantees, again, not between Israel and neighboring states, but between Israel and the whole Arab world. I, as the first ambassador to Israel, understand very well the need of the average Israeli citizen to feel that his or her person and security are guaranteed, and the Arab Peace Initiative does exactly that. It tells Israelis: your security will be guaranteed not by the Palestinians but by all of us, by the three hundred plus million Arabs in that region. And the third is an end to the conflict, and an end to claims. No further Arab is going to come and say, 'We are going to claim part of pre-1967 Israel,' once a two-state solution is implemented and an end is brought to the occupation. And the fourth and most important compromise is an agreed solution to the refugee problem. The word 'agreed' is

How would the Arabs provide such guarantees? What would they mean? How would they work? Nobody has elaborated on this. Once again, without well-thought-out ideas, it seems that Israel would be trading tangible land for an abstract and intangible idea.

But that is not how peace will be made. Realists argue less for active engagement in the peace process and more for the United States to simply offer the outcome or the blueprint to peace, as if that is how peace is made. Neoconservatives don't really believe that peace is possible, and so they favored the disengagement that guided the Bush administration for so long. The problem with the neoconservatives' approach is not only that we have seen the price of disengagement. The real problem is that the neoconservatives make their disbelief in peacemaking a self-fulfilling prophecy. They won't test the proposition, believing the Arabs are hopeless on peace, and so they rule it out without ever knowing. The realists, being divorced from reality, want peace but think it can be produced on the cheap with blueprints and slogans but not the real investment that is required. They hold the Israelis responsible for making concessions, but largely give the Arabs a pass, too often accepting rhetorical commitments at face value. Worse, they, too, create their own self-fulfilling prophecies by assuming that the two sides are incapable of peacemaking and therefore the United States must act in their place.

So what is the right way to pursue peace? We turn now to our prescription for peacemaking.

---

not a coincidence. It was put there to give a clear indication that no Arab is talking about four or five million Palestinians going back to Israel. And despite the violence of the last six years and despite the lack of a political process within the last six years, not a single Arab state withdrew its signature. The Arab Peace Initiative is still on the table today. Any attempts to solve the problem once and for all, through addressing the needs of both sides, because let's be candid: solutions that take care of the needs of one side and not the other are not going to work!" Marwan Muasher, "Is the Two State Solution Still Relevant?" Speech at the Weinberg Founders Conference, Washington Institute for Near East Policy, September 19–21, 2008. Audio and video recording found at: http://www.washingtoninstitute.org/templateC07.php?CID=423.

Chapter Six

ENGAGEMENT WITHOUT
ILLUSIONS: GIVING PEACE
A CHANCE

P ursuing peace in the Middle East is important for America's national security interests in the region. We say this not out of a misguided sense of linkage. We say it because the Palestinian-Israeli conflict is and will remain evocative for Arabs and Muslims throughout the world. We say it because the conflict does create anger and a profound sense of grievance—and radical Islamists play on that grievance to recruit, to keep Arab regimes on the defensive, and to try to create a revolutionary new order in the Middle East. We say it as well because it is time to end or at least transform this conflict—both because it is right to do on its own merits and because the perpetuation of the conflict breeds a sense of hopelessness in the region and that certainly also plays into the hands of Iran, Hizbollah, and Hamas.

However, as we have shown, the neoconservative mythology has led its theorists to dismiss even the possibility of peace. Apart from blinding them to the existence of those in the Arab world who might be partners for peace, their guiding myth leads them to underestimate the consequences of allowing a psychologically powerful issue to appear to have no prospects of being addressed. Ironically, they also fail to see how hopelessness on this conflict can put Israel in an increasingly untenable position. Note, for example, that many Palestinian intellectuals and political figures are now saying that they prefer to let the Palestinian Authority collapse or dissolve and make Israel responsible for meeting the economic and social needs of the Palestinians—indeed, to oblige Israel to absorb the Palestinians and have a one-state outcome in which the Palestinians eventually become the majority.[1]

Letting the conflict fester is thus not an option. But the realists are just as bad and just as misguided. Their mythology promotes engagement on the cheap without a recognition of the context. Their attachment to blueprints ignores the consequences of building expectations when the prospects of success are limited. What is more, after two terms of the Bush administration's penchant for transformational objectives that it was incapable of achieving, the last thing we need is to embrace positions or aims that we are unable to deliver. If anything, U.S. policy must now be guided by a new, grounded pragmatism. America needs to restore its credibility and reputation for effectiveness. Who will respond to us if we continue to proclaim objectives we cannot achieve?

So we need to pursue Middle East peace, but we need to do it in a way that is practical and likely to produce results that can be seen and felt. It sounds simple, but it is not—especially after six years of disengagement and two years of largely incompetent engagement.

DEFINING AMERICA'S ROLE IN PEACEMAKING

The starting point for defining our role is to acknowledge that realists may be right about one thing: it is not so easy for the parties—Israelis, Palestinians, and Arabs—to resolve the conflict completely on their own. If they could have, they would have done so already. That does not mean that the United States can take their place in peacemaking; we cannot. Ultimately, the parties must invest in the agreement, have a stake in protecting it, and feel that they own it—otherwise they won't stand by it. But the United States does need to help produce any agreement that they will reach in negotiations.

The United States is needed to do several things. One of the most important roles we play is that of being a clarifier in any negotiation process. Even for parties that know each other well—and the Israelis and Palestinians who are talking to each other today have reached this point—there is still a tendency to misread what the other intends. In any negotiation, there is a presumption that the other side is trying to manipulate the process to its advantage. There is a natural tendency to believe that every position presented is driven by an ulterior motive. In our experience dealing with both sides, we have seen each presuming to read into what the other side is actually trying to do with an idea or a proposal. And, as Dennis found often in the negotiations, the worst was almost always perceived when the intent was actually something very different.

Palestinians read every Israeli idea on security as being an Israeli device to preserve control and avoid giving Palestinians real independence. They did not see a genuine Israeli need being described; instead they saw an Israeli exaggeration. For their part, Israelis read every Palestinian idea as a way of avoiding responsibilities for imposing real law and order—rather than a Palestinian desire to try to meet what the Israelis were asking but in a way that they found politically sustainable. Often, each believed they were offering something genuine—and it was left to the United States to explain what the other side actually intended. In that role, we would say, "You may or may not accept the idea, but please understand what is really driving it—it is not what you perceive to be the case."

In conflicts of this sort—historic, national, and ethno-religious—the tendency to read the worst into the other side's intent is almost a given. Being on the scene to clarify the actual intent will be an ongoing U.S. role and responsibility. This also fits with the more demanding task of protecting and insulating the negotiating process. Playing the clarifying role helps to smooth the negotiations and prevent them from getting off track because of misperceptions. That is certainly one way of preserving the process. The more challenging role is to protect the process from inevitable shocks. One area where the Clinton administration did not receive enough credit for its efforts was its handling of the process after major terror events in Israel, or the 1999 killing of Palestinians at the Hebron tomb, or the 1996 opening of the Hasmonean tunnel in Jerusalem—and the turmoil that followed each.

In these and countless other cases, the U.S. role was to work with both sides to limit the fallout, to get appropriate statements of condemnation of the event, to produce specific corrective responses on the ground from one side or the other, and to work out how talks would resume.[2] During the years of 1996–99, the U.S. role was essentially that of a crisis manager, constantly finding ways to keep both sides talking and dealing with one another when the potential for collapse remained high.

To be sure, the role is not to preserve talks only for their own sake. Rather, it is to preserve a negotiating process that is moving toward agreements and tangible results. Depending on the context, the protective role may take on greater weight, but it remains only one of the tasks the United States needs to play to promote real progress.

During the Oslo process—and certainly during part of the Bush administration—producing needed financial assistance has been a critical U.S. role, particularly for the Palestinians. Mobilizing donors is unlikely to be done by anyone else—though the record is surely mixed in assessing how it has been done to date. Arab states have limited the scope of their promises and often not delivered what they promised (for example, the Saudis and Kuwaitis have pledged a few hundred million dollars— less than Norway—and are often very slow to deliver on their pledges). However, no one else on the international stage has been particularly good at taking the lead and mobilizing large donor efforts for the Palestinians—and when it comes to Israeli needs, primarily military assistance, it is only the United States that plays this role.

Here again, the U.S. role may be critical for sustaining a process and also for generating the kind of rewards or benefits that can help the Israeli and Palestinian publics see the payoffs of making peace. Others will also provide financial assistance—certainly the Europeans have been the largest financial backers of the Palestinians—but it is typically left to the United States to provide security assurances and material support to Israel as well as to help mobilize a campaign for the Palestinians.

In this sense, the U.S. role is to provide reassurance—that security and economic needs will be met, in terms of guarantees against potential threats, and about political support from us and from the international community. Historically, letters of assurance were often needed at critical points to get all parties to take steps or cross historic thresholds. This was true with the Israelis going back to the interim agreements with Egypt in the 1970s, with all the parties to the Madrid Conference in 1991, and throughout the Oslo process and in the negotiations between the Israelis and the Syrians. For its part, the Bush administration provided a letter of assurance to Prime Minister Sharon in April 2004 before he finalized his decision on Israeli withdrawal from Gaza in 2005—but the administration later seemed to walk back at least some of its content in an oral statement by President Bush designed to reassure President Abbas.

The point is that America has many roles to play in helping the parties reach peace—from clarifying, to mobilizing financial and political support, to protecting and insulating, to assuring and guaranteeing.

Providing such guarantees can relate to the agreement itself—meaning the readiness to guarantee the implementation of the terms of the agreement—or it can relate to guarantees against the potential risks associated with carrying out the agreement.[3] Offering assurances and guarantees will necessarily be one of the roles the United States plays in promoting peace.

There is, of course, one role we have not discussed, and that is being a broker or mediator of the negotiating process. Clearly, brokers can be more or less ambitious. They can facilitate discussions, they can be a go-between and pass messages, they can seek to distill differences and then offer proposals to narrow the gaps, or they can actually put their own comprehensive proposals on the table. America has played all these roles at different times. With President Carter at Camp David and beyond, the United States brokered the agreement; President Clinton, at Camp David and then with the Clinton Parameters, tried first to narrow the differences and then offered his own comprehensive bridging proposal.

The question is not whether the United States should also play the brokering or mediating role; the more we are involved in the process with the parties, the more it becomes natural, even if only through the process of clarifying positions, to begin to offer ideas on overcoming gaps.

But how we play this role should be shaped by two very different realities. The first relates to where the parties are in the process. Presenting American ideas too early can preempt what the parties must do on their own, both to invest in the negotiations and to reveal to us what really matters to them.

Every negotiation involves wants and needs. Settling historic conflicts is about reconciling the needs of each side, not their wants. We must be immersed deeply enough in the negotiations—and have done enough to draw each side out—to be able to distinguish between their wants and needs. Moreover, in order to get a real sense of what they must have in order to make a deal, there is simply no alternative to thrashing out and testing the limits of different ideas and combinations of tradeoffs—and that, too, takes time and deep immersion in the process.

To be sure, our ideas or bridging proposals are more likely to succeed if the two sides have been trying to reach agreement, have not been able to do so, and seek or ask for American bridging ideas. When Dennis brokered the Hebron deal in 1997, this is exactly what happened at the end of twenty-one days of shuttling between and working with the two sides.[4]

There is a second and more profound reality, and that relates to the scope of what we are proposing. It is one thing to offer bridging proposals for more limited agreements. Today, the realists would say it is time for an American blueprint to resolve everything. They would argue that the peace process can no longer move in small, incremental steps; that only knowing the endgame "can mobilize moderates and isolate rejectionists"; and that it is time to settle everything.[5]

In the last chapter, we observed that the realists tend to push for a blueprint in the abstract, disconnected from whether it has any chance of being accepted or not. For us that represents treating peace as an abstraction and divorcing it from the context in which it has to be produced. The scope of what we decide to do in a broker or mediator's role needs to be governed by the context.

What is possible now? Can American brokering ideas transform the environment? Some believe, for example, that if Palestinian moderates don't see how the conflict can end, they won't be able to justify taking the tough steps on security that are required to confront rejectionists. There is something to this argument. But it tends to overlook at least two factors: first, merely offering a political endgame—or political horizon for how the conflict ends—may not be enough if that horizon seems totally removed from day-to-day realities. Can Palestinians truly believe they will have an independent state and the Arab neighborhoods of East Jerusalem as their capital if they cannot move from Nablus to Jenin, or if they continue to face Israeli checkpoints outside of each of their cities and towns? Given what the Palestinian public sees as the false promise of Oslo, if life doesn't change when such a blueprint or horizon is offered, it will view it with great cynicism—and that won't empower Palestinian moderates, it will further weaken them.

Second, the United States at this point cannot afford to raise expectations again. At the time President Bush and Secretary Rice pushed for the Annapolis process and declared their objective of reaching a peace agreement within a year (and their confidence in being able to do so), Arab leaders told them it was fine to set this goal, but only if they were actually going to achieve it. If they did not, Secretary Rice was told, no one will believe anything the United States later declares on the process.[6]

Again, bear in mind the effect of the last eight years of policy and missteps in the region as a whole. A new American president will bear this legacy; he will not be given a pass. He will not start with a clean slate on which he can make bold promises. In the Middle East, we will have to show that our words are not empty. We will have to prove our effectiveness, prove that when we say something, it will actually happen.

This brings us back to the central point of peacemaking: context matters. What we must do now is understand the circumstances and shape a strategy that reflects the current realities even while it is geared toward changing them. Statecraft requires marrying objectives and means; it requires reality-based, not faith-based or ideologically driven, assessments. We have to see the world as it is, not as we wish it to be. That does not require giving up ambitious objectives. But before we can change an unacceptable reality, we have to understand it first. So our starting point must be to understand the context and shape our objective—and our strategy for achieving it—accordingly.

THE CONTEXT FOR PEACEMAKING

Today, we face multiple limitations in trying to produce peace between Israel and its neighbors. Start with the Palestinians: the Palestinian Authority holds sway in only part of its territory. Hamas controls Gaza and rejects the very idea of a two-state solution. There is no prospect any time soon of the Palestinian Authority reasserting its control over the area. Any agreement between Israel and the PA on peace may have to include Gaza—no Palestinian leadership would retain any credibility if it looked as if it was ready to forsake Gaza—but such an agreement will exist on paper and not be implementable, at least as it relates to Gaza, for some time to come.

This is an obvious limitation, but not the only or necessarily even the most important obstacle to peacemaking between Israelis and Palestinians. We believe the most formidable obstacle is the disbelief that exists on both sides. The fact that the Israeli and Palestinian publics no longer believe that peace is possible disempowers their leaders. No political leader is likely to take on history and mythology on such core issues as Jerusalem and refugees if he or she believes that the public will reject it when they do. That does not mean that leaders cannot lead, but they have to have some reason to believe that the public will follow them.

Why do the publics disbelieve? Let's look at each in turn. In the case of the Israelis, several factors have contributed to their disbelief. First, there is the failing of Oslo. From their standpoint, rightly or wrongly, Israelis saw in Ehud Barak someone who was prepared to stretch to meet Palestinian needs, first at Camp David and then in accepting the more far-reaching Clinton Parameters. Israelis saw a readiness to make unprecedented concessions on withdrawal and Jerusalem, and the Palestinian response was not only rejection but violence. The Palestinian response— or to be fair, the Arafat rejection and support or countenance for violence— convinced the vast majority of Israelis that the Palestinians were not prepared for peace, were not ready to accept Israel, and had not given up on rejection. Nothing has done more to discredit the Israeli peace camp in Israel than the combination of the Arafat rejection of the Clinton Parameters and the intifada. In fact, most Israelis concluded that if the Palestinians were not prepared to accept the Clinton Parameters, then they were not prepared to accept anything.

Second, there has been the effect of the unilateral Israeli withdrawals from Lebanon and Gaza. Though the withdrawals were carried out by two different prime ministers, Barak and Sharon, and for two very different reasons, the Israeli public has now drawn similar conclusions about the consequences of withdrawing from Arab lands. With regard to Lebanon, Israel departed in May 2000; the UN confirmed that Israel had fulfilled its obligations under UNSC resolution 425, having withdrawn to the international border. Yet what was the result in the eyes of the Israeli public? Hizbollah claimed a great victory; its power grew greatly in Lebanon; and in the summer of 2006, it provoked a conflict by coming across the border, kidnapping Israeli soldiers, and, in the ensuing war, hitting Israel with four thousand rockets.[7]

If anything, the Gaza withdrawal has soured the Israeli public even more. It has done so not simply because of the previous Lebanon experience, but because it came after Arafat was gone, involved the Palestinians directly, and seemed to confirm all the worst lessons of Lebanon. What's more, unlike Lebanon, there was real public resistance to the Gaza withdrawal; Prime Minister Ariel Sharon pulled all the settlements and settlers out of Gaza—there had been none in Lebanon—and the settler movement resisted this mightily, fearing it could be a preview of what would happen in the West Bank. It was an emotionally difficult thing for the Israeli public, but many took pride in being able to do it. And yet what was the result? Rocket fire did not stop out of Gaza for even one day after the withdrawal, making life miserable for Israelis living in towns like Sderot—and this was true even before Hamas seized control. But Hamas did take control, and the lesson for the Israeli public seemed to be, "If we were to withdraw from the West Bank, the same thing would happen there, and Hamas would also take over." However, as every Israeli also knows, Gaza lies along Israel's periphery and the West Bank sits astride Israel's heartland. Rockets fired from the West Bank would make every Israeli community vulnerable on a daily basis just like Sderot—and that is simply not tolerable.

In short, the Israeli disbelief has emerged from a number of searing lessons. Unfortunately, the Israeli perceptions have a mirror image on the Palestinian side. The reasons may be different, but they are also real and powerful. For Palestinians, Oslo's failure is also profound. For them, Oslo was supposed to deliver the end of occupation. Israelis may feel Palestinians betrayed Oslo, which was supposed to end terror and produce their acceptance of coexistence. Palestinians, however, feel that Oslo, instead of freeing them from Israeli control, actually deepened Israeli occupation. It did not stop the settlements. Palestinians believed they would get the Israelis to leave the West Bank and Gaza—or at least stop increasing their presence there—and yet for most of Oslo they saw the opposite: more Israeli building of settlements, almost a doubling in the numbers of settlers, more roads to serve settlers only, and more limitations on Palestinian freedom of movement as a result. Palestinian terror led to closures, meaning Palestinians could not work in Israel the way they once had.

The sense of betrayal on the Palestinian side is just as great as on the Israeli side. While Israelis feel they have had no choice but to impose restrictions on Palestinians because of terror, Palestinians see Israeli actions as being deliberately punitive and not related to security. They saw Israeli obligations under Oslo flouted—prisoners not released, withdrawals not taking place as scheduled, and the status of the territory constantly being changed to Israeli advantage, in effect prejudging the negotiations and their purpose. And with the collapse of Oslo during the Bush years, Palestinians saw draconian measures applied to them—with devastating consequences for their economy, for their ability to move anywhere in the West Bank or live anything like a normal life.

Again, Israelis may see their security measures—a security barrier, checkpoints limiting mobility for people and commerce, and undercover operations to make arrests—as a natural and necessary response to prevent Palestinian terror, but Palestinians see it differently. They blame Hamas and Islamic jihad far less and the Israelis far more for their predicament. With Palestinian per capita income dropping 40 percent from 2001 to 2006—it dropped 25 percent in the Great Depression in the United States, by way of comparison—life has become very difficult.[8] For Palestinians, it has been much easier to focus on their anger and sense of grievance than the possibilities of coexistence with Israelis—and to draw the conclusion that Israel is simply not willing to give up control.

Given this context, even the Israeli withdrawal from Gaza did not make a favorable impression on Palestinians. This was in part because Hamas—much like Hizbollah before them—claimed that their "resistance" or violence was responsible for driving Israel out, and in part also because Palestinians created a new narrative that the Israelis were giving up something they did not want—Gaza—in order to keep something they did want, namely, the West Bank. It did not help that even though the Gaza withdrawal came after Mahmoud Abbas had been elected president of the PA on a platform of nonviolence, Palestinians were not seeing any payoff or improvements in terms of their day-to-day existence. Little was done to manage the withdrawal from Gaza in a way that would have given Abbas credit for it. In fact, nothing was done to make it appear as if his moderation and his negotiations with the Israelis had produced this. Sharon had made the decision to withdraw, and he did not want the Palestinians to be able to tell him how to do so. In his eyes, if he had to take tough decisions vis-à-vis his own hard-line constituency, then let Abbas do something similar if he wanted Israel to carry out the withdrawal in a way that would specifically benefit him.

If Sharon was not prepared to be responsive to Abbas, given his own very real domestic challenges, the Bush administration needed to intervene. It needed to see how important it was for Abbas—a new Palestinian leader without the authority or charisma of the icon he had replaced—to show results. It needed to realize that the Gaza withdrawal was a historic moment that should be seized to reestablish belief in peacemaking; and it needed to realize that both Sharon and Abbas would need the withdrawal to be vindicated. But the administration, still governed by its neoconservative, disengagement instincts, was unable to see what was necessary or to act on it—and it squandered this moment.

The administration sought to create a new opening with its decision to reengage in the peace process in January 2007, a decision that led to the Annapolis conference in late November of that year. But this too ended up representing another missed opportunity to try to restore at least a sense of possibility about peace. To be fair, U.S. reengagement at this time did not encounter nearly as powerful an opening as that available in 2005; unlike 2005, there was no Israeli action like withdrawal from Arab lands to be seized upon. Also unlike 2005, when Abbas had just been elected and had a clean slate with the Palestinian public, by 2007 he had already lost much of his luster, having delivered nothing on daily life or Israeli behavior—and having been weakened by the Hamas election in 2006. And on the Israeli side, unlike 2005, when Israel's leader, Ariel Sharon, had great standing and authority, by January 2007, Israel's prime minister, Ehud Olmert, had very little of either. He had been profoundly weakened by the mishandling of the war with Hizbollah in the summer of 2006—and it was clear the Israeli public had little confidence in him.

So launching an initiative in January 2007 was bound to be far more difficult. If anything, the circumstances should have put even more of a premium on thinking the initiative through and focusing on achieving something tangible. When publics have lost faith in peacemaking for all the reasons noted above, it is not simple to restore it. Loss of faith and belief is far more profound than simply loss of confidence. It will not be restored overnight, but only gradually—and even then it takes tangible demonstrations of change to produce it. From this standpoint, had Secretary Rice focused on laying the groundwork, on building a foundation, on producing what Israeli and Palestinian publics would have noticed, she might have done much for peacemaking. Instead, she sought a political horizon and did next to nothing to change any realities that the two publics might have felt. Only when it became clear there would be no political horizon or endgame presented at the Annapolis conference did she switch to saying the purpose was to launch negotiations.

The problem was, there was no day-after strategy to show that this new negotiating process would produce change. And it did not. Both sides saw more of the same. In the first two months after Annapolis, there were several terror attacks against Israelis in the West Bank (actually connected to those in the Palestinian security forces), and Palestinians saw new announcements on settlement construction. While large amounts of assistance were pledged, very little materialized in terms of noticeable economic improvements. Rather than change—when their skepticism required something dramatic to give them a reason to believe the process should be given a chance—each public saw more of what had made them cynical in the first place.

Over the course of 2008–2009, there have been limited improvements economically but no significant changes in employment or mobility for Palestinians. And, though the United States and the European Union have trained some battalions of security forces for the PA—and they are operating in Jenin, Nablus, and Ramallah—the Israeli military and security forces see little evidence of activity against terror in the West Bank, and that is what the Israeli public hears. At the same time, there has been a political process. Secretary Rice did push for a negotiating process, and after some fits and starts, it did begin.

But this process takes place in private and is divorced from the public realities. These talks have been serious but are not translatable precisely because of the weakness of the leaders and the absence of an environment that would give them confidence to reveal compromises and feel that those might be supported.

Such is the context for peacemaking between Israelis and Palestinians as we look ahead.

WHAT TO DO ON ISRAELI-PALESTINIAN PEACE

If disbelief and cynicism about peace continue to govern both Israeli and Palestinian publics, the key to giving peacemaking a chance is to provide the publics with a reason to take a second look. They will not be persuaded by pronouncements or grand declarations; they have heard them before and will discount them. But they can be persuaded at least to take notice if they see behaviors that matter to them.

That is what is required today. Both publics need to see something from the other side that is meaningful to them. Of course, what may be most meaningful to them may be beyond what either side can politically pull off: Israelis most want to see Palestinians actually fight terror, not condone it or facilitate it; Palestinians want to see no restrictions on their movements, all Palestinian prisoners released, and all settlement activity halted.

Neither side is politically able (or willing) to do these things, particularly in the current context. But the point is to try to change that context and change what is politically possible. So a starting point might be to work behind the scenes and get each side in parallel to take a step that is possible for them and yet would be noticed by the other's public. For example, the Palestinian Authority may not have the means or the will to go after terrorist infrastructure, but it does have the means to declare an end to incitement to violence against Israelis in the schools, the media, and the mosques—and follow through on it on a daily, public basis. This would mean stopping sermons by PA-paid imams that call for violence (something now being tried by the PA), publicly criticizing or condemning articles that are inciting, and making sure that there are not banners glorifying *shahids*, or martyrs, in the schools—which unfortunately is a common practice.

Were all these steps taken, reflecting a clear policy, the Israeli public would take notice. By the same token, if the Israelis were to take dramatic steps to ease the movement of people and commerce, it would be noticed by the Palestinian public. We are not saying that Israel will lift checkpoints any more than that the PA will go after terror infrastructure. They will not, and we are not suggesting that they take steps that jeopardize their security and increase the chance of bombs going off in their cities again. But movement through all the major checkpoints around Palestinian cities and towns is inefficient and maddening for Palestinians, because all the lanes for movement are rarely open. At the Qalandia and Bethlehem checkpoints, for example, there are as many as five lanes available for movement of Palestinians, yet typically only one is open. Open all the lanes, and suddenly delays for Palestinians can be cut by 80 percent. Israel does have the means to do this—by accelerating their nascent effort to privatize the security at the checkpoints, just as they have done at Ben-Gurion Airport. Similarly, they can make far more use of scanners and containers on trucks at the commercial crossing points to remove the costly offload and onload procedures that add time and expense to all commerce.

If each side were to begin by taking these steps—none of which are beyond their capabilities—their actions would be noticed by the other's public. We don't raise these ideas as a substitute for a political process or for additional steps that need to be taken. Rather, we raise them because while an integrated process that combines economic, security, and political elements is a prerequisite for real progress, each of these elements will be easier to pursue if the publics on each side begin to have a sense that something is changing and something new is possible.

Any strategy for changing the context for peacemaking must operate at all these levels. A political negotiating process that is not connected to changes on the ground will have little or no credibility. Changes on the ground that are not connected to a political process will seem like ends in themselves not leading anywhere. The failure of the Bush administration was not its inability to see that all these elements were necessary, but to think they did not have to be connected in a seamless whole.

Having former British prime minister Tony Blair serve as an envoy to promote the Palestinian economy for the Quartet made sense, but not if he had no responsibility for the security issues; appointing three different U.S. generals for security issues implied that the security matters were disconnected when in fact the security and economic realities are completely tied. If Palestinian mobility is going to be limited for security reasons, then commerce and certainly outside investment in the Palestinian economy are going to be truncated as well.

So integration must be the hallmark of any strategy for restoring the Israeli-Palestinian effort on peace, and it must be guided by producing changes on the ground that will be noticed—and will affect—each public. Changing the Palestinian approach to incitement and the Israeli handling of checkpoints are tactical moves that should be pursued quickly but also in parallel with steps on the Palestinian economy and security. For all the donor promises and private sector efforts now under way that offer the potential for improvements over time, there is very little that is being felt by the Palestinian public now. The PA is still scrambling to meet its monthly payrolls—and the PA remains the largest employer in the West Bank. But unemployment remains high, new employment opportunities are emerging very, very slowly, and something much more dramatic is needed in this area. Significant new job creation would provide an unmistakable demonstration that people will be going back to work, that the efforts of the PA are paying off, and that a return to violence will jeopardize these gains.

There is and has been one area where significant and meaningful jobs could be created, and that is in the housing area. Palestinians used to make up the backbone of the Israeli construction industry, but, for security reasons, they are no longer allowed to work in Israel in any appreciable numbers. Housing needs in the West Bank are real, and Palestinians with the right kind of financing and investment could launch major projects. Some of the housing projects could even be tied not to rehabilitation but to new housing in refugee camps, which make up about 9 percent of the population in the West Bank—something that would be good for Palestinians and also send a signal to Israelis about Palestinian practicality with regard to the future.[9]

In 2005, the United Arab Emirates (UAE) announced at least $100 million in funding for Khalifa bin Zayed city in Gaza. They had previously funded Gaza housing developments to the tune of $55 million; these were designed, contracted, and built by Palestinians.[10] What if ten such projects for the West Bank could be funded immediately by the Gulf Cooperation Council states—Saudi Arabia, Kuwait, the UAE, Qatar, Bahrain, and Oman? Notwithstanding the drop in the price of oil, these states would not find it difficult to provide such financing. While it might be out of character, the fact is that they claim to care about the Palestinians. A new administration should approach them and present this as part of a broader approach that would involve a multidimensional strategy in which we, they, and the Israelis and Palestinians all had responsibilities to assume. We would make clear that we would fulfill ours (and would have to show we were beginning to do so), but providing immediate funding for construction would be part of their responsibilities—and it would be difficult to understand or not criticize publicly if they were not prepared to help the Palestinians financially in this way.[11]

Putting Palestinians back to work on a dramatic scale could build momentum and contribute to changing the psychology. But if we don't affect the security situation, and the way the Israeli military now approaches it, little will change economically or politically—and no negotiation will be likely to succeed. And here we face a very difficult problem. The Israeli military at one point accepted the Oslo process; this process transformed the Israeli approach to security. Prior to Oslo, the Israelis defined their security needs in terms of what they would do unilaterally. With Oslo, the Israelis were defining their needs with the Palestinians mutually. Many of the leading officers in the IDF believed in Oslo, but with the advent of the intifada, and the involvement of many of the Palestinian security forces in it, the Israeli military felt betrayed, and today it has returned to the unilateral mind-set.

The IDF does not believe that the PA and its security forces will ever perform or live up to their obligations when it comes to fighting terror. In the past year, Palestinian prime minister Fayyad's efforts to establish law and order and show that the PA could deliver stability for its own citizens has led to the insertion of the Palestinian security forces into Nablus, Jenin, and even Hebron. The Israeli military and security forces have cooperated with these moves, but continue to see only a Palestinian readiness to deal with crime and not terror. They see no command-control structure, they see no real political backing for Palestinian officers to go after sensitive targets, and they see no legal apparatus to try those who might be arrested—leading to the perpetuation of the revolving door of arrest and release of terror operatives.

For their part, Palestinian security forces claim the Israelis give them little opportunity to do what is necessary—and even in places like Nablus and Jenin, Israeli forces have intervened and made arrests in ways that undercut their credibility. PA forces have not wanted to look like Israel's police force, doing Israel's bidding against Palestinians. Nor, if they have established their presence and begun to act, do they want Israeli incursions that make them appear irrelevant and safely ignored by Israel. And yet the kind of quiet coordination that would avoid embarrassing the PA forces is, for the most part, not taking place. Though there are exceptions and there is some coordination at the local level around Jenin and Hebron, the IDF at the senior levels simply does not deal with the Palestinian security forces.

So long as that is the case, the IDF will not focus on what Palestinian forces might need, the pressures they are under, the way they might evolve, or even the tests the IDF could establish to see if they are capable of changing. In conversations we have had with senior Palestinian security officers, they have been willing to acknowledge that the IDF is right to question them, given their past behaviors, but argue that they should be given a chance now. They argue as well that the Hamas coup in Gaza was a wake-up call for them and that they know what they are up against with Hamas. Preventing Hamas from coming to power in the West Bank is a shared interest with the Israelis—but, in their words, the Israelis won't serve that shared interest if they undercut them and make it impossible for them to play a credible role.

The argument sounds good, but given the history of PA acquiescence in terror, the Israelis won't buy words, they will only buy behaviors. Certainly, the PA's performance in preserving calm in the West Bank during the early 2009 conflict with Hamas in Gaza in which large numbers of Palestinians were killed, should build the credibility of the Palestinian forces in Israeli eyes. Still, the IDF will wonder how the PA will do in actually fighting terror. In light of that perspective, it is essential to deal with the security issues practically, and the best way to do that is at two different levels. At a professional, functional level there is a need to establish a senior level security group involving leading members of the IDF with the senior PA security forces. They need not just to meet regularly but to develop a joint work plan on security for the West Bank; the plan would lay out an agreed approach for what the PA would be expected do on all security issues, including terror, and where, when, and how they would act. They would agree in the near term on capabilities the Palestinian forces would need and where and under what circumstances the IDF would still act. Both Prime Minister Fayyad and President Abbas have told us that if there is a "ticking bomb," they understand that if the PA can't act, Israel will. But Abbas and Fayyad must also agree on who has clear authority on the Palestinian side to act, and the Palestinian officers who meet with the Israelis must have the capability to agree to the necessary plans and procedures—and then to follow through on them.

Such an approach will certainly address some of the complaints that the Israelis have about the Palestinian security forces and would not require the IDF to accept on faith that the PA forces will act. They will have a plan, with a sequence—which, of course, can be adjusted depending on circumstances—and they will be able to see whether the Palestinians are performing. By the same token, the Palestinian forces would also have some assurance that the IDF will not be undercutting them.

If this approach works, the Israelis will know they have a security partner; if it does not, the Israelis will know it, and will also know that they did not preempt the possibility that Palestinians would play such a role at some point.

Aside from the near-term practical reasons for such an approach, it will be essential for overcoming what is a fundamental conceptual divide on security that is bound to bedevil the negotiations. There will be no agreement on a two-state solution if there is not a common approach to security. Today, however, both sides have drawn exactly opposite conclusions from the last eight years. At the time of Camp David and the Clinton Parameters, the Israeli military did not have dealing with rockets as one of their prime security concerns. After being hit by four thousand rockets from Hizbollah and being unable to stop the more than twenty-five hundred rockets after Israel left Gaza in 2005, one of the main Israeli security preoccupations is ensuring that the West Bank cannot be a platform for rocket attacks into Israel.

The IDF understands that given the proximity of the West Bank to all of Israel's major population centers, rocket attacks from the West Bank would make literally every Israeli community vulnerable to such attacks; they would even raise questions about being able to operate Ben-Gurion Airport, Israel's only international airport. The conclusion that the IDF draws is that it must retain complete freedom of action in the West Bank—as well as control over all the potential border crossing points—to prevent such an eventuality as well as to stop terrorist bombs in Israel.

The Palestinian lessons from the years since 2001 are exactly the opposite. The Palestinians feel suffocated under Israeli control. And they conclude that they cannot have an independent state if there is even one Israeli soldier on their territory. They will accept international forces to meet Israeli security concerns, but not an Israeli presence. For the Israelis, no international forces will ever be rigorous enough; they will certainly never act to root out terror cells in the refugee camps or the cities and towns of the West Bank the way the Israelis do on a nightly basis today. The lessons of Lebanon, where Hizbollah has been allowed to rebuild and greatly add to its military and rocket capability notwithstanding the presence of fifteen thousand UN soldiers, certainly add to the Israeli unwillingness to put their fate in the hands of international security. In fact, for the Israelis, the issue is not just the failure of the international forces to halt the likely buildup of rockets and their launching into Israel; it is also that once international forces are interposed, they also block Israel from dealing with the problem lest they hit the international troops.

This basic conceptual divide will only be overcome if the Israelis see there is a serious Palestinian approach to security and if joint answers are conceived to address core missions. Palestinians must demonstrate that they understand there will be no independence if they do not perform in a certain fashion. We don't mean to suggest that solving the security problem will be simple; hardly, but the security issue will underpin everything else. There will be no sustainable improvement on the economy and there will be no peace agreement if it is not addressed in a way that creates a relationship between the Israeli and Palestinian security forces—and, in the end, puts the Israeli military in a position in which its leaders will say that a peace agreement does not jeopardize Israeli security.

To be sure, Palestinian security forces will be more inclined to do what the Israelis feel is necessary if they see how it is part of settling the conflict and producing their state. The argument that Palestinians have made from the very beginning of Oslo was that they could crack down on rejectionists, but only if it was in the service of achieving their national independence and statehood. In other words, to accept confrontation internally there had to be a Palestinian, not Israeli, reason for doing it. Whether the Hamas readiness to internally confront Fatah and other Palestinians and take over Gaza has changed that mind-set is not clear.

What is clear is that the security dimension needs to be connected to a political process that gives strong reason to believe the core issues will be resolved. When realists claim there is a need for a blueprint, there certainly would be some resonance with Palestinians—and even for Israelis who want to know what is the end point.

But like everything else, the political process—or even blueprint—cannot stand on its own. It must be rooted in something to be credible. For a time, we both believed there was value in producing a statement of principles that embodied the core tradeoffs for solving the conflict. We thought a short document that highlighted that Israel would get what it needed on security and refugees—ensuring Israel's future as a Jewish state—and that Palestinians would get what they needed on borders and Jerusalem—meaning the state would be viable and would have Arab neighborhoods of East Jerusalem as its capital—made sense.

It would provide each side with the general contours of an agreement while leaving the details to be negotiated. It would offer hope that a solution was possible while meeting the core needs of both sides. It would offer a clear counterpoint to the Iranian-Hizbollah-Hamas argument that there can be no two-state solution and that struggle is the answer—particularly if the international community and the Arab world embraced this statement of principles.

This was what Secretary Rice probably had in mind. The problem was that the context did not exist to make it credible, much less to produce it. There was little basis to make the two publics believe; and absent that, there was a very real danger that such a document could be rejected by both publics if offered—as it might well be—for approval in a referendum. In fact, those heading the negotiating teams, Israeli foreign minister Tzipi Livni and former Palestinian prime minister Ahmed Koreia, both opposed the idea of simply negotiating general principles. They both felt that to make an agreement credible, it had to be detailed enough to show that it was thought through, and that fundamental questions were not being left open and subject to very different interpretations and the possibility of no agreement at all. Moreover, precisely because of the disbelief of the publics and the legacy of Oslo, they each believed that a high level of detail was needed to show the agreement was real and was more likely to be implemented as a result.

While their approach made sense, it also ensured that there was little prospect of reaching an agreement on all the core issues, precisely because of the weakness of the leaders and the disbelief of the publics. But they have worked hard, and their negotiations can provide a basis on which the Obama administration can proceed.

So we come back to where we started. The Obama administration is likely to inherit negotiations that in private have narrowed differences on functional issues like what state-to-state relations (e.g. on health, agriculture, environment, and trade) would be. They have probably also narrowed the differences on the border—with both sides accepting that Israel will annex an area for settlement blocs and that there will be a territorial swap to compensate at least in part for the annexation. They don't agree on the size of the settlement blocs or the scope of the compensation, and there remain significant gaps on security, refugees, and Jerusalem. Nonetheless, a very useful negotiating basis has been established.

The Obama administration should support that basis and seek to build more of a public and private context to give the negotiations credibility. That is why the efforts to get each side to take a step (or steps) that the other side's public would notice, to do something dramatic on the

Palestinian economy, and to create a senior security working group should be immediate priorities. Certainly, as part of discussions with the two sides about these steps, other steps may be considered. For example, if an Israeli moratorium on settlement expansion for several months could help Palestinians, the administration might seek to produce it, provided it could parlay the moratorium into steps that the Arab states would take to reach out to Israel in return—something that would show Israel was not making a unilateral concession but was getting something for it in terms of relations with Arab states not now at peace with Israel.

Similarly, the consultations with the two sides should focus on how the administration could offer the biggest help to the negotiating process. Since the administration would be inheriting a negotiating process rather than initiating it, the two parties should define what kind of a brokering role they want the United States to play. They should decide whether there are other steps they seek from the region or the international community. For example, is there a role on security issues with the Palestinians that Jordan can play, or that the United States and Europe are prepared to play, that both sides agree could be useful for bolstering the current process? Are there circumstances in which a follow-on to the Annapolis conference could be of benefit, to report progress and to gain specific international endorsement of that progress—and be a more concrete counterpoint to Iran and its narrative of rejection? Could such an endorsement or some other international activity be seen as further benefiting the PA and creating greater pressures on Hamas to change its behavior?

Lastly, the new administration in consultation with the parties could also consider the value of a partial agreement on the borders. Specifically, it could see whether it was possible to resolve the territorial issues and agree on a map for the West Bank, one in which there would be annexation of roughly 5 percent of the West Bank for settlement blocs and a territorial swap of approximately the same amount to compensate Palestinians for the annexation. While the issues of Jerusalem and refugees would still have to be resolved, and the implementation of the territorial agreement would take some time to carry out, the value of the territorial issue being largely finalized is that both sides would know the borders. In such circumstances, settlements, as a corrosive symbol, would no longer exacerbate the psychological environment for peacemaking and be a constant source of grievance to the Palestinians—and that would be worth a great deal.

All of these possible approaches by the Obama administration assume, of course, that everything proceeds in a linear direction. If it does, our recommendations offer the soundest basis on which to proceed. But there could be some intervening shocks or profound political changes, and there remains the question of what to do about Hamas.

WHAT TO DO ABOUT HAMAS
AND OTHER CONTINGENCIES

Hamas remains a real challenge, and that challenge cannot be wished away. The logic of the current approach is to make the West Bank bloom, Gaza wither, and the PA produce an agreement that fulfills Palestinian national aspirations. In such a scenario, the secular leadership of the PA and Fatah would have delivered and Hamas would have been shown to be a failure by comparison and incapable of offering a future. In truth, if such an outcome could be produced, it would create great pressure on Hamas from the Palestinian public, and probably trigger great fissures within the Hamas movement. Hamas, after all, may have strong ideological roots, but it is not necessarily homogeneous as a movement, and divisions within it will become more pronounced the more Hamas seems disconnected from Palestinian society.

It makes sense to follow such an approach. But at least two points must be kept in mind. First, at this stage the West Bank is not blooming and the PA is not seen as delivering. Hamas may not be, either—and that may account for its loss of support—but the PA and Fatah are not building their following. The strategy of changing the realities on the ground, dramatically improving the economy, and giving the public a reason to believe again—the steps we have been describing and suggesting—could make a difference. It won't happen by itself. It will take a determined effort by the new administration. And this strategy should be informed by the recognition that it is necessary not only for shaping the public context for peacemaking but also for competing with Hamas. The more effective the PA becomes in delivering social services at the grass roots, improving economic well-being generally, and showing it can alter Israeli behavior, the stronger and more competitive it will become vis-à-vis Hamas.

However, there is a second, paradoxical factor that must also be considered. Hamas is unlikely to acquiesce in a situation in which it is being undercut. So long as the PA is not competitive and the prospects of peace seem distant, Hamas may not have much incentive to explode everything again—either by launching rockets deeper into Israel from Gaza or by carrying out terror spectaculars. Listen to Israeli security officials, and they will tell you Hamas is still trying to carry out bombings in Israel and the Israelis are stopping them. But Hamas generally observed a cease-fire out of Gaza during the summer and fall of 2008, partly because they sought a respite and partly because they wanted the siege of Gaza to be lifted, given pressure from the Palestinian public. But will Hamas stick to the cease-fire if the PA strategy for competing with Hamas begins to succeed or the prospects for peace suddenly look real? And if they don't, and fighting and large numbers of Palestinian casualties result from Israeli retaliation—which is almost inevitable if there is a Hamas resumption of rocket fire and it goes deeper into Israel—won't the PA cut off all talks at that point? After all, no Palestinian will want to be seen negotiating with Israel if Israel is killing large numbers of Palestinians in Gaza, even if Hamas has provoked it.

Was this why Hamas chose to end the truce that its leaders had generally observed from June to December 2008?

Probably not: Hamas was unhappy that the truce had not led to a real opening of the crossing points and an end to the siege of Gaza. Israel continued to limit the flow of goods into Gaza at least in part to maintain pressure on Hamas to release its kidnapped soldier Gilad Shalit. Moreover, throughout the truce period, Hamas permitted intermittent rocket fire into Israel, which responded by closing the crossing points each time this happened.

As a result, life remained very difficult in Gaza. Hamas's leaders also appear to have made a basic calculation: with elections approaching, Israel would shy away from the high costs of a military campaign in Gaza, allowing Hamas to use renewed rocket fire as leverage on Israel to end the siege. If this happened, it would once again validate Hamas, proving it knew how to use force to achieve its aims and change Israel's behavior.

This proved to be a horrendous miscalculation. The fragile truce expired on December 18, 2008, and for twenty-two days, Israel conducted a devastating air and then ground campaign in Gaza before declaring a unilateral cease-fire. Hamas was not destroyed as an organization nor did it lose control over Gaza. Palestinian and Arab anger toward Israel was deep and profound over the scale of destruction in Gaza and the deaths of more than 1,300 Palestinians.

That Hamas used mosques, hospitals, schools, and homes as their battleground and hiding places—and the civilian population as human shields—did not lessen the rage that many Arab publics felt toward Israel. But it did generate criticism toward Hamas and also created an opening for the Palestinian Authority and Arab regimes to offer a different future for Palestinians. It also offered the chance to portray an unmistakable contrast between Hamas and the Palestinian Authority—a contrast in which Hamas and the Islamists promised only a future of death, destruction, and poverty while the PA offered the possibility of reconstruction, normal lives for Palestinians, and a path toward achieving national aspirations.

Will such a contrast shape the reality in 2009 and beyond? It is too soon to say. It will take much support for the PA, including from Israel, and the achievement of demonstrable results from the PA's leaders and institutions. It will also take active Arab support and recognition that management of the reconstruction process in Gaza is to be controlled by the PA. The outcome of national unity talks among Palestinian factions could also prove to be very important. For those who believe that a prerequisite for peace is Palestinian unity, the question will be who determines the ground rules of reconciliation. If it is Hamas, there is good reason to be concerned. Note the words of Hamas spokesman Osama Hamdan, who is an ally of Hamas leader Khaled Mashal in Damascus, and the explicit conditions he has for reconciliation with Fatah: "Those who committed mistakes must correct their mistakes through a clear and frank declaration to stop security coordination with the occupation [Israel], release [Hamas] prisoners, and later end negotiations [with Israel] because the peace process is irreversibly over. . . . It's time for us to talk about a reconciliation based on a resistance program to liberate the territory and regain rights." As usual, Hamas leaves vague whether the target area that it seeks to free by dint of force is the West Bank and Gaza, or Israel.

Finally, much will depend on whether the cease-fire holds and whether Hamas is prevented from rebuilding itself militarily, especially when it comes to acquiring longer-range rockets that could reach Tel Aviv. If Hamas acquires this capability, notwithstanding international commitments on smuggling designed to prevent it, there will be the very real danger that the cease-fire will break; if it does, and Tel Aviv or Ben Gurion Airport is hit, everything will be transformed. In such circumstances, the next round of fighting will be far worse than this one was and Israel may well feel compelled to reoccupy Gaza in order to prevent being held hostage by the ever-present threat of Hamas rocket strikes. If the Israelis do feel the need to go back into Gaza, any strategy for the West Bank will have little prospect of succeeding for some time to come.

To sum up, the best course—not one that typically prevails in the Middle East—is to pursue our strategy in the West Bank, seek to make the PA far more effective, hold the shaky cease-fire in Gaza, and not to alter the approach to Hamas unless it alters its behavior. It is one thing to allow life to ease in Gaza—making it harder for Hamas to portray itself as a victim—and another to allow Hamas to gain massive investment there or recognition from the outside. Over time, the key to marginalizing Hamas may be not only having the PA appear to succeed, including on managing the reconstruction in Gaza, but also gaining Arab state backing for the PA vis-à-vis Hamas. If Arab states come to believe that Hamas positions preclude any prospect of restoring Palestinian unity, Arab leaders may back the PA in a politically meaningful way.

Apart from the uncertainties with Hamas, there are also political unknowns with both Palestinians and Israelis. President Abbas's term ends in 2009; sorting out the question of new elections and their timing could take much of the year. If nothing else, if Abbas's term is ending, will he be as willing to contemplate far-reaching compromises on core issues like refugees? Similarly, in Israel, a new government will emerge in the spring of 2009. At the time of this writing, it is not possible to predict the capabilities and inclinations of that government—though it is likely to be based on a center-right and not center-left coalition. Depending on the makeup of that government, there may not be much enthusiasm for a conference in which Israeli concessions might be exposed as a way of showing where the negotiations to date have narrowed the differences and progress has been made.

The larger point here is that there are political uncertainties among both the Israelis and Palestinians. There could be successor governments on either or both sides that are unwilling to pursue final status negotiations in 2009. Should any of these circumstances obtain, the new U.S. administration will have to take stock of the situation and conduct discussions with both sides—as well as Arab leaders and the Europeans—to decide what steps might make sense. Arab leaders might have to assume the role of giving a new Palestinian leader greater backing and support to build up his legitimacy—something that the administration might require as a condition for its own willingness to assume much greater responsibility.

One last contingency needs to be discussed. Earlier we mentioned that some leading Palestinian intellectuals and political figures are now calling for the Palestinian Authority to be dissolved. Some believe it is becoming weaker and that it is fruitless to try to preserve it. Some argue that this is a nonviolent way to put great pressure on Israel, particularly because Israel as the occupying power would then have to assume responsibility for all the socioeconomic needs of the Palestinian population. Others see it not as a means to put pressure on Israel to become more responsive to the Palestinian Authority, but rather as the pathway to a one-state solution in which the Palestinian population eventually becomes the majority between the Mediterranean Sea and the Jordan River—and Israel loses its rationale as a Jewish state and becomes a binational state.

While Palestinian figures can theorize about such possibilities, and Israelis should not ignore the consequences of the PA being so weak or discredited that it collapses—leaving a void that must be filled—Israeli leaders will not allow Israel to become a binational state. If the PA collapses, or if there is little prospect of a negotiation for a political settlement and the Palestinian population becomes radicalized, a new Israeli approach to disengagement from the West Bank is likely to emerge over time. To avoid the danger that withdrawal will produce a Gaza-type outcome, which would then leave all of Israel vulnerable to rocket fire, and yet to prevent the demographic dangers of a binational state, Israel could decide to withdraw all its settlements to the east of the security barrier but to leave behind the IDF to preserve security and prevent the West Bank from becoming a platform for rocket or terror attacks. Israel, in this circumstance, would say it is up to Palestinians and the international community to meet their own needs and even to build a state in the roughly 92 percent of the West Bank that would be free of Israeli settlers but not free of an Israeli security presence.

In effect, Israel would be reframing the issue from occupation to security. Its leaders could even say that the security barrier need not represent the final political border. But it would be up to Palestinians to demonstrate that they were willing and able, on their own or with the backing of others, to assume responsibility in a way that would permit the withdrawal of Israeli soldiers. Statehood would be available to Palestinians, but they would have to earn it, and Israel could not be expected to withdraw its forces until someone could demonstrate they were willing and able to ensure that the West Bank would not be a launching pad for attacks against Israel.

This, too, is an approach that sounds good in theory but would be practically hard to produce. But this approach could come to define the future if the PA collapses or there is no prospect of negotiating peace. No one should have any illusions that the status quo will somehow be preserved. One way or the other, it will give way—and when it does, as difficult politically as it may be for Israelis to withdraw settlers but not soldiers without an agreement, they may do so to preserve the Jewish character of the state. If we want to avoid this eventuality, the new administration needs to shape a new public context, promote major economic projects including housing in the West Bank, construct a new mutual approach to security, and build on the current political negotiating process. None of this will simply emerge by itself.

ISRAEL AND SYRIA

Turkey has been managing an indirect negotiation between Israel and Syria. While indirect negotiations can set the stage for direct talks—and may shape an agenda that gives them promise—the current set of discussions will not produce an agreement. Neither side will make major compromises in such a forum. The Syrians will not do so because they want something larger from an agreement than Turkey can promise them: large economic payoffs and international acceptability that can come only from a U.S.-brokered agreement.[12] For their part, the Israelis are not going to concede anything significant without hearing directly from the Syrians what they would get in return—and what the Israelis now want is not withdrawal from the Golan Heights for calm in return. The Golan Heights has been Israel's quietest border since 1974. Israel wants Syria to make a strategic turn away from conflict by dissociating itself from Iran, Hizbollah, and Hamas.

In Israeli eyes, that would represent a change in the strategic landscape in the Middle East and would justify withdrawal. The peace with Syria would isolate Iran (from its only Arab state ally), dramatically weaken Hizbollah (as it would lose its source of arms and Syrian protection), and raise the difficulties of Hamas trying to compete with the PA. Hamas's external leadership now bases itself in Damascus; where would it go after Syrian peace with Israel? Certainly not to Lebanon, where it would be highly vulnerable, and not to the Gulf states, where it might or might not be welcome but would surely be vulnerable to Israel's reach; Tehran would be the only safe option, and that is a long way from Palestine.

The question is whether Syria, in order to recover the Golan Heights (and gain international acceptance and real economic benefits), is ready to separate itself from Iran, Hizbollah, and Hamas. Neoconservatives will say no—the regime in Damascus will never make such a choice and shouldn't be believed if it suggests it might; realists will say yes—the regime is largely secular, and its real interests lie in peace and connections to the international and Arab mainstream and not with Iran and its allies. Frankly, it is hard to know who is right. It is even possible that the Syrian regime itself does not know—and will know only when facing a real choice.

It is interesting that the Israelis feel the need to test the possibilities. And it is also interesting that the Israelis and Syrians had enough of a common stake in the indirect negotiations to coordinate a public statement through the Turkish government acknowledging that they were negotiating. Coordinated statements between the Israeli and Syrian governments are rare. Given all this, it makes sense to test, to probe, and to see whether an agreement is possible.

That, of course, runs against the grain of the Bush administration, but the Obama administration should pursue the possibility. In doing so, however, it should not forget the lessons of the past. In 1996, after the Rabin assassination, the negotiations that the Clinton administration organized and managed at the Wye River Plantation between the Israelis and Syrians showed great promise; they were done in by four terrorist bombs in nine days (and a month later Hizbollah's launching of Katyushas into Israel). Hamas's bombs and Hizbollah's escalation together doomed Shimon Peres's election bid; he was determined at the time to do a deal with Syria, and yet Syria's clients—Hamas and Hizbollah—subverted the opportunity. There are conflicting views as to whether it was Iran that directed such attacks from afar, but it is hard to escape the view that Syria has given to nonstate actors, and perhaps to Tehran, a veto on decision-making in Damascus. This view is something that Syria needs to fix. Throughout the 1990s, whenever the peace process was making progress, terrorist bombs often derailed it. Bashar al-Asad needs to know from the Obama administration that while it is serious about promoting an Israeli-Syrian agreement, it is not going to invest in a major way if either Hamas or Hizbollah is free to subvert the negotiating process at any time of their choosing. Syria will need, in the first instance, to show that it will not let this happen again.

CONCLUSION

Peacemaking at the start of 2009 and beyond will not be easy. The Bush years have left a woeful legacy. The forces that reject peace are far stronger than they have been, with Iran's coercive capabilities growing, Hizbollah with veto power over the Lebanese government and an arsenal of forty thousand rockets, and Hamas in control of Gaza. The forces favoring coexistence are far weaker, with the Palestinian Authority divided, Israel (prior to elections) lacking a strong leader with moral authority, and America seen as having been largely ineffective and unable to translate its commitments into reality.

Many Arab leaders, either as an excuse or because they genuinely fear the consequences of going out on a limb for an America that has seemed more adept at undermining than helping them, will seek U.S. demonstrations of its ability to deliver before signing on to its initiatives. If nothing else, this tells us that the context in general (and not just between Israeli and Palestinian publics) is not good for peacemaking.

That reality should sober us. We should be careful about launching transformational and strong declaratory objectives if we will be unable to enact them. We must prepare the ground before we decide what to do. In this chapter, we have tried to make it clear that we don't have the luxury of doing nothing on peacemaking but that our efforts must be informed by clear-headed, not wishful, thinking.

The neoconservative instinct to disengage has contributed to the woeful set of circumstances we now have to confront. Their premise of the Arabs accepting Israel becomes less likely in circumstances where we disengage. If we deny moderates in the Arab world the possibility of success or hope, what do we expect to happen to their publics? We leave radicalization and conflict as the only alternatives.

The realist instinct to launch blueprints that we can't produce will only add to our image of being ineffectual. We need the opposite. We need to create some models of success, or at least progress, and early on.

But to do that we must see the world as it is. We must remain committed to the importance of trying to produce peace. Those who think it is futile even to try for peace make hopelessness a self-fulfilling prophecy, without ever knowing whether there was an alternative. Those who pursue peace, but with no illusions, hedge against the uncertainties. They give peace a chance because they understand we must—and yet they protect themselves if peace remains beyond their grasp.

Chapter Seven

COMPETING MYTHOLOGIES
ABOUT IRAN

To this point, we have explained the fundamental failings of linkage and why it offers a distorted view of reality in the Middle East. We have also shown how different American administrations, having been misled by the linkage mythology, pursued policies that failed and were bound to fail. While linkage may be wrongheaded, and its emphasis on the Palestinian issue as the cornerstone of everything in the Middle East may distort reality, the Arab-Israeli conflict remains important. As we have tried to show, there are right and wrong ways to approach it and be effective. We believe in engagement on peace, understanding the context and the multiplicity of ways that the United States can and should promote peace.

In general, we tend to see engagement without illusion as a guiding principle for dealing with the major state-based threats and challenges America faces in the broader Middle East. In the next few chapters, we explore how best to deal with Iran. There is no state today that poses a greater threat to America's interests in the Middle East. It is interesting that in the 2008 campaign, both candidates described Iran's getting nuclear weapons as a "game changer." In other words, it would change the balance of power in the region in a profound way. The stakes are high. Whether on Middle East peace, Iraq, energy, terror, or nuclear proliferation to nonstate and state actors, Iran poses challenges to our interests and our hopes.

The U.S. problems with Iran go back many years. Starting with the 1979 revolution, the Islamic Republic of Iran has bedeviled American policy and policymakers. From the Carter administration through the George W. Bush presidency, American leaders have sought without success to change Iran's behavior. Engagement has been tried and failed in the Carter, Reagan, and Clinton administrations. A policy of isolation and containment has similarly been found wanting in many of those same administrations—and clearly isolation has not succeeded in either of the Bush administrations.

While no doubt some of the difficulties have been a function of the internal dynamics within the Iranian leadership and the ongoing battles between the more revolutionary and more pragmatically minded constituencies, the question is whether there is a path that could be more productive. One thing is certain: never has it been more urgent for the United States to find an effective way to alter Iranian behavior. With Iranian hostility toward the United States and its interests unabated, and with the Iranian regime moving inexorably toward becoming a nuclear power, the United States no longer has the luxury of being unable to affect what the Iranians do. Indeed, the United States and the international community now face a crossroads and need urgently to choose a new, more effective path.

So what should the United States be doing? In this chapter and the next, we explore two profoundly different mind-sets about Iran and what should guide our policy toward it. Those who embrace these mind-sets— these competing mythologies—are guided by very different assumptions about the dangers that a nuclear Iran would pose; they see Iran through very different lenses. They reflect what has been an ongoing debate over whether to engage revolutionary Iran or to isolate and undo it, with neither side able to point to successes in their preferred way of approaching the challenge of the Islamic Republic. These two opposing camps or schools of thought might best be characterized as "engagers" versus "regime changers." Ironically, these two schools of thought coexisted uneasily in the Bush administration, and, given their diametrically opposed views and policy prescriptions, often (particularly in the first term) produced policy paralysis as a result.

Put another way, both camps have policy ideas influenced by different sets of myths about the nature of Iran's leadership and the extent of what is possible in dealing with it. The engagers see the religious leaders in Iran as essentially pragmatic; whatever their rhetoric, they are perceived by the engagers as ultimately persuadable. The regime changers see Iran's political leaders as shaped by an ideology that trumps reason.

The first school says that Iran is like any other state and therefore it can be treated like any other state. As such, since deterrence worked during the Cold War with the Soviet Union, it will work with Iran. The international community need not be so concerned about Iran's becoming a nuclear weapons state; on the contrary, we must *engage* Iran, and in the worst case, if agreements prove difficult to achieve, we can settle for containment. The second school argues that Iran is not only unlike any other state, but it is led by a revolutionary rogue leadership that has declared war on us. It cannot be deterred; worse, its behavior cannot be altered. It will never accept anything less than our defeat. Iran thus cannot be engaged, and any such effort to engage it will be doomed to fail. Nothing short of regime change can be acceptable.

As with any mythology, there is an element of truth in each of these schools of thought and the assumptions that guide them. We will examine the key assumptions behind each mind-set and why they are held, point out their fallacies, and then offer a third way to guide our policy toward Iran and the challenges it poses.

THE ENGAGERS/REALISTS: IRAN IS LIKE ANY OTHER STATE

Realists like Zbigniew Brzezinski, John Mearsheimer, Stephen Walt, and Barry Posen make the case that Iran is motivated by power and interests like any other state. They don't ignore egregious Iranian behaviors, but neither do they find the Iranians very different from those whose behaviors we have rejected or abhorred in the past. Nor do they see them as very different from those powers that the United States has been able to deter in the past. Many in the West saw the Soviet Union and China as ideologically driven, but were convinced that the reality of facing assured destruction if they used their nuclear weapons against U.S. interests had a sobering affect and limited their aggressive behavior.

As Zbigniew Brzezinski has written, "Deterrence has worked in US-Soviet relations, in US-Chinese relations. . . . The notion that Iran would someday just hand over the bomb to some terrorist conveniently ignores the fact that doing so would be tantamount to suicide for all of Iran. . . ."[1] For those like Brzezinski, Iran is no more prone to commit suicide than the Soviet Union was. Many of the realists argue that the Soviet Union was once also defined as being a revolutionary power bent on world domination. As time went by and its leaders were seen as more pragmatic than revolutionary and deterrence seemed to work, the Soviet Union came to be seen as an adversary but one that was not irrational. It was subject to pressures and inducements and the strategic logic of the nuclear age. The United States could live with it and manage competition and even conflict.

Interestingly, for a time China appeared to be very different. China, under its leader Mao Tse-tung, conjured up fears of complete irrationality. It seemed to respect no limits or conventions. The Soviets came to be perceived as the rational Communists; the Chinese were seen as irrational, and there was a fear that they might not be deterred by the prospect of massive destruction. Indeed, as Mao implied in 1957, China's leaders might be prepared to sacrifice 300 million people—nearly half its population at the time—to achieve "the victory of the world and the Chinese revolution."[2]

The prospect of China's developing the nuclear bomb and deciding to use it for the sake of the revolution was so alarming that the Kennedy administration considered approaching the Soviets about carrying out joint military action to forestall the development of Chinese nuclear capabilities. Stewart Alsop, a journalist close to President Kennedy and quite familiar with his thinking, wrote of the "madness of Mao Tse-tung" and advocated military strikes to prevent China from going nuclear.[3] However, the Kennedy administration ultimately decided that the price of military action was too high and its gains too limited to justify military strikes against the fledgling Chinese nuclear infrastructure. Instead, when the Chinese finally tested a nuclear bomb in 1964, President Lyndon Johnson reaffirmed U.S. defense commitments in Asia and declared that the new Chinese capability had "been fully taken into account in planning our own defense program and our own nuclear capability," and that China's new status would "have no effect on the readiness of the United States to respond to . . . aggression."[4]

President Johnson's declaration made it clear that China's possession of nuclear weapons did not change the strategic landscape, and that his administration would stick by its prior commitments. In effect, he was signaling to the Chinese that their nuclear capability would still be dwarfed by the American arsenal and they would not only gain nothing but could lose everything. The logic of deterrence and mutual assured destruction would apply to China even through the period of the Cultural Revolution, when it seemed to be guided more by ideology than by rational considerations. But its revolutionary ardor would wane, and, in the eyes of the realists, deterrence (and engagement) contributed to a transformation of China's behavior.

For the realists, Iran, too, can subordinate its ideology to practical considerations much the way the Soviets and Chinese have done previously. It is seen as no more ideologically motivated than either of these two Marxist-Leninist states and just as likely to adjust its behavior. Indeed, realists will argue that for all the posturing of Iran's leadership, it is basically guided by pragmatic instincts and the realities of power.

There certainly are acknowledged experts on Iran who, while not necessarily part of the realist camp, believe that Iran's leaders are highly ideological but still capable of making pragmatic choices, especially when it comes to regime survival. Karim Sadjadpour, for one, believes that Ali Khamenei—Iran's Supreme Leader—is guided by Islamic ideology and deep hostility to the United States, and yet he also points out that Khamenei has "ruled the country by consensus rather than decree, with his own survival and that of the theocratic system as his top priorities."[5] Indeed, as Sadjadpour has observed elsewhere, regime survival is paramount, and "even hardliners in Tehran who would like to export the revolution, who want to transform Iran into the dominant regional power, and who seek Israel's demise, seek—first and foremost—to stay in power."[6]

To be sure, regime survival is also enshrined in an important theological dictum of the Islamic Republic. As Mehdi Khalaji, a specialist on Iran and a Shiite theologian by training, has pointed out, "the guardianship of the jurist" has been employed by the ruling elite since 1979. This concept not only marries political and religious decision making in the regime, but also allows the Shiite jurists to overrule Islamic law when, in Khalaji's words, it serves "the interest of the regime."[7]

While "the guardianship of the jurist" theoretically creates a religious justification for pragmatism, analysis of the regime's actual behavior offers examples in which Islamic ideology appears to guide it and other examples in which the interests of the regime trump ideological considerations. Note, for example, that Islamic solidarity is trumpeted in supporting the Palestinian cause and delegitimizing Israel, while the

Chechen cause is ignored lest Russia be antagonized. Muslim unity is used to provide essentially unlimited support for Hizbollah and Hamas, while Christian Armenia is supported in its war in Nagorno-Karabakh against Shia-Muslim Azerbaijan; and Iran, as Sadjadpour observes, endlessly denounces America for its "godlessness," yet is willing to align itself with socialist leaders like Hugo Chávez and Fidel Castro.[8]

To some observers, these positions indicate that even if ideology plays a significant role in its decision making, the Iranian leadership weighs its interests carefully as it decides on a course of action. For all of the Iranian leadership's professed hostility toward Israel, which is profound and seems a pillar of the regime's strategic orientation, there is a school of thought that suggests revolutionary Iran will be pragmatic should it possess nuclear weapons. Barry Posen, for one, argues that an essentially rational Iranian leadership would be deterred by the Israeli capability to respond to an Iranian nuclear attack by destroying Iran's eight largest cities, its oil industry, and its capacity to operate as a functioning society. In Posen's words, "little in the behavior of the leaders of revolutionary Iran . . . suggests that they would see this as a good trade."[9]

For the realists, Iran's leadership is and will remain fundamentally rational. By rational, they mean that the Iranian government makes decisions on a cost-benefit basis. To be more precise, they posit that the way Iranian leaders arrive at their decisions follows the same basic logic that drives U.S. leaders, and that the Iranian assessment of costs and benefits is not only similar to the American one, but is knowable to American policymakers.

Deterrence theory, after all, was always based on an inherent rationality embodied in much of game theory.[10] Rationality was largely unaffected by cultural differences. Surely those who have written about applying deterrence strategy to the challenge of Iran, including Zbigniew Brzezinski, Barry Posen, John Mearsheimer, and Stephen Walt, do not deny the existence of cultural differences. Rather, they basically argue that when it comes to questions of national power, interests, and survival, cultural differences largely become less relevant—and that they do so in the case of Iran.

The realists are guided by one other critical assumption in arguing for deterrence and engagement: the costs of the United States' using military force to prevent Iran from going nuclear are simply too high.

Whether measured in terms of Iran's ability to retaliate against our forces in Iraq, or to strike at Saudi oil facilities and cause an even greater oil shock worldwide, or to foster a backlash against us in an already angry Arab and Muslim world, or to trigger greater terror against us using Hizbollah or others, the costs are simply unacceptable. For Zbigniew Brzezinski, it is not only the costs—which, as he observes, would make the "misadventure in Iraq look trivial"—it is also that "even keeping the military option on the table impedes the kinds of negotiations" that could change Iranian behavior.[11]

For many of the realists, even efforts to engage in coercion of Iran are bound to be counterproductive. This is ironic for two reasons: first, because coercion is an implicit part of any deterrent relationship, since deterrence is built on a presumed threat, and second, because coercion has always characterized Iranian behavior toward the outside world. Even if one is willing to accept the argument that in many cases the Iranian leaders may be driven by defensive motivations, it is hard to deny the proposition that coercion is embedded in Iran's approach to others. One constantly sees warnings from Iranian leaders of the consequences of behaviors Iran will interpret as hostile.[12] As a leading Arab Gulf state ambassador told us recently, Iran's leaders present three faces to the region: one in which exporting the revolution remains a live option, a second in which promoting turmoil is simply a given, particularly if they are not happy with you, and a third in which they are also, of course, willing to reach agreement and do business with you. They are, this Arab official observed, a "little like your mafia—willing to offer you insurance for good behavior."[13]

Lest one think this behavior is reserved only for the Arabs, it is worth recalling a not-so-subtle threat President Ahmadinejad made against the Europeans over their policies. In Ahmadinejad's words, "We have advised the Europeans that the Americans are far away, but you are the neighbors of the nations in the region. . . . We inform you that the nations are like an ocean that is welling up, and if a storm begins, the storm will not stay limited to Palestine and you may get hurt."[14] To be sure, Iran has engaged in coercion and terror against Israel for the past twenty-five years, funding Hizbollah with weapons, training, and financial assistance and also providing money and arms to Hamas and Islamic Jihad, despite the fact that Israel has never attacked Iran.

Ultimately, if coercion is part of the way Iranian leaders approach the outside world, they are bound to understand it—even if they will not like it when it is applied to them. From this standpoint, coercion ought to be part of the realist approach to deterrence and containment if those who are advocating such a posture are to be consistent in emphasizing each as the appropriate response to Iran's becoming a nuclear weapons state.

Are there reasons not to be so sanguine about the effectiveness of deterrence and containment for dealing with a nuclear Iran? The short answer is yes. The key realist assumptions about applying deterrence to Iran the way it was applied to the Soviets or Chinese can be questioned, because today's circumstances are quite different from those operating during the Cold War. In the Middle East today a nuclear Iran could lead to a regional arms race at a time of open conflicts. Furthermore, the element of messianic ideology embraced by important segments of the Iranian leadership raises legitimate questions about the stability of deterrence and the certainty that weapons would neither be used nor transferred—and whether Iran is in fact like any other state. Finally, there is the question of what can actually be deterred. Deterring overt attacks may be one thing, but how about preventing coercion and intimidation by an Iran that has a nuclear shield to prevent responses against it when it employs militias like Hizbollah or Hamas or the Mahdi Army to threaten others with terror or instability?

While using force to prevent Iran from going nuclear may well be a very expensive and unattractive option, the myth that deterrence is a kind of given because Iran is no different from those states that have been deterred in the past is based on a number of false assumptions. As a result, treating deterrence of a nuclear Iran as a given because it is seen to be like any other state is not only misguided, it is misleading to the point that it may complicate the ability to actually deter Iran. And it would certainly make it far harder to alter Iran's behavior.

THE FALLACIES OF THE REALIST MYTH ABOUT IRAN

A natural starting point for outlining some of the fallacies of the realist assumptions is on the very issue of deterrence and how it operated in the Cold War. Deterrence, it should be noted, was premised not only on shared rationality. It was premised also on the ability to "understand the other's thinking and accurately anticipate its behavior."[15]

While observers may idealize how deterrence functioned during the Cold War in this regard, it is worth recalling that in the Cuban Missile Crisis the United States and the Soviet Union were brought to the brink of nuclear war precisely because Soviet premier Nikita Khrushchev miscalculated and thought he could get away with placing nuclear armed missiles in Cuba and offset American strategic advantages by doing so. He was certainly wrong, but he was not alone in his miscalculations and his lack of awareness of what the other side might do. President Kennedy's management of the crisis may have been masterful, but there was much he did not know during the crisis that could easily have triggered an escalation to nuclear war. For example, he did not know that the Soviet submarines against which the U.S. Navy dropped depth charges during the crisis were armed with nuclear torpedoes and that the commanders of those subs were authorized to fire these torpedoes if their hulls were penetrated. In fact, the unknowns and dangers in the Cuban Missile Crisis were far greater than anyone knew at the time—so much so that President Kennedy's secretary of defense, Robert McNamara, following a discussion with former U.S. and Russian officials about the crisis forty years after those events, declared:

> For many years, I considered the Cuban missile crisis to be the best-managed foreign policy crisis of the last half-century. I still believe that President Kennedy's actions during decisive moments of the crisis helped to prevent a nuclear war. But now I conclude that, however astutely the crisis may have been managed, by the end of those extraordinary 13 days—October 16–October 28, 1962—luck also played a significant role in the avoidance of nuclear war by a hair's breadth.[16]

While deterrence held in this instance, escaping nuclear war by only a hair's breadth with a country with which the United States had direct communications is very different from doing it with a country like Iran with which we communicate only through others. During the Cold War, the nuclear threats were comparable and mutual, and American leaders possessed a degree of familiarity with the country they were attempting to deter. During the Cold War, in the words of Keith Payne—a longtime deterrence theorist—deterrence was about strategic forces and having undistorted communications with important elements of the leadership of the other side. During the Cold War, the United States communicated deterrence "redlines" through formal government-to-government communiqués, speeches, and démarches. Payne asks the rhetorical question whether that will be true for the United States and Iran, or for Israel and Iran.[17]

It may not be. Even if deterrence was more tenuous in the Cold War than previously thought, with the enduring potential for miscalculation, American administrations were nonetheless far better positioned to communicate with the Soviets and to avoid misunderstandings. American policymakers could be far more certain that the Soviet leaders knew the messages they were conveying and understood them, particularly because there were channels to get feedback. With Iran, the story is simply different. Is there reason to believe the Iranians understand well American messages conveyed through others? Do they think we "get" what they want us to understand from what they convey indirectly to us? And if they think we understand but we do not, are not the risks of deterrence's failing quite high? There are reasons to be concerned about the answers to all these questions.

Judith Yaphe and Charles Lutes, analysts at the National Defense University, have discussed the absence of communications and its effect on deterrence not only between the United States and Iran but also between Iran and Israel. They see a dramatically different context and conclude that it will be "difficult to establish a controlled deterrence relationship, as existed between Washington and Moscow in the Cold War."[18] Worse, they believe that "the lack of direct communication between Iran and the United States, Israel, and its own neighbors, makes Iran's ability to recognize their redlines a great danger."[19]

One well-placed Israeli scholar, Gerald Steinberg, agrees, but, with a particular focus on Iran and Israel, adds that it is not just the lack of direct communication that is the problem; it is, he suggests, also the relative isolation of Iran's decision makers, "the fog that surrounds" how they make decisions and their "faith-based revisionist objectives." He goes on to warn that even if Iran's leaders are "not suicidal," it will be hard to achieve stable deterrence because there is such a "high potential for misperceptions regarding Israel's intentions and red-lines and so many [potential] triggers for crises."[20]

The potential for Iran to misread or discount redlines—whether American or Israeli—is exacerbated by both American and Israeli instances of seemingly establishing and then retreating from their so-called redlines over the last several years. Israeli leaders consistently talked about not being able to tolerate Iran's crossing the point of no return on nuclear development—meaning the point at which it could develop fissionable material without assistance from the outside and would become a nuclear power.[21] Yet Israel has not, in fact, done anything as Iran crossed that threshold; note, for example, that Iran with its current process has already produced more than 1,010 kilos of low enriched uranium (LEU) without any Israeli response.[22]

Similarly, the Bush administration failed to respond as Iran approached declared redlines. For example, President Bush declared in June 2003 that his administration "will not tolerate the construction of a nuclear weapon [by Iran]."[23] Secretary of State Rice repeated this declaration in 2006.[24] Vice President Dick Cheney was unequivocal in asserting in October 2007 that we would not "allow" Iran to develop nuclear weapons.[25] And yet we have imposed no serious price on Iran as it resumed uranium conversion activities at Isfahan in August 2005, broke International Atomic Energy Agency (IAEA) seals at Natanz in January 2006, began heavy water production at Arak in August 2006, or announced in April 2008 that it was now installing six thousand of the second-generation IR-2 centrifuges—centrifuges that have been developed secretly either at Natanz or another, unknown facility and that are vastly more efficient than the 3,800 now operating.[26]

While there have been three UN Security Council sanctions resolutions, none of them directly affects the functioning of the Iranian economy. Thus, Iran has been willing to continue to defy the international community's demands that it stop its nuclear-related activities. If redlines are supposed to indicate that an intolerable price will be paid if one crosses them, Iran, at least at this point, doesn't believe it. And the Bush administration gave them no reason to believe it. The administration too often made strong statements and didn't act on them vis-à-vis Iran, leaving the impression that it did not understand the difference between a redline and pink line.

But it is important for Iranian leaders to understand that difference. For example, if the Obama administration establishes possession of nuclear weapons as a redline, the Iranians must understand the price they would pay for crossing it. Similarly, if a different redline is established—namely, the use or transfer of nuclear arms—the Iranians must see that such action would mean they are crossing a redline and not a pink line and understand that the consequences will be devastating should they do so. The realists would certainly argue that Iranian leaders will understand the difference between defying the international community generally and the United States specifically over developing a nuclear capability, and that they will not delude themselves into thinking they could escape the consequences of use or transfer of such weapons.

Yet here again U.S. policymakers need to see the Iranians as they are, not as they wish them to be. Can they be so certain that the Iranians will have tight command-and-control structures in place? Will they have a limited number of weapons sites that are completely secured? Will decisions on use follow a strict chain of command? Will there be permissive action links (PALs) or locks on warheads with codes that local commanders will not possess?

Today there is no one outside Iran who could give definitive answers to any of these questions. Even within Iran, there is little evidence that such questions are even being considered. Since the Iranians claim they are not interested in developing nuclear weapons—only fuel to power reactors and generate electricity—it should come as no surprise that there are few signs that these questions are now being raised, much less answered.

What is known? To begin with, the Islamic Revolutionary Guard Corps (IRGC) controls the nuclear program today. The Supreme Leader has doubtless assigned to those in the Revolutionary Guard considered to be the most trustworthy the task of protecting the nuclear program and facilities—and presumably that would remain the case should the decision be made to assemble nuclear weapons. While the IRGC may be the most loyal to the regime, Ray Takeyh—an expert on Iran who does not favor confrontation with its leaders—has described the Revolutionary Guard as a "125,000 strong force [that] is commanded by reactionary ideologues who are committed to the values and philosophical outlook of the clerical militants."27 Another specialist on Iran, Gregory Giles, similarly observes that even if the IRGC defines its main mission as safeguarding the regime, its members are associated with extremist clerics like Ayatollah Mesbah Yazdi, and it is the leading edge of Iran's terror apparatus. Giles wonders "how Iran's nuclear force operators [in the IRGC] would respond to religious edicts, or *fatwas*, from their personal spiritual guides that were at odds with orders [from Khamenei]."[28]

If the past is any indication, we should not be so confident about unmistakable control by a highly disciplined and unified Iranian leadership. During the Iran-Iraq War, for example, the IRGC often acted on its own. The IRGC attacked oil tankers even after receiving, and acknowledging, explicit instructions not to do so.[29] They did much the same in launching missile attacks against Kuwait even though this was not the government's policy. In almost all such cases, the actions were linked to political infighting in Tehran.[30]

To be sure, nuclear weapons are likely to be seen differently. But one cannot rule out that religious and ideological zealots in the IRGC could gain access to such weapons. The challenge is different from what we faced with the Soviets during the Cold War. While fears may have been conjured up from time to time about rogue military actors in Moscow (or Beijing), the dominance of the Communist Party over the military was never in question. In the Soviet Union, the MPA and the KGB constituted the political watchdogs in the military itself and the security apparatus, to ensure that the Communist Party's primacy was never challenged by the military and that a putsch was out of the question.

One might argue that the IRGC has a similar role within Iran; it is there to safeguard the regime and make sure that the Iranian military never becomes a threat. But what if the IRGC itself is a party to political infighting or jockeying for power? And what if the debates end up not just being about the export of the revolution but about acting on religious duty and opportunity?

From this standpoint, the issues may involve both the question of controllability of the nuclear weapons and the question of whether all those in the leadership are likely to be deterred by the prospect of assured destruction. Even during the Cold War, there were some theorists, such as Colin Gray, who felt that assured destruction might not deter the Soviets if they thought they could win a nuclear war with the United States. Since their measure was survival of the political system, Gray and others focused on the Soviet civil defense program as indicating that the Soviets thought they might be able to "survive and recover rapidly from a nuclear war."[31]

The Iranians are not likely to believe that they can survive a nuclear war with the United States. But how might they compare themselves to Israel? Akbar Hashemi Rafsanjani, the former Iranian president and someone seen in the West as a pragmatist, declared at one point that "even one nuclear bomb inside Israel will destroy everything. However, it will only harm the Islamic world. It is not irrational to contemplate such an eventuality."[32]

That Rafsanjani has said it is not irrational to consider such a possibility again suggests a cost-benefit assessment. The problem, of course, is that here the possible benefit of destroying Israel makes the cost of absorbing nuclear retaliation from Israel worth it. Maybe this is just bravado. Maybe the Iranians do not appreciate what the Israelis could actually inflict on them—at least not the way Barry Posen (cited earlier) assesses it. In any case, if the Iranian leadership knew that if they attacked Israel with nuclear weapons, the United States would, in the words of then-Senator Hillary Clinton, "obliterate" them in response, Iran's leaders would realize the folly of such an attack.

However, even here there are two basic problems with believing that deterrence will be straightforward and relatively easy to achieve. First, the Iranians may accept that direct attacks are too costly, but indirect attacks through Hizbollah or Hamas against Israel might not be. Nuclear or dirty bombs could be given to them by those in the IRGC who are committed to Israel's destruction, and the regime could deny any responsibility. There is the danger that Iranian leaders, including those not driven by ideological imperatives, could believe that America will not find it easy to use weapons against Iran if Iran's leaders deny any involvement in an attack on Israel and if the only evidence that the United States can muster is circumstantial and not ironclad. So who controls the weapons in Iran—as well as the ideology of those who might be able to gain access to them—could determine the effectiveness of deterrence.

And ideology cannot be so easily dismissed as a motivator of actions that we might consider irrational. Some longtime observers of Iran and the Middle East, such as Professor Bernard Lewis are convinced that our calculus on assured destruction will not apply to the Iranians, given the ideology of important segments of the elite. Lewis observes:

[During the Cold War] both sides had nuclear weapons. Neither side used them because both sides knew the other side would respond in kind. This will not work with a fanatic [like Ahmadinejad]. For him, mutual assured destruction is not a deterrent, it is an inducement. We know already they do not give a damn about killing their own people in great numbers. We have seen it again and again. In the final scenario, and this applies all the more strongly if they kill large numbers of their own people, they are doing them a favor. They are giving them a quick free pass to heaven and all its delights. . . . [33]

To be sure, many other specialists on Iran will argue, as already noted, that regime survival matters first and foremost to the Iranian elite and that most members of the elite won't roll the dice with their own future. While this is no doubt true, it is also true that there are important members of the elite who are motivated by the belief that they must facilitate the return of the Hidden Imam. These are not fringe members of the leadership. They include President Ahmadinejad, a number of senior clerics, and some members of the IRGC. Ahmadinejad has been particularly outspoken about the Hidden Imam, frequently speaking of the need to prepare for his imminent return. He even claimed in a 2005 meeting with a nonaligned foreign minister who was cautioning him on the dangers of Iran's policies that his interlocutor need not worry because "these are signs of the appearance of the Imam Mahdi who will appear in the next two years."[34]

Shiites believe that the Twelfth Imam, known as the Mahdi, went into hiding over a thousand years ago and will return one day to save the world from injustice. The Mahdi is the Shiite savior or messiah, and it is believed that he will return to usher in a world of justice and purity. All evil will be extirpated and pain and suffering will be removed. His return "will signal the triumph of the faithful over all enemies" and create an opening to paradise for all good Muslims.[35]

President Ahmadinejad leaves little doubt about his devotion to the Hidden Imam and the meaning of his return: "[T]he entire universe has been created for that holy event to take place; the day when all the prophets and martyrs will come to help the Imam."[36] But for Ahmadinejad this is not an abstraction or a distant vision—he often refers to the Mahdi's presence and his guiding spirit even now: "[W]e see the hand of [his] holy

management every day. God knows that we see it. I don't exaggerate. . . .
I believe that the Imam is managing the affairs. . . ."[37]

Furthermore, he has linked Iran's nuclear development directly to
the Mahdi: "Do you remember when imam [Khomeini] said that wher-
ever we go, at each phase of the [Islamic] Revolution we can see a divine
hand has been taking care of things? We can see. Iran's nuclear achievement is the biggest miracle of contemporary history. . . . The big powers
are still astonished. . . . Iran has become nuclear before their eyes, despite
their will. It is not an accident. We behold the hand of the Imam [Mahdi],
we behold it in many occasions."[38]

When criticized by some in the Iranian elite over his beliefs and his
constant references to the return of the Hidden Imam, Ahmadinejad has
responded, saying in one instance, "I know that close minded people
don't believe these things. . . ."[39] But he does believe "these things" and
has attacked his critics, declaring, "Some people make fun of these beliefs; this is because their hearts are devoid of faith. These modern day
pagans are heathens. They pretend to be intellectuals, but don't have the
understanding of a goat."[40]

Interestingly, some of Ahmadinejad's critics are also clerics. The
cleric Hassan Rouhani, the former nuclear negotiator and ex-secretary of
Iran's Supreme National Security Council, has criticized Ahmadinejad's
government for "encouraging superstitious practices."[41] He has bluntly
attacked those who speak of the imminent reappearance of the Mahdi,
saying: "Two or three years ago another circus show was launched when
some officials called to put up podiums for the Imam Mahdi in Tehran.
There were also those who advanced the idea that the Imam was going to
appear in the next two years, and with the passage of time, it is clear today they were liars."[42] Both of Rouhani's references are to Ahmadinejad,
the first to when he was mayor of Tehran and the second to his prediction
noted above in his meeting with a visiting foreign minister.

Both the criticisms of Ahmadinejad's beliefs about the Mahdi and his
responses to them suggest that when it comes to the Hidden Imam, he is
not posturing, but truly believes what he says. This is not just a theoretical dispute between Ahmadinejad and Rouhani. It could have relevance
for Iran's behavior—no doubt the very reason Rouhani feels the need to
attack it. Indeed, it could have relevance for whether deterrence can really work with a nuclear Iran.

Consider that in the Shiite texts on the Mahdi's return, there is an end-of-days or apocalyptic reality that accompanies his reappearance. The victory over all enemies of Islam will involve killing at least a third of the world's population, and, as Mehdi Khalaji points out, none of the Shiite texts say that the Mahdi will kill only combatants.[43]

The great danger is that Ahmadinejad and those who believe in the apocalyptic vision of the Mahdi's return also believe that they have an obligation to facilitate his reappearance. Again to quote Mehdi Khalaji, who studied for fourteen years in Qom to become a cleric: many of those in the middle ranks of the Revolutionary Guard "consider themselves 'soldiers of the Mahdi' who bear the responsibility of paving the way for the return. These groups are the heirs of those who favor world Islam. . . . They believe a true Shiite cannot merely await the Mahdi without actively engaging in a series of measures to prepare his return."[44]

Do Ahmadinejad and those in the IRGC who believe in the apocalyptic vision believe that annihilating Israel is a necessary first step toward preparing the return of the Hidden Imam? Ahmadinejad's own words should give us pause in this regard. In speaking in 2007 about how the "Zionist entity" (the way he typically refers to Israel) would collapse soon, Ahmadinejad seemed to tell the Israeli people not only of their imminent demise but also how that demise was connected to the return of the Mahdi: "Today I declare by a louder voice, though your eyes and ears are closed, that all the world sees that you are going to be drawn, because justice and the pioneer of justice is on his way."[45] On the occasion of Israel's sixtieth anniversary in May 2008, Ahmadinejad referred less to the Mahdi and more to the need to eliminate Israel as soon as there was an opening to do so: "[T]he peoples of the region would not miss the narrowest opportunity to annihilate this false regime [Israel] . . . the nations of the region despise this false and criminal regime."[46] Might not Iran's development of a nuclear capability provide something more than the "narrowest opportunity" he refers to?

None of this means that deterrence could not work with Iran. After all, there are those in the Iranian leadership, including the Supreme Leader, who put the survival of the regime as their first priority. They are probably the mainstream of the leadership. They are likely to be deterred from the overt use of nuclear weapons. They may agree that transferring the weapons to groups like Hizbollah or Hamas could be suicidal for them.

But this assumption—and deterrence itself—cannot be taken for granted or treated as a given. The United States and others must adopt policies and actions that will leave the Iranian leadership with no doubts about the consequences of the use or transfer of nuclear weapons or dirty bombs—and those consequences must be devastating in the view of Iranian leaders. There must be no ambiguity about accountability; indeed, Iranian leaders must not think that they can deny involvement or responsibility for the transfer of a weapon, or suggest that rogue elements were responsible and they were not, and thus escape the consequences.

When past U.S. administrations have suggested that those responsible for taking over the embassy in 1979, or those who carried out the Khobar Tower bombings, or those who are arming or training militias in Iraq or providing the explosives that kill U.S. forces, are rogue elements and may not be the political leadership in Iran, they were signaling that deniability might work with us. American leaders cannot be parsing the regime in this fashion. The Iranian leadership must know there is no escaping responsibility and they will be held accountable for the action of any element of the Iranian regime should it ever involve the use or transfer of nuclear weapons or dirty bombs.

For this stance to be credible, the United States must not only have a consistent posture of making clear that the actions of any Iranian regime elements will be the responsibility of the government and its leaders; the United States and the international community must also have the nuclear forensic ability to determine the origin of any nuclear weapon that has been used. This will require developing not just an American capability, but also an international capability (perhaps through the development of a consortium) that will be able unmistakably to identify the signature of every nuclear weapon and be able to state unequivocally whose stockpile it has come from. Only then will Iranian leaders know there is no escaping the consequences.

Finally, Iranian leaders must believe American redlines. We cannot afford to be devaluing our word. Threats should not be made if they are not going to be acted upon. And surely we must find better channels for communication if we hope to be sure that the Iranians are hearing and interpreting our messages the way we intend them to be heard and understood.

All this suggests that deterrence will take much more thought than the realists give to it. It requires a strategy and coordination with others. It requires knowing how to affect Iranian perceptions and knowing as well how to get the Iranians to decide, for their own reasons, not to assemble a nuclear weapon, if for no other reason than the uncertainty of knowing whether such weapons can be controlled internally. A strategy for deterrence must be guided by the possibility of dissuasion in which Iranian leaders see a set of costs that raise doubts in their minds about the value of the weapons—whether in terms of the risk of usage, the loss of control, the arming of Iran's neighbors, the increase of countervailing military presence in the region, the extension of a nuclear guarantee to the neighboring states, the complete economic and political isolation of Iran should it decide to test nuclear weapons, or any combination of these factors.

One part of this strategy might require finding a way for others—perhaps the British or French—to talk to the Iranian leaders about command-control mechanisms, including PALs; this, too, could be part of a strategy for reminding the Iranian leaders that control may not be such a given for them and could thus be useful in convincing them that they have more to lose than gain in crossing the threshold of actually assembling nuclear weapons.

Even doing all this does not mean that deterrence and containment can be carried out in a way that prevents a nuclear Iran from changing the landscape of the Middle East in very dangerous ways. Surely if Iran possessed fissionable material but did not assemble weapons—or at least maintained ambiguity about whether it possessed nuclear capabilities—it might have less impact in the area. The problem, however, is that a nuclear Iran, an Iran capable of a nuclear weapon breakout very quickly, even if deterrable, will still cast a shadow over the region. Its capacity to coerce will affect the behaviors of others.

And this is a problem the realists tend to assume away. They argue that the U.S. nuclear umbrella will deter Iran's threats to its neighbors. It may well deter overt attacks; maybe with the right declaratory policy and the right nuclear forensic capability, we may also deter the transfer of nuclear weapons or materials to militias like Hizbollah or Hamas. But what of covert threats or threats to destabilize their neighbors?

The threats we may be most able to deter may be the ones that least concern Iran's neighbors. The ones that most concern them are likely to relate to coercion and to be driven by an Iran that feels emboldened because its nuclear weapons render overt threats against it less credible. Iran's neighbors are likely to see Iranian threats to promote subversion through local Shiite populations or to use Hizbollah to carry out bombings as real dangers—made more imminent and dangerous if Iran has a nuclear shield behind which to operate. (Bear in mind that Hizbollah has already demonstrated that it acts not just against Israel but on a regional basis; for example, it played a role in the Khobar Tower bombings in Saudi Arabia and has been active in training Shia militias in Iraq.[47])

Once Iran has nuclear weapons—or the capacity to assemble them quickly—its coercive power is bound to affect the choices its neighbors feel they have. Will this lead them to cut ties with the United States, or to seek the removal of America's forces from the Gulf, or to become more responsive to what Iran wants on oil production and pricing policies? Barry Posen answers "no" because Saudi Arabia, for example, will know that "if it succumbed to Iran's blandishments once, and severed its connections to the United States, it essentially would become a satellite of Iran, and there would be no end to Iran's demands."[48]

Posen may be right. And yet when one looks at the behavior of regional states, they focus first and foremost on internal stability—the area where we are least able to offer them security assurances. If they believe Iran can affect their internal stability—and the United States is more of a problem than an asset from this standpoint—they will look for ways to hedge their bets. They will seek to avoid what Iran may consider provocative steps, and they will accommodate when they feel it necessary. That does not mean that the Saudis and others will make themselves satellites of Iran; it does mean, however, that they will seek to give Iran less of a reason to threaten them and will be less inclined to challenge Iran.

Maybe this won't express itself so clearly in terms of ties to the United States, particularly if the Gulf states want Iran to know it can push them too far. But when it comes to being responsive to U.S. requests if Iran views these requests as hostile, will our putative friends in the Gulf be responsive to us? Iranian concerns will be given greater weight and ours will be given less across the range of issues in the region.

The issue on which we are likely to see the greatest impact is peace with Israel. When Iran threatens any state or the Palestinian leadership with great harm if they compromise with Israel, who will be willing to take such steps? Legitimizing compromise with Israel remains difficult in the Arab world in any case, but it still remains possible. That possibility is certain to recede if Iran acquires a nuclear capability and becomes even more willing to make its influence felt. Recall that Ahmadinejad declared, "Anybody who takes a step toward Israel will burn in the fire of the Islamic nation's fury."[49] An Iran with a nuclear capability is likely to be seen as far more likely to act on Ahmadinejad's words and mobilize threats to destabilize those in the region who would think about peace.

Peace may not be the only casualty of an Iran that goes nuclear; so might nonproliferation policy in the Middle East. The Saudis, Jordanians, and Egyptians have all begun to speak about developing nuclear power— and they echo the words of the Iranians when they do so. None of them have any illusions about Iran's real nuclear aims. All of them are likely to be more insecure once Iran has nuclear weapons or the ability to assemble them quickly. They may not be prepared to settle for U.S. guarantees to deter or counter the Iranians. Indeed, the Congressional Research Service in a 2008 study concluded that the Saudis and others may prefer to have their own nuclear capability in response to the development of Iranian nuclear weapons.[50]

The Saudis in particular could decide that as the main Sunni competitor with Iran, they must also have a nuclear capability to offset the imagery of Iranian-Shiite power. This would serve not only to counter any increased Iranian coercive capability, but also to show that Iran is not on the march and that the Shiites do not have either a technological edge or mystical advantages over the Sunnis.[51]

While it is certainly true that Saudi Arabia does not now have a nuclear infrastructure, the Saudis could choose to buy nuclear weapons from Pakistan or to pay the Pakistanis to station nuclear weapons on their soil. These two Sunni countries have long had a close and at times secret military relationship. Once Saudi Arabia buys or acquires nuclear weapons, will Egypt accept the reality that Saudi Arabia would be the only Arab state to have nuclear arms on its soil? That seems unlikely. As if to give credence to that point, a senior Egyptian official recently told us in very blunt terms: "If Iran goes nuclear, it will be the end of the NPT [Nuclear Non-proliferation Treaty]." That we could be looking at a nuclear Middle East should be a source of great concern. In the words of the president of the Council on Foreign Relations, Richard Haass, "More fingers on more triggers and more nuclear material in a part of the world associated with instability would be a strategic nightmare."[52]

If nothing else, we are reminded that Iran going nuclear—even if deterrence could be made to work in the case of overt threats—is not desirable. To make deterrence work will require a tough declaratory policy, as well as the ability to convince the Iranians that they will never escape accountability and that ultimately they may lose more by going nuclear than by stopping short of doing so. Dissuasion won't be easy but might be achievable, particularly if we can play on Iranian vulnerabilities—something we explore in chapter 9.

But even if we can make deterrence and containment effective, which is clearly not a given, there will still be the challenge of offsetting Iranian coercion and preventing proliferation in the region. A nuclear umbrella of assurances, a readiness to say that if Iran would raise its nuclear status we would preempt, a set of strategic discussions with the Saudis and others to focus on how to address Iranian threats—while also making clear what *they* will lose by going nuclear—would all have to be part of a broader effort to cope with an Iran that goes nuclear. So we can clearly see how the realist mythology that Iran is like any other state and deterrence will work misses the point.

Apart from the fact that deterrence cannot be taken as a given, there will be other significant consequences in the region should Iran go nuclear. Iranian coercive power will grow and alter the landscape of the region, making peace far less achievable and regional behaviors far less amenable to our interests.

Having explored the realist mythology and the dangerous assumptions that guide it, it is appropriate at this point to turn our attention to the neoconservatives and address their myths and their shortcomings.

Chapter Eight

THE NEOCONSERVATIVE VIEW
OF IRAN: A ROGUE REGIME THAT
MUST BE CHANGED

We believe that the regional consequences of Iran going nuclear require a serious effort to prevent it—including the possibility of direct engagement with Iran. Neoconservatives have a very different mind-set and approach. Unlike the realists (or the authors), the neoconservatives are convinced that deterrence can never work with revolutionary Iran. Worse, they think any effort to negotiate with the Iranians will be exploited by Iran, which, in their eyes, has an interest in using talks but never living up to any agreements.

For the neoconservatives, it is impossible to dissuade Iran from going nuclear and impossible to deter them once they have done so. Some of the neoconservatives believe that an Iran with nuclear weapons is such a calamity that military force must be used to prevent it. Others believe that the only answer is to change the regime—anything less is doomed to fail. For observers such as Michael Ledeen, Richard Perle, Norman Podhoretz, and others (including many who served at the highest levels of the George W. Bush administration), Iran may have leaders from time to time who appear more moderate or pragmatic, but the essence and purpose of the regime have remained essentially the same since the 1979 Islamic Revolution.

Michael Ledeen, an author and longtime activist with Iranian dissidents, has probably captured the core beliefs of the neoconservatives better than anyone else when it comes to Iran. In his words, Iran is "an enemy that never hid its intention to destroy us."[1] For Ledeen, it is an illusion to believe there is any value in engaging Iran, for the mullahs "don't share our dreams, they dream only of our destruction."[2] He cites chapter and verse of how the Iranians have used all of our efforts to engage them to undermine us, and suggests that we in the West have consistently deluded ourselves into believing that Iran will change. American and European diplomats insist, in his words, that "negotiations can eventually tame the Islamic Republic. It won't work. Only the defeat of the Islamic Republic can accomplish that goal because it would demonstrate that the mullahs do not have divine support for their global jihad."[3]

Ledeen and others make the point that the mullahs are convinced they will succeed in their aim to destroy us, and they have little difficulty citing Iranian statements to prove their point. One such example, cited by Ledeen, was a commentary on the official Web site of the Iranian broadcasting system which forecast the demise of the Western world and our political culture: "It seems that in the same way that . . . Imam Khomenei predicted the fall of communism, we must get ready to search for the liberal democratic civilization in the history museums."[4]

In a very similar vein, Richard Perle pointed out that the Iranians know what they want: nuclear weapons and the means to deliver them; suppression of freedom at home and the spread of terrorism abroad; and, in their words, the "shattering and fall of the ideology and thoughts of liberal democratic systems."[5]

For the neoconservatives, this is an ideological struggle but only the Iranians are waging it. We must wake up and see what is confronting us. The Islamic Republic will not quit.

The neoconservative warnings may seem extreme, but to be fair, it is worth noting that then-secretary general of the UN Kofi Annan and his aides were shocked by the comments that President Ahmadinejad made to them when they visited Iran in 2006. During the course of complaining about how the UN was structured in a way that both unfairly and inappropriately favored the Western powers, Ahmadinejad asserted that it was time to change things because "while America and Britain won the last world war, Iran would win the next one."[6] Iran, in other words, was the new power on the world stage and would effectively eclipse the old powers.

The neoconservatives are not inventing the hostility of senior Iranian officials, including Supreme Leader Ali Khamenei, toward the United States. Khamenei has repeatedly said that he believes that the United States seeks global dictatorship and seeks to further its own interests by dominating others. Some say his views are the same as those of the father of the Islamic Revolution, Ayatollah Ruhollah Khomeini, who likened the relations between the United States and Iran to those between a "wolf and a sheep."[7] Not surprisingly, the Supreme Leader has said that "conflict between the two [United States and Iran] is something natural and unavoidable."[8] One could interpret Khamenei's comments as a defensive reaction to perceived American hostility and a kind of Iranian "preemptive rejection" of the United States: you try to impose on us, you reject us, you do not respect our needs or interests, and you want to change our regime—therefore conflict between us is inevitable.

Neoconservatives see Khamenei's stance very differently. They do not see it as a defensive Iranian reaction. On the contrary, they see the unrelenting use of terror abroad, repression at home, and efforts to export the Islamic revolution and dominate the Middle East as signs of an ideological fervor that will never be satisfied until Iran emerges victorious and the West is defeated. Neoconservatives point out that Iran's leaders believe they can emerge victorious because much as "Islam" defeated the Soviet Union in Afghanistan, so too will it force America, "the twentieth century's other superpower," to submit in Iraq.[9] Given the nature of this struggle, the neoconservatives conclude that there is "no way to negotiate a reasonable modus operandi with such people, since their war on us derives from ultimate issues, not geopolitical disagreements."[10]

Even on lesser yet still important challenges such as the Iranian pursuit of nuclear weapons, the neoconservatives see no way to negotiate with Iran's leaders to get them to forgo their desire to have nuclear capability. Neoconservatives believe that the acquisition of nuclear weapons is too important to the Iranian objective of achieving dominance in the region; and in any case, regardless of what Iran's leaders may say or agree to, the Iranians will hide what they are doing—as they did for nearly twenty years—and preserve a clandestine option to "break out" when it suits them. While the Bush administration was not willing to talk directly to Iran on the nuclear issue (until it joined other powers for a meeting at the end of the administration's tenure), it supported the effort of the Europeans to do so, and incurred the wrath of neoconservatives in the process.[11] Andrew McCarthy of the Foundation for the Defense of Democracies criticized the Bush administration for seeking a negotiated outcome and for "offering the kitchen sink to the mullahs in a surely futile plea that they drop their nuclear ambitions."[12]

The neoconservatives argue that military force, rather than negotiations, is the only answer to Iranian nuclear ambitions. They recognize that an Iran with nuclear weapons will change the world as we know it (and very dangerously so), and since there is no other way to prevent it, military force is the only answer. William Kristol of the *Weekly Standard* has advocated immediate military strikes against Iran, asking, "Why wait? Does anyone think a nuclear Iran can be contained? That the current regime will negotiate in good faith? It would be easier to act sooner rather than later. Yes, there would be repercussions—and they would be healthy ones, showing a strong America that has rejected further appeasement."[13]

Others focus less on the nuclear issue and more on regime change as the only answer. As Michael Ledeen has written, American policy has been "based on an illusion: that the Islamic Republic could renounce terrorism, perhaps treat its own people better and ultimately become a normal country. The simple unpleasant truth is that it is hard to find a historical case in which a revolutionary regime has voluntarily and successfully moderated its behavior. Regime change is necessary for that to happen. . . ."[14]

The essence of the neoconservative argument is that revolutionary Iran can never become a "normal country" no matter how much we may wish it; the answer, therefore, is regime change. For the neoconservatives, regime change is not some pipe dream. It is an achievable reality.

Richard Perle, the chairman of the Pentagon's Defense Policy Board's Advisory Committee from 2001 to 2003, writes of how the Islamic Republic has sunk "into political, economic and social decline. Opponents of the regime have been calling for a referendum on whether to continue as an Islamic theocracy or join the world of modern, secular democracies. They are sure of the outcome."[15]

Perle is not suggesting that the mullahs will allow such a referendum; rather, he is citing the unpopularity of the regime and the potential created for undermining or replacing it. Ledeen, too, cites polling that shows the unhappiness of the Iranian public and refers to the many demonstrations and protests against the regime that continue despite tough crackdowns by the government. He goes on to say that the "Iranian people need three things from us to catalyze their wide-ranging protests into an effective revolutionary force: hope, information, and some material support."[16]

Practically speaking, this means, according to Ledeen, that we should broadcast interviews about Shiism into Iran, drawing special attention to Shiite clerics in Iraq who clearly oppose the Ayatollah Khomeini worldview and the nature of the Iranian theocracy. This would demonstrate that the Islamic Republic's version of Shiism is rejected by clerical authorities. In addition, our broadcasts should constantly report "Iranian news"—as people in Isfahan "need to know what is happening in Tehran, Tabriz, and Shiraz, and vice versa."[17] The more the Iranian public knows, the more they may become prone to act. And finally, we should find a way to get what might be described as today's means of mobilizing mass actions (satellite phones, laptops, servers, phone cards, and other electronic communications devices) to those likely to drive such demonstrations: students, teachers, truck drivers, oil and textile workers. Ledeen argues that the final days of the regime are likely to be days of "mass demonstrations and a shutdown of the country's productive enterprises. The latter requires large-scale strikes," and that of course will require "encouraging private enterprises and free trade-union organizations to build strike funds for workers."[18]

Sound fanciful? Ledeen and other neoconservatives are convinced that the regime is vulnerable. The fact that the Islamic Republic arrested a number of Iranian Americans—one of whom was a sixty-seven-year-old grandmother—and held them for nearly ten months in 2007 on charges of espionage suggests that the regime feels vulnerable. None of those arrested believed in subverting or confronting the Iranian regime; all worked on civil society programs, and yet these programs were portrayed as somehow connected to trying to foment a "velvet revolution."[19]

Some specialists on Iran who are not neoconservatives do, in fact, call attention to the Supreme Leader's preoccupation with the "velvet revolutions" of Eastern Europe that spawned abrupt change led by "pro-Western" intellectuals.[20] Iran scholar Patrick Clawson of the Washington Institute for Near East Policy likes to say that Ali Khamenei, the Supreme Leader, worries more about a cultural invasion than a military invasion—"he fears Hollywood more than he fears Washington."[21] Karim Sadjadpour points to Khamenei's concerns about a political and cultural onslaught that would produce cleavages among Iran's political elites and use Western "vice" and cultural influence to undermine traditional society and foment "ethnic and sectarian unrest."[22]

If nothing else, the Iranian leadership's fears of a velvet revolution suggest that the neoconservative arguments about the vulnerabilities of the Iranian regime should not simply be dismissed. Whether, as they argue, the regime can be easily uprooted, however, may be another matter; the subjective fears of a regime do not automatically translate into its teetering on the brink of survival and waiting to be pushed over the edge.

But that imagery of a vulnerable Iranian regime was precisely what was perceived by those making decisions in the Bush administration in May 2003. At that time, the Iranian regime appears to have reached out to the administration with a proposal in the form of a fax on the nuclear issue and the broad array of other differences between America and Iran. Yet it was simply dismissed. Why? What was in the fax?

THE IRANIAN FAX AND THE NEOCONSERVATIVE REASON FOR ITS REJECTION

In May 2003, a few weeks after American forces had removed Saddam Hussein and defeated the Iraqi military, a fax was sent to the State Department with a cover letter from the Swiss ambassador to Iran, Tim Guldimann. Since the United States and Iran do not maintain formal diplomatic relations, the Swiss represent U.S. interests in Iran and act as the official channel used to convey and receive messages from the Iranians.

The Guldimann cover note explained that the accompanying proposal had been approved by the highest authorities in the Iranian system, including the Supreme Leader, Ali Khamenei. The fax laid out a comprehensive proposal for dealing with the differences between the United States and Iran, presenting both Iranian and U.S. aims to be put on the table and the establishment of three working groups on disarmament, regional security, and economic cooperation. The disarmament working group was to create a road map for "full transparency . . . and guarantees to abstain from WMD on the one side [Iran] with access to western technology." The terrorism working group was to work toward a plan for achieving the aims of "enhanced [Iranian] action against al Qaeda" and Iranian "support for Middle Eastern peace"—with the acknowledgment that U.S. aims included the stoppage of material support to Hamas and Islamic Jihad and the transformation of Hizbollah into a "mere political organization in Lebanon." Finally, the economic working group was to develop a road map for the "abolishment of sanctions and solution of frozen assets."[23]

Here was the so-called grand bargain being outlined by the Iranians with each side's aims and purposes laid out in a very clear fashion. For example, the first Iranian aim was to have the United States refrain "from supporting change of the political system by direct interference from outside"; and the first U.S. goal was to have full transparency to ensure that there are "no Iranian endeavors to develop or possess WMD."[24]

The text of the fax was drafted by Sadegh Kharrazi, then Iran's ambassador to France and the nephew of Iran's foreign minister at that time, Kamal Kharrazi. Had the United States been seeking talks and trying to prepare them, this is the kind of agenda we would have proposed to see if the negotiations could be worthwhile. Truth be told, there probably would have been great doubt that such a clear agenda could have been achieved, particularly with working groups and their goals stated so explicitly and with the aim of a public statement outlining the broad areas of agreement to be published after the first meeting. In all likelihood, that might have been seen as more than the traffic would bear.

And yet this is what the Iranians apparently proposed. Why say apparently? Because there are those who believe that only part of the Iranian regime was really behind this proposal.[25] Was the Swiss ambassador exaggerating? We will never know, because the State Department chose to ignore the proposal and to reprimand the Swiss ambassador for overstepping his role as an intermediary in conveying it in the first place.[26]

Maybe Guldimann was exaggerating or, in the words of then deputy secretary of state, Richard Armitage, maybe "the Swiss ambassador in Tehran was so intent . . . on bettering relations between 'the Great Satan,' the United States, and Iran that we came to have some questions about where the Iranian message ended and the Swiss message may begin." But there was no willingness to try to find out or to test the possibilities raised by this proposal.[27] Why? Because, in the words of Richard Haass, who was then the head of the Policy Planning Staff in the State Department, "the bias was toward a policy of regime change."[28] The top Bush administration officials were convinced that "the Iranian government was on the verge of collapse," and the worst thing to do would be to give it prolonged life by negotiating with it.[29] The neoconservative assumptions were guiding the Bush administration at this time and led to the rejection of an initiative by the Iranians at a juncture when they were not spinning centrifuges, not enriching uranium, and not a nuclear power.

The irony is that the Iranians apparently made this proposal because they were afraid that they might be next after Iraq. According to Trita Parsi, an expert at the Carnegie Endowment for International Peace who was talking to Iranian officials (and who subsequently obtained the fax from them), the U.S. military victory in Iraq frightened the Iranians—after all, U.S. forces routed the Iraqi military in three weeks, and this was a force the Iranians had not been able to defeat over the course of an eight-year war. As we will discuss shortly, Sadegh Kharrazi, the drafter of the proposal, lent credence to Parsi's interpretation.[30] The United States had leverage and did not use it because regime change is what the administration sought in Iran, and it read the proposal as an indication that the regime was desperate. In the eyes of the neoconservatives in the administration, the regime was on the brink of falling and only our engagement could save it. We cannot guarantee that negotiations with Iran in 2003 would have been successful, but would it have hurt the United States to probe and find out? We did not engage the regime. It is still here; and it is enriching uranium at an ever increasing pace.

We will return to a discussion of the Iranian motivations for the initiative and what it tells us about Islamic Republic leaders, but first it makes sense to look more closely at the assumptions behind the neoconservative mythology and the basic problems with them.

THE FALLACIES OF THE NEOCONSERVATIVE MYTHS ABOUT IRAN

For the neoconservatives, changing the regime in Iran is both necessary and achievable. They may not be wrong that Iranian leaders are aware of their vulnerabilities, but there is a big leap between that and regime change. There is no automaticity. For several decades now, it has been a staple of much neoconservative thinking that the Iranian regime is just waiting to be pushed and it will collapse.

And yet the Islamic Republic is still around. It is about to turn thirty years old. Yes, there are signs that it is not popular. But it has also demonstrated staying power. While the neoconservatives could be right, there is also a strong possibility that they are wrong.

The same people who told us that Iraq would be a cakewalk are also telling us that it will not take much to produce regime change in Iran. So by all means do not engage Iran. On the contrary, work harder to subvert it.

But since they were so wrong about Iraq being a cakewalk, should we not be questioning their assumptions on Iran? And if they are also wrong about Iran, what would be some of the costs of pursuing regime change? Or, to take another of their assumptions, what might be the costs of using force against Iran to prevent it from going nuclear? In either case, the costs are likely to be far higher than the neoconservatives seem either to acknowledge or to consider.

Ironically, what seems to guide the neoconservatives is an almost fatalistic optimism. Because America's purposes are right, and its power and obligations great, our success is nearly ordained. The Bush administration was governed by this mind-set in going into Iraq; it acted on the assumption that when Saddam Hussein fell, everything would fall into place and not fall apart. Its assessment of the situation in Iraq was faith-based, not reality-based.

On Iran, the neoconservative assumptions seem very similar. Just push and there will be an unleashing of the masses, and they will simply force a collapse of the regime—much as the shah's regime collapsed in the face of mass demonstrations and a massive shutdown of the society.

But what if the will of the mullahs and those who are ideologically committed to the regime—the Revolutionary Guard and the Basij religious militias—is unrelenting? What if they are truly determined to try to hold on to power? Maybe their power and hold can be eroded, but it is hard to predict with any certainty how quickly this could take place or how and when this would be translated into the end of the regime. What is not hard to predict with certainty is the danger of trying to bring down a regime that possesses nuclear weapons.

And here there is a basic danger that the neoconservative thinkers seemingly fail to consider: the Islamic Republic is likely to possess nuclear weapons before the regime can be changed. Context is everything. Time is not a neutral variable. We cannot know how quickly the regime can be changed—and the neoconservatives cannot predict this with any reliability—but we can predict that Iran will achieve nuclear weapons capability once it is able to accumulate enough fissionable material. While the guesses vary on this, the Iranians, according to one expert who has typically been conservative in his estimates, are now making considerable advances and, if they go all out, are likely to be in a position to assemble a nuclear bomb by the end of 2009.[31] Even if this estimate is too optimistic, the Iranian ability to produce nuclear weapons is bound to proceed far more quickly than our efforts to produce regime change. Indeed, the more the Iranian leaders see that regime change is the American objective, the more they will have a stake in accelerating their efforts to go nuclear, if for no other reason than believing that nuclear weapons will afford the regime greater protection against overt and covert threats to it.

Worse, should the Iranians develop nuclear weapons, the prospect of their use goes up if the regime believes they have little to lose. The most dangerous combination for the region and the world is for the Iranians to have nukes and to see us actively trying to subvert the regime. In such circumstances, our threats to Iran of the consequences of using such weapons are likely to be much less impressive to them—after all, in their eyes we are trying to destroy them in any case. Conversely, they may choose in such circumstances to threaten the use of such weapons as a lever to get us to desist from all such efforts to subvert them.

Might this not get all of Iran's neighbors pressuring us to reach an accommodation with the regime rather than continuing to provoke it? It is hard to escape the conclusion that the neoconservative assumption about regime change and its efficacy makes less and less sense the closer the Iranians get to having nuclear weapons. The desire to have a different Iranian regime may become greater, but the capability to achieve it is likely to decrease and become increasingly dangerous.

To be sure, that could argue for another neoconservative position: the need to use military force against the burgeoning Iranian nuclear capability before it is too late. Precisely because it is too dangerous to have the Islamic Republic with nuclear weapons if regime change is not possible in the near term, those like William Kristol and Norman Podhoretz believe that force must be used sooner rather than later. While others, such as Michael Ledeen, continue to believe that regime change without overt military intervention is the better option, the Kristol-Podhoretz school of thought believes that waiting is not an option. They may well be right about the dangers of Iran going nuclear, but once again one sees an instinct to downplay the costs of such an act. Kristol's comment noted above acknowledged that there would be repercussions, but they would be good repercussions.

Yet there are surely many repercussions that will not be good. The costs of using force against the Iranians cannot be wished away, much as the costs were wished away before the Bush administration went to war in Iraq. Iran, after all, has many retaliatory options, beginning in Iraq. The Iranians can make life (and particularly the lives of U.S. soldiers) in Iraq far more difficult. They can dramatically increase the flow of weaponry and explosives into Iraq and do much more to foment the militias they support to attack American forces. We have seen only a small token of what the Iranians could do toward our forces and toward destabilizing Iraq—and don't think that Iraq's government is not fully mindful of how much more Iran can do to destabilize Iraq if it truly seeks to do so. (Note how careful the Iraqi government has been not to confront Iran over the provisions of arms, monies, and matériel to militias, including the so-called special units of the Mahdi Army.)

Beyond making life far worse in Iraq, the Iranians could choose to open up northern and southern fronts against Israel with Hizbollah and Hamas. Hizbollah may be far more of an Iranian creature than Hamas— with Iranian commentary describing Hizbollah as an appendage of the Islamic Republic[32]—but even Hamas's agenda could be served by ratcheting up pressure against Israel out of Gaza; Iran has now supplied Hamas with close to a hundred longer-range rockets capable of hitting deeper into Israel.[33] Of course, this number and Hamas's overall capability pale in comparison to Hizbollah's nearly forty thousand rockets, of which large numbers can now reach Tel Aviv and even Dimona, the location of Israel's nuclear reactor.[34]

In addition, Iran has several other deeply troubling options for destabilizing the region and the international economy. It can increase terrorism and use terror to threaten its Arab neighbors; it could fire rockets at key Saudi or Kuwaiti or UAE oil facilities or terminals. Even if Iranian attacks did not put them out of commission, the risk premiums and the oil futures markets might easily drive up the price of oil again and, in so doing, compound our already severe economic crisis.

None of this is to say that the costs to Iran might not be very daunting. The more extreme the Iranian responses, the more we could attack the Iranian economic and transportation infrastructure without hitting its oil and natural gas sector. Perhaps such attacks or their prospect will deter Iranian escalation. Perhaps the Iranian leaders will fear the consequences of such attacks. But can we count on such attacks weakening their hold on power, or strengthening it? Will such American attacks foster a nationalist backlash from Iranians coming to the instinctive defense of the homeland and generating a broad coalescence around the mullahs and their hold on power?

Here again, the answer is not necessarily self-evident. Maybe it is also not self-evident to the Iranian leadership. What is clear, however, is that the repercussions from U.S. military strikes against Iran create all sorts of unknowns that are bound to be anything but good. This does not even begin to touch on what could be a wider emotional backlash in Arab and Muslim countries against our attacks. This could be widespread, particularly if the conflict drags on and large numbers of Iranian civilian casualties result. Given the already hostile view that many throughout the Muslim world now hold of us—in no small part because of the war in Iraq—a war with Iran might trigger much more enduring anger toward the United States. Even if al-Qaeda and Iran are not partners, there can be little doubt that al-Qaeda exploits anger and frustration to build its following among Muslims who may already be prone to believe al-Qaeda's propaganda that we are at war with Islam.

It is easy to see all the things that could go very wrong in the aftermath of a military strike against a burgeoning Iranian nuclear capability. Still, it is also possible that more limited strikes and large forces and options held in reserve could temper the Iranian retaliation. The Iranian leadership might be deterred from widespread responses if only limited strikes against nuclear facilities were launched but with the threat of much more systematic and intensive attacks likely to follow should Iran respond or escalate.

Moreover, the context in which attacks take place could also heavily influence the nature of the response worldwide to our actions. In this sense, the regional and global reaction to U.S. military action against Iran could look very different if we had first conducted our own direct negotiations with Iran—and the Iranians had rejected all reasonable efforts to forge an agreement that would provide them with civil nuclear power and a variety of other political and economic benefits in return for unmistakably giving up once and for all their pursuit of nuclear weapons.

One last question to ask about the consequences of using force against the Iranian nuclear facilities is what the effect will be on Iran's nuclear aspirations. The risks and dangers associated with Iranian responses might ultimately be deemed acceptable if the Iranian nuclear program was being destroyed once and for all. But that, too, seems very unlikely. The Iranians have now developed the know-how, and that cannot be destroyed. Though costly, the infrastructure could be rebuilt, and the Iranian nuclear efforts would probably become far more covert in the aftermath of military strikes against them. At most, such attacks would probably set back the program several years. Perhaps neoconservatives would argue the utility of buying time on the grounds that the opportunity for regime change could then be exploited without the inherent dangers of trying to change a regime that already has nukes.

But even this argument falls victim to the wishful-thinking character of most of the neoconservative assumptions. Indeed, as noted above, there is the very real possibility that a military strike could trigger a nationalist backlash that strengthens and doesn't weaken the regime.

In the end, the risks of using military action to forestall an Iranian nuclear program need to be weighed against the risks of having to live with an Iran with nuclear weapons. As we saw in the last chapter, those risks are profound and cannot be wished away.

It is not only the neoconservatives who are guided by an almost fatalist wishful thinking. The realists, too, assume away the threat of a nuclear Iran, too prepared to ignore what makes Iran different from the Soviet Union and what makes the current regional and international circumstances different from the conditions that characterized the bipolar Cold War era.

Yet a desire to avoid force as a first option based on wariness of unintended consequences could easily signal a lack of American will. Regardless of the options we pursue, it is essential that the Iranians not perceive an absence of United States resolve. Indeed, if the story of the 2003 fax tells us anything, it is that it was the fear of American force that may have led Tehran to a more moderate position.

Thus, the threat of military force could be significant. Ultimately, much could depend on whether force is used as an instrument of first resort or is reserved as a possible last resort. If force is utilized before diplomatic options are explored, it delegitimizes us in the international arena. Yet if used as a last resort, it will appear far more legitimate and the consequences could be different. Regardless, one thing is clear: an Iran that acquires a nuclear weapons capability would materially change the balance of power in the Middle East, emboldening radicals and intimidating moderates and creating risks of nuclear proliferation to nonstate actors.

If we cannot live with an Iran with nukes, and yet military actions create a wide array of intended and unintended (and dangerous) consequences, is there not a third way? Is it not possible to dissuade the Iranians from going nuclear? Neoconservatives are certain that there is no way to dissuade Iranians from going nuclear—and, of course, given how far the Iranians have now advanced down the road of nuclear development, they may be right.

However, even such a leading proponent of regime change as Michael Ledeen has explained how the Islamic Republic has adjusted its behavior when it felt the costs of not doing so were too high. Ledeen points to Khomeini's words on "swallowing the bitter pill" of having to accept the end of the war with Iraq in 1988—an end he accepted, according to Ledeen, because of a combination of losses (twenty thousand Iranian soldiers being killed by Iraqi nerve gas and other conventional military defeats) and a series of U.S. actions, in response to Iranian mines and threats to our naval forces in the Persian Gulf, that resulted in the sinking of two Iranian frigates and several small speedboats, the downing of an Iranian F-4 fighter aircraft, the destruction of three Iranian oil platforms, and the shooting down of an Iranian civilian airliner (which the Iranians assumed was not accidental). Khomeini, Ledeen argues, saw the losses and perceived U.S. involvement as leaving him little choice but to end the war.[35]

In other words, perceived costs altered Iranian behavior. Not surprisingly, others who are not neoconservatives argue that diplomatic and economic pressures and incentives can moderate Iranian behavior. Ray Takeyh explains that the Iranian policies of assassinating dissidents living in Europe and supporting opposition forces in the Gulf sheikdoms reached a high point in the early 1990s. But these policies were reversed when, in response to the conviction of Iranian agents for the assassination of Kurdish leaders in Germany, Europeans withdrew envoys and Germany imposed trade restrictions in 1997, and the Saudis and others made the end of Iranian support for opposition groups a condition for normalizing relations.[36]

The Iranian fax is a more contemporary example of the regime signaling its readiness to change its behavior. In this case, the Iranians seemingly offered to address all U.S. concerns—on nuclear weapons, on terror, on opposition to peace and support for Hamas and Hizbollah—in return for our meeting their concerns on regime change, recognition of their place in the region, civil nuclear power, an end to economic boycotts, and full economic relations. Sadegh Kharrazi, the main drafter of the proposal, gave a speech in 2007 in which he explained the thinking behind the faxed letter that was conveyed to the Bush administration. He said:

> [I]n 2003, there was a wall of mistrust between Iran and America and *in any second there was the possibility for an American attack!* For that reason with my suggestion the 8th government wrote a letter to America and announced *our agreements with some of America's policies in the Middle East such as peace in Palestine and the need for transformation of Hizbollah of Lebanon to a political party and also making the nuclear activities of Iran more transparent* . . . but the wall of mistrust between America and Iran was too high and the Americans did not even consider the letter [emphasis added]."[37]

Here is an extraordinary admission that this far-reaching proposal resulted far less from the expectation or prospect of some inducement than from the reality of Iranian fears. Iranian leaders feared they might be the next targets after Iraq. They surely did not mourn the removal of Saddam Hussein (who in eight years of war imposed such horrendous costs on the Islamic Republic), but, as another Iranian official said at the time, "The fact that Saddam Hussein was toppled in twenty-one days is something that should concern all countries in the region."[38]

It certainly concerned the Iranians—and those concerns produced an apparent readiness to strike a bargain with America in which the Islamic Republic's leadership was prepared to alter its behavior fundamentally both on the nuclear issue and its support for terror. To be sure, it would receive important benefits related to regime acceptance and acknowledgment of its place in any regional security arrangements. But that is the essence of negotiations—each side adjusts behavior and receives something for doing so. Let us be clear: at this time, it was perceived American leverage and Iranian concerns about that leverage (and the potential for very direct U.S. military action) that led to the Iranian offer.

The neoconservatives might well argue that the Iranian offer was just a tactic, that the Iranians were trying to "buy off" a threat and thus their adjustments in behavior would have been temporary and lasted only until they thought American leaders were no longer paying attention. Perhaps the neoconservatives are right—perhaps the hostility of the leaders of the Iranian regime ensures that all adjustments will be tactical.

Still, the readiness to respond to pressure suggests that Iranian behavior can be influenced and that their leaders might find it in their interests to defer their nuclear ambitions if they see the price as being too high and the gains of staying on their current path too limited. Ray Takeyh argues that Iran is an essentially pragmatic power that bases its foreign policy on radical revolutionary values.[39] The combination of basic pragmatism as it relates to the regime's core interests plus a continuing revolutionary set of values means that both tendencies will play themselves out in Iranian behaviors.

The neoconservatives miss this reality because they only see the revolutionary impulses that drive the Iranian leadership. But the reality is more complex. In fact, Islamic ideology, national interests, and factional politics not only produce a strange alchemy but almost guarantee that Iranian foreign policy will rarely move in a linear fashion. As we have seen, the Iranian leadership will adjust its behavior, but one also has to shape policy in a way that takes account of the balance of forces in that leadership.

There are certainly those in the leadership who will never reconcile themselves to the United States and who favor confrontation, believing that confrontation justifies greater controls domestically and preserves ideological zeal and purity. Anoush Ehteshami, a seasoned observer of the Iranian political scene, has written about what he describes as the "Iranian neo-conservatives"—a constituency in the leadership that he says is closely associated with Iran's security apparatus and the radical factions of the clerical establishment. In his words, their ideological zeal drives them and they are keen "to export the fruits of Iran's Islamic revolution to the rest of the region and beyond."[40]

Ruhollah Hosseinian, someone who is an Iranian hardliner, has stated that Iran's ideological commitments guarantee problems with the Western world: "We should also not have the false belief that the world imperialists will be happy with us if we stay true to our revolutionary ideals."[41] In other words, confrontation with the United States and its allies is inevitable, and if so, all the more reason to have a nuclear capability. One Iranian commentary seems implicitly to make the point that Iran needs a nuclear capability for its own reasons of deterrence: "In the contemporary world, it is obvious that having access to advanced weapons [nukes] shall cause deterrence and therefore security and will neutralize the evil wishes of great powers to attack other nations and countries."[42] Yahya Rahim Safavi, the former head of the IRGC, was much more explicit in this regard: "Can we withstand America's threats and domineering attitudes with a policy of détente? Will we be able to protect the Islamic Republic from international Zionism by signing conventions banning the proliferation of chemical and nuclear weapons?"[43]

For the Iranian hardliners, nuclear weapons clearly have a considerable attraction, and they won't be easily dissuaded from developing them. For this constituency, it is essentially an article of faith that the Islamic Republic must challenge the world and not be integrated into it. But there are many others in the Iranian elite who see the world and Iran's needs very differently. They see unacceptably high costs in being excluded from the international system—and dissuasion might work with them.

For these members of the Iranian elite, survival of the regime is paramount. They seek to preserve the system, and they understand that having a connection to the international financial system and the global economy is essential. And they seem to understand well that confronting the outside world will isolate and not integrate Iran internationally. Consider the words of Hassan Rouhani: "Foreign policy does not mean chanting slogans. Foreign policy does not mean using fiery words. Foreign policy does not mean increasing threats against us. We cannot say we want to be developed but, at the same time, we don't want to interact with the international community."[44] Similarly, the Iranian economist Saeed Leylaz, writing in the Iranian daily *Kargozaran*, explained that Iran's economic problems would continue so long as it was isolated when it needed imports from abroad, even declaring, "We say nuclear energy is our right. The problem is rooted in the contradiction between our diplomacy and economic policies."[45]

The Supreme Leader Ali Khamenei, Iran's most important decision maker, seems less mindful of being integrated into the international system. On the contrary, he often seems preoccupied with ensuring Iran's self-sufficiency in order to guarantee that Iran is not dependent on the outside world.[46] Yet his decision-making style is typically consensual, favoring some basic agreement among the different forces within the elite. Moreover, at least according to the Swiss ambassador to Iran, he authorized the comprehensive proposal in the May 2003 fax that the Swiss conveyed to the Bush administration. He seemingly saw the need to adjust Iran's behavior given its situation and the danger that was perceived coming from Washington in the aftermath of its defeat of the Iraqi army.

Khamenei almost seems to embody the conflicting revolutionary and pragmatic tendencies that one sees within the Iranian elite. But his suspicion of the United States is deep-seated, and he is convinced that America cannot accept an independent-minded Islamic government: "The United States government has not lost its insatiable greed for domination of our country."[47] Such perceptions also make him leery of giving in to American pressures, particularly since he believes the U.S. government is interested in changing not Iranian behaviors but the Iranian regime. Khamenei thus fears where concessions to the United States are likely to lead:

If the officials of a country get daunted by the bullying of the arrogant powers, and, as a result, begin to retreat from their own principles and make concessions to those powers, *these concessions will never come to an end!* First, they will pressure you into recognizing such and such an illegitimate regime, then they will force you not to call your constitution Islamic! They will never stop obtaining concessions from you through pressure and intimidation, and you will be forced to retreat from your values and principles step by step! Indeed, the end to U.S. pressure and intimidation will only come when Iranian officials announce they are ready to compromise Islam and their popular government of the Islamic Republic, and the United States may bring to power in the country whoever it wants![48]

Khamenei made this statement at the end of May 2003. He made it in the aftermath of the U.S. rejection of Iran's comprehensive proposal offered at the beginning of that month. If his words mean anything, they mean that the administration's rejection confirmed his views about the danger of making concessions to us; after all, any concessions could never go far enough to satisfy us, were bound to be seen as a sign of the regime's weakness, and, if anything, would simply add to the American impulse to push for regime change. No doubt the U.S. rejection probably also did much to discredit those in the leadership who had pushed for such compromises.

There are certainly Western specialists on Iran who believe that the hard-liners in the elite are strengthened by Western pressures and their more pragmatic opponents are strengthened when there are signs of our readiness to compromise. Sounds good in theory, but it is hard to point to examples in the nuclear negotiations in which our readiness to compromise has strengthened the hand of the pragmatists. And yet it is hard to deny the effect that the rejection of the fax proposal appears to have had on Khamenei.

Maybe what we are seeing is that the *context* in which proposals are made or rejected is critical. In May 2003, the Iranians were seeing the application of U.S. power in Iraq and were scared about what it might mean for them. They were prepared to make far-reaching proposals that clearly would have required basic changes in their own behaviors. Had the Bush administration responded, it is possible that our relationship with Iran—and certainly its nuclear efforts—would not only be at a very different point today, but also we might not be in a position of having to address the prospect of an Iran with nuclear weapons any time soon.

The problem today is that the context has changed. The Iranians are far less fearful of the United States, having seen us become bogged down in Iraq with a great deal of domestic criticism about the war. Apart from having less reason to be concerned about our threats, their own position and leverage in the region seem to have grown with Hizbollah's greater weight in Lebanon, Hamas's increased strength in Gaza, and Iran's troublemaking capacities in Iraq. Does all this suggest that Iran would have less interest in U.S. offers? The answer probably depends, at least in part, on how far-reaching the offers are. The more the Iranians have to fear about the consequences of turning down far-reaching offers, the more they may find the offers meaningful.

In this sense, the keys to affecting the behavior of those in the Iranian elite may lie not only in the international context but also in the domestic one within Iran. We have already seen how external fears appear to have generated a readiness to change behavior in May 2003. Could domestic pressures make inducements from the outside much harder to resist? Could the costs of forgoing offers that clearly serve Iran's interests create internal pressures to be responsive, particularly if the economic conditions in the country were seriously deteriorating? It is worth noting that some Iranians have already pointed to the high costs of Iran's nuclear program and what Iran is losing by pursuing it. Ahmad Shirzad, an Iranian physicist, raised the opportunity costs of pursuing the nuclear agenda at a time when Iran was experiencing power outages in the winter of 2008. According to Shirzad, the $5 billion spent on the nuclear program could have been better spent on developing Iran's rich natural gas deposits.[49]

Even the Supreme Leader, with all his hostility to the United States, in early 2008 suggested that relations with America might prove possible in the future if they served the regime's interests: "Cutting ties with America is among our basic policies. However, we have never said that the relations will remain severed forever . . . relations with America [have] no benefit for the Iranian nation for now. Undoubtedly, the day [that] relations with America prove beneficial for the Iranian nation I will be the first one to approve of that."[50]

In other words, the domestic and international context could well affect the Iranian calculus. The neoconservatives fail to grasp this possibility. They are too wedded to their myths that it is pointless to engage the Islamic Republic and that Iran can never be dissuaded from its pursuit of nuclear weapons. As such, they operate on the assumptions that regime change and/or the use of force are the only options—and these assumptions could once again lead us down a dangerously misguided path, particularly when dissuasion may yet be a possibility.

However, if our discussion of the realist assumptions has told us anything, it is that dissuasion and even deterrence will not be easy. The approach to each must be carefully considered and developed. Even then, there is no certainty of success—Iran may be truly committed to having a nuclear weapons capability. Somehow, any approach must recognize the twin revolutionary and pragmatic tendencies that pulse through the Iranian elite. And it must find a way to affect the balance between these tendencies so that those who are more pragmatic alter the Iranian policies from within.

In the next chapter, we offer an approach for how best to deal with Iran and its burgeoning nuclear capability. We said at the outset of these chapters on Iran that we are facing a crossroads; it is time to pick a new path that avoids the inherent pitfalls built into the mind-sets of the neoconservatives and realists and the policy prescriptions that follow from them.

Chapter Nine

A NEW APPROACH FOR
DEALING WITH IRAN

Fashioning the right approach to Iran is no simple matter. The realists and the neoconservatives respond to different elements of the Iranian regime. The realists essentially focus on the pragmatists, while the neoconservatives are riveted on the radical revolutionary side of the regime. The mind-set of each captures one aspect of the Iranian reality but misses a part of what shapes Iranian behavior. If it is to succeed, American strategy must be informed by the dual impulses and tendencies that guide Iranian policy.

In this chapter, our aim is to identify the approach that gives us the best chance to alter Iran's behavior. If there are competing tendencies and constituencies that influence Iranian behavior, our approach must take account of both sets of impulses. As with any effort at statecraft, if we are to affect Iran's behavior (and the often competing elements that shape it), we must understand Iran's vulnerabilities and our points of leverage. The neoconservatives tend to look at Iran's vulnerabilities only as a basis on which to change the regime; the realists tend to look at them as a reason not to be fearful of Iran, believing that we—more than they—need to adjust behavior.

Yet we have a profound need to alter Iran's behavior on its nuclear program and in the region, and our discussion of how to do so will examine Iran's vulnerabilities and how best to play upon them. But no approach to Iran, no policy that can work, takes place in a vacuum. We need to look again at the context in which we must operate. We need to consider why our stakes are so high in getting the policy right. We need to review both what the Bush administration tried to do and how its policy evolved from what might be described as a weak neoconservative posture to a weak realist effort—never fully embracing either approach but at least beginning a process of working with others internationally. And we need to look at the efforts of the international community both to engage the Iranians and to sanction them, if for no other reason than to understand what has been tried and found wanting. Only then will we be well positioned to offer our judgment of which option is most likely to work, the key assumptions that guide it, and why it stands the best chance of success.

OUR STAKES IN CHANGING IRAN'S BEHAVIOR

Iran has certainly posed challenges and threats to America's interests since the Iranian Revolution in 1979. But in the 1980s, Iran was consumed and drained by eight and a half years of war with Iraq. Even after the 1991 U.S. defeat of Saddam Hussein in the first Gulf War, Iraq remained a threat and a counterweight to Iran. But that counterweight disappeared with the American removal of Saddam's regime in 2003. And today Iran seems to be on a roll in the region, effectively challenging America's interests throughout the Middle East. From Iraq to Lebanon to the Palestinian Authority and Israel, Iran's policies are not only at odds with ours, but seem designed to frustrate and undermine U.S. goals and partners. Listen to Arab governments in the area in private, and one hears—as we often do—laments about Iran's growing strength in the region and its ability to exploit militancy and anger in the Middle East to put these regimes on the defensive. The fact that the complaints about Iran are made more in private than in public says something about Iran's coercive capacity in the region already.

Nuclear weapons capability would surely add to Iran's ability to twist arms in the region. Arab and Israeli leaders with whom we have spoken explain that should Iran possess nuclear weapons, they fear that the landscape of the region will be fundamentally altered. Iranian leaders, they argue, will feel emboldened to use terror and terror groups to threaten or subvert others in the area, including particularly those who might be inclined to pursue peace with Israel, knowing that their nukes provide an umbrella of protection or a built-in deterrent against responses.

To be sure, Israelis are worried not only about an increasing Iranian coercive capability and the dampening effect it will have on those in the

Arab world who would contemplate the compromises necessary for making peace. They see an Iranian nuclear weapons capability as posing an existential threat to the state of Israel. Tell the Israelis that Iran will act rationally, knowing that Israel can retaliate with a devastating nuclear counterstrike if Iran or its proxies ever used nuclear or dirty bombs against Israel, and they are not reassured. For starters, they point to the language of Iranian president Ahmadinejad, who has denied the Holocaust and Israel's right to exist; declared that Israel (or "the Zionist entity," as he refers to it) will be "wiped off the face of the map"; and proclaimed that the countdown to its destruction is close at hand. Israelis take small comfort from those who are seen as more pragmatic than Ahmadinejad in the Iranian leadership, such as former Iranian president Akbar Hashemi Rafsanjani. Even he, they point out, has said that Iran could absorb many nuclear bombs and survive, while Israel, given its small size, could not survive even one.

It is not just Israel's small geographic size and concentrated population that worry Israelis. It is the ideological-messianic fervor of at least some in the Iranian leadership. The Israelis question whether that segment of the Iranian leadership (which believes in the apocalyptic return of the Hidden Imam) can actually be deterred and believe that they cannot run the risk of trying to find out. For Israel, the issue extends beyond the ideological bent of the regime. Iran refuses to negotiate with Israel, since it does not recognize Israel's existence. Consequently, Israelis do not believe they have a diplomatic option even if they wanted one. As a result, the risk of an Israeli preemptive military action to blunt or delay the Iranian nuclear program is quite high. Shaul Mofaz, former head of the Israeli military and a member of the Israeli cabinet, has gone so far as to declare, "If Iran continues with its program for developing nuclear weapons, we will attack it. The sanctions are ineffective."[1]

That alone might argue for an intensive American effort to prevent Iran from developing or acquiring a nuclear weapons capability. Only if Israeli policymakers believe that U.S. and European policymakers are likely to be far more effective in preventing the Islamic Republic from acquiring nuclear weapons will the Israelis be less inclined to strike Iran independently. As important as it is to avoid such an Israeli action, given all its possible consequences, there are other reasons to prevent Iran from going nuclear. For one thing, the fear of increased Iranian coercive capabilities—particularly as they relate to being more aggressive in pushing a Shia agenda or even subversion in states like Saudi Arabia—is likely to produce a perceived need for a counter nuclear capability. In chapter 7, we spoke of the likelihood that Saudi Arabia would feel the need to acquire its own nuclear capability, and if it did so, it would almost certainly have a cascading affect in the Middle East. From this standpoint, Iran going nuclear creates the very real prospect that the Middle East will become a nuclear-armed region, and the last thing we should want is for this region—characterized by conflicts and instability, with dangerous nonstate actors and great potential for war through miscalculation and escalation—to be filled with states possessing nuclear weapons. Not only is this a frightening specter, but if states in the Middle East go nuclear, what is the likely effect on the nuclear nonproliferation regime more generally? If the prohibitions on going nuclear break down in the Middle East, will they not disappear elsewhere? Will a nuclear Middle East not spell the end of the NPT? And with its likely demise, will we not see the end of one of the few international pillars that has truly preserved stability?

The answers to these questions are unfortunately self-evident and reveal why our stakes in preventing Iran from going nuclear are so high. The Bush administration certainly understood this, and its policy was to prevent it.

THE EVOLUTION OF THE BUSH ADMINISTRATION'S APPROACH

During the first term of the Bush administration, there was never a single, clear-cut policy toward Iran. Did we want regime change, or a change in the behavior of the regime? There were two schools of thought, and President Bush never made a choice between the two. Consequently, there were elements of both present in the policy. For example, we would engage Iran on Afghanistan, but then include them in the "axis of evil." Similarly, leading officials in the State Department were prepared to contemplate a "grand bargain" and engagement as the way to resolve the nuclear issue, even as those in the Pentagon and the White House rejected any readiness to make a deal with the Iranian government—emphasizing that any such deal would come at the expense of the true democrats in Iran and prolong the life of this unsavory regime. These neoconservative elements held sway within the administration at the time of the faxed Iranian proposal and mandated its rejection.

The basic problem for the regime changers was that the pace of Iran's nuclear developments was certain to outstrip their efforts to promote the undoing of the regime. They might oppose any engagement with Iran; they might favor only pressure on Iran; and they might hope that Iran would be next after Iraq. But in the meantime Iran was proceeding with its nuclear program, and the regime changers were unable to alter that reality.

However, British, French, and German engagement with Iran gave those in the administration who favored engagement a vehicle to support. At one point, the EU-3's efforts seemed to be producing results as the Iranians agreed to suspend their program to complete the nuclear fuel cycle in return for seeing what inducements the Europeans might provide. The Bush administration was kept informed of the European efforts. In fact, the British, French, and Germans sought to coordinate fully with the administration, realizing that Iranians wanted not only what Europe could provide but also key "goods" from the United States: the unfreezing of Iranian assets, lifting of our unilateral sanctions, and specific security assurances.

But formal coordination (not to mention any U.S. incentives for Iran) was beyond what the administration was prepared to undertake in its first term. The regime changers (that is, the neoconservatives) had sufficient influence to ensure that no U.S. assurances or inducements could be offered and no direct coordination or planning with the EU-3 was possible. That began to change in the second term. Even during the transition between terms, President Bush began "signaling to foreign leaders visiting him in the Oval Office that he knew much had gone wrong in his first term, and he had empowered Rice to put a new emphasis on consultation and teamwork with allies."[2] He echoed this theme during his February 2005 trip to Europe, and after that trip he authorized coordination with the EU-3 on Iranian policy and permitted them to offer limited incentives to the Iranians on America's behalf.

There would be no direct U.S. engagement with Iran on the nuclear issue, but the United States now began to coordinate with the Europeans on all steps toward Iran. The essence of the approach was to let the Europeans talk to Iran, warn the Iranians of the consequences, including sanctions to be imposed if they persisted in their nuclear efforts, and offer limited inducements to the Iranians to cease their program. Interestingly, the Iranian resumption of conversion of uranium ore to uranium gas (hexafluoride) did not stop the United States from continuing to coordinate with the Europeans—even when the British, French, and Germans resumed their talks with Iran. The Europeans had warned the Iranians in the summer of 2005 that the conversion process was a redline and if they resumed it, the Europeans would stop negotiations with Iran on the nuclear issue. The Europeans held the line for nearly six months but then relented; nonetheless, when the trio backed off and resumed their direct talks, notwithstanding the unabated Iranian conversion efforts, the United States maintained their readiness to coordinate directly.

With the Europeans in the lead, the administration worked to build an international consensus on the need for Iran to stop its nuclear developments and the need to isolate it if it did not. In fact, the administration established a regular coordinating forum of six, with the British, French, Germans, Russians, and Chinese. Early efforts focused principally on the IAEA, but also involved the European Union's talks with Iran, led by the EU's representative, Javier Solana.

Iranian nonresponsiveness to the IAEA led the agency to refer the matter to the United Nations Security Council in early 2006, setting the stage for a discussion of sanctions. The administration scaled back its own desire to press immediately for sanctions (and later for those sanctions to be far-reaching) in order to preserve a united front against Iran. The administration also took two additional steps to set the stage for punitive sanctions. First, Secretary of State Condoleezza Rice announced in the spring of 2006 that the United States would talk directly to Iran on the nuclear issue if Iran would suspend its enrichment activities. Second, shortly thereafter, in June, the administration signed off on an incentives package (which included light-water reactors for Iran) that the Europeans offered the Iranians in return for stopping enrichment. The Iranians were given until the end of July 2006 to respond to this incentive package, with the proviso that if they did not suspend enrichment, they would become subject to Chapter VII, or mandatory and enforceable Security Council sanctions.

The Iranians rejected the European offer, claiming that enrichment was their right, that they could not be pressured into surrendering it, and that sanctions would not hurt Iran but would reduce its readiness to cooperate with the IAEA. In fact, the Iranians rejected all proposals designed to get them to give up their goal of completing the nuclear fuel cycle from conversion through uranium enrichment.³ Yet even after Iran's rejection of the European inducements package, there was no rush to adopt sanctions. Serious discussions of sanctions did not commence until the fall in the Security Council, and it was not until December 23, 2006, that UNSC resolution 1737 was adopted.

INTERNATIONAL COMMUNITY EFFORTS TO CURB THE IRANIAN NUCLEAR PROGRAM

This first resolution, 1737, fell far short of what the administration sought. It wanted the resolution effectively to render Iran isolated politically, psychologically, and economically. It wanted financial institutions in both the public and private sectors not to be able to do business with Iran; it wanted to impose a travel ban on any Iranian officials or those tied to the government. It wanted the resolution to squeeze Iran and play on its economic vulnerabilities—particularly its dependence on outside investment and the need for considerable technology transfer for its decaying oil and natural gas infrastructure. It also wanted to play on the Iranian self-image that its standing and importance could never make it a pariah like North Korea.

But neither Russia nor China was prepared to go this far. Both argued against putting Iran in the corner, and both sought to protect their commercial dealings with Iran. Rather than lose the possibility of producing a Chapter VII sanctions resolution against the Iranian nuclear program, the administration (and the Europeans) accepted a resolution with much less impact or reach. The resolution focused narrowly on imposing penalties or restrictions on the nuclear and missile-related industries in Iran by prohibiting the sale of equipment or technologies that could contribute to either the Iran enrichment activities or nuclear weapons delivery systems. To add bite to these restrictions, the resolution also went after leading Iranian companies and individuals involved in these activities, mandating that the assets or funds of a total of ten Iranian entities or companies as well as eleven individuals be frozen. Finally, the resolution not only created a committee of all the Security Council members to follow up on the resolution (while empowering it to add Iranian entities or individuals subject to an asset freeze as it saw fit), but also asked the director general of the IAEA to report back in sixty days on whether Iran had complied with the resolution and suspended its enrichment and reprocessing activities.[4]

While President Ahmadinejad was dismissive of the resolution, he became subject to much more biting criticism within the leadership, with one newspaper associated with Supreme Leader Ali Khamenei even suggesting that Ahmadinejad's posture on the nuclear issue was designed to divert attention from his failed domestic policies.[5] From this standpoint, the significance of the resolution was less the immediate impact it had on Iran's economy—which, after all, was not targeted—and more the concerns it raised about the possibility of much greater costs being imposed over time if Iran did not cease its nuclear activities. In this connection, the weakness of the Iranian economy, made far worse by mismanagement and Ahmadinejad's misguided policies, created very real vulnerabilities that raised the risks of proceeding with the nuclear program over the opposition of the international community.

Had there been a follow-up resolution that began to restrict Iranian access to credit, the choices for the Iranian leadership could have been drawn far more sharply. The sixty-day reporting requirement created an obvious clock to begin working on the next resolution when Iran failed to comply—and such work did begin. Once again the process was slow and complicated within the Security Council, and once again the administration opted to accept a second resolution that failed to go after the Iranian economy but did preserve an international consensus against the Iranian nuclear ambitions. Resolution 1747 was adopted on March 24, 2007; it expanded the number of Iranian entities and individuals whose assets would be frozen, and also outlined potential restrictions on Iran's sale or procurement of conventional arms.[6]

The logic seemed to be geared toward affecting those most directly involved in the nuclear energy and missile industries in Iran and the military and Revolutionary Guard Corps as well. This was a basis that preserved unity within the UN Security Council and kept the Russians and Chinese on board while allowing the Bush administration to keep Iran isolated. Unfortunately, it did not alter Iranian behavior, as Iran continued to build gas centrifuges and pursue enrichment activities.

Though 1747 also had a sixty-day reporting requirement on Iranian compliance built into it, there was no immediate move toward adopting a third resolution—once again signaling Iranian leaders that no real economic pressures would be put on Iran. With Iran not responding, the others not prepared to put additional pressures on Iran, and the Bush administration unwilling to break ranks at this point, a move was made to offer the Iranians an inducement. The United States in May 2007 joined with the European trio, the Russians, and the Chinese and had Javier Solana present the Iranians with a new proposal. Solana proposed that the two sides would begin negotiations at the working level, and at this point there would be a "double freeze": Iran would not install additional centrifuges, and the UN Security Council would not impose additional sanctions. When ministerial talks began, there would be a "double suspension" in which Iran would suspend all enrichment and reprocessing and the UN would suspend all sanctions.[7] The proposal, formally titled "The Way Forward to Negotiations," not only offered Iran binding assurances for the supply of nuclear fuel but also discussed the timing and methods of uranium enrichment for Iran in the future.[8]

For the Bush administration to accept such a proposal represented quite a leap. Yet notwithstanding what the Europeans also considered to be a "generous offer," the Iranians did not even respond to it. Solana was to raise it again in October in his ongoing discussions with the Iranians, and this time around the Iranians rejected it.

In the intervening period, in the summer of 2007, Iran did reach an agreement with the IAEA to provide answers by the end of the year to all the outstanding questions posed to it by the agency on its nuclear-related activities—one of the aims embedded in Resolutions 1737 and 1747.[9] While the Bush administration expressed concerns about the vagueness of this process, it nonetheless agreed in a September 2007 meeting with the British, French, Germans, Russians, and Chinese to wait until the end of November to pursue a third UNSC resolution.[10] In so doing, the administration joined with the others in being willing to give both the IAEA and Javier Solana a chance to produce some progress before pressing for more sanctions at the UN.

Additional sanctions, however, seemed quite likely when in the last week of November there were two unmistakable setbacks to producing responsiveness from the Iranians. First, Dr. Mohamed ElBaradei, director general of the IAEA, reported that Iran had crossed the threshold of operating three thousand uranium-enriching centrifuges—a threshold that is often identified as representing a scale of infrastructure necessary for producing fissile material for nuclear weapons. ElBaradei reported that while Iran was providing answers that clarified some issues with the IAEA, Iran's restrictions on agency inspectors prevented the IAEA from being able to determine whether Iran's program was designed to generate electricity or to produce weapons.[11] Second, Javier Solana, after meeting with the new Iranian negotiator, Saeed Jalili, made it very clear that there was no progress: "I have to admit that after five hours of meetings, I expected more, and therefore I am disappointed."[12] According to participants in the meeting, Jalili, a deputy foreign minister known to be close to President Ahmadinejad, told Solana, "Everything in the past is past, and with me, you start over. . . . None of your proposals have any standing."[13]

In the immediate aftermath of these two developments, the six countries—the United States, Britain, France, Germany, Russia, and China—began work on a new UNSC resolution based on a draft British text.[14] The consensus to produce a third UNSC resolution immediately did not mean that differences had disappeared on how tough to make the penalties on Iran. The Russians and Chinese continued to resist imposing tough economic sanctions, with the Russians believing that pushing for more inclusive inspections was more important than imposing penalties and the Chinese not wanting to inhibit their own soaring trade with Iran. And yet even their willingness to adopt a third UNSC resolution was soon dramatically undercut by a new development: the National Intelligence Estimate (NIE) on the Iranian nuclear program.

THE NATIONAL INTELLIGENCE ESTIMATE AND ITS IMPACT

The December 3, 2007, public release of the NIE titled "Iran: Nuclear Intentions and Capabilities" transformed the landscape on dealing with Iran. The report asserted that Iran had halted its nuclear weapons program in 2003. In making this statement, it created the impression that Iran was not pursuing nuclear weapons and was not a near-term threat. This produced a slew of obvious questions: If Iran was not a near-term threat, why pursue sanctions? Why build pressure on that regime? And, of course, why should all options, including the military, be on the table?

The report was a collective effort of the intelligence community. It probably reflected a desire to ensure that intelligence could not be used to justify a war on Iran the way the Bush administration had used the intelligence community to justify going to war in Iraq. However, given the way the NIE was drafted, it was bound to create several ironies and have a number of unintended consequences. It is ironic that Iran was *not* sanctioned by the United Nations for its covert nuclear weapons program; it *was* sanctioned for its open pursuit of uranium enrichment, which, if continued over time (something the NIE acknowledged was occurring), could be used to develop nuclear weapons. It is also ironic that the NIE concluded that Iran had stopped its weapons program in 2003 "primarily in response to international pressures," which "indicates Tehran's decisions are guided by a cost-benefit approach."[15] Perhaps the greatest irony of all is that by framing its judgments the way it did—emphasizing the covert nuclear weapons program and efforts rather than the overt enrichment developments—the NIE inadvertently succeeded in considerably reducing the "cost" factor in the ongoing international approach to Iran.

Though the British, French, and Germans generally tried to hold the line, the international reaction after the NIE was markedly different from what it had been before. One almost needs to divide the approach toward dealing with Iran into the pre-NIE and post-NIE periods. Pre-NIE, Russia and China were prepared to act immediately on a third UNSC sanctions resolution against Iran; post-NIE, they both raised questions about doing so and postponed consideration of such a resolution. It took until March 3, 2008, to adopt the third Security Council resolution (1803), and like its predecessors, the resolution was quite limited and sent a signal as much for what it did not cover as for what it did.[16]

Pre-NIE, the Saudis were trying to raise the pressure on the Iranians over their nuclear program. In early November 2007, Saud al-Faisal, the Saudi foreign minister, called on Iran to respond to a Gulf Cooperation Council (GCC) proposal to "create a consortium for all users of enriched uranium in the Middle East. The consortium will distribute according to needs . . . and ensure no use of this enriched uranium for atomic weapons."[17] Faisal suggested that Switzerland could be the site of the enrichment plant for the consortium and made clear that this proposal, which he revealed had been conveyed privately to Iran one year earlier but had not produced a response, would answer the Iranian desire for civil nuclear power and not prejudice Iranian rights in any way.[18] Why go public at this point unless the purpose was to put pressure on Iran?

But that was pre-NIE; post-NIE, there has been no additional mention of the proposal. On the contrary, the GCC invited Ahmadinejad to attend their December meeting (an unprecedented invitation), and King Abdullah of Saudi Arabia also invited the Iranian president to go to Mecca—hardly signs of increasing pressure on Iran. Similarly, after keeping Iran at arm's length, Egypt invited Iranian official Ali Larijani to Cairo for discussions after the NIE; and former Egyptian ambassador to the United States Ahmad Maher wrote in a January 2008 commentary that Israel, not Iran, was the problem for the Arab world and that the "disputes between Arabs and Iran" can be resolved "through a dialogue."[19]

In Iran itself, one also sees a pre-NIE reality and a different post-NIE reality. Ahmadinejad was clearly on the defensive prior to the NIE, and he went on the offensive after it. He seized on the NIE, proclaiming a great victory and at one point referring to the intelligence report as a "declaration of surrender."[20] But he was not content only to claim a great victory over the United States and others who opposed the Iranian nuclear activities; according to his office's news service, he also "belittled" those in Iran who had criticized the high cost Iran was said to be paying over the nuclear issue.[21]

If nothing else, those like Rafsanjani who were warning about the costs of Ahmadinejad's nuclear approach seem to have been undercut. Certainly, their complaints that he was actually threatening Iran's security with his belligerent language lost credibility, and following the publication of the NIE, he was subjected to far less criticism for "his inflammatory rhetoric."[22]

Even more to the point, Ali Khamenei, the Supreme Leader, became much more vocal in his support for Ahmadinejad on the nuclear issue after the NIE—actually lauding the "personal role of the president and his resistance in the nuclear case."[23] In addition, the Supreme Leader began to assert his responsibility for decision making on the nuclear question. In a January 3, 2008, speech, Khamenei for the first time "admitted that Iran's shift in nuclear policy—which began right after Ahmadinejad came to office—was by his order."[24] Whether coincidence or not, the Supreme Leader also assumed a more visible role on the nuclear issue post-NIE, meeting with Dr. ElBaradei on January 12.[25] While it is probably too much to claim that the NIE has changed Khamenei's view, his readiness to be clearly identified with the nuclear program nonetheless became far more apparent.[26]

It is hard to escape the conclusion that the leverage and choices that could be employed vis-à-vis Iran in the aftermath of the NIE have been reduced. Having fewer choices or options, however, does not mean we have none. Iran still has vulnerabilities and interests that might be susceptible to both positive and negative incentives and disincentives.

IRAN'S VULNERABILITIES AND OUR DIPLOMATIC CHOICES

Our basic objective toward Iran should be to prevent it from developing nuclear weapons and to alter its destabilizing, antipeace policies in the Middle East. Do we have the means and the leverage to do so? In the aftermath of the NIE and Iran's continuing enrichment developments, that remains unclear, but Iran certainly has some very basic vulnerabilities.

Iran's Vulnerabilities

Iran's oil output is declining at a time when its domestic consumption is increasing rapidly. At present, Iran is falling more than 300,000 barrels per day (b/d) below its OPEC export quota, not because Iran's leaders do not want to meet their quota but because they cannot meet it. When one considers that Iran derives 80 percent of its export income from its sale of oil, and that those revenues provide at least 75 percent of the government's total revenues, it is not hard to see the potential for leverage.[27]

Mehdi Varzi, a former Iranian diplomat and National Iranian Oil Company official, has gone so far as to say, "Oil is as important as the nuclear issue; it will affect the very survival of the regime."[28] One senior

British official, who very much agrees with this sentiment, told one of us that "if you want to affect the Mullahs, let them see that they are not going to have the money to subsidize the civilian economy—and the key to that is cutting off investment and technology transfer to the energy sector." In effect, this official was saying that should the mullahs, who are primarily concerned with preserving their power and privilege, come to believe that Iran's economic lifeline is going to be cut and the oil revenues are going to dry up, they may well decide that the nuclear program is not worth the cost.

Mehdi Varzi and our British colleague may or may not be correct, but one thing is certain: the Iranians need massive investment and technological help from the outside to prevent the continuing decline of their oil output. Kazem Vaziri-Hamaneh, Iran's oil minister in 2006, put the decline of output at 500,000 b/d each year.[29] This decline—married to growing internal consumption—creates an unmistakable squeeze that has led some analysts to suggest that Iran's oil income could actually disappear by 2014 or 2015.[30]

Of course, Iran could impose strict conservation measures, and it could gain access to outside technical expertise to help reverse the natural decline in many of its oil fields. It could also get foreign oil companies to invest in developing new fields that require more sophisticated techniques and technologies to exploit. But real conservation may provoke a domestic political backlash, particularly with internal consumption having tripled since 1980 and Iranians expecting to be able to benefit from their energy resources. Ahmadinejad claimed that he would bring the oil revenues to every table; instead, he has brought rationing of gasoline, high inflation, high unemployment, and international isolation.

One measure of the isolation is that Iran was unable to sign any firm oil or gas contracts for the first two and a half years of Ahmadinejad's tenure.[31] Only in the aftermath of the NIE were the Iranians able to resume signing contracts with Malaysia, China, Italy, Austria, and Switzerland to develop oil and natural gas fields, and the biggest of these deals—the one with Malaysia—eventually will require Western subcontractors to produce and market the liquefied natural gas.[32] The signings of these deals indicate the ongoing interest that foreign companies have in investing in onshore and offshore exploration blocks, but as Jeroen van der Veer, the chief executive of Royal Dutch Shell, explained, "We have a dilemma."

Iran's oil and natural gas reserves are too big to ignore, but "we have all the short-term political concerns, as you can see."[33] Those "short-term" concerns have been made more acute by unilateral U.S. sanctions, which, among other things, are designed as much for their psychological as for their practical impact (e.g., the U.S. posture is geared toward raising questions about the danger and the cost of investing in Iranian front companies). In the words of then-Secretary of the Treasury Henry Paulson:

> In dealing with Iran, it is nearly impossible to know one's customer and be assured that one is not unwittingly facilitating the regime's reckless behavior and conduct. The recent warning by the Financial Action Task Force, the world's premier standard setting body for countering terrorism finance and money laundering, *confirms the extraordinary risks that accompany those who do business with Iran* [emphasis added].[34]

And there can be no doubt that even the unilateral U.S. sanctions on three Iranian banks and the Revolutionary Guard—with the implication that we will sanction any company doing business with the IRGC—are having an effect. Iranian economist Saeed Leylaz has said, "Sanctions are like icebergs. Only 10 percent of the effect is directly attributable to the Security Council. Ninety percent is fear of the U.S."[35] European businesses are cutting back on trade with and investment in Iran, and the result is that prices on most goods are going up dramatically in Iran. According to one report, the prices on most commodities rose roughly 50 percent in the early months of 2008 (even before the dramatic spike in oil prices), largely because many foreign manufacturers and distributors became more wary of doing business directly with Iran lest they come under greater scrutiny from the U.S. Treasury Department.[36]

Will this produce a change in Iranian behavior? There is no sign of it to date. But it is interesting that Iran's well-connected *bazaari* class of merchants are being hit hard, and apparently one such group complained to the Supreme Leader that sanctions were "hurting their bottom line."[37] Moreover, in October 2008, widespread protests actually led to strikes by *bazaaris* against government economic policies and prompted a prominent Iranian sociologist to remark, "[T]his is a sign of economic and social chaos resulted by the government's policies [and] no one feels safe in a situation where there is recession, inflation, unemployment and economic crisis. All traders feel threatened."[38]

The economic vulnerability is clear. The potential to squeeze the Iranians more on their oil revenues is also obvious, and it need not involve trying to cut off Iranian exports, which would drive prices far higher. It would, however, require cutting off all credit and outside investment in the oil sector, and it could also include embargoing refined gasoline products, something that might have a very significant impact, given the Iranians' need to import approximately 40 percent of the gasoline they use. The Chinese and Russians have shown great reluctance to go along with anything so drastic, and of course simply squeezing Iran does not guarantee responsiveness. Indeed, there are those who believe the only way to produce a change in Iranian behavior is to offer meaningful inducements while engaging the Iranian leadership. Here it is worth recalling that the Supreme Leader, Ali Khamenei, now appears to be taking a much more open and direct role on the nuclear issue. Even if he generally has preferred to operate on the basis of involving all the relevant elites when it comes to the nuclear issue, there is no question that the Supreme Leader, not the president of Iran, is the chief decision maker.[39]

Is it time to engage Khamenei and Iran, or is the best option to squeeze tighter? Or are there other alternatives or mixes of options that could still change Iran's behavior?

Diplomatic Options

Option 1. Tighten the Noose. This is the path the Bush administration preferred. The administration pushed for and got adoption of a third sanctions resolution at the UN—once again settling for sanctions that did not really target the Iranian economy for the sake of getting a resolution. While accepting less at the UN, the administration pushed European governments to lean on banks, investment houses, and energy companies to prevent any new deals. As already noted, this has had at least some impact.

Prior to the NIE, President Nicolas Sarkozy of France was encouraging EU-wide sanctions that would go well beyond the UN sanctions in cutting the economic lifeline to Iran. His argument was that much more needed to be done to force the Iranian leadership to see that the price of pursuing their nuclear program was simply too high—and, indeed, if it was not done, the risk of military action to prevent Iran from going nuclear would inevitably increase. He was not arguing for the use of force; rather, he was trying to mobilize opinion in Europe to show that if more was not done economically to squeeze the Iranians and make them see the cost of the nuclear effort, those who saw Iran's nuclear program as a profound threat might see force as the only option.

While Sarkozy has backed off this posture since the NIE, the idea of pushing for additional EU-wide sanctions remains on the table. And they would certainly have an impact in Iran. European companies may generally be cutting back and fearing the risk of investment in Iran, but a number of European governments are still providing several billion dollars of credit guarantees to their companies doing business in Iran. The figure was approximately $18 billion in 2005,[40] and while it has since been significantly reduced, Italian, Spanish, Austrian, and some German firms are still benefiting from such guarantees.

So long as credit guarantees are still available, it will be hard to convince the Iranians that they will be subject to much stiffer economic pressures and that their economic lifeline will be cut off. Indeed, while Iran is obviously feeling increasing pressures from America's unilateral sanctions and efforts with the Europeans and others, it is interesting that when the Iranians held a conference in Tehran this past year to offer their own sweeteners on possible oil exploration contracts, dozens of European, Russian, and Chinese oil companies attended. According to Gholam Hossein Nozari, the managing director of Iran's national oil company, this was a "sure sign companies do not cower to U.S. pressure."[41]

Clearly, if one is pursuing the option of tightening the economic noose, more needs to be done. One means of doing so would be to enlist the Saudis. They have a very high stake in Iran not going nuclear. While the NIE made them less willing to challenge the Iranians publicly, or even to be seen as part of an open effort to contain or isolate Iran, there clearly are private ways to employ Saudi financial clout. For example, the Saudis have tremendous holdings in Europe, and they could go privately to the relevant European governments, the key banking and investment houses, and the major energy companies and make clear that those who cut all ties to the Iranians would be rewarded by the Saudis and those who don't would fall into disfavor and receive no investments or business.

Something similar could be done with both the Chinese and the Russians. It is particularly important to do so with the Chinese, who have been driven by a mercantile mentality and are drawing special complaints from the Europeans for rushing to replace European companies whenever they pull back from Iran. China may seem to be a difficult case because it does receive about 13 percent of its oil from Iran. But make no mistake, if the Chinese had to choose between Iran and Saudi Arabia, they would choose the Saudis. They have massive new investments in Saudi petrochemicals and are jointly financing new oil refineries, and the Saudis have agreed to fill a strategic petroleum reserve for China. Business is business, and the Chinese have a higher stake in Saudi Arabia than in Iran. Again, the Saudis need not broadcast what they are doing—but they do need to be enlisted to quietly pressure the Chinese to change their approach to Iran lest they lose out on a profitable future with Saudi Arabia.

The Saudis could also influence the United Arab Emirates. The UAE's commercial ties to Iran are growing, and Iranian companies are relocating to Dubai in an effort to circumvent the existing sanctions. While the UAE may fear coming under great Iranian pressure if they simply cut back on exports to Iran, which rose to $12 billion in 2006, the international community could give the emirates some cover. The UN could decide, for example, that it will create a monitoring team to oversee compliance with the sanctions imposed in resolutions 1737, 1747, and 1803; the UN has done this with many other sanction resolutions, and it could establish such a team in the UAE. In Dubai's "free-wheeling business environment," a UN monitoring team could identify Iran's efforts to use the UAE to get around the sanctions and give the UAE an explanation for why it must cut down on illicit Iranian activity.[42]

There clearly is room to do much more to tighten the economic noose around Iran and sharpen the choices the Iranian leadership must make. Not everything need be done through United Nations Security Council resolutions—indeed, that route has probably already been exhausted. Formal and informal sanctions, informal jawboning, and finding ways to get the Saudis to use their clout could all add to the pressures.

But is pressure alone likely to work? One could argue that if applied much more systematically and targeted effectively, it might yet. Perhaps, but pressure alone may only succeed in creating a siege mentality in the Iranian regime and thus strengthen the hand of the hard-liners. Pressure that squeezes the regime far more effectively without tying it to an open door, or to something from which Iranian leaders could also gain, may simply convince Iranian leaders that we seek only their humiliation. Pressure that offers only humiliation, meaning admission of defeat, is likely to make it easier for the hard-liners to argue that giving in to it will only whet the appetite of those in the United States who will be satisfied with nothing less than regime change. President Ahmadinejad appeared to make this very point in responding to his internal critics on why Iran should not concede on the nuclear question given the pressure: "If we would take one step back in our confrontation with the arrogant powers regarding our nuclear program, we would have to keep taking more and more steps back till the very end."[43]

The problem with the tightening-the-noose option is that the Iranian leadership may choose confrontation, believing it has nothing to lose. Furthermore, this option is not likely to work fast enough to prevent the Iranians from going nuclear. Pressure has not worked so far, and another year of enrichment has already made Iran a nuclear power state if not yet a nuclear weapons state. If its leaders see only pressure, which they may see as tied to a regime-change strategy, they may be inclined to go all out, and should they do so, they theoretically could have at least one bomb by the end of 2009. So maybe it is time to try a different path.

Option 2. Engagement Without Conditions. Secretary of State Condoleezza Rice might have argued that the Bush administration did not seek a pressure-only approach; after all, the administration supported the incentives package in the summer of 2006, was willing to back the "double freeze" proposal in May 2007 (and its refinement in June 2008), opened up a trilateral dialogue with Iran on Iraq, and proclaimed a readiness to discuss all issues if Iran would only suspend its enrichment activities.

However, critics of the administration paint a very different picture—one, they say, that is what the Iranians see.[44] From Tehran, the picture looks like one of unrelenting efforts to isolate or pressure Iran. Even when Iran tried to be responsive after 9/11 on al-Qaeda and Afghanistan, it received no recognition or reciprocation, only the charge that it was part of the "axis of evil." When it apparently conveyed privately a readiness to put all issues on the table, including its nuclear program and support for Hizbollah and Hamas, in 2003, it was rebuffed with a simple rejection. While dialogue was being rejected, hostility was being projected through the attempt to promote a wall of Sunni Arab containment and economic pressures.

Critics of the Bush administration policy argue that the pressure-only or isolation policies are doomed to fail and have built up a reservoir of deep suspicion throughout the Iranian elite. Given that, they argue for an engagement-without-conditions approach.

Analysts Mark Brzezinski and Ray Takeyh believe that the NIE's findings create an opening, not a problem. In their words, "That Iran ceased work on its nuclear program several years ago is positive, as it provides an opportunity to start negotiations with Tehran without any preconditions. Moreover, it allows both parties to come to the negotiating table with a constructive tone."[45] They and other critics of the Bush administration approach see value in creating an environment for the talks in which neither side is seeking to pressure the other, "making veiled threats," or dismissing the other's security concerns.[46]

Preconditions would be inconsistent with trying to foster such an atmosphere for the talks. Moreover, to make such talks work, the critics argue for negotiations that will be comprehensive in scope, not incremental. They believe the agenda should cover the full array of concerns of both sides:

- Iran wants recognition of its legitimate security and regional interests, a U.S. commitment to accept the regime and give up efforts to change it, a recovery of its frozen assets, an end to economic embargoes, and the right to have civil nuclear power.
- The United States wants Iran to give up its pursuit of nuclear weapons, its support for terrorist groups and militias that threaten or hold existing governments hostage, and its efforts to prevent Arab-Israeli peace.

For the critics who favor engagement without conditions, the tradeoffs are not difficult to imagine. In return for American acceptance of the legitimacy of the Iranian regime and resuming economic ties with it, Iran would have to stop providing all military equipment and training to Hizbollah, Hamas, and other regional militias and publicly commit to a two-state solution to the Arab-Israeli conflict. In return for U.S. support for Iran's civil nuclear program, Iran would have to accept an intrusive inspection regime based on having permanent inspectors operating on a

24-hour-a-day, no-notice system of inspections. In return for U.S. acceptance of Iran's role in Iraq, Iran should be prepared to help to work out understandings not only between the Shia and Sunnis within Iraq but also with the Saudis to make such understandings more likely to hold. Finally, in return for our accepting Iran's regional position, Iran would need to join an effort with its neighbors to create a new regional security system resolving territorial disputes, accepting existing borders, limiting arms acquisitions, and opening trade.[47]

Most of those who favor this engagement option believe that Iran's behavior can be modified. They see Iran as "an unexceptional opportunistic power seeking to exert preponderance in its immediate neighborhood."[48] While that might ordinarily argue for the use of carrots and sticks to affect Iran's choices, the engagers without conditions feel that Iranian suspicions are simply too high, their leverage toward their neighbors too great, their cash reserves too substantial, and their nuclear program too far along for them to respond to our "sticks."

But is all that true? Usually when regimes say pressure won't work on them, that is precisely what they are trying to head off. President Ahmadinejad would not be facing some of his domestic criticism if not for concerns that his provocative posture, including specifically on the nuclear issue, was costly to Iran. Ali Akbar Velayati, the Supreme Leader's senior foreign policy adviser, has recently gone so far as to say that President Ahmadinejad, "without mentioning the president by name . . . should avoid 'illogical declarations and slogans' that undermine relations with the world."[49] Moreover, even when oil prices were high, they did not erase the basic vulnerabilities of the economy or reduce unhappiness about it. Fuel heating shortages in the winter of 2008 triggered a torrent of new criticisms of Ahmadinejad's economic policies; even earlier, Ayatollah Mahmoud Hashemi Shahroudi, the judiciary chief and one of Iran's leading clerics, blasted the president for what he termed "heavy blows to the Iranian [economic] system."[50] And now, with oil prices having dropped dramatically, President Ahmadinejad has been attacked for squandering Iran's financial reserves.

This is not to argue against engaging the Iranians. But it is to argue that engagement should not necessarily dispense with preserving pressures on the Iranian regime. To engage with no pressure might well convince the regime that the United States is conceding up front and there is thus no need to respond to what we seek. It almost certainly would convince them of our weakness. In our experience in negotiating with Middle Eastern parties—admittedly Arabs and Israelis, not Iranians—the tendency when one side thought it was on a roll and in a strong position was to believe that there was no need for it to compromise; ironically, when it found itself in a weakened position or on the defensive, it would tend to think that it could not afford to compromise. What that experience would argue for with the Iranians is preserving pressure but also providing face-savers and inducements at the same time.

Option 3. The Hybrid Approach: Engagement Without Conditions but with Pressures. When we say engagement without conditions, we mean that there would be no preconditions for the United States talking to Iran. Iran would not, for example, have to suspend its uranium enrichment first. But to avoid having Iran misread this as a sign of weakness, pressures must be maintained. Iran must see that though the United States is no longer imposing a precondition for talks, it has succeeded in adding to pressures on Iran even while it is offering a way to reach an accommodation.

The logic of this option is that Iran must see that the costs of pursuing the nuclear option are real and will not go away, but that Iran has a door to walk through. Iran must see what is to be gained by giving up the pursuit of nuclear weapons—and those gains must be meaningful to the Iranian leadership. The hybrid option is designed to concentrate the minds of Iranian leaders on what they stand to lose, without humiliating them.

This option ends the image that there is a price just for talking to the United States, but does not leave the impression that America has caved in and effectively given up as talks begin—or that negotiations can provide a legitimate umbrella under which nukes can still be pursued.

So how to talk and preserve the pressures without making either side appear weak? One way to do so would be for the United States to go to the Europeans and offer to join the talks with Iran without Iran having to suspend uranium enrichment. To avoid misleading the Iranians into thinking they had won, we would, in effect, be imposing conditions not on Iran but on Europe for the talks. The European Union would adopt more stringent sanctions on investments, credits, and technology transfer vis-à-vis Iran in general, or at least on the Iranian energy sector. The Iranians would be informed that the United States is joining the talks but that these sanctions are now being adopted by all European countries or would be soon.

Would the Europeans go for it? It is possible. The EU negotiators have been convinced for some time that there is a deal to be struck with Iran, but only if the United States is directly at the table. They believe that while Iran does seek economic and political benefits from the Europeans, the big prize is with the Americans. It is not just the frozen assets, but the conviction that the United States is determined to subvert the regime and that no deal is possible until the United States provides security assurances and guarantees to Iran directly.[51]

For applying the hybrid option in this fashion, what matters is not whether the EU view is correct. What matters is that the EU representatives are convinced that this is what will move the Iranians. Moreover, the EU's readiness to go along with the U.S. condition that its members adopt tough sanctions as the price for getting the United States to the table will, no doubt, also depend on a U.S. commitment to negotiate seriously on a comprehensive proposal that would include many of the tradeoffs noted above in option 2. There would be one key difference in the comprehensive proposal that would be proffered as part of the hybrid option: here, acceptance of Iran's being a civil nuclear power would require not simply acceptance of intrusive inspections, but also a ban on stockpiling low-enriched uranium and a requirement to have it shipped out of the country to an IAEA facility. In other words, in option 3, the nuclear part of the comprehensive proposal would be geared more to guarding against an Iranian breakout capability as well as providing for verification procedures designed to prevent the existence of covert or clandestine nuclear programs in Iran.[52]

There could be one other problem in getting the EU to go along. If the NIE has convinced most Europeans that the United States is less likely to use force against Iran, they may feel less urgency and less need to put additional pressure on Iran. Indeed, many in Europe may feel that they can live with an Iran with nuclear weapons and that containment is an acceptable posture. If so, they may balk at applying more sanctions, particularly because it means absorbing real economic costs.

In such an eventuality, there may be value in enlisting Israel to send a high-level delegation privately to key European capitals to make the point that while others may feel they can live with a nuclear Iran, Israel feels it does not have that luxury. Not, by the way, because its leaders might not prefer it, but because Iran does not seem willing to let Israel exist. The Israeli message would be that if you want to avoid the use of force, "we need to see that you are going to raise the costs to Iran in a way that is likely to be meaningful to the Iranian leaders."

To be sure, another way to increase the likelihood of getting European responsiveness on increased pressure would be to enlist the Saudis and their financial clout. The point here is that the sources of pressure identified in the "tighten the noose" option must also be incorporated into the hybrid option. It really is an amalgam of options 1 and 2. The Saudis need to be enlisted to act not as a favor to the United States—since they are not inclined to do us any favors—but because their own interests in preventing Iran from going nuclear are so potent. As noted earlier, the Saudis do have real leverage toward both the Europeans and Chinese, and it needs to be employed even as we engage the Iranians.

The Russians, too, could be enlisted in this option. The Russians could provide both significant pressures and inducements. If the Russians made it clear to the Iranians that they would not protect them from greater external pressure but could offer them a way out—especially if it looked as if pressures would increase from the outside—the Iranian leaders might very well change their calculus.

Getting the Russians to play this role will not be easy or necessarily cheap—and our readiness to engage them and consider certain inducements to them after their behavior in the war in Georgia has certainly not been made easier. But in the aftermath of Georgia, the Russians have seen their stock market decline dramatically and investment from the outside fall precipitously—and while the Russians seem keen on asserting their national pride and prerogatives, it is possible that they may want to demonstrate where cooperation with them is in the West's collective interests.

From this perspective, the Russians might be interested in a joint approach on Iran. Certainly, the Russians have no desire for Iran to go nuclear, and yet they have been careful not to push the Iranians too hard. Is it because they are concerned that if they do, the Iranians will make trouble for them in their Muslim periphery? Or is it because the Russians have a different agenda in the Middle East now, and becoming an alternative or counterweight to the United States is taking on more importance?

Or is it because they don't believe it is possible to stop the Iranian program, only contain it? Or is it because the Russians want something if they are going to play such a role? Maybe all four factors are involved in some form.

If so, there could be several creative ways to engage the Russians on issues they have raised as being very important to them. Missile defense in Eastern Europe or NATO expansion involving Ukraine or Georgia have been elevated into symbolic issues in which Russian interests are at stake, and the West appears to be trying to contain Russia and deny the Russians their natural areas of influence—at least according to the political narrative that first former Russian president Vladimir Putin and now his successor Dmitry Medvedev have articulated. While more complicated in the aftermath of Georgia, trade-offs that address Russian interests could be considered on these or other issues if the Russians demonstrate they are prepared to apply real pressure on Iran.

In theory, the ballistic missile defense deployments in Poland and the Czech Republic are designed to provide protection from Iranian missiles. If the Russians would act to reduce the Iranian threat, these sites might not be so necessary. Such a trade-off with the Russians was not acceptable to the Bush administration, given its commitment to antimissile defenses. But this or alternative trade-offs on NATO expansion might be acceptable to the Obama administration and ought at least to be considered pending consultations with the Czechs, the Poles, and our other NATO allies. These are delicate political issues with the Czechs, Poles, Ukrainians, and others in the alliance, and quiet consultations first will be essential before actually going down this road. (Needless to say, we think it is important to maintain close relations with our Eastern European allies who have mobilized their publics in support of close ties with the United States, and we do not want to undercut them or raise further doubts about our credibility.)

There are two other possible inducements for the Russians: offer to help them assume a leading position as a supplier of nuclear fuels internationally—something that could mean a great deal financially to them; or allow them to take the lead in doing the deal with the Iranians on stopping their nuclear program. This would respond to the Russian political and psychological need to show they are playing a major new role internationally, effectively recapturing their lost status on the world stage. Each of these inducements has certain downsides: among other things, could we be so confident about Russian safeguards, and could we really count on the Russians not surprising us with what they might offer the Iranians or how they might try to play us off against the Europeans?

While these risks might be manageable, they remind us that as we involve others who have leverage, we need to think through who we can effectively work with, who has reasons of their own to act, and how we can most productively integrate others into a common strategy to alter Iran's behavior. Any such strategy needs to focus not just on the levers but also on how we should go about engaging the Iranians if we are employing either options 2 or 3.

HOW TO SET UP ENGAGEMENT WITH THE IRANIANS AND NEGOTIATE EFFECTIVELY

In discussing the hybrid option, we mentioned that the Iranians could be informed that the United States was joining the talks directly even as they were being told about increased EU sanctions. That is, of course, one way to prepare the ground for U.S. engagement with Iran. But there are other ways to do so that would be relevant for either the "engage without conditions" or "engage with pressure" option. For example, engagement, whether without conditions or with pressure, should still be prepared. An agenda should be created before the Americans first come to the table. One way to do so would be to have the Europeans quietly have discussions with the Iranians on a more comprehensive agenda, which goes beyond the nuclear issue, to prepare for U.S. inclusion in the talks. Another way could involve some of the existing "track two" channels, which could be used to set the stage for official contacts. This is how the Oslo process evolved, with prenegotiations in an ongoing academic channel taking on issues and creating milestones for gradually bringing officials to the talks.

While each of these ways could be effective, we prefer another approach. We recommend trying to set up a direct, secret back channel. Keeping it completely private would protect each side from premature exposure and would not require either side to publicly explain such a move before it was ready. It would strike the Iranians as more significant and dramatic than working through either the Europeans or non-officials— something that is quite familiar. It has the additional value that a discreet channel, which is protected, makes it possible to have a thorough discussion and to see whether there is a common agenda that can be constructed.[53]

Assuming it is possible to produce such an official, discreet back channel with the Iranians, one good way to begin such a discussion would be to ask the Iranian representative to explain how his government sees U.S. goals toward Iran and how he thinks the Americans perceive Iranian goals toward the United States. Any such interaction must find a way to show the Iranians that we are prepared to listen and to try to understand Iranian concerns and respond to them, but that ultimately no progress can be made if our concerns cannot also be understood and addressed.

Maybe, given the history, it will be difficult to set up such a direct channel that is also authoritative. We will want the channel to connect to Ali Khamenei, the Supreme Leader; otherwise it will fail the test of being authoritative. To authenticate the credibility of those involved, we will certainly need to establish some early tests. Maybe we will need the Europeans (or others) to help set up the channel. And maybe, even if we engage the Iranians, we will find that however we do so, and whatever we try, the engagement simply does not work.

We will need to hedge bets and set the stage for alternative policies designed either to prevent Iran from going nuclear or to blunt the impact if they do. Those represent two different policy choices with very different implications. Whichever path we take will be more sustainable if we have directly engaged Iran first. Tougher policies—either military or meaningful containment—will be easier to sell internationally and domestically if we have diplomatically tried to resolve our differences with Iran in a serious and credible fashion.

In fact, if negotiations fail to prevent the Iranians from changing their current path, it will be important to show not only that the United States negotiated directly with Iran but also how much was actually offered. The package of inducements offered to Iran should be both fully coordinated with others and made public at an appropriate moment. Such an approach may build pressures within Iran not to forgo the opportunity that has been presented, while also ensuring that the onus is put on Iran for creating a crisis and also for making conflict more likely.

In this sense, should force end up being used against the Iranian nuclear capability, it will be very important to set the context so that the perception internationally is that the action is legitimate. Ironically, the more that Iranian leaders know they are isolated and have brought the risk of military action on themselves, the more they might be dissuaded from taking steps to go nuclear. From this standpoint, negotiations should also be seen as part of a dissuasion strategy—a strategy in which the Iranians see both what they stand to lose from going nuclear and what they stand to gain from not going nuclear.

Iranians might be dissuaded from going nuclear if they knew that they would become less secure in doing so. If, for example, they saw that their neighbors would be receiving more arms from the outside, better counterterror capabilities, theater missile defenses that could counter Iranian missiles, and commitments to come to their defense in the event of attacks from Iran, the Iranian leadership might have to ask itself what exactly it was gaining from going nuclear. Similarly, if continuing down the nuclear path was going to bring greater U.S. and European forces geographically closer to Iran (note that France is now establishing a naval facility in the UAE) and the prospect that Iran would face increased preemptive and retaliatory capabilities nearby, Iranian leaders again would have to consider the efficacy of their moves. (Even if a military strike is a last resort, it may be advisable to pre-position and enhance American military forces in the region and maintain contingency planning.)

These moves should be foreshadowed in any direct talks that we have with the Iranians. Negotiations involve not just the offer of possible inducements but also the explanation of what is going to happen if agreement cannot be reached, including the possible use of force. If the Iranians thought in May 2003 that they might be next after Iraq—and that fear may have triggered a forthcoming Iranian proposal—we are reminded that the threat of force can be a way to make diplomacy more effective. Diplomacy backed by coercion has always been a part of statecraft done well. When we say that we are not taking force off the table, that must be more than a slogan; it is essential that the Iranians continue to believe that they might well be playing with fire if they persist in their pursuit of nuclear weapons.

In the end, it is important to try to get the Iranians to see that negotiations offer them a pathway out of a threatening cul-de-sac. But for that to be the case, the negotiations with the Iranians cannot be open-ended; there should be an agreement with the EU, the Russians, and Middle Eastern states such as the Saudis and Israelis that if agreement is not reached within a set period of time, the negotiations may be ended—or at least that some of the "dissuasion steps" will begin to be implemented in the region. Time is of the essence, given the pace of the Iranian nuclear program, and diplomacy should be conducted with a sense of urgency.

If negotiations fail, we will certainly face hard choices. However, the context both at home and abroad for either the use of force against Iran or a robust policy of deterrence will look dramatically different should good-faith, direct negotiations be tried and fail. To be sure, additional moves could be taken and also revealed in advance in the negotiations. One such move might be a Kennedy-like statement on Iran: just as President Kennedy declared during the Cuban Missile Crisis that any nuclear missile launched by Cuba against a country in the Western Hemisphere would be regarded as an attack by the Soviet Union on the United States, requiring a full retaliatory response on the Soviet Union, so too could we say that any such nuclear attack from Iran or its proxies against any American ally will be regarded as an attack against the United States and bring full retaliation on Iran.[54]

Such a declaration would be a bold move that would also highlight the danger of Iran going nuclear for the Iranians and the world. This step, or some of the ones mentioned earlier, could be part of efforts to reach agreement with Iran but also part of a larger strategy that is designed to produce deterrence or set the stage for the use of force if agreement proves not to be possible.

Ultimately, statecraft involves the use of all our tools and assets, including diplomacy (both public and private), economic leverage, and the application of coercion. Neoconservatives and realists also understand the scope of the tools available to the United States in trying to affect Iranian behavior. The difference with the approach we have outlined here is that we would combine rewards and penalties and play upon Iranian desires and fears to affect their calculus. We would also build hedges into the strategy, trying to reach agreement in the first instance but setting the stage for deterrence or the use of force if agreement proves impossible—something we also see as part of our engagement approach.

Sometimes even the best efforts at statecraft do not work, and that could prove to be the case with Iran. But before we come to that conclusion, it is time to try a serious approach to statecraft that neither rejects diplomacy (as the neoconservatives do) nor acquiesces to the Iranians (as the realists are inclined to do).

Chapter Ten

REALIST FALLACIES
IN DIPLOMACY: ENGAGING
HIZBOLLAH AND HAMAS

To self-described foreign policy realists, the behavior of nonstate actors is essentially irrelevant to whether or not they ought to be engaged. In answer to questions such as whom to engage and under what conditions, the realists would say: talk to everyone, without qualification. Unfortunately, this approach too often leads to the misconception or mythology that you can make peace with anyone.

Two members of the realist school, former national security advisors Zbigniew Brzezinski and Brent Scowcroft, have repeatedly said that they favor engaging Hamas. Along with a few other policymakers, they signed a joint statement in 2007 that declared: "We believe that a genuine dialogue with the organization [Hamas] is far preferable to isolation."[1] At the core of their idea is the view that diplomatic engagement provides the prospects of progress and moderation, while isolation does not.

Their support of this idea came as the Bush administration was strongly criticized for not engaging Iran and Syria. If one should engage these troublesome regimes, why not Hizbollah and Hamas? Isn't it inconsistent to support the engagement of some and not others, when all may be considered bad actors on the international stage?

Yet there is a difference between engaging state and nonstate actors, and it is one of the realists' greatest mythologies to believe that political engagement with Islamist nonstate actors (who practice terrorism) is essential to pursuing peace in the Middle East. Their mistaken belief is that these groups can be persuaded to foster such peace.

Misdirected, ill-timed engagement, however, will not come cost-free. It will exact high costs on policy. And the relationship between nonstate actors and the often fragile regimes or nascent democracies that house them is tenuous at best. Such dynamics need to be carefully analyzed before any diplomatic steps are taken.

In this chapter, we outline the concepts behind the realists' key arguments for engagement with nonstate actors—with a focus on Hizbollah and Hamas—and explain why these assumptions are misguided. We will show why the realists are mistaken in believing that the United States should engage state and nonstate actors alike—even as, in 2008, the Bush administration was mistaken to not engage Iran and Syria.

THE DIFFERENCES BETWEEN STATE AND NONSTATE ACTORS

To begin with, it is essential to draw a distinction between states, such as Iran and Syria, and nonstate actors, such as Hizbollah and Hamas. States exist on the world stage and their recognition is not in question. By not talking to them, we do not delegitimize them. Their standing remains. Our interest is to make the outlandish behavior of rogue states the focal point of international attention, not our lack of engagement with them. Paradoxically, our willingness to engage such states makes it easier to adopt a tougher policy toward them if they are not responsive. If after we show good-faith readiness to engage them it is still impossible to reach an agreement, the onus for this failure is far more likely to be put on these rogue states.

There are other reasons to draw distinctions between states and nonstate actors when considering engagement. For one thing, states have defined and tangible interests. Their gains and losses are far easier to measure than those of nonstate actors, and the use of incentives and disincentives—the lifeblood of negotiations—are far more likely to have an effect on their behavior.

For another thing, states can be held accountable. Unlike nonstate actors, states have a central address. It is clear who bears responsibility for certain actions. Even if leaders are not answerable to their own citizens, such as in nondemocratic states, they can be held accountable in an international context. For instance, they may be subject to sanctions or isolation or other penalties or rewards. This does not guarantee that states will behave in a perfectly rational manner. Some are reckless in their behavior, and others may simply miscalculate. Nonetheless, the combination of states' definable interests and international accountability strengthens the rationale for engaging them in diplomatic negotiation.

For nonstate actors, the situation is fundamentally different. There is no central address, but they are constantly seeking recognition. They want to be an arbiter. They want international standing. They want to use this standing not to assume responsibility but to create the sense that the achievement of their purposes is inevitable. International recognition grants legitimacy and gives momentum to their agendas—and helps shield these agendas from deeper questioning.

Organizations such as Hamas often like to meet with high-profile figures such as Jimmy Carter to increase the recognition conferred upon them. Nonstate actors know that they gain from such meetings. They want to demonstrate that it is the world that must adjust to them, and not the other way around. While it may be necessary to use third parties to communicate with such groups regarding tactical cease-fires and the like, such indirect communication is not the equivalent of engagement. The latter is an important card that should not be given away for free.

Moreover, in contrast to states, the interests of nonstate actors are often ideologically driven. In the context of this book, we are not seeking to catalogue how all nonstate actors believe and act. In the specific context of the Middle East and the Arab-Israel conflict, we can say that two nonstate actors, Hizbollah and Hamas, are often motivated by factors far removed from political interests and accountability. Rather, their missions consist of ideological agendas that they seek to impose by force.

Because they lack a central address and definable accountability, nonstate actors must be judged differently. It is unlikely that those who advocate suicide bombings and initiate wars without the approval of their host governments can be deterred in the same ways as those governments. Nonstate actors are more likely to think along ideological than pragmatic lines, and assuming the role of the victim often adds to their appeal or the narrative they seek to promote. Indeed, for both Hizbollah and Hamas, winning is often the product of merely surviving—for example, they see fighting Israel and surviving as a great accomplishment, particularly when compared to the existing Arab regimes, which always seem to lose in any confrontation with Israel. If they can provoke Israel into inflicting civilian casualties in the process, so much the better in their eyes. With such an orientation and with such strong, ideologically driven behaviors, it is essential to establish preconditions before the United States considers talking to such groups.

In addition to their rejection of coexistence with Israel and their use and support of terror, both Hamas and Hizbollah create another problem. Each challenges its host government, and over the last few years both have seen great value in taking part in elections as a way of enhancing their political power. While they are keen to use democratic machinery to build their legitimacy, they refuse to play by the rules of the democratic game. They fiercely resist any effort to disband their respective private militias and become purely political actors. Indeed, they have already demonstrated their readiness to use their weapons when the political process and circumstances do not suit them—witness Hamas's coup in Gaza in 2007 and Hizbollah's use of force against the Lebanese government in 2008.

Consequently they pose nearly impossible challenges to extremely fragile regional experiments in democracy. While the Oslo Accords forbade rejectionist parties from running in elections, the Palestinian Authority (PA) was too weak to enforce that rule (and the Bush administration made no effort to see it enforced even as it insisted that the elections be held); not surprisingly, Hamas ran and won (with a plurality of 44.45 percent) in 2006. No nascent democracy can sustain itself in the presence of private militias that have no compunction about acting outside of and in direct contradiction to state authority. These groups may win at least some power by promising an alternative to corruption, but once in power they pursue their own narrow agendas, which are not only corrupt but destructive. And once they have planted themselves in these democratic systems, as a determined minority, they can use the force at their disposal to intimidate and effectively veto any decision—or effectively pursue any path they want without regard to its consequences for the state.

There is a simple way to test whether such groups are ready to be part of something larger or whether they merely want to exploit the state for certain benefits. Are they willing to give the state what the sociologist Max Weber called "a monopoly over the use of force"?[2] Groups such as the Islamic Action Front in Jordan and the Muslim Brotherhood in Egypt eschew the use of violence in the democratic system. In contrast, Hamas and Hizbollah do not, adamantly refusing to dismantle their own militias.

Jordan's former foreign minister, Marwan Muasher, explained the consequence of this behavior when he stated, "Any political party in the Arab world must pursue their objectives through peaceful means. . . . If Hizbollah or Hamas want to be in power, I think they are more than entitled to be that, but they cannot carry arms with one hand and be in the system with the other. . . . Otherwise, people will feel that these arms might be used against them and they will feel equally the need to arm themselves."[3]

These groups are in effect declaring their independence from any political system; they can always opt out and act on their own terms. At their core, they are dedicated to advancing their own ideological interests by any means necessary instead of being part of any truly democratic or independent polity. Their commitment to sectarian ideology over the national good may be one of the most powerful arguments against diplomatic engagement with them.

Those in the realist school of thought, unfortunately, tend to approach the idea of engagement in a vacuum. They do not give much consideration to how engagement with Islamist groups might impact fragile experiments in democracy. This may be because it is power rather than democracy that animates the realists. They think that all American foreign policy must be driven by tangible interests, be they military or economic, and not by Western values. They do not have a moral lens for looking at foreign policy. Moreover, they rarely see any connection between the internal dynamics of a society and that country's outward behavior. For example, in their eyes, democratization in the Arab world is at best an irrelevancy for the United States. At worst, it is a serious impediment for close ties between the United States and the Arab regimes. Therefore, since Saudi Arabia is critical to the United States as an oil supplier, why anger the Saudi royal family by raising the issue of democracy? The Saudi royal family will invariably view democratization as a threat, as it could dilute or even eliminate its power. The democratic power that may come to the fore might not provide oil or could be anti-American. Thus, it is best for the United States to avoid raising any issue that could interfere with American economic interests.

One should not caricature the realists' position by insisting that they are uninterested in democracy. Rather, the instinct of the realists is to downplay democratic processes abroad or invoke other superseding interests. They compound their problem, however, by also appearing to be oblivious to the impact that U.S. diplomatic engagement with such groups would have on moderates who favor coexistence with others, including Israel. These moderates are America's natural partners in the region. They constitute the majority of the Palestinian and Lebanese populations—namely, those who back the PA and the government of Lebanon. Unconditional engagement completely undermines those moderates who risk their lives in support of coexistence. In such a context, moderates will be quickly viewed inside their country as quislings or collaborators. Moderation will be viewed internally as unprincipled weakness, and the effectiveness of moderates will evaporate. Moderation wins domestic political support when it is a vehicle to achieving national aims. If there are other parties who sound more nationalistic and have international legitimacy, who will look to the moderates, and why not use terror to deal with grievances? Of course, the impasse in peace negotiations could achieve the same negative impact on the moderates. This is one of the reasons why we favor an active peace process. However, it is counterproductive to engage such groups, as we hurt the people we want to help and help the people whom we should want to hurt.

In short, the realists are wrong in not making distinctions between states and nonstate actors. They are wrong in not making a distinction between Islamists who will play by democratic rules and those such as Hamas and Hizbollah who do not. They are wrong in underestimating the implications of such engagement for moderate partners in the region who are willing to accept coexistence.

It makes little sense to engage such groups. In saying this, we are not ruling out direct engagement if these groups meet certain conditions. But there is good reason to insist that they meet threshold criteria before they are to reap the benefits of diplomacy. Such criteria were met by the Palestine Liberation Organization (PLO) in the late 1980s, paving the way for engagement with the United States and ultimately for the Oslo Accords with Israel in 1993. It is up to the international community to use all available leverage and demonstrate that such nonstate groups are the ones who must change their behavior, not the international community.

In at least some cases, the international community has in fact operated in this fashion. Consider the case of Hamas. The restrictions imposed on it after the 2006 elections, which Hamas won, were adopted by the 'Quartet'—the United States, the European Union, Russia, and the United Nations. Very few experts would have expected the other three members to stick with the United States almost three years after the Quartet imposed such sanctions. Given the animosity toward the Bush administration and a traditional tilt among the other three members of the Quartet toward the Palestinians, a split seemed inevitable. But sanctions have remained contingent upon Hamas's renunciation of violence, recognition of the existence of Israel, and acceptance of past Israeli-Palestinian agreements. To date, the members of the Quartet—with the exception of the Russians, who meet with Hamas leaders—have not accepted the realist argument for engaging Hamas. So long as the basic orientation and purposes of Hamas and Hizbollah do not change, it would be self-defeating to accept the realist argument for engaging them.

LOOKING MORE CLOSELY
AT HIZBOLLAH AND HAMAS

Both Hizbollah and Hamas prioritize their sectarian ideology and use their private militias to defiantly impose their will on the rest of their countrymen. There is ample evidence that these groups marry ideology and a militia in order to try to impose their will on their host governments. Hizbollah never gave up its weapons after the signing of the Taif Accord in 1989, when the other Lebanese factions disarmed. Is it a surprise that both groups, who claim that their weapons are needed against Israel, actually used these weapons against their own people? In each case, unfortunately, the force has been devastatingly effective.

Undoubtedly Hizbollah appreciates the economic and political benefits that being part of the Lebanese government confers. However, at the same time, it does not feel bound by the Lebanese government or its policies. This was evident in the summer of 2006, when Hizbollah felt it was within its power to take an entire country to war by crossing an international border—demarcated by the UN—into Israel, killing Israeli soldiers, kidnapping others, and triggering Israel's retaliation. Hizbollah never consulted the Lebanese government, of which it is a part. As demonstrated in the 2006 war, Hizbollah apparently believes that issues of war and peace lie within its purview and do not require the approval of the government.

In this connection, Lebanese interior minister Ahmad Fatfat issued thinly veiled criticism of Hizbollah in the month after the thirty-four-day war's conclusion when he declared, "The use of strategic weapons to strike at the depth of another country is tantamount to inviting that country to strike at the Lebanese depth. This is something that cannot be delegated to a single side within the state; it is the right of the state to decide this."[4]

But Hizbollah felt no obligation to respect the right of the state. The same held true for the PLO when it was based in Jordan from 1968 to 1970, and then Lebanon after that until 1982. Hizbollah's leaders followed their own agenda, using extensive funding provided by Tehran, as well as Iranian and Syrian weapons. The group repeated the same pattern two years later, shocking many both in and outside Lebanon. In the spring of 2008, Hizbollah set off intra-Lebanese fighting when the Lebanese government sought to exercise its sovereignty over all telecommunications in the country and tried to close down, or at least control, a separate fiber optic communication network operated by the group.

Referring to this network, Lebanese communications minister Marwan Hamadah charged Hizbollah with establishing "a general communications network all over Lebanon under their control and under Iranian control."[5] Hamadah blamed Hizbollah for acting independently of Lebanon and insisted that the Lebanese government's objectives were modest. He went on to draw a larger point about Hizbollah's operating independently of the Lebanese government in security matters: "We have never asked Hizbollah to hand over its arms. We asked it to come to the negotiations table and draw up a defense policy in coordination with the Lebanese Army, provided that the war-and-peace decision remains the prerogative of the Lebanese central government, as it is in all countries of the world."[6]

For its part, Hizbollah refused to cut its Iranian-funded telecommunications system, which is independent of the Lebanese government. It also demanded that the government reinstate a pro-Hizbollah general to oversee Beirut airport security.[7] This was critical for Hizbollah, apparently, as it wished to preserve its ability to smuggle resources and supplies into Lebanon from other countries, including Iran.

When confronted on these points, Hizbollah was willing to cross a redline that all the other battle-scarred factions in Lebanon's civil war of 1975–90 pledged not to cross—intentional, large-scale killing of fellow Lebanese. During the May 2008 conflict, which left eighty dead, Lebanese prime minister Fouad Siniora branded Hizbollah as worse than Israel, saying, "Even the Israeli enemy never dared to do to Beirut what Hizbollah has done."[8]

May 2008 provides us with a lesson on how Hizbollah operates. While there are some who claim Hizbollah's political and military wings work separately and are disconnected from each other, there is no evidence to support this argument. On the contrary, Hizbollah's strength has always been its ability to leverage its power in both directions. It uses its armed forces against the existing government, and it uses its political position to insulate these forces. This dual leverage was evident in May 2008, when its militia fired on Lebanese civilians and Sunni militiamen associated with the March 14 Alliance. Hizbollah knew the Lebanese Armed Forces (LAF) would not fire back, as the LAF's leaders had instructed the army to avoid internal conflict. Since the other militias disbanded in 1989, in keeping with the requirements of the Taif Accord, Hizbollah had no counterweight, particularly as the army was not prepared to intervene against it. The group's military action broke a political stalemate within Lebanon—to Hizbollah's advantage. Talks were hastily held in Qatar—not in Saudi Arabia, as had occurred in the past. This was not coincidental, given Qatar's close ties with Iran. In these talks, Hizbollah won its demands to change the electoral system to its advantage and be given a veto over all Lebanese national security decisions. In short, military means were used to secure political power.

Repeatedly, Hizbollah has aligned itself with the Lebanese government only when doing so would meet its own ends. In 2000 the group took credit for Israel's unilateral withdrawal from Lebanon, and its political support skyrocketed. Then, at the end of the 2006 war, Hizbollah insisted that UN Security Council Resolution 1701 not authorize a UN force to disarm southern Lebanon independent of the authority of the Lebanese government and the LAF. Their rationale was obvious. Hizbollah has enough political sway to know that the LAF will not use the UN force as a lever against them. Therefore, the UN force would only be allowed to operate to the extent it did not interfere with Hizbollah's weaponry. Israeli foreign minister Tzipi Livni named this as the most contentious point in the diplomacy focused on ending the war. Hizbollah's success in insisting upon this point undercut any possible effectiveness of the UN force and enabled Hizbollah not only to rebuild its forces but to massively expand the number of rockets it now possesses. Thus, Hizbollah's political clout secured its military might.

However one looks at it, the political and military wings of Hizbollah are not separate forces. When the Dutch government wondered whether it should designate the entire organization a terror group, it reached the conclusion that "Hizbollah's political and terrorist wings are controlled by one coordinating council" and that therefore "there is indeed a link between these parts of the organization."[9] The Dutch conclusion was not unprecedented. The United States, Australia, and Canada also hold that the political wing of Hizbollah is a terrorist group.

It is pointless to believe that we can engage one part of an organization at the expense of the other—and it sends the wrong message. As terrorism expert Bruce Hoffman notes, "Our problem is that Hizbollah's path to legitimacy has been purchased with the blood of over 300 dead Americans, and the model that its leaders are now actively seeking to export challenges the axiom that terrorism doesn't work. As long as the Hizbollah model goes unchallenged, we will have no hope of persuading other aggrieved groups that terror is a repugnant and useless tool for gaining legitimate political power."[10]

Just as Hizbollah acts to weaken the Lebanese government, challenge it, and undercut its effectiveness and legitimacy, so too does Hamas seek to erode and diminish the PA and its decisions. Hamas answers only to its own ideological agenda. When Israel left Gaza in 2005 and PA president Mahmoud Abbas urged Palestinians to demonstrate to the world that they could manage Gaza in a peaceful manner, Hamas claimed for itself the right to fire rockets into Israel even though it did not have PA government clearance. Rocket fire continued unabated. What began as an action against Israel turned against the PA itself. By the summer of 2007, Hamas staged a coup in Gaza during which it threw PA members out windows and off roofs and took over the security services and television station. Many Palestinians thought Hamas would never be guilty of starting a *fitna*, or civil strife, but the group crossed that line with little or no hesitation.

In fact, Hamas continued to use force against the Palestinian population during 2008. It took advantage of a six-month cease-fire with Israel to consolidate control over the Gaza Strip. This included attacks on rival clan strongholds that resulted in high numbers of casualties, including women and children. It also chose to place its munitions stockpiles and rocket launchers in densely populated civilian areas, particularly in sensitive locations such as schools and mosques. The extensive use of human shields produced predictable results. When Hamas ended the cease-fire in December and proceeded to fire hundreds of rockets into southern Israel, Israel retaliated to degrade Hamas weapons capability by bombing tunnels on the Egypt-Gaza border that were being used to smuggle missiles capable of reaching the outskirts of Tel Aviv. Tragically, 1,300 Palestinians were killed. Even as Operation Cast Lead was under way, Hamas continued to execute Fatah sympathizers, as well as those accused of the very broad charge of "collaboration with Israel."

How do weak moderate regimes deal with such internal challenges? Mahmoud Abbas recognized the danger of such groups when he said, "A political party plus a militia is unacceptable."[11] Unfortunately, Abbas later conceded this issue under pressure from Hamas. Whether in the PA or the Lebanese government, moderate elements have frequently lacked the capability to assert their authority over Islamist parties. These fragile regimes do not have developed state institutions, whereas the Islamist parties have a deep ideological commitment that gives them an air of authenticity. Yet it is counterproductive to allow these Islamist groups to dictate the terms of engagement. In the case of the Palestinians, their democratic system was so fragile that Abbas may not have had the leverage to insist upon key issues. But the international community has leverage in dealing with such groups, and this should not be lost by making political engagement unconditional. By not setting fair criteria, we empower those people whose behavior is abhorrent—even as we undermine our friends.

REALISTS' CORE ARGUMENTS IN THE CONTEXT OF THE MIDDLE EAST

A myth of the realists is that one should engage Hamas and Hizbollah, believing the ideology of these groups is irrelevant and it is imperative to engage everyone in the Middle East who is perceived to have power. The realists make different arguments to support this view. Embedded in their arguments is an assumption that the act of negotiation is a transformative experience for any actor, regardless of agenda or past actions.

One argument against preconditions states that the prior intent of the other party is irrelevant. You make peace with your enemies, not your friends. According to this view, Hizbollah and Hamas, while not moderate by any means, are worthy interlocutors because the dynamic of negotiations changes everything. If only these groups were brought inside the political tent, they would become constructive partners in promoting peace and ending tragic conflict. Drawing upon historical precedents such as Britain's experience with Sinn Fein of Northern Ireland, this argument insists that the dynamism of negotiations is such that ideologically implacable foes ultimately abandon their agendas for the greater practical rewards of peace. Zbigniew Brzezinski has written, "Missing from much of the public debate is discussion of the simple fact that lurking behind every terroristic act is a specific political antecedent. That does not justify either the perpetrator or his political cause. Nonetheless, the fact is that almost all terrorist activity originates from some political conflict and is sustained by it as well. That is true of the Irish Republican Army in Northern Ireland, the Basques in Spain, the Palestinians in the West Bank and Gaza, the Muslims in Kashmir and so forth."[12] The conclusion is clear: engagement will end the conflict, so talk to everyone— the more extreme, the more relevant to the object of peace.

Ahmed Yousef, a Hamas official often touted as one of the pragmatists in the group, has also used the IRA example. Yousef stated, "After all, the IRA agreed to halt its military struggle to free Northern Ireland from British rule without recognizing British sovereignty. Irish Republicans continue to aspire to a united Ireland, free of British rule, but rely upon peaceful methods. Had the IRA been forced to renounce its vision of reuniting Ireland before negotiations could occur, peace would never have prevailed. Why should more be demanded of the Palestinians?"[13]

A second, related argument is built around the realist assumption that ideology is largely a cloak for power. Thus ideology is merely a useful tool for Hamas and Hizbollah. Moreover, political engagement will create and highlight internal fissures, strengthening the more pragmatic elements in these groups who are willing to make peace while weakening the more radical ones—and engagement can defuse or address grievances. According to this view, diplomatic engagement is a small price to pay given the potential benefit of ending all conflicts. Engagement is not a reward for good behavior, but rather an instrument to advance the objectives of peace and moderation. Indeed, John Mearsheimer and Stephen Walt have made this case both to impugn Israel's intentions and to argue for dealing with Hamas. Note their words: "If the Israelis were genuinely interested in reaching a peace agreement with the Palestinians, they could work with the Arab League, Abbas, and the more moderate elements within Hamas to push the peace process forward and isolate—or maybe even convert—the rejectionists in Hamas and other radical groups like Islamic Jihad."[14] In other words, rejectionists don't reject out of belief but rather out of grievance and circumstance.

Yet another argument used to justify negotiations with groups such as Hizbollah and Hamas is that these groups were elected and are therefore entitled to be included in negotiations, regardless of their views. Failure to engage will only boomerang and create a public backlash in the societies of which these groups are a part. Consequently, nonengagement and isolation is a self-defeating policy because it is likely to bolster radicalization and violence—not moderation, as intended. One needs to engage the groups that are rooted in the social fabric of their land—be it Gaza, the West Bank, or Lebanon—and thereby acknowledge political realities on the ground. Rami Khouri, editor-at-large of Beirut's *Daily Star*, declared, "Hamas is a major and legitimate player and was also democratically elected. It cannot be avoided."[15] Brzezinski goes further, criticizing the consequences of exclusion after the elections by saying, "We have exercised our power to insist on elections in Palestine, which Hamas did win. Once they won, we then engaged in a policy not only of ostracism, but of financial boycott, in effect undermining it, and creating more tension and radicalism and poverty in Gaza, which was susceptible to exploitation by Hamas."[16]

While these arguments (and the assumptions that guide them) have a surface plausibility, they once again fail to meet the test of reality in the Middle East in general and in the Arab-Israeli context in particular. It may seem paradoxical, but the core realist arguments are all too often divorced from reality. To demonstrate how and why they fail to reflect real-world conditions, we will address them one by one and explain why they fail the reality test—particularly when it comes to insisting on unconditional engagement with Hamas and Hizbollah.

Realist myth no. 1. All preconditions to engagement must be avoided.

According to this view, intentions and ideology are irrelevant. All negotiations—even between enemies—are beneficial. It is therefore best to negotiate without any preconditions because these can only be obstacles to peace. Proponents of this approach, such as Brzezinski and Ahmed Yousef, have, as noted above, used the case of Northern Ireland as an example of its success. In Northern Ireland, Great Britain unsuccessfully tried to subdue the Irish Republican Army (IRA). The military option failed, and alternative peace efforts to negotiate with nonmilitants were also unsuccessful. Talks with the IRA, on the other hand, succeeded. For the realists, the analogy is clear: Israel has not defeated Hamas and Hizbollah, therefore Israel should talk to both of them.

Yet there is a problem with the analogy. It is worth noting some obvious differences at the outset. First, neither the IRA nor Sinn Fein had as one of its goals the destruction of Great Britain. Rather, these groups merely sought the unification of Ireland. Sinn Fein, a political party associated with the IRA, was committed to achieving a united Ireland. Even if it supported force as a means to achieving this goal, the goal itself was potentially compatible with that of Great Britain, whose existence was never threatened. While the violent method used to achieve the IRA's and Sinn Fein's objectives was abhorrent, British withdrawal from Northern Ireland would not affect British survival. Hizbollah and Hamas, by contrast, are not prepared to tolerate Israel's existence in principle or in practice.

Second, and again keeping in mind the question of whether or how the example of Northern Ireland might be applicable to the Middle East, it is worth noting the instrumental role that the Irish government played in the peace talks. This could be instructive in the context of the Middle East. Dublin has consistently provided the type of leadership that the Arab states, sadly, have not. The Irish government worked closely with Britain in a bid to solve the conflict. Specifically, the former had no problem speaking of the inadmissibility of violence as part of the peace process in Northern Ireland. It listed clear criteria for any party that wanted to be considered a legitimate partner in solving the conflict.

In contrast, while some Arab states privately shun Hamas or Hizbollah, they do not condemn these groups' ideology in public. They may condemn an individual attack or the loss of innocent lives, but they avoid condemning either group by name or as a perpetrator of terrorism—or declare that violence is wrong, because they will never say that resistance is wrong.[17] Such states would never tolerate armed Islamist militias in their own countries like those that exist in Lebanon and Gaza. In addition, some regional states such as Iran and Syria actively arm these groups; the contrast with Dublin's assumption of a leading role and its readiness to spell out acceptable and unacceptable behavior could not be more striking.

But the main reason why this is a failed analogy is that Sinn Fein did in fact fulfill very explicit preconditions for peace talks. Indeed, the preconditions of the 1990s were far more stringent than those insisted upon today in the case of Hamas. In other words, the story of Northern Ireland actually *proves* the importance of preconditions.

Because preconditions are so central to the story of diplomatic success in Northern Ireland, and because the realists argue that if the terrorist IRA could be engaged, then so too can Hamas, it is worth explaining the history of the Good Friday process in some detail.

DIPLOMACY'S GOOD FRIDAY SUCCESS: BACKGROUND AND LESSONS

On December 15, 1993, in what became known as the Downing Street Declaration, the leaders of Britain and Ireland defined the objectives of the peace process, including who would be eligible to discuss the fate of Northern Ireland. The declaration states: "The achievement of peace must involve a permanent end to the use of, or support for, paramilitary violence. They confirm that, in these circumstances, democratically mandated parties which establish a commitment to exclusively peaceful methods and which have shown that they abide by the democratic process, are free to participate fully in democratic politics and to join in dialogue in due course between the Governments and the political parties on the way ahead."[18] The IRA declared a cease-fire on August 30, 1994, in a statement that explicitly favored a peace process: "Recognizing the potential of the current situation and in order to enhance the democratic peace process and to underline our commitment to its success, the leadership [of the IRA] have decided that from midnight there will be a complete cessation of military operations."[19]

Yet it was not enough for the IRA to commit itself to a "complete cessation of military operations" and the success of the peace process. On March 7, 1995, Britain insisted that the IRA agree to decommission arms, with a tangible plan of how this would be accomplished. British secretary of state for Northern Ireland Sir Patrick Mayhew announced that the credibility of the peace process was tied to the start of disarmament: "In order to test the practical arrangements and to demonstrate good faith, the actual decommissioning of some arms [is necessary] as a tangible confidence building measure and to signal the start of the process."[20] Britain did not only want the IRA to commit itself to the *principle* of decommissioning; it wanted to see group members give up their weapons. Progress was slow due to occasional violations of the cease-fire, and also due to British political turbulence as the Conservative Party was replaced by a Labour government under Tony Blair. However, by 1997, a new cease-fire was instated.

On August 26, 1997, the British and Irish governments agreed to the formation of the Independent International Commission on Decommissioning. But the IRA resisted the British demand for it to turn over its weapons before negotiations began. George Mitchell, the U.S. peace negotiator for Northern Ireland, understood that a group that maintains weapons during a delicate political process is seeking to use violence and arms as leverage on this process. Note Mitchell's words: "For years, the republican movement pursued a dual strategy of both the bullet and the ballot box: Use the political process to make what gains were possible, and at the same time maintain the use, and the threat of violence to move the political process along. Indeed, it was an article of faith among some republicans that the British government would change its Northern Ireland policy only as a reaction to violence, especially in Britain."[21] To address this issue, Mitchell crafted what became known as the Mitchell Principles. These stated the following:

> To reach an agreed political settlement and to take the gun out of Irish politics, there must be commitment and adherence to fundamental principles of democracy and nonviolence. Participants in an all-party negotiations should affirm their commitment to such

principles. Accordingly, we recommend that the parties to such negotiations affirm their total and absolute commitment:

a. To democratic and exclusively peaceful means of resolving political issues;
b. To the total disarmament of all paramilitary organizations;
c. To agree that such disarmament must be verifiable to the satisfaction of an independent commission;
d. To renounce for themselves, and to oppose any effort by others, to use force, or threaten to use force, to influence the course or the outcome of all-party negotiations;
e. To agree to abide by the terms of any agreement reached in all-party negotiations and to resort to democratic and exclusively peaceful methods in trying to alter any aspect of that outcome with which they may disagree; and
f. To urge that "punishment" killings and beatings stop and take effective steps to prevent such actions.[22]

The IRA did not rush to accept the Mitchell Principles, even though it did reiterate its commitment to the cease-fire in the summer of 1997. Then British prime minister Blair stated that if the IRA violated the cease-fire, Sinn Fein could not be part of a peace process. Only on September 9, 1997, did Sinn Fein accept the Mitchell Principles, and at that point it was permitted to join the Irish peace process and Sinn Fein leader Gerry Adams was able to meet Blair.

Needless to say, the Mitchell Principles go far beyond the conditions of the Quartet regarding Hamas. If realists want to apply the case of Northern Ireland and the IRA to Hamas, then it would be essential for political representatives of Hamas (or for that matter Hizbollah) to take a public stand calling for peace, renouncing the use of force, and agreeing to give up their weapons at some point in the process. If Hamas or Hizbollah were to act like Sinn Fein it would be a powerful development in the Middle East. It would dramatically improve the climate surrounding peace talks, proving to a distrustful public that the future can be different from the past.

One final point is worth noting: the IRA's decision to accept a cease-fire and enable Sinn Fein to participate in the 1997 peace talks came at a time when it was under considerable military pressure. It was not the IRA of earlier years, when terror attacks were more frequent and public support stronger. Thus another lesson worth drawing is that not yielding to terrorism benefited Britain over time, as the IRA realized that it would be advantageous to enable Sinn Fein to accept the Mitchell Principles and enter the peace talks. David Trimble, a moderate Irish Protestant political leader, later said, "There was always push and pull with this business of republicans coming into politics. The push was the success of the security forces and disenchantment of the core support the IRA had relied on. There was a pull factor, too, in the attraction of politics and the possibility of political success."[23]

In contrast, Hamas's and Hizbollah's militant capability is more serious than the IRA's power ever was. Consequently, its threat of force is greater. Or, as two analysts—Steve Simon and Jonathan Stevenson—put it, "Hamas is not Sinn Fein: it is more a rigid militia than a pragmatic political party, and it will conclusively relent only in response to force."[24] These groups will not change their basic ideology unless they face external pressure. Otherwise, they have no incentive to do so. While the diplomatic door should be held open to Hamas and Hizbollah, the onus is on them to meet the needed preconditions in order to ensure the success of diplomacy.

Realist myth no. 2. Hamas and Hizbollah are worthy of diplomatic engagement because they are pragmatic at heart.

Another key argument is that Hamas and Hizbollah are worthy of engagement because their ideological commitments are not so strong as to rule out pragmatism. Such questioning of these groups' ideological fervor is compatible with the signature realist belief that politics is all about power, and values are irrelevant. Ideological arguments must be malleable since they only disguise an otherwise understandable search for power. The intellectual godfather of the realist school, Hans J. Morgenthau, stated this view clearly when he said, "The main signpost that helps political realism to find its way through the landscape of international politics is the concept of interest defined in terms of power." In the realist view, even violence and terror are only instruments that lead to diplomatic negotiation.

The realists' discomfort with ideology reflects a traditional discomfort of the American people. Indeed, Americans are under the impression that their pragmatism is mirrored by everyone else in the world. It is easier to believe that all groups are motivated by legitimate grievances that can be redressed in a rational manner. This discomfort with ideology has evolved, however, since September 11, 2001, when Americans realized that some groups are so fanatical that they fly planes into buildings. One does not have to argue that Hamas is part of al-Qaeda's international jihadist movement to claim that it may be just as strongly committed to an ideological platform of its own.

American pragmatism will find Hamas's and Hizbollah's ideological commitments very troubling, and it is tempting to just wish such troubles away. These groups' willingness to declare cease-fires to serve tactical purposes is often taken by the realists as a sign that Hamas and Hizbollah are in fact filled with "closet" pragmatists. It is true that both groups are capable of demonstrating short-term tactical flexibility. As Hamas seeks to consolidate its authority and prove to the people of Gaza that it is capable of governing, the group's only hope of maintaining a "business-as-usual" façade is to call for an occasional cease-fire—usually under military pressure from Israel. Yet it is hard to equate this self-interest with pragmatism when it comes to the larger question of coexistence with Israel.[25] This was vividly demonstrated in December 2008, when Hamas ended the Egyptian-brokered cease-fire and launched hundreds of rockets at southern Israel. An uneasy quiet was restored only after the IDF had destroyed nearly all Hamas military targets and killed their third-in-command.

The view that Hamas is not wedded to its militant goal of destroying Israel was apparent during the 2008 visit by former president Jimmy Carter to the Middle East. Unlike Brzezinski, his former national security advisor, Carter would not consider himself a realist. Yet for many years he believed in the necessity of engaging Hamas. This view was most clearly presented during his 2008 visit. After meeting with the Hamas leadership in Damascus, including the head of its political bureau, Khaled Mashal, Carter returned to Jerusalem and insisted that he had a written commitment from Hamas that it would abide by a PA-Israeli peace agreement so long as it was submitted to the Palestinians for a referendum. Carter viewed this statement as a vindication of his view that Hamas should be engaged. The former president told the Israel Council on Foreign

Relations, "[I]f President Abbas succeeds in negotiating a final status agreement with Israel, Hamas will accept the decision made by the Palestinian people and their will through a referendum . . . or by a newly-elected Palestinian national council . . . even if Hamas is opposed to the agreement. Verbatim, this is their language."[26]

Within just a few hours, however, Mashal gave a televised address from Damascus that contradicted Carter's statement. Among other things, Mashal stated that Hamas would not recognize Israel even if a peace agreement won in a worldwide Palestinian referendum. Mashal went on to declare, "We approve of a state that exists on the borders of 4 June 1967, with Jerusalem as its capital, with real sovereignty, without any settlements, and with the full right to return, but without recognizing Israel."[27] In other words, Israel would receive no recognition, but a state could be accepted next to Israel. However, "the full right to return" is coded language for the right of an estimated few million Palestinian refugees and their descendents to flood Israel.[28] Mashal knows very well that the right of return that he advocates would, unless qualified and limited, destroy the Jewish character of Israel and make it a binational state. He also knows that Israeli leaders will not be complicit in their own destruction.

But even this did not go far enough for Mashal. He further distanced himself from Carter's statement by referring to the "prisoners' document," a well-publicized document cobbled together by some Fatah and Hamas prisoners in an Israeli jail in 2006. The document states that any referendum on peace will have to include all the Palestinians in the world, including those living abroad. In other words, Mashal's concept of a referendum is that millions of Palestinians around the world should be able to vote, outnumbering the Palestinians living in the West Bank and Gaza. He is assuming that Palestinian expatriates would turn down an agreement that only gives them the right to return to a newly created Palestinian state and not to their former homes in Israel. This referendum idea is therefore a nonstarter.[29] Mashal's insistence on the "full right to return" of Palestinian refugees and an unwise and unworkable referendum rendered the substantive part of Carter's talks meaningless. But if one does not understand the coded language, one might believe the visit was successful—President Carter certainly thought so.

Riad al-Malki, the foreign minister of the Palestinian Authority, was not fooled by the Carter visit. Note his words, "President Carter came to the region thinking he could achieve something. Unfortunately President Carter left without anything concrete." He added, "Hamas offered nothing to President Carter. They reiterated the same positions. There was no change on the part of Hamas."[30]

Yet the meetings had great value for Hamas, and won it a public relations victory (Carter is the only former U.S. president to meet with the group's leaders). Western visitors—journalists and others—have met with Mashal and believed they have come to a diplomatic breakthrough, then immediately realized the Hamas proposal was actually hollow. Hamas is happy to repeat this scenario because it believes it conditions the American public and the international community to the reality of having to deal with them without having to shift its position at all. In other words, contrary to the view of those who favor engagement based on the assertion that Hamas actually wants peace, engagement has historically proven to be a futile exercise. Hamas has sadly proven itself to be disingenuous time and again—or, stated differently, has been prepared to go to great lengths to prove that its belief system really does matter.

ADDITIONAL INDICATORS OF HIZBOLLAH'S AND HAMAS'S IDEOLOGICAL FERVOR

There are surely other signs of how committed Hizbollah and Hamas are to their ideological positions. Consider how each responded to Israel's unilateral withdrawal from Lebanon and Gaza. Both Hamas and Hizbollah interpreted Israeli withdrawal from Lebanon and Gaza as a sign of weakness to be exploited, not an Israeli step toward coexistence to be encouraged. Each emphasized that Israel's departure from Lebanon in 2000 and Gaza in 2005 was not a sign that Israel wanted to end occupation of Arab lands and coexist with its Arab neighbors, but that Israel was weak and their violence needed to be intensified. Hizbollah's leader, Hassan Nasrallah, was quick to take credit for Israel's exit. In a speech he gave in the immediate aftermath of the Israeli exit from Lebanon in May 2000, Nasrallah emphasized that the Israelis' move could be read as an outright Israeli defeat and reflected Israel's weakness, not its readiness to end conflict or end the occupation of Arab lands. Speaking before thirty thousand supporters in the south Lebanese town of Bint Jbeil on May 25,

2000, Nasrallah declared, "Israel may own nuclear weapons and heavy weaponry, but by God, it is weaker than a spider's web."[31] According to Nasrallah, Israel looks menacing, but one merely needs to flick at it and it will collapse. The spiderweb metaphor became the preferred imagery for Hizbollah to describe the appearance, but not the fact, of Israeli power.

In the same speech, Nasrallah called on the Palestinians to choose violence over negotiation, and many have wondered whether this admonition helped trigger the Palestinian intifada some four months later.[32] Unfortunately, the perception that Israeli moderation or Israeli concessions equal weakness fits into Nasrallah's preconceived view of Israel's Westernized society. In a speech given less than two months before he launched the cross-border raid into Israel that triggered the war of that summer of 2006, Nasrallah described Israeli society by saying, "Another weakness is that both as individuals and as a collective, they are described by Allah as 'the people who guard their lives most.' Their strong adherence to this world, with all its vanities and pleasures, constitutes a weakness. In contrast, our people and our nation's willingness to sacrifice their blood, souls, children, fathers, and families for the sake of the nation's honor, life, and happiness has always been one of our nation's strengths."[33]

Nasrallah's words reflect a mind-set, and it is a mind-set shared by Hamas. Much like Hizbollah, Hamas also emphasized Israel's defeat in withdrawing unilaterally from Gaza. If Hamas was not largely driven by ideology but rather by core pragmatic elements motivated by legitimate grievance, would it not have sought to provide Israel with incentives to continue withdrawal beyond Gaza and from the West Bank as well? Israel uprooted all eight thousand Jewish settlers from Gaza in 2005, and yet during Hamas's rise to power (January 2006 to April 2008), more than 2,500 rockets were launched from Gaza, landing in Israeli cities and villages. Israel no longer occupies Gaza, but the rockets have largely continued—under Hamas's control. Some say that the rockets are a response to Israeli retaliation. But it is easy to disprove this. If there were no rockets, the odds are very high that Israel would have no reason to retaliate. Even during periods without Israeli retaliation, the rocket fire has continued.

Like Hamas, Hizbollah continued to fire at Israel after that nation had already withdrawn from the occupied land. After all, Israel exited Lebanon in 2000, overseen by the UN to ensure the exit was complete. Yet Hizbollah staged a cross-border raid and triggered the 2006 war with

Israel. It seems Hizbollah does not need the grievance of an occupation to keep firing at Israel and stockpiling tens of thousands of rockets.

This is not to suggest that Hamas and Hizbollah are run by fanatics who can never discern their own tactical self-interest. From time to time, Hamas and Hizbollah agree to cease-fires. But, by their own admission, one should not confuse short-term tactics with long-term strategy. Khaled Mashal, in an interview with al-Jazeera television in the spring of 2008, stated that Egypt had proposed a six-month truce between the Hamas rulers of Gaza and Israel. He said his group was ready to cooperate, but added: "It is a tactic in conducting the struggle. . . . It is normal for any resistance . . . to sometimes escalate, other times retreat a bit. . . . Hamas is known for that. In 2003, there was a cease-fire and then the operations were resumed."[34] As noted previously, Hamas did, in fact, repeat this pattern when the cease-fire ended in December 2008.

The ideological commitment of these groups is genuine and central. Indeed, if it were not central to the group's identity, Hamas would jettison ideology for international favor and fewer restrictions. Yet it refuses, despite the material benefit this would grant its leaders. Hizbollah, too, would have wider international legitimacy if it compromised its agenda. The reality is that Islamist groups like Hamas and Hizbollah have a real credo. These movements fuse religious and nationalist interests while exploiting a grievance or a set of grievances. And their ideological appeal has enabled them to acquire weaponry and financial assistance from Iran.

Hizbollah's genuine ideological commitment and fealty to Iran are sometimes couched in theocratic terms. For instance, in October 2004, a top Hizbollah official, Nawwaf al-Moussavi, told a colleague in the Hizbollah-dominated Dahiyeh, or southern suburbs, of Beirut that Hizbollah sees Iranian Supreme Leader Ayatollah Khamenei as its *vali al-faqih* (jurist-leader) and offers him unlimited obedience. Al-Moussavi said that "Nasrallah believes in *velayat al-faqih* [the guardianship of the jurist or the political supremacy of the religious leader]. He [Nasrallah] says that if *vali al-faqih* orders me to divorce my wife, according to the theory of *velayat al-faqih*, I have to do so."[35] Nasrallah's professed obedience to Iranian imperatives—even when they contradict Hizbollah's own inclinations— is one more indicator that Hizbollah is an ideologically driven movement, guided by its belief system and not by any potential for moderation or pragmatism.

Even Hizbollah's former leader, Sheikh Subhi al-Tufeili, who headed the group from 1989 to 1991, offered a critique of the group's foreign-dominated agenda. At the end of 2006, he told the Kuwaiti daily *al-Siyassa* that Hizbollah has evolved from an organization dedicated to fighting Israel to one that takes orders from Iran. Al-Tufeili stated, "It wasn't like this in the beginning. Hizbollah's activity was limited to resistance [operations]. . . . But, unfortunately, the problem has developed today to the point where they have succeeded in changing Hizbollah from a resistance force into a tool to be used in [whatever] direction they want." When asked pointedly whether Hizbollah takes orders from outside, Al-Tufeili replied, "Yes, Hizbollah is a tool, and it is an integral part of the Iranian intelligence apparatus." Al-Tufeili added, "Iran is the main nerve in the activity today in Lebanon. All Hizbollah activity [is financed] by Iranian funds. Syria has an important role, but Iran is the main and primary support of [the Lebanese opposition]."[36]

And one other thing is certainly clear about Hizbollah today: it shares Iran's fundamental hostility to Israel. Nasrallah's ideological animus toward Israel is clear and profound. He does not accept the legitimacy of Israel under any borders, and denies the possibility of any form of coexistence with Israel or the Jews. He repeats this often. In one interview with Egyptian Television, Nasrallah declared:

One of the central reasons for creating Hizbollah was to challenge the Zionist program in the region. Hizbollah still preserves this principle, and when an Egyptian journalist visited me after the liberation and asked me if the destruction of Israel and the liberation of Palestine and Jerusalem were Hizbollah's goal, I replied: "That is the principal objective of Hizbollah, and it is no less sacred than our [ultimate] goal. The generation that lived through the creation of this entity is still alive. This generation watches documentaries and reads documents that show that the land conquered was called Palestine, not Israel." We face an entity that conquered the land of another people, drove them out of their land, and committed horrendous massacres. As we see, this is an illegal state; it is a cancerous entity and the root of all the crises and wars, and cannot be a factor in bringing about a true and just peace in this region. Therefore, we cannot acknowledge the existence of a state called Israel, not even far in the future, as some people have tried to suggest. Time does not cancel the legitimacy of the Palestinian claim.[37]

Nasrallah also openly speaks about capturing Jerusalem, even though it is far from Lebanon. In 2000, he said, "We have liberated the south [Lebanon], next we'll liberate Jerusalem."[38] He has repeated this objective subsequently on a variety of occasions.

The ideological underpinnings of Hamas are different if no less deeply rooted. The Islamic Resistance Movement (of which the Arabic acronym is HAMAS) began as the Palestinian branch of the Muslim Brotherhood, which was founded in Egypt in 1928. Its goal was to create a theocratic state based on the Koran. In Egypt the Muslim Brotherhood officially stated its opposition to violence as a means to reach a theocratic state. But when it was established in Gaza in the 1980s, the group would evolve. At first it was dedicated to establishing a theocratic Islamic state that would span Israel, the West Bank, and Gaza. Palestinians are fond of pointing out that Israel welcomed Hamas in its earliest years, believing it would serve as a counterpoint to Palestinian nationalism. But as Hamas became violent, Israel turned against the group very quickly.

Hamas officials repeatedly make clear that their goal is not merely ending the occupation of the West Bank and Gaza, but ensuring that Israel too becomes part of an Islamic state. Meanwhile, the original Hamas policy of objecting to violence, born from the connection to the Muslim Brotherhood, gave way to the most virulent form of terrorism and anti-Semitism. The Hamas Charter of 1988 is filled with calls to kill Jews; Zionism is seen as a secret society like the Freemasons. The charter states (Article 13): "There is no solution for the Palestinian question except through Jihad. Initiatives, proposals and international conferences are all a waste of time and vain endeavors."

Furthermore, Hamas has translated its violent ideology into violent action. Suicide bombings occurred throughout much of the 1990s, reaching a crescendo, with more than a hundred gruesome attacks, during the second intifada between 2000 and 2004. Hamas is known for its glorification of suicide attacks. This is arguably the group's most hideous contribution to Palestinian public life, as it has created a culture of death among its adherents. Sadly, it is not rare to see parades of masked Palestinian youths wearing cardboard versions of TNT suicide belts. Even Palestinian babies are sometimes dressed up as *shahids* (martyrs) with explosive belts. During the height of the second Palestinian intifada from 2000 to 2004, posters of suicide bombers—local heroes—were plastered all over Gaza. Even in Germany during World War II, there was no comparable glorification of state-sponsored killers. Japanese kamikaze pilots may have received comparable adulation, but they were viewed at home as pointedly hitting only military targets and not women and children. Some Palestinian intellectuals have petitioned against the practice of suicide bombing, but their pleas have fallen on deaf ears.

Hamas has used mosques to recruit suicide bombers against Israel. Tragically, the glorification of suicide bombing gets a boost from Islamist militant preachers. For example, the Palestinian mufti (chief cleric in charge of holy places) of Jerusalem, Ikram Sabri, said at the very start of the second intifada in late 2000:

> I feel the martyr is lucky because the angels usher him to his wedding in heaven. I feel the earth moves under the occupiers' feet. . . . There is no doubt that a child [martyr] suggests that the new generation will carry on the mission with determination. The younger the martyr—the greater and the more I respect him. . . . They [mothers of martyrs] willingly sacrifice their offspring for the sake of freedom. It is a great display of the power of belief. The mother is participating in the great reward of the Jihad to liberate al-Aqsa. . . . I talked to a young man [who] said: ". . . I want to marry the black-eyed [beautiful] women of heaven." The next day he became a martyr. I am sure his mother was filled with joy about his heavenly marriage. Such a son must have such a mother.[39]

The Hamas movement ideology is not just fueled by religious fervor in mosques, but also driven by financial assistance from a variety of foreign supporters, including an ideological Iran, which provides it with funding, training, and weapons. Taken together, its militant, ideological commitment is linked to the broader objective of obtaining an Islamist state in all of historic Palestine.

Realists tend to dismiss the ideological underpinnings of both Hizbollah and Hamas. Leaving aside how much they actually know about the credos of each group, the realists cannot bring themselves to believe that ideas and belief systems count for more than the desire for power. Accordingly, the realists would like to believe that these groups are cynical about ideology. For the realists, the only reason that these groups act as they do is because they have little or no stake in the existing power structure. In Walt and Mearsheimer's writings, they indicate that the lack of peace can be attributed to Israel. They do not focus much on Hamas, but suggest that a peaceful Israel could co-opt more moderate elements of Hamas into the circle of peace. Hamas's ideology is given no weight, suggesting that if they are given their share, they will desist from extremism. Since everything is about power, Hamas would have no reason to be a spoiler if there were a power-sharing arrangement. Indeed, this seemed to be the view of Saudi Arabia in 2007, when it sponsored the Mecca Agreement for power sharing between Fatah and Hamas. The Saudis hoped to keep Iran outside the Arab sphere of influence by providing Hamas with an incentive to moderate its positions.

Yet recent experience suggests that bringing groups such as Hamas and Hizbollah inside the tent does not necessarily moderate their behavior or reinforce their acceptance of the rules of the game. For example, Hamas has insisted that Mahmoud Abbas should be the peace negotiator, but at the same time outlines clear constraints on Abbas's authority. These limits are set out in the previously mentioned "prisoners' document." This eighteen-point plan leaves recognition of Israel deliberately ambiguous, while explicitly stating the need for all refugees to be allowed to return to Israel and for any referendum on an agreement to be voted on by all Palestinians in the diaspora. We have already referred to this formula as being an unworkable one for peace. And yet Hamas insisted on the plan's acceptance before it would join the short-lived unity government with Fatah in 2007. Even when the Mecca power-sharing agreement brought Hamas firmly inside the tent, the organization still proved a spoiler from the inside when its violent takeover in Gaza caused the unity government to collapse in June 2007.

While internal political cohesion is nice in theory, it is nearly always a prescription for foreign policy paralysis in the Arab-Israeli context. The same has been true on the Israeli side. There were national unity governments joining Likud and Labor between 1984 and 1990, but no movement on peace with the Palestinians. The London agreement reached by then

Israeli foreign minister Shimon Peres and Jordan's King Hussein in 1987 was scuttled by then Israeli prime minister Yitzhak Shamir. The price of unity is the avoidance of major initiatives, which will always be controversial. Therefore, there is no reason to believe that a "big-tent" approach will be successful.

It would be nice if the realists were correct that these groups view ideology as merely an instrument of power. But as we have shown, ideology has always trumped other priorities for Hizbollah and Hamas. To be sure, these groups understand that their populaces are not purely driven by ideology, and they have sought to build their support in the past by providing social services and fighting corruption. To win the 2006 elections, Hamas exploited anger against Fatah's corruption and utilized the promise of an improved social safety net to expand its political base. But these were strategies largely directed at winning power.

Once in office, Hamas thought that it could have it both ways: maintain international support and its ideology. Yet since assuming office, it has been constrained from growing further and has even shrunk, precisely because of its inability to break international sanctions. Hamas was forced to choose between its ideology and its provision of social services. This was a choice it sought to avert. Yet when forced, it chose to reverse its priorities rather than compromise its ideology. When times became more difficult, it chose to provide services only to its own hard-core constituency. During the summer of 2007, for example, the United Nations in Gaza sponsored two hundred thousand Gaza children in United Nations–led summer camps all season long, according to John Ging, who heads UN efforts in Gaza. By contrast, he said, Hamas had only forty thousand kids in Hamas-led summer camps for one week. Sadly for the realists, it seems these groups have a more instrumental view of social services than they do of ideology.

If there is another lesson here, it is that a key objective should be to empower the nonradical elements as the providers of social services. Neither Hamas nor Hizbollah should remain in their perceived position as the alternative vehicle to deliver social services to a broader population. It is important to strengthen those moderates who are not motivated by ideology but rather seek problem-solving solutions when it comes to the Arab-Israel conflict, social services, and fighting corruption. It is incumbent upon Fatah in the Palestinian arena, the non-Hizbollah elements in the Lebanese arena, and other like-minded parties to be seen as being effective on these issues—and for those who care about a future not dominated by Islamists to help the non-Islamists to deliver programs and services and not just words.

Realist myth no. 3. Isolation is counterproductive, as it ignores political realities on the ground and the communal grievances that Hamas and Hizbollah represent.

Related to the realist myth that *inclusion* undermines extremists is the view that *exclusion* will produce a public backlash. While the first realist myth casts negotiations as a transformative experience for Hamas or Hizbollah and the second emphasizes the pragmatic nature of these Islamist groups, the third stresses the risks of a policy of isolation. This argument does not insist that negotiations will change these groups, but rather that failure to engage is self-defeating—that winning elections and being part of the social fabric of their regions entitles these groups to negotiations regardless of their views or actions. These groups have wide public support, so the argument goes, therefore the world must adjust to them, not the other way around.

According to this view, isolating Hamas is counterproductive; diplomatic engagement is the best policy, since Hamas is an elected part of Palestinian society. A similar argument can be made regarding Hizbollah, which was founded on the idea that its members, the Lebanese Shiites, have been discriminated against in the Lebanese political system over decades.[40]

This argument is both factually untrue and counterproductive. Despite the dire predictions of the realists and others, public backlash has not materialized. From the moment the Quartet imposed sanctions on Hamas in January 2006, critics predicted that Palestinian anger against the restrictions would lead to such a backlash. Former president Carter wrote, "The likely results will be to alienate the already oppressed and innocent Palestinians, to incite violence, and to increase the domestic influence and international esteem of Hamas."[41] In short, the prediction was that support for Hamas would skyrocket in defiance. The Palestinians would rally to its side against international pressure.

But this did not happen. According to a variety of polls, support for Hamas has steadily dropped since reaching a high-water mark upon its election in January 2006. According to polls by An-Najah National University in Nablus and the Palestinian Center for Policy Survey and Research (PCPSR), based in Ramallah, public support for Hamas has dropped not just in the West Bank, but even on its home turf of Gaza.[42]

In an October 2008 poll conducted by the Palestinian-run Jerusalem Media and Communications Center (JMCC), a plurality of Palestinians living in Hamas-dominated Gaza thought that the economic conditions had improved in the West Bank under the Palestinian Authority of Prime Minister Salam Fayyad while these same people by an overwhelming number of 76 percent thought the Hamas-led government of Ismail Haniyeh had presided over deteriorated economic conditions. The same Gazans thought the Fayyad government was having success in advancing reform, while they said Hamas was failing in Gaza. One month later, in another JMCC poll, Gazans said they were twice as likely to vote for Fatah as they were for Hamas in Palestine Legislative Council elections. (Only 16.6 percent of Palestinians supported Hamas. The decline has been steady, as was noted by the Palestinian journalist Daoud Kuttab.)

A number of issues have contributed to Hamas's increasing unpopularity, at least prior to the Israel-Hamas war of December 2008–January 2009. First, the group hoped it could keep its campaign promise to raise the standard of living and halt Palestinian corruption. Hamas sought to divide Europe from the United States and break the restrictions. By doing so, Hamas would prove that it could maintain its call for the destruction of Israel while providing the Palestinians with a more normal life in Gaza. But that was not possible. Despite serious tensions during the Bush administration between the United States and the EU over issues ranging from Iraq to climate change, the two parties have held together on the issue of Hamas. Hamas was forced to choose between its ideology and its ability to govern, and, as we have repeatedly shown, it chose the former. The Palestinian populace did not seem to approve of Hamas's choice, and public support dropped.

Second, the Palestinian public did not like the fact that Hamas used violence against fellow Palestinians to seize control of Gaza in June 2007. There are pictures of Hamas members throwing Fatah members out windows and shooting at their kneecaps. A poll conducted by the PCPSR shows that 73 percent of Palestinians opposed Hamas's takeover, while only 22 percent supported it.

Third, in the aftermath of the Gaza takeover, the West Bank has done better economically than Gaza. The Palestinian Donors Conference, convened in Paris at the end of 2007, brought in commitments of over $7 billion to the West Bank. Of course, pledges do not always translate into material assistance and delivery, and there is a lag between commitments and actual improvements on the ground. Still, the Palestinian people began to see economic differences between the West Bank and Gaza.

The backlash argument is not proved in the case of Lebanon, either. Neither the Lebanese general public nor the Shiite public is enthralled by Hizbollah's ideological direction. Middle East historian Fouad Ajami, who grew up as a Shiite in Lebanon, writes of a dichotomy between Hizbollah and the public:

> There would be distinct roles for the Lebanese state and for [Nasrallah's] "resistance movement." The first would assume the burden of order and governing, while his movement would carry the banner of the armed struggle against Israel. This kind of contradiction can't be papered over. Nasrallah and his lieutenants must fully grasp their precarious position: They feed off mayhem and strife, while the country yearns for a break from its feuds.
>
> It is doubtful that the Shiites will always follow Nasrallah to the barricades, and those who do so will expect material sustenance from Hezbollah. There are estimates that Hezbollah provides employment for 40,000 of its wards and schooling for 100,000 children. This is no small burden, even for a movement sustained by Iranian subsidies. Nor is it the case that the majority of the Shiites want the strictures and the rigor of Qom and Tehran dominating their world. True, the underclass and the newly urbanized in the Shiite suburbs may have taken to the dress code, style, and religious ritual of the Iranian theocracy. But the majority must wish a break from all that. Hezbollah will not be able to run away with Lebanon.[43]

Failure to engage has not enabled these militant groups to generate a public backlash in their favor. By the same token, talks without preconditions would embolden the extremists and undermine the moderates. If Hamas were to be engaged, Palestinians who stuck out their neck for a two-state solution would be branded as quislings. By engaging Hizbollah, we would be undermining Lebanese moderates. As Ajami writes, "It would be reasonable to assume that the weight of Sunni sentiment would shift toward the jihadists, were they to conclude that the mild-mannered Sunni politicians cannot win a test of wills, and arms, against Hizbollah."[44] The damage could easily extend beyond Lebanon, Gaza, and the West Bank. Might not the Islamic Action Front in Amman or the Muslim Brotherhood in Cairo change their postures and call for the destruction of peace treaties with Israel? After all, why have a full-blown treaty? U.S. unconditional engagement with these groups would create a precedent that could have far-reaching consequences.

Finally, what about the realist argument that our respect for democracy requires that Hamas and Hizbollah be engaged? Certainly, in the case of Hamas, it won the parliamentary election of January 2006. But if Hamas does not change its commitment to terror and violence, why does its winning an election require us to change our principles, particularly when doing so could be so counterproductive to those moderates who believe in peace? Similarly, simply because Hamas won the election does not mean it should be receiving assistance from the donor community. International assistance is not an entitlement. The donors conference was organized to promote investment in Israeli-Palestinian coexistence. Hamas would ask that the international community keep its ideal of coexistence and simply fork over the cash—regardless of their behavior.

We believe that the world does not owe Hamas any international assistance or diplomatic services. When former British prime minister Tony Blair was asked in 2002 if the world had no option but to work with Yasir Arafat, he replied that the Palestinians can elect whomever they please, but the international community is not going to waste time in working with individuals who have demonstrated that they are not interested in delivering on the cause of peace. In short, nobody should expend time and effort on dead-end diplomacy with Hamas and Hizbollah. If there is no commitment, however grudging, to the cause of coexistence, the odds are that parties will not make the subsequent hard choices in the negotiations themselves.

THE FOLLY OF ACCOMMODATING REJECTIONISM

The real-world tests of the three arguments underpinning the realist case for engagement do not inspire great confidence. U.S. policymakers must be careful not to accept the mythology of the realist critics embodied in their arguments. There is no substitute for direct cooperation between moderates with common interests. Converging interests exist today between Israeli and Palestinian moderates: Israel opposes Hamas because it is sworn to Israel's destruction, while the Palestinian moderates view Hamas as dragging them back to the Middle Ages and away from the challenges of modern life. Ultimately, successful engagement must be predicated upon these common interests. Therefore, empowering Palestinian moderates should remain at the heart of an Israeli-Palestinian strategy. If done correctly, this could shrink the appeal of Hamas to only its smallest, hard-core base.

In other words, we are not in denial that more moderate supporters exist and at the same time, we do not think either Hamas or Hizbollah can just be wished away. On the contrary, we are very cognizant of the weight and power of Hamas (and for that matter Hizbollah) and the grave dangers they pose for trying to achieve peace. They are unlikely to give up their belief system and moderate themselves. Bringing them inside the tent, therefore, won't give peace a chance; it will likely undo and discredit peacemaking. But keeping them outside the tent requires a serious effort at competing with them. And the best way to do that is to show not only that they don't deliver, but that their more moderate competitors actually do.

In practical terms, that means that the international community must find ways to help empower the alternatives such as the PA or the Lebanese government so they deliver real services and programs and not just words. More must be done to enhance their effectiveness and their capacity for good governance. And to build hope and a sense of possibility— which is the antidote to the frustration and hopelessness that Hamas and Hizbollah prey on—there needs to be a peace process that has real promise. There needs to be a reality that is changing for the better and that shows tangible results from peacemaking. None of this is possible without the international community helping and also remaining very firm on the unacceptability of terror. In other words, the alternatives to

Hamas and Hizbollah have to become more credible, and Hamas and Hizbollah have to be seen as unable to deliver what they promise—unless, of course, they are prepared to change their behavior.

In the final analysis, we should not close the door to Islamist groups if they are prepared to moderate themselves. The great irony is that the more competitive the moderate alternatives become internally, the more Hamas and Hizbollah will have to decide whether they must adjust their behaviors. They will not necessarily give in to the outside world's demand for change, but they can ill afford to ignore pressure from within. So for the Palestinian rejectionists, if they wish to change their ways toward accommodation, they could then be welcomed. The choice is theirs.

The Lebanese arena requires understanding that Hizbollah is driven more by ideology and its ties to Iran than by any accountability to either the Lebanese government or public sentiment. The realists fail to understand this reality, and their arguments are thus fundamentally flawed—they amount to little more than myths that rewrite reality but don't reflect it. Rejectionism is real. It is not an illusion, and it cannot be accommodated.

Chapter Eleven

THE U.S.-ISRAELI ALLIANCE: AN IMPORTANT COUNTERWEIGHT TO RADICALISM IN THE MIDDLE EAST

For realists, interests matter most; values, though desirable, are decidedly secondary. According to the realist view of American interests in the Middle East, Israel is a burden to the United States, not an asset. Many realists hold this belief—this myth—as an unchallengeable principle. Few have argued for it more forcefully than the University of Chicago's John Mearsheimer and Harvard University's Stephen Walt, who go so far as to say that the United States is mistaken to have such a close association with Israel—an argument and a belief that forms the core of their highly controversial book, *The Israel Lobby and U.S. Foreign Policy* (expanded from an article printed in the *London Review of Books* in March 2006).

While Mearsheimer and Walt concede that during the Cold War, Israel may have been an asset to the United States, they suggest that in the post–Cold War period, whatever value it had has long since been replaced by costs. In their words, "Backing Israel may have yielded strategic benefits in the past, but the benefits have declined sharply in recent years while the economic and diplomatic costs have increased. Instead of being a strategic asset, in fact, Israel has become a strategic liability."[1] Their argument is that securing oil and good relations with the Arab world should be the primary U.S. goal in the Middle East, and our association with and strong support for Israel impede this aim.

Specifically, they write that Arab and Muslim antipathy toward the United States results from their identifying the United States with Israel.

This comes at a heavy cost, they assert, given the extent to which Americans have become the targets of terrorism. If the United States could halt its support for Israel, U.S. relations would improve with both leaders and citizens of the oil-rich region. They argue, "If Israel possessed vital natural resources (such as oil or natural gas), or if it occupied a critical geographic location, the United States might want to provide support in order to maintain good relations and keep it out of unfriendly hands. In short, aid to Israel would be easy to explain if it helped make Americans more secure or more prosperous. Israel's strategic value to the United States would be further enhanced if backing it won America additional friends around the world and did not undermine U.S. relations with other strategically important countries."[2]

But are their assertions right? Are they rooted in reality or—like so many realist views—paradoxically divorced from it? Let us turn to a discussion of where and why their arguments fail and reflect mythology rather than reality.

PRACTICAL BENEFITS OF THE U.S.-ISRAELI RELATIONSHIP

Among other things, Mearsheimer, Walt, and their realist cohorts fail in their basic definition of U.S. national interests, not seeing that they comprise both pragmatic and value-centered elements. We will put values aside (until later in this chapter) and focus on Mearsheimer and Walt's definition of *interests*. Our knowledge of the Mideast suggests that the situation is far more complex than they appreciate.

In truth, their approach appears to reflect the traditionalist, Arabist school in the U.S. State Department. This school was most prominent at the inception of Israel and in the decades that followed. As we outlined in our arguments against the concept of linkage (chapter 3), Arabists viewed Israel as an impediment to the United States' ability to establish close ties with the Arab world. According to their zero-sum thinking, every step toward Israel necessarily represented a step away from the Arabs. In other words, ties to one side ensured distance from the other. But just as the linkage arguments were belied by the reality in the region, so too we see that the Arab regimes do not in fact think this way. Their actions are driven by their own national interests, not an automatic—or even a reflexive—zero-sum outlook. If the Arabs do not limit themselves to this approach, why should the United States?

Though not as common as in earlier years, vestiges of Arabist rationales still linger among some U.S. thinkers and even a few policy makers. And among realists like Mearsheimer and Walt, the zero-sum view thrives. They fear that close ties with Israel can only alienate Arab regimes. The zero-sum mind-set reflects an inability to appreciate the complex dynamics of the Middle East. Not only has the U.S.-Israeli relationship not been a liability for either country, it has been, at least to some extent, an asset to the Arab regimes, as a strategic counterweight to radicalism. Radicals, led by Iran, are enemies not only of the United States and Israel but also of key Arab regimes. The Saudis and all six Gulf states believe that Iran has hegemonic designs on Arab oil. Senior officials in these states, as well as their counterparts in Egypt, Jordan, and Lebanon, also fear Iran for security, territorial, and ideological reasons. They see Iran as hostile to the Arabs for reasons relating to a mix of historical incursions by Persia into the Arab world, aspirations for regional dominance, and sectarian differences. They fear that Iran will funnel money to militant organizations, such as Hizbollah and Hamas, so that these proxies will destabilize the Arab regimes and gain Iran a foothold in a Sunni Arab world. Iran could, in their eyes, also foment social unrest among Shiite communities who happen to live in the oil-sensitive areas of Saudi Arabia and Bahrain. Finally, the Arab regimes fear that Iranian support from abroad could fuel local extremism. After all, if Iran can fund a Sunni Hamas, why could it not fund the Muslim Brotherhood in Egypt or the Islamic Action Front in Jordan? Yet it is the United States and Israel that are often the most likely to act—or at least serve as the strongest countervailing forces—against Hamas and Hizbollah and perhaps against Iran, leaving Arab regimes to benefit while still maintaining an arm's distance. Few Arab governments actually believe that a weak Israel would serve their national interests.

Apart from the value of Israeli strength as a potential inhibitor to Iranian aggression—even in the eyes of Arab leaders—the U.S.-Israel alliance has, over the years, contributed to American interests in Middle Eastern stability in another way. It has actually served as an effective deterrent against war. It has made the idea of an Arab-Israeli interstate conflict—prevalent between 1948 and 1973—no longer realistic. President Anwar Sadat of Egypt used the close U.S.-Israeli relationship to justify his turn away from war, saying he could fight Israel but not America. Now the forces pushing for battle are not Arab states but the Islamist forces— the Iranian regime, Hizbollah, and Hamas.

There is another point that ought to be raised when looking at the realist argument about the adverse consequences of the U.S.-Israeli relationship and the need to dissociate as a result. While realists are quick to raise the costs of association, they ignore the possible impact of dissociation.

Were America to actually distance itself from Israel, consider the impact on U.S. credibility. There have been few American relationships around the globe that have been publicly reaffirmed more consistently or fervently than the U.S. commitments to Israel. How would our commitments to others be viewed if we walked away from Israel? If, as the realists want, the United States distanced itself from Israel, why would any Arab regime believe that a U.S. commitment to its nation could be counted on? This question would be asked by ally and adversary alike. It would be the greatest windfall imaginable to the strongest Islamist elements, whether al-Qaeda or Iran, who would see it as a validation. It would lend a sense of momentum or inevitability to their cause, and countries throughout the region would view future U.S. actions through this lens. After all, it is not coincidental that Iran calls Israel "little Satan" and the United States "big Satan." For the Iranian regime, weakening Israel is just a means to weaken the position of the United States in the Middle East—in hopes of enhancing its own role in the region. Al-Qaeda, too, wants to weaken the United States' role in the region, since it sees Washington as propping up its Arab allies, many of which are al-Qaeda's foes. It is not hard to imagine how the Islamists would portray an American departure from Israel: as a retreat before their power—much the way they portayed Israel's unilateral withdrawal from Lebanon in 2000 and unilateral pullback from Gaza in 2005.

As we observed above, these same Arab states benefit from the presence of a strong Israel. Yes, they would like the Arab-Israeli conflict to be addressed. On an emotional level, they may even want Israel to disappear; however, they are aware that this is not only impractical but undesirable. Israel serves as a strategic counterweight to radical regimes and entities that the major Arab states find threatening. Because a strong Israel counters these entities, it protects moderate regimes while allowing them to avoid direct confrontation—without being identified with Israel.

This might seem to be a provocative idea, but we believe history bears it out. For example, in 1970—at the behest of the United States, whose military was tied down in Vietnam, and with the permission of Jordan—the Israeli army mobilized to ensure that a more radical Syria would not successfully invade and topple the Hashemite regime of Jordan's King Hussein. Israel has remained an implicit protector of Jordan since that time—and not only against threats from Syria. During Saddam Hussein's rule, Israel let it be known that any entry of Iraqi forces into Jordan would be a casus belli. Moreover, Israel has been a factor in many other regional conflicts, finding ways to provide covert support when radical or extremist states were threatening more moderate or conservative regimes (the Israeli role in providing covert support to the royalists during the conflict in Yemen is but one such example, albeit one that was not successful).

This not to say that Israel is necessarily a great friend of Arab regimes or that it does not cause them embarrassment, but that most do not see Israel as a threat and are aware of how its military strength can be of use to them. For the purposes of showing how much the realists misread the region—and why they have therefore developed erroneous arguments about the costs of association with Israel—it is worth taking a closer look at Arab and Israeli interests and where they actually converge.

CONVERGING ARAB-ISRAELI INTERESTS IN THE REGION

One does not need to look only at the distant past to find examples of where Israel and a number of its Arab neighbors have found common cause. In the post-9/11 world, there are numerous cases of converging interests between Israel and Arab regimes, shaped by a perception of common enemies. Four recent cases highlight this point: (1) the 2007 Israeli bombing of the Syrian reactor, (2) the Arab reaction to Hizbollah's triggering of a war with Israel in 2006, (3) Arab reactions to Iran's effort to build a nuclear program, and (4) comparable attitudes toward Hamas.

Israel's Bombing of the Syrian Nuclear Reactor

On September 6, 2007, Israeli jets bombed a reactor that Damascus had constructed with the assistance of North Korea, located in northeastern Syria along the Euphrates River near the town of al-Kibar. According to U.S. officials, this plutonium reactor was nearing operational capability but required the reprocessing of nuclear fuel.[3] In the Middle East, sometimes the best news is not what *has* happened but rather what has *not* happened. Israel never publicly took credit for bombing the reactor. This could have triggered denunciations or—worse—created the conditions for a possible war with Syria. Israel therefore remained silent. More interestingly, Arab regimes did so as well. If Israel did not take credit, the Arab regimes did not have to condemn, and indeed not a single Arab government uttered even one word of condemnation against this action.

Arab silence spoke volumes about the views of most Arab governments. In fact, the Arab states—other than Syria itself—were not at all unhappy about Israel's action; the enmity of many Arab regimes toward neighboring Syria dates back to 1980, when Syria was the only Arab state to back Iran in the eight-year Iran-Iraq War. Many Arab leaders even boycotted the Arab summit in Damascus in 2008, again reflecting general unhappiness with Syria's support for and identification with Iran. In general, most Arab governments want Israel to be strong when it comes to encounters with Iran, Syria, Hizbollah, and Hamas—and it is fair to say that Arab silence was designed to send a message to the regime in Damascus that the Arab world felt Syria was being taught a useful lesson.

Hizbollah: A Shared Threat

Another example of the converging interests of Arab states and Israel was the Israel-Hizbollah war of 2006. Hizbollah went to war without the vote of the Lebanese government—it was a unilateral decision, facilitated by Iranian weapons. Many Arab regimes were distressed by Israel's lackluster military performance and the inconclusive outcome of this war: the Arabs wanted Hizbollah to be defeated, not to emerge stronger from the conflict, as they fear the emergence of Iran-backed Islamist militias that are used as instruments for upending the existing order in the region.

In an unprecedented fashion, Arab regimes blamed Hizbollah for being reckless in launching the 2006 war against Israel—a dramatic stance in a region where the regimes reflexively blame Israel for confrontations with Arabs and have historically justified "resistance" against Israeli occupation. A number of commentaries in the Arab press were quite clear in explaining the criticism of Hizbollah. Note the words of Ashraf al-Ajrami in the Palestinian daily *al-Ayyam*:

> The Arab countries, particularly Saudi Arabia, Egypt, and Jordan, believe that no party has the right to drag the entire region to a military confrontation with Israel. These countries believe that there is no room for mistakes and adventures. The Arabs are worried about Iran's plans in the region, especially with regard to Iraq and the development of nuclear weapons, and their attempts to influence events in Lebanon and Palestine. A large number of Arab countries, particularly in the Gulf, see Iran as a future adversary.[4]

The Saudis minced no words in attacking Hizbollah's behavior. On July 14, 2006, the Saudi press agency issued the following official dispatch:

> The Kingdom stood firmly with the Resistance in Lebanon until Israeli occupation of South Lebanon ended. Viewing with deep concern the bloody, painful events currently taking place in Palestine and Lebanon, the Kingdom would like to clearly announce that difference should be drawn between legitimate resistance and miscalculated adventures carried out by elements inside the state and those behind them without consultation with the legitimate authority in their state and without consultation or coordination with Arab countries, thus creating a gravely dangerous situation exposing all Arab countries and their achievements to destruction with those countries having no say. The Kingdom views that it is time that these elements alone bear the full responsibility of these irresponsible acts and should alone shoulder the burden of ending the crisis they have created.[5]

Again, bear in mind that historically, even when Arab regimes might have felt this way, they would not have expressed such views in public.

Their readiness to do so reveals much about their perception of Iran and the threat it represents. In this instance, the Saudis were appalled by the Hizbollah action for several reasons. First, the action was taken without consulting any Arab governments, including that of Lebanon, which has been supported by Sunni Arab states. Second, the Saudis perceive Hizbollah as Iran's proxy and did not want to see Iran handed an excuse to launch a proxy border conflict with Israel. Along with other Arab regimes, they are troubled by Iran's muscle flexing and do not want to see that nation ascendant in the Middle East. Third, they feared that Hizbollah might use the conflict to subvert the Lebanese regime and give Iran a stronger foothold and greater leverage in the Arab-Israeli conflict.

So, notwithstanding a conflict with Israel, the Saudis, Egyptians, Jordanians, and others in the Arab League took Hizbollah to task and initially blamed it for the conflict. More recently, Arab regimes have again been provoked by Hizbollah's actions against the Lebanese government in May 2008—seeing it as a challenge and threat no less than Israel does. Hizbollah forces temporarily occupied Beirut, and nearly 100 Lebanese were killed and 250 wounded in the worst fighting since the country's fifteen-year civil war, which ended in 1991. We noted earlier that when Hizbollah turned its guns on fellow Lebanese citizens, Lebanese prime minister Fouad Siniora criticized Hizbollah, blaming the organization for breaching its pledge to not engage in internecine fighting and publicly saying it was acting worse than the Israelis. But Arab leaders were equally tough. During the Arab foreign ministers' meeting on May 12, 2008, held to discuss the crisis in Lebanon, Saudi foreign minister Saud al-Faisal compared Hizbollah leader Hassan Nasrallah to former Israeli prime minister Ariel Sharon, saying that "they both had agreed to invade Beirut." He added: "The legitimate government in Lebanon is facing a large-scale war, [and] we cannot stand idly by." He went on to say that "Iran has undertaken to run that war" and that "Hizbollah intended to forcibly [transform] Lebanon into a state with a 'rule of the jurisprudent.'" And he concluded, "We must do everything in our power to end this war and to save Lebanon, even if this would involve forming an Arab force to rapidly deploy throughout Lebanon, to restore its security and defend the current legitimate government."[6]

The Egyptians echoed Saud's words, as illustrated by an article written by Muhammad Ali Ibrahim, editor of *al-Gumhouriyya* and a member of parliament. In it he wrote that Nasrallah was a new example of "Islamic fascism," whose other representatives are Hamas leader Khaled Mashal in Gaza and Muslim Brotherhood guide Mahdi Akef in Egypt, and added that its main aims were to institute the political agenda of its funders to topple the "secular" states, and to establish an Islamic caliphate, even over the dead bodies of the citizens of Lebanon, Egypt, or any other "secular" state.[7]

The Threat of an Ascendant Iran

Iran's support for Hamas has added to Arab regimes' fears of Iran. When this support is combined with Iran's emerging nuclear program, Arab leaders see an Iran that appears to be on the march, without hesitation to do all it can to put pressure on them. Indeed, when Qatar called a pan-Arab summit in January 2009 to formulate a unified position on Israel's Operation Cast Lead, both Egypt and Saudi Arabia boycotted, partly out of concern that the summit would be used as an opportunity to expand Iran's influence in Arab affairs. Whatever one's views of a Palestinian national unity government between Hamas and Fatah, it is true that Saudi Arabia's King Abdullah justified his efforts to broker such an outcome in what was dubbed the Mecca Agreement on the basis of keeping the Palestinian issue outside Iran's sphere of influence.

Clearly, then, Israel and the Arabs have a shared desire to curb Iran's sphere of influence. In particular, both share a deep-seated fear that the nation's nuclear program could launch an arms race in the region and even lead to the provision of nuclear materials to nonstate actors by Iran. They also recognize that a nuclear Iran would have a shield behind which it could engage in much greater coercion of its neighbors with little fear that there would be recourse against it. Saudi liberal columnist Saleh Rashed said the Saudis should not be embarrassed by the convergence of Saudi and Israeli interests when it comes to Iran. He writes:

> At present, we are suffering from two things: Iran's attempts [to gain] regional hegemony, and its attempt to impose its influence via its sectarian allies—the fifth column of Arab Shi'ite fundamentalists. Imagine what Iran's influence, hegemony, and fifth column would be like if Iran had a nuclear bomb. Perhaps it is a strange

coincidence that, this time around, our strategic interests coincide with those of Israel. The regime of the mullahs in Iran is our enemy, and at the same time it is an enemy not just of Israel, but of world peace and security. I know that the Arab demagogues stand together indiscriminately with anyone who is against Israel and America. But we need to not be swept away by these demagogues as we were in the past. This time, the absolute priority must be our strategic security in the Gulf, which is threatened by Iran— even if this comes at the expense of the Palestinian cause. In politics, nothing prevents you from allying with the devil for the sake of your interests. This is what confronting the Iranian danger— which is close—demands of us. This issue, in my estimation, cannot suffer delay or hesitation. Every passing day benefits Iran.[8]

Curbing Hamas

In the same context, there is also an unstated convergence of interests between the Palestinian Authority and Israel regarding Hamas. Israel sees Hamas as an irredentist group calling for Israel's destruction, and members of the PA view the group as seeking to drive the Palestinian people back to medieval times. Given the Israeli occupation, the PA cannot openly state that there is a convergence of interests; however, this has been, in effect, operationalized—in the West Bank, the PA focuses on the economy, while Israel and the PA jointly focus on security. Indeed, the PA has been moving against Hamas charities—the backbone of the Hamas infrastructure in the West Bank—with the help of Israeli information about where the money is coming from and how it is being used.

POSSIBLE IMPLICATIONS OF SHARED ARAB-ISRAELI INTERESTS

All of the above suggests that the reality is more complex than either Mearsheimer or Walt cares to depict or understand. Arab and Israeli interests often converge, and their differing levels of cooperation successfully constrain various radical organizations. The logical counterargument is that Hizbollah and Hamas were formed as a reaction to Israeli occupation, and therefore Israel is as much a part of the problem as part of the solution. There is an element of truth to this; however, the growth of Islamist groups transcends the Israeli-Palestinian conflict. Such Islamist organizations have emerged amid the failure of pan-Arabism. Given a variety of grievances, including Shiite disempowerment in Lebanon and corruption in Gaza, the emergence of such opposition groups in the Palestinian and Lebanese arenas was probably inevitable.

There should be no mistake: if Israel disappeared tomorrow, this would create a power vacuum that could (and likely would) be filled by radicals. Israel is certainly not loved in the region, and Israeli behavior toward the Palestinians is a problem for Arab leaders and often puts them on the defensive. Arabs will consistently complain about Israel and seek American pressure to change Israel's behavior toward the Palestinians. But U.S. dissociation from Israel would raise more questions than it answers for nearly every Arab government. By the same token, a peace agreement between Israelis and Arabs would almost certainly lead to more overt forms of cooperation in their convergent interests. Here is one more strong argument for an active peace process.

The implementation of policies based on convergent Arab and Israeli interests is possible because, in essence, Arab states know Israel does not pose an existential threat to them. The best indication of this reality is Israel's nuclear capability. The Israelis developed a nuclear reactor in Dimona in the 1960s and since that time have maintained that they would never be the first to introduce nuclear weapons into the region. Nevertheless, Arab leaders have assumed for decades that Israel had a nuclear weapon. And yet Arab states, for the most part, have not sought to match Israel's nuclear capability with their own nuclear programs. This is no small matter. If Israel really threatened the Arab states with its nuclear capability, wouldn't the Arab states use their mighty economic resources from the Persian Gulf to move heaven and earth and engage in an all-out nuclear arms race in the Middle East?[9] The Arabs have noted that Israel has never threatened them with nuclear weapons, even when it was briefly losing the 1973 war against Egypt. As one Arab official told us confidentially, "We know that Israel has a bomb in the basement, but Israel keeps it in the basement. On the other hand, if the Iranians get the bomb, they will wave it. This will cause problems."

Most Arab leaders certainly see Iran in this light. The vision of nukes in the hands of Iran's leaders sets off great alarm bells. As we noted earlier, one senior Egyptian told us that if Iran gets a nuclear-weapons capability, it would be the end of the Nuclear Non-Proliferation Treaty. And, as King Abdullah of Saudi Arabia has reportedly told Vladimir Putin, if Iran goes nuclear, so will Saudi Arabia.[10] The contrast with Israel is striking.

The converging Arab-Israeli interest in curbing radicalism may not make the two sides allies—after all, these countries have fought each other in periodic Middle East regional wars—but it is still a significant development. It demonstrates that a distance has been traversed since the time between 1948 and 1973. As noted above, the regional wars stopped because, in the eyes of Arabs and Israelis alike, they became too costly, both militarily and economically.

THE U.S.-ISRAELI ALLIANCE: A KEY TO DETERRENCE IN THE REGION

The close military ties between the United States and Israel in the 1970s and 1980s certainly contributed to making the recurring Arab-Israeli wars that dominated the headlines between 1948 and 1973 nearly unthinkable today. Critically, U.S. ties with a strong Israel have averted the need for the United States to intervene militarily in Arab-Israeli wars: the ties themselves have prevented any conflict requiring intervention. As analyst Martin Kramer and others have noted, this arrangement should be ideal for realists, who like the idea of the United States being able to hold the sway of power in the region without committing its troops to battle. Israel's ethos has always been the right to defend itself, by itself. It is proud that no American soldier has had to die in its defense.

But the close U.S.-Israel relationship has done more than avert war and foster deterrence. In Egypt's case, it made the regime realize that only the United States could help it regain the land it had lost on the battlefield. This realization was not lost on others in the region, and as a result, the United States became the dominant Western player in peace-process mediation. The American position in the Middle East gained from our being the one nation that could broker peace.

Led by Egyptian president Hosni Mubarak, who fought as head of the Egyptian Air Force in the 1973 war, Arab leaders came to believe that wars with Israel are futile. This idea was tested with the outbreak of the second intifada in September 2000. Fresh Israeli-Palestinian clashes were now being viewed on Arab satellite television, and there was an emotional outpouring on all sides. On the eve of the Arab summit to address this renewed conflict, Mubarak sought to stave off those who wanted the Arab summit to be focused on taking steps toward war with Israel or the breaking of ties. At a press conference on the eve of the summit, hosted by Mubarak in Cairo, the Egyptian leader spoke forcefully against the prospect of war. As noted previously, Mubarak made it clear that war was futile. It did not solve the conflict.[II]

In fact, Mubarak's view is that war is self-defeating for Egypt; in his eyes, Egyptians have sacrificed a lot for the Palestinian cause. With Anwar Sadat's historic visit and the ensuing diplomacy, Egypt—with America's active peace mediation—was able to regain every inch of its land. This provided Syria with a model and also an imperative: with Egypt—the largest Arab state—out of the war coalition, Syria could no longer effectively wage war.

It is hard to escape the critical insight that the closeness of U.S.-Israeli relations has served not only as a powerful deterrent against war in the Middle East, but also as a spur to conflict resolution. After all, if there is no military option for large-scale war between states, it forces the parties to solve problems peacefully. Close U.S.-Israel ties avoided bloodshed, led both Egypt and Jordan (which fought in 1948 and 1967 but not in 1973) to solve their conflicts peacefully with Israel, and helped bring Syria to the peace table. Poor U.S.-Israeli relations would have sent the opposite signal, certainly opening the door to incessant fighting. Needless to say, wars are devastating on a variety of levels—and expensive, as Mubarak notes.

To be sure, Syria's evolution toward avoiding war with Israel probably involved more than only the closeness of U.S.-Israeli ties. It was also motivated at least in part by Soviet leader Mikhail Gorbachev's unwillingness to provide what Hafez al-Asad, then president of Syria, called "strategic parity." In other words, the Soviet Union would not provide the materials or the support for Syria to gain strength equivalent to or countervailing Israel's. Critical to Gorbachev's calculation—and relevant for our purposes—was that, given U.S. support for Israel, he would have to pay a high financial price to back Syria—and even a price in the coin of U.S.-Soviet relations. Gorbachev wanted to cut Soviet losses in the Middle East, not get drawn into possible conflicts in the region and escalated tensions with the United States. His "new thinking" in foreign policy ruled out continued backing of Syria's ambitions vis-à-vis Israel, and he told al-Asad as much during the Syrian leader's visit to Moscow in May 1987.

Significantly, the close U.S.-Israeli ties affected not only Egypt but also the Soviet Union and its leader, and led at least in part to Gorbachev's new posture—and Gorbachev's posture made it clear to al-Asad that he had few choices at the end of the Cold War; indeed, in his eyes, his patron disappeared while Israel's became the sole remaining superpower. In this context, al-Asad's explanation for why he would head to a 1991 Madrid peace conference becomes very clear: "In Arabic we say, 'Do you want grapes or do you want to fight the vineyard keeper?' We want the grapes."[12] Syria could not hope to defeat Israel in battle, and this deterred further wars involving Damascus as well as Cairo.

In looking more closely at the period after the 1973 war, it is striking how wrong the Arabist arguments turned out to be. Rather than harming U.S. relations with the Arabs—the essence of the Arabist assumption—steps toward Israel benefited America. Ironically, it was precisely the close U.S.-Israeli relationship after the war that enabled the United States to become a decisive diplomatic player in the Middle East. What began as a surprise attack against Israel in 1973 ended just over two weeks later with Israel on the outskirts of Cairo and Damascus. Egypt passed messages to Kissinger at the start of the war that its objectives were limited. Yet Sadat saw a benefit in launching the war. When the United States ultimately backed Israel with the belated airlift, Sadat certainly saw the futility of war. In the aftermath of war, Sadat also saw that America was the only one capable of affecting Israeli behavior. As a result, the United States became the mediator, first between Egypt and Israel, and later between Israel and Syria.

To be fair, Mearsheimer and Walt, unlike the Arabists, concede this point when they write: "Backing Israel to the hilt would make it impossible to gain the land and demonstrate the limited value of Soviet support. This strategy bore fruit in the 1970s, when Egyptian president Anwar Sadat severed ties with Moscow and realigned with the United States, a breakthrough that paved the way to the Egyptian-Israel peace treaty of 1979. Israel's repeated victories including over two Soviet clients in 1973 also forced the Soviets to expend precious resources rearming their clients after each defeat, a task that the overstretched Soviets could ill afford."[13]

They also concede that Israeli confrontation with the Arab states during the period 1948–73 would lead to Israel's passing on important intelligence about the Soviet Union. Mearsheimer and Walt write, "By providing the United States with intelligence about Soviet capabilities, Soviet client states, and the Middle East more generally, Israel facilitated the broader U.S. campaign against the Soviet Union."[14] Much of that intelligence relationship remains classified, making it difficult for outside analysts— including the realists—to evaluate its successes.[15]

ISRAEL AS AN ASSET IN THE COLD WAR

Here there is a larger point to be made. Israel was an unquestioned strategic asset during the Cold War. Declassified information has revealed that Israeli defense experts gave the United States access to Soviet equipment captured in the 1967 and 1973 war and provided a Soviet MiG-21 turned over by an Iraqi defector. Israel also shared advanced technology it obtained, and the U.S. and Israeli defense industries worked together to adjust U.S. weapons to counter what we learned from the captured Soviet capabilities. In addition, the two countries shared intelligence on counterterrorism and almost all other areas of mutual interest. This should come as no surprise, since the Soviet Union and the Eastern Bloc trained Middle Eastern terrorists in the 1970s and 1980s.[16]

In the 1980s, during the Reagan administration, the scope of cooperation between the United States and Israel took on a more strategic and institutional character. Though a secret strategic dialogue was begun in the Carter administration (in which Dennis Ross was a participant), the readiness to go public about such cooperation—particularly given mutual concerns about Soviet military capabilities in the Middle East and about Soviet backing for a number of Arab states—led to a number of understandings during President Reagan's time. The Memorandum of Understanding that was reached in 1981 launched a series of such agreements and institutional arrangements between the American and Israeli military and defense establishments. The United States would soon be pre-positioning stockpiles of supplies in Israel for American use in contingencies throughout the Middle Eastern theater of operations. Joint air and naval exercises became increasingly frequent. The U.S. Marine Corps engaged in live-fire exercises and practiced beach assaults in Israel as well. By 1989, Israel's defense minister, Yitzhak Rabin, would reveal that the United States and Israel had conducted twenty-seven or twenty-eight combined exercises and that U.S. Marine Corps exercises were being held at the battalion level.[17] When in the 1980s the Soviet Mediterranean Squadron designated the Syrian port of Tartus as its main submarine base, Israel offered Haifa, which had begun to provide port services for U.S. ships in 1977, to the U.S. Sixth Fleet.

As stated earlier in this chapter, the realists concede that Israel was a strategic asset for the United States during the Cold War. As Mearsheimer and Walt write, "This justification for supporting Israel is factually correct, and Israel may well have been a net strategic asset during this period."[18] But given their overall view that Israel has been a liability, it is not surprising that they also blame Israel for giving the Arabs a reason to align with the Soviets in the first place.

For example, part of the realist narrative about the Middle East is that if it were not for Israel, the Soviets would not have had an opening in the Middle East. They claim that Egypt sought arms from the Soviets in 1955 because of Israel. This was twelve years before the 1967 war, during which Israel occupied Palestinian territory. At the time, the United States had an arms embargo in place against both the Israelis and the Arabs. The embargo actually benefited the Arabs in 1948, because they, unlike Israel, had preexisting standing armies. This was a time when the Arab states, including Egypt, did not accept the existence of Israel under any borders. Yet it is rather astounding that Mearsheimer and Walt write, "Given their continuing *conflict* [emphasis added] with Israel and America's reluctance to provide them with arms, Israel's main Arab adversaries had *little choice* [emphasis added] but to seek help from the Soviets, despite their own misgivings about moving closer to Moscow." This was not a border conflict. Egypt's grievance was not about a raid from Gaza in 1955, as Mearsheimer and Walt suggest (a raid precipitated by a series of Palestinian attacks into Israel that killed eleven Israelis), but rather about Israel's very existence. More importantly—and this again reveals how little they know about the political dynamics in the region—the arms deal was also about the Egyptian desire to break the Western arms monopoly. It was about Nasser's domestic needs and desire to catapult himself to prominence in the region. As part of that strategy, Nasser wanted to demonstrate that (unlike others in the region) he could do something the Western powers—the colonial powers—did not like; indeed, he could humiliate those who had humiliated the Arabs for so long. This was the same rationale that led to his decision in 1956 to nationalize the Suez Canal, in which Britain and France had been major shareholders for decades.

Overall, the realists want to denigrate what Israel has provided for the United States. While they may not deny that there was some value to our relationship during the Cold War, they argue that Israel unwittingly fostered Soviet access to the Middle East even during that period. Moreover, their noting that there may have been value in the past is meant to highlight a contrast with today. And in the present they see only cost in our association with Israel, no benefit. They set a bar that almost no country could meet while denying that Israel has been a factor in securing the oil-rich Persian Gulf—the area they define as being the core of our interests in the Middle East. In truth, the Gulf region has required a major infusion of U.S. ships and personnel—but it is also true that since Israel has eliminated the need for a U.S. troop presence in the Levant part of the region since 1973, it has made U.S. deployments to the Gulf substantially easier than they might have been if there were great instability requiring substantial American forces in the eastern Mediterranean.

In concluding this part of the discussion, it is certainly fair to say that the realists offer an overly simplistic and skewed view of the region. Israel may not be the military asset it was during the Cold War, but it nonetheless continues to play an important role and serve American interests and policy in the Middle East. Together, a strong Israel and a strong United States have effectively deterred conflict and prevented bloodshed, and—we hope—will continue to successfully curb radicalism, including the new dangers posed by Iran's search for regional ascendance. And as far as peace goes, it is the relationship the United States has with Israel that sets it apart from all other would-be peacemakers. No one else has more potential to affect Israeli behavior, which leads most Arab and Palestinian leaders to look to Washington to play the decisive role in peacemaking.

BEYOND INTERESTS: THE ROLE OF VALUES
IN THE U.S.-ISRAELI RELATIONSHIP

American foreign policy has never been driven solely by "interests." We have always had a self-image that we stand for greater causes and greater goods. Our historical sense of "exceptionalism" has meant that foreign policy could not be justified only in narrow terms. Henry Kissinger was challenged on his policy of détente with the Soviet Union because it seemed devoid of values. Kissinger himself has written about how particular policies can only be sustained politically if they are consistent with our values.

Realists seem to believe that they are the only ones capable of defining America's interests, and they resist the idea that values ought to play a role in our foreign policy. The fact is that values are a part of who we are, of what we define as being important to us. When it comes to Israel, it is impossible not to see a values connection.

The connection between Israel and the United States has deep roots. As the author Michael Oren documents in his book *Power, Faith and Fantasy: America in the Middle East 1776 to the Present*, American attitudes toward the Middle East have been intertwined with religion. Oren notes that the first Protestant missionaries departed Boston for the Middle East in 1819 with the objective of restoring the Holy Land to Jewish sovereignty.[19] This theme has deep roots. Woodrow Wilson was captivated by the idea of a Jewish homeland. When the British sought his views while they were considering whether to issue the famed Balfour Declaration of 1917, Wilson said: "To think that I the son of the manse should be able to restore the Holy Land to its people."[20] In much the same vein as we noted earlier, President Harry Truman would later on compare himself to King Cyrus, who enabled the Jewish people to return to their homeland some 2,500 years ago.[21]

The link has not been just religious and cultural. In the wake of the Holocaust—the nadir of depravity and genocide in the twentieth century—the United States felt a responsibility to the Jewish people and their yearning for a state of their own. This attitude played a significant role in President Harry Truman's decision to reject the advice of his senior cabinet officials and recognize Israel when it declared itself a state. There was not just a sense of responsibility, but a deeper bond and spiritual connection.

Our bonds with Israel are not just a function of feeling a debt because of the Holocaust. They reflect the reality of shared values, as polls among Americans consistently demonstrate. Israel is a sister democracy in a region that has largely been hostile to democracy. Perhaps because of that, Israel's enemies are almost always America's enemies as well. Indeed, much like the canary in the coal mine, Israel, it seems, is often the first to be threatened by those who threaten us. Throughout the twentieth century that was certainly the case, as those who threatened the Jewish people and Israel also threatened the United States. This is not because the Jewish people or Israel were the cause of those threats or triggered the enmity. Instead, these enemies attacked in Israel the same freedom and religious liberties enjoyed by U.S. citizens.

What matters most, shared values or shared interests? Clearly, both matter. Americans see in Israel a country that is like us, but in a hostile neighborhood. It warrants our support because of shared values—but often those shared values are the very reason we share common enemies. Is it any accident that we have faced common enemies—from the Nazis to the Soviets, and now the radical Islamists? The Nazis blamed the Jews for the ills of interwar Germany, beginning in the mid-1930s, and America's "Greatest Generation" was called on to fight the Nazis in World War II. The Soviets sought to stamp out religious and cultural life in the Soviet Union for a variety of religious minorities, including the Jews, dating back to the 1920s. This assault reached a crescendo in the late 1940s and early 1950s before Stalin's death. Apparently fearing that a new state of Israel, born in 1948, would ally with the West, Stalin launched an anti-Semitic drive that year to eliminate "rootless cosmopolitans." Senior Soviet officials subsequently concocted a story that Jewish doctors planned to poison the Soviet leadership. In the aftermath of Stalin's death in 1953, the so-called "doctors' plot" was dismissed as utterly baseless. From 1967 until just prior to the demise of the Soviet Union, Moscow had no ties with Israel and did much to halt free Jewish emigration. U.S.-Soviet interaction had its ups and downs, but the Cold War was the organizing principle guiding U.S. foreign policy from the end of World War II until the Berlin Wall fell in 1989.

Iran is another case in which the enemy of America is the enemy of Israel. Once again, it is as much our values as anything else that drives Iran's basic enmity toward the United States. As we have noted elsewhere, when Iran became an Islamic republic under Ayatollah Khomeini in the late 1970s, Israel was called the "little Satan," the United States the "big Satan." At the time, the United States was not hated because of Israel. If anything, the reverse was true. Israel was seen as an outpost of "American imperialism." Of course, radical Islamist groups such as Iran-backed Hizbollah did not need to attack the United States because of Israel. Hizbollah killed 241 Marines in the Beirut barracks bombing of 1983 and was responsible for the hijacking of TWA flight 847 in 1985.

Al-Qaeda also opposed the United States initially because of the large U.S. military presence in Saudi Arabia. It only later came to oppose Israel, sometimes claiming the issue was the Palestinians, other times claiming opposition to any non-Muslim presence in the Mideast. (Over time, it would claim that it opposed the United States because of its support for Israel.)

There is a very basic point that stands at the core of U.S.-Israel relations. The relationship between the United States and Israel now stretches to over more than sixty years—sixty years of good relations, of economic and strategic cooperation, and of deepening friendship between these two countries and two peoples. Few other nations have been as consistently supportive of the United States, and so unconditionally. Israel has never threatened the United States, either directly or by sheltering its enemies. It is difficult to find a country whose voting record at the United Nations more closely resembles the United States' than Israel. As was discussed earlier, whereas Arab regimes that see themselves on the side of the United States frequently cultivate anti-Americanism among their people, both the Israel government and Israeli people are unabashedly pro-American. Israeli president Shimon Peres, Nobel Peace Prize laureate and senior statesman, is fond of saying that Israel is unique in that part of the world because its response to aid from the United States is gratitude. Israel has never requested that its relationship to the United States be defined by preconditions that might make us loath to continue the relationship, nor has it asked that the relationship be exclusive so as to limit close bilateral ties between Washington and the Arab states.

Do Israeli efforts to preserve their security have consequences that sometimes put us in a difficult position with Arab regimes? Absolutely. However, given all of the above, what reason could possibly induce the United States to walk away from such a stalwart ally? The realists seem to miss the fundamental point that allies do not always have interests that align perfectly. What seems necessary for one may seem inopportune or problematic for the other. For instance, the United States would prefer that Israel halt all settlement activity, whereas Israel, for a variety of reasons, has continued settlement construction. However, contrary to the realist view, and in light of our convergent interests, we ought to be deepening our relationship with Israel so that we can work more closely to resolve challenges and address new opportunities in ways that maximize the benefit to both sides.

Ultimately, we believe that the United States and Israel have forged an alliance that has remained strong and has served the interests of the Middle East as a whole. While a comprehensive list of the practical benefits of the U.S.-Israeli relationship, both past and present, exceeds the scope of this chapter—even this entire book—such a list would not tell the whole story. Unlike Mearsheimer and Walt, we do not believe interests alone should drive U.S. policy. Even if we were to think on purely realist terms, the shared interests of the United States and Israel—and, as we have seen, of many Arab states as well—further a cooperation that deters conflict and helps stabilize the Middle East. In the face of terrorism and radical threats on all sides, it is fair to say that this relationship has been rooted in shared interests no less than shared values.

Chapter Twelve

PROMOTING DEMOCRACY
IN THE MIDDLE EAST: MYTH,
REALITY, OR NECESSITY?

If there was a signature issue of the George W. Bush presidency, it was democracy promotion. President Bush proclaimed in his second inaugural address that "the best hope for peace in our world is the expansion of freedom in all the world." Knowing that there could not be an exclusively military answer to the war on terror, the president saw democracy promotion, particularly in the Middle East, as the best way to "drain the swamp" that produced terrorists. And for his second term, he defined democratization in the Middle East as the organizing principle that would guide his last four years in office. While the president certainly seemed to believe in and repeat his calls for it, the principle over time seemed to become more of a slogan than an operational guideline of policy.

Perhaps reality imposed itself on the Bush administration. The more it pushed for elections in the Palestinian territories and Lebanon, the more undesirable results it saw. It is doubtful that Bush believed his vision for democracy would lead to Hizbollah's taking more than a quarter of the vote in 2005 and Hamas's winning elections in the West Bank and Gaza in 2006. Hizbollah's success had terrible consequences for Lebanon's democracy and governmental stability; within eighteen months of Hamas's victory in the polls, it violently took control of Gaza.

Such developments seem to have led the Bush administration to retreat on its signature issue and dismiss the validity of promoting democracy in the Middle East as a principle or even an objective. Some argue that the region is not ready for serious political reform. Combined with the unpopularity of President Bush, there has been a tendency to discredit the ideal and suggest that for the Middle East, democracy is and will remain more an illusion than anything that can be translated into reality.

We think it is far too soon to draw such a conclusion. No doubt the idea was oversold, reflecting a neoconservative lack of understanding of the region and its possibilities. There was certainly very little grasp of the context and the challenges that would be faced in an implementation of democratic principles and an exaggerated emphasis on early elections. As a result, the Bush administration approach was bound to fail, its actions based far too much on myth and far too little on reality.

The so-called realists leaped on this quickly. They bristle at the notion that they are uninterested in having democracy succeed in the Middle East. Yet at the same time they see little advantage in pressing in this direction. For realists, it seems clear that the issue of democracy extends beyond the issue of the Iraq War, in which the democratization effort was linked to American use of force. For them, the issue seems much deeper, and does not seem to be a worthy enterprise for the United States to invest in. Mearsheimer writes, "[D]emocracies as well as non-democracies like having nuclear deterrents, and both kinds of states support terrorism when it suits their interests."[1] Neoconservatives, however, had more at stake. They had believed that a quick, massive defeat of Iraq would send such shock waves throughout the region—and that dictatorial regimes would be so frightened—that authoritarians would be swept away in a democratic tide. Needless to say, this has not yet occurred.

Unfortunately, the neoconservatives' plan was not grounded in regional realities. An undifferentiated view of all states in the region—whether weak or strong—plagued diplomatic efforts. Additionally, policymakers did not sufficiently convey to the American public that this was a long-term objective, whose progress could only be measured in small increments. Yes, one heard an occasional phrase in a speech of President Bush or Secretary of State Rice that this was a "generational struggle," but this message was too easily lost in general expectations and the sweep of rhetoric.

There will be some who say the entire effort was a fallback when weapons of mass destruction in Iraq were not found and a retrospective need arose at the end of 2003 to look for an overarching rationale for the occupation of Iraq, for a new organizing principle. Whatever the motivation, we think it is important that the cause of political and economic reform be pursued in the Middle East with a clear understanding that it will be a long-term effort that will take the work of several administrations. Given this reality, future administrations should retain political and economic reform as a component, albeit not necessarily the centerpiece, of their Middle East policy.

With this in mind, a new administration needs to resist the traditional Washington "pendulum" effect, swinging to the opposite end of the most recent policy. Bush's democratization policy was clearly flawed—and largely based on myth—but we should avoid a return to the realist fallacy of ignoring the domestic dynamics of a country as long as its external behavior is acceptable. A more nuanced approach is needed between the two poles, an approach that sees democratization as a long-term goal and promotes it in a sustainable manner that is flexible and aware of the different conditions present in different types of regimes. Such an approach would not only respond to the reality in the region, but also reflect the right mix of our values and our interests.

DEMOCRATIZATION AND OUR STAKES IN THE MIDDLE EAST

Why is this effort toward democratization so important? It goes without saying that it is necessary in order to maintain and support U.S. values. Democratization is consistent with the American ideal of individual liberty; ultimately, we seek to support a Middle East that is more just and humane. Such support is part of the American political tradition and predates Wilsonian idealism in the early part of the twentieth century. It can be seen even in the nineteenth-century efforts of American Protestants to set up missions and, later, colleges in disparate parts of the Middle East. The roots are deep. Indeed, even more recently, although Americans have been disappointed by the pace of Iraqi democracy, the Pew Global Attitudes Poll in April 2007 showed that 60 percent of Americans wanted the United States to promote democracy around the world, while only 34 percent demurred.[2] Policies that reflect our values are almost by definition easier to sustain over time.

Policy realists should understand that political and economic reform as a principle not only serves our values, but is also critical for our interests in the region. It is this dimension that we would like to address.

Realists take the future vitality of the oil regimes as a given. In the short run, these regimes seem impregnable, given that their intelligence services—employed to repress dissent—are often the most efficient part of the regime. But are they likely to survive over time? Absent reform, it is an open question. Over time, many of these regimes could crumble, and the future of this crucial region could well remain in doubt. Without the legitimacy of more democratic governance, these states are bound to be greater targets for assault by Islamists such as al-Qaeda, or by Iranian-backed movements with militias such as Hizbollah and the Mahdi Army.

Given the importance of Middle Eastern oil until alternative energy sources are developed in sufficient quantity, the stakes could not be higher. For the next ten to twenty years, the Middle East will remain vital to the economic interests of the United States and the international economy more generally. Until alternative energy sources prove sufficient, the United States will need to work with Middle East regimes to maintain a constant flow of oil at reasonable prices. Furthermore, American partnership with many of these regimes in dealing with regional challenges such as Iran or disruptions to the Arab-Israel peace process will also remain important. While the contributions of Arab leaders to addressing these regional problems have tended to be limited, they have a role to play.

Somehow the United States must find a way to work with these leaders and their regimes on shared problems such as terror and peace even while American leaders push to promote political reform; the two go hand in hand. Al-Qaeda rejects these regimes and their leaders, modernity in general, and any possibility of coexistence.

While we see the need to work with existing regimes, we part company with the realists because unlike them, we believe the days of authoritarian regimes in the region are numbered. Perhaps due to their lack of understanding of regional realities, realists tend to gloss over the internal dynamics of these countries. The realists do not understand, or fail to acknowledge, that there have been profound political costs for our ignoring the domestic political dynamics in the authoritarian and semiauthoritarian states. Turning a blind eye to how Middle Eastern regimes deal with their own people not only abets countless acts of brutality, but also allows the chasm between those who govern and those who are governed to widen.

And unfortunately, the lack of democratization or accountability has meant there are no constraints on leaders, and this has fostered deep alienation. "By ignoring the political will of their people, the results were not a perpetuation of the status quo. Rather, it led to the ascendance of the Islamists across the region," stated Hala Mustafa, an Egyptian intellectual and editor of the Cairo-based *Democracy Journal*. She noted, for example, that Ayman al-Zawahiri, widely considered to be Osama bin Laden's deputy, was a leader of Egypt's Islamic Jihad. Zawahiri was a medical doctor from an established middle-class family. His problem was not poverty, nor was it bin Laden's, who emerged from one of the wealthiest families in Saudi Arabia. In this sense, terrorism has emerged at least in part as a response to the dearth of accountability of Mideast rulers toward the governed. Profound alienation provided fertile soil for al-Qaeda's efforts to enlist recruits—culminating with September 11, 2001. What the acts of that day taught us is that—thanks to technology—grievances in one country, however far away, can have an impact on the United States.

In other words, if people are fundamentally alienated under governance systems that deprive them of all rights, a backlash becomes almost certain. This backlash can be focused against the regimes themselves—or not. In an era where protest movements tend to be defined by the Islamists, this backlash can lead to terrorist acts either against the regime or against the country that is seen to underwrite the regime: the United States. After all, bin Laden thought attacking the United States would remove the props for the current Arab regimes.

There are too many negative signs on the horizon for these regimes to ignore. As the Arab Human Development Reports have repeatedly made clear, Arabs are suffering from an educational, economic, and democratic deficit. Problems include corruption, cronyism—which limits wealth to a privileged few—and a lack of private sector employment prospects at a time of an Arab youth bulge. The net effect is to exacerbate a sense of domestic grievance that favors the Islamists—the most organized protest group—in Arab countries.

Moreover, such a backlash may become more likely given demographic trends, socioeconomic problems, and established elites with no interest in a rational distribution of national wealth. This issue is not necessarily linked to poverty, but to a lack of dignity and hope, as evidenced by terrorists from middle-class backgrounds.

Globalization can be unsettling in a variety of ways. It creates rising expectations as more people see what other countries have and what their own societies lack. In an age when every Arab watches al-Jazeera or other satellite channels and when so many have access to the Internet, the expectation gap is bound to be wide. Where travel is possible, it is disorienting to see major differences. The Hamburg cell that helped perpetrate 9/11 was comprised of an educated group of people, but dislocation had its impact. Moreover, globalization is bound to be unsettling for societies that are rooted in traditional mores. These trends are going to intensify. Therefore, there is little alternative to reform, even if it is measured and not rapid.

From this standpoint, political and economic reform, if implemented effectively, could be both an antidote to terror and a lifeline for aging regimes seeking to avoid future domestic discontent. This should have been the message that the Saudis and Moroccans took from homegrown terrorism in their own countries in 2003 and 2004. This alone ought to create a pragmatic rationale for pursuing political reform in the Middle East. No U.S. administration can allow the idea of political reform to be discredited, regardless of the results of the Bush administration. Indeed, Secretary of State Rice was correct when she declared, "Let us not romanticize the old bargains of the Middle East—for they yielded neither justice nor stability."[3]

Historically, Arab regimes have sought to cope with problems of internal dissent and economic disparity by employing a deflection strategy. This has led to the paradoxical situation in which the United States maintains working relations with (and even offers security assurances to) Arab rulers even as those rulers continue to blame their domestic woes on the United States and other external enemies. Moving forward, the United States has a compelling interest to end this dichotomy.

Seeking to promote sustainable democratization should be the key in this regard. The Bush administration was not wrong to see democratization as a crucial component in the war against terrorism. Alienation and anger—which the Islamists exploit—will not disappear unless there is a greater sense of inclusion and participation within Muslim societies. If the United States wants to work against the ascendance of Islamism in the Middle East, it needs to work with these regimes (and pressure them as necessary) to engage in political and economic reform. And—of vital importance—these regimes (assuming they recognize the need for reform and true inclusion) will see that they have an interest in working with the United States toward this end. In so doing they will not be doing America a favor, but rather serving their own interests.

WHAT WENT WRONG?

So if democracy promotion was a good idea, how and why did it go wrong? After a major push by the Bush administration, why did it fail? Why has democratization become synonymous with the naïveté that promoted radicalism instead of undercutting it?

First Mistake—Ignoring Regional Realities

Above all, the Bush administration and the neoconservatives seemed to have no feel for the realities on the ground in the Middle East—realities that make democratization a complex effort in the best of circumstances. The administration misread the problem and drew the wrong lessons from the past. For example, at the start of the diplomatic drive, Secretary Rice, among others, would attack those who she felt were saying that the Arabs were not capable of democracy. She indicated that she saw this as a form of racism, noting that democracy was advancing everywhere around the globe. But she failed to point out that the biggest problem in the Mideast is not the will or capacity of the people, but the resistance of the rulers who head functioning regimes. In many respects, major democratic gains in recent decades came as a result of regimes that either completely collapsed or that were isolated and vulnerable to major grassroots movements. Allied victory in World War II meant the collapse of regimes in Germany, Japan, and Italy. The same was true four decades later, when all the Eastern Bloc regimes crumbled at the end of the Cold War. In other words, the success of political reform came as a function not just of a willing populace, but of a lack of resistance by the regime in question. Democratic transition also occurred in countries such as Chile, the Philippines, and South Korea. In these countries, both key factors were present—strong grassroots democratic movements (with authentic and credible institutions) and regimes that were rather isolated and vulnerable to pressure.

Yet the Middle East is fundamentally different from the defeated Axis powers at the end of World War II or the Eastern Bloc Communist regimes at the end of the Cold War. The authoritarian regimes of the Middle East are not defeated. Some neoconservatives mistakenly drew a direct line from the democratic revolutions of late-1980s Eastern Europe to the Middle East today. Neoconservatives saw themselves as the heirs of Reaganism—some were even in the government at that time—and they brought the same attitude to their Middle East policy. But the realities of the Middle East are more complex: in the Middle East, many opposition leaders were not trade unionists such as Lech Walesa. There was no willing Catholic Church under the energetic leadership of Pope John Paul II. Instead, the opposition in these regimes has been led by Islamists seeking a theocratic state and, by dint of ideology, largely hostile to the United States.

Since the Middle East of today is so different from the other places where authoritarian regimes have collapsed, the question is what should be done in relation to these regimes. It would be an unfair caricature to say that the neoconservatives wanted regime change across the entire Middle East. They hoped the toppling of Saddam Hussein would be an earthquake that would frighten the regimes and inspire opposition. Yet outside of Iraq and Iran, their approach might be described as one of attrition more than anything else. Joshua Muravchik is probably the most prominent democratic theorist of the neoconservatives, and in 2004 he wrote:

> To foment democracy in the Middle East, overthrowing the regime of Saddam Hussein was a good start. His was the most entrenched, recalcitrant, murderous, and dangerous of the Arab tyrannies. And historically Iraq stands second only to Egypt as a pole of influence in the Arab world. If U.S. efforts to implant democracy in Iraq take hold, as they did so successfully elsewhere in the post World War II occupations, this will greatly encourage democrats in the other Arab countries. And it will greatly increase the pressure for concessions felt by their rulers.[4]

Muravchik also writes, "Outside of Iraq, America will use such nonmilitary methods as diplomatic pressure, foreign aid, increased international radio and television broadcasting, and direct assistance to democracy advocates. By these means it will try to foster a regional tide of democratization that will bring the Middle East into sync with the rest of the world."5

While Muravchik is surely right when he emphasizes such stratagems, they are not sufficient in and of themselves. True, Muravchik explicitly mentions diplomatic pressure and thereby implies diplomatic engagement. Yet from other neoconservative statements, it seems as if they believe it is quixotic to view Middle East regimes as partners in political reform.

To be fair, there is reason for such skepticism. Arab leaders have maintained their rule through various degrees of repression, and even semiauthoritarian leaders are unlikely to stop it and join reform projects that they see as undermining their control. External pressure is needed to promote change.

But external pressure is a half-measure; it is a necessary but not sufficient condition for promoting necessary reforms. There must be a mixed approach, preserving working relationships with these regimes and at the same time prodding them to engage in reform. During the Cold War, the United States retained ties with Eastern Bloc regimes while championing the cause of dissidents. The United States understood that this could not be an either/or proposition. And this remains true today in the Middle East. So long as Middle Eastern regimes believe the United States is not bent upon regime change, most will live with the duality in American foreign policy.

Again, consider the lessons from the past. The United States was able to shine a spotlight on brave dissidents in the Cold War and contain pernicious Soviet influence but at the same time found ways to maintain a working relationship to solve mutual problems. It cannot be ignored that at times the United States used economic leverage to back its support for dissidents, as in the case of the Jackson-Vanik Trade Amendment in 1974, which contributed to the exodus of Soviet Jews.

The Bush administration forgot this lesson of the Cold War. Engaging the Soviets did not preclude support for or meetings with dissidents. Yet the Bush administration seemed to believe that reform and engagement were either/or propositions. In 2005, Secretary Rice cancelled a visit to Egypt due to the imprisonment of key dissidents. That was a symbolic statement. But by 2006, all vestiges of such a policy disappeared as the

Bush administration dropped its democratization program and engaged all types of Middle East regimes (with the exception of Syria and Iran, but for reasons unlinked to democracy). It was as if the secretary of state simply gave up on the policy. Public support of dissidents largely disappeared and engagement with regimes took precedence. Indeed, in the final months of the Bush administration, Rice visited Libya, which is a police state but which abandoned its weapons of mass of destruction programs.

Was anything asked of Libya on domestic issues? No, nothing was asked of the regime on domestic issues. With other regimes, has the U.S. been at all willing to develop an agenda for reform or at least discussion of it? Again, apparently not. One of the things missing in the Bush administration was any tangible sign that it sought, or in any way pushed for, or ever held probing dialogues at the highest levels with these regimes about issues of incremental political and economic reform.

Make no mistake. Our commitment to diplomatic engagement of this sort does not mean that we are enamored with these regimes. We know their failings very well, but we have little interest in pushing regime change without knowing the consequences—or in seeing Islamists replace the existing regimes. We cannot wish away our stakes in stability in the oil-laden Middle East. At the same time, we do not think engagement has to come at the price of not raising the issues of political and economic reform in a very honest dialogue. Sometimes that focus is public, and sometimes it is private. Given the enormity of their domestic challenges, we believe the stakes are as high for these regimes as they are for the United States and the rest of the world.

The key is to make sure that such reform is not merely cosmetic, since every Arab regime likes to trumpet both at home and abroad that it is engaged in reform. Egypt and Saudi Arabia—the region's two largest states—do not have all the leverage, even as the United States is faced with the real needs of preserving access to oil, countering terrorism, and halting Iranian radicals and their nuclear program. The United States gives more than $2 billion per year to Egypt, while Saudi Arabia benefits from the security umbrella provided by the United States. The essence of statecraft is to identify your leverage and use it to affect the calculus of others through a variety of incentives and disincentives. Could this mean more or less foreign aid for a country such as Egypt? Could it mean not always responding quickly to arms requests from the Saudis? It depends on the circumstances.

Second Mistake—Focusing on Weak States and Promoting Early Elections

The Bush administration was also prone to pushing reform without a clear guide and without any sense of where it might work. It was as if they thought one shoe would fit all sizes. Where was the assessment of which states might be sturdy enough to withstand unconditional rapid democratization? Why was there no effort to assess the probability of democratic success in different states? As democracy theorist Thomas Carothers points out, some basic elements of regional state structures made many Middle East countries poor candidates for instant democracy: low levels of economic development, concentrated sources of national wealth (such as oil), identity-based divisions (particularly over religion), little historical experience with political pluralism, and a nondemocratic neighborhood. Carothers goes further and makes a crucial point, saying: "In certain situations, democratization does need to wait for state-building. Where a state has completely collapsed or failed under the lash of civil conflict or other accumulated or acute calamities, moving rapidly toward open political competition and elections makes no sense. The state will need to have at least minimal functional capacity as well as something resembling a monopoly of force before such a country can pull itself onto the path of sustainable, pluralistic political development."[6] Certainly that has been the case for the Palestinians. Mahmoud Abbas, as president of the Palestinian Authority, might declare a policy of one authority, one law, and one gun, but he lacked the capability to enforce it.

But the Bush administration ignored such weakness. Not heeding the insights of analysts like Carothers, the administration pushed for democratization in Lebanon and in the West Bank and Gaza. Neither has a functioning state apparatus, nor do the authorities there have a monopoly on the use of force. Hizbollah ensures that the central Lebanese government does not have that capability, and Hamas ensures that the PA is constrained. In both, elections produced disastrous results. After Hamas won, while maintaining its guns, it was only a matter of time before it would use its forces for political purposes—and it did so in a violently staged takeover of the Gaza Strip. In Lebanon, much the same happened. As Hizbollah kept its fully armed militia, it paralyzed the working of the Lebanese government and—after turning its guns on fellow Lebanese— won a veto on all Lebanese decision making.

There was no realization by the U.S. administration that pressing for immediate elections would create unintended consequences. This was particularly true in the case of the Palestinians. By forcing the elections in the West Bank and Gaza in January 2006, the Bush administration ended up crippling its entire democratization initiative.

The possibility of Hamas running with its guns and rejectionist platform was foreseen in the Oslo II accord in 1995 and ruled out. The United States helped negotiate Oslo II between Israelis and Palestinians and is one of its signatories. Yet during their October 2005 meeting, President Bush gave Palestinian leader Mahmoud Abbas a green light for Hamas to run in the upcoming elections. In other words, the United States agreed to violate existing rules that Israelis and Palestinians had already agreed upon. Annex II, article III, paragraph 2 of Oslo II states: "The nomination of any candidates, parties or coalitions will be refused, and such nomination or registration once made will be canceled, if such candidates, parties or coalitions: commit or advocate racism; or pursue the implementation of their aims by unlawful or non-democratic means." Indeed, Hamas did not participate in the 1996 elections, and its call for an election boycott was defied by the vast majority of the Palestinian people (85 percent), who chose to vote.

Unfortunately, as noted above, the Bush administration did not insist that the Oslo II terms be upheld. It could have forced Hamas to meet electoral standards as groups do throughout the world. Such groups can be political parties or militias, but they cannot be both. When participating in elections, by design you are choosing ballots over bullets. Hamas should have had to choose. Yet it was not forced to choose, so it was able to have it both ways—and with horrific results. This was a terrible mistake on the part of the United States. It is of course possible that Hamas would have refused to make the choice, but in that case the onus of electoral nonparticipation would have been on it. Instead, Hamas gained legitimacy through a system it actively disdained. The net effect is that it used its militia to bolster its political standing, and conversely used its political standing to insulate its militia: precisely the sort of result democratization was supposed to forestall.

When we discussed in chapter 10 the issue of whether to engage Hamas or Hizbollah, we observed that these groups, by keeping their guns, are consciously declaring their independence from any political system. They can always opt out and act on their own terms. At their core, they are dedicated to advancing their own ideological interests by any means necessary instead of being part of any truly democratic or independent polity. In this light, it seems fair to say that Secretary Rice, writing in *Foreign Affairs* during the summer of 2008, had it backward when she stated: "The participation of armed groups in elections is problematic. But the lesson is not that there should not be elections. Rather, there should be standards, like the ones to which the international community has held Hamas *after the fact* [emphasis added]: you can be a terrorist group or you can be a political party, but you cannot be both. As difficult as the problem is, it cannot be the case that people are denied the right to vote just because the outcome might be unpleasant to us."[7] But in this case, the issue was their weapons more than their views; it was their unwillingness to meet the basic criteria for elections that had been established in the 1995 Interim Agreement.

Since Secretary Rice knew very well before the 2006 election that Hamas was not going to give up its militia, why didn't she at least say at that time that their participation was inconsistent with the criteria for who could participate? Why didn't she insist on holding them to the requirements of an agreement the United States had signed, not as an observer, but as a mediator? In fact, Bush and Rice ignored Israel's insistence that the decision to include Hamas was a violation of Oslo II. Yet in effect she writes in *Foreign Affairs* that the issue is Hamas's participation—after the fact, and after the elections have given it the veneer of legitimacy. This makes no sense.

No less confusing were Bush's own remarks just after the January 2006 elections. In virtually the same breath, he seemed to contradict himself. At a White House press conference, he declared:

So the Palestinians had an election yesterday, and the results of which remind me about the power of democracy. You see, when you give people the vote, you give people a chance to express themselves at the polls—and if they're unhappy with the status quo, they'll let you know. That's the great thing about democracy, it provides a look into society.

And yesterday the turnout was significant, as I understand it. And there was a peaceful process as people went to the polls, and that's positive. But what was also positive is, is that it's a wake-up call to the leadership. Obviously, people were not happy with the status quo. The people are demanding honest government. The people want services. They want to be able to raise their children in an environment in which they can get a decent education and they can find health care.

And so the elections should open the eyes of the old guard there in the Palestinian territories. I like the competition of ideas. I like people who have to go out and say, "Vote for me, and here's what I'm going to do." There's something healthy about a system that does that. And so the elections yesterday were very interesting.

On the other hand, I don't see how you can be a partner in peace if you advocate the destruction of a country as part of your platform. And I know you can't be a partner in peace if you have a—if your party has got an armed wing. The elections just took place. We will watch very carefully about the formation of the government. But I will continue to remind people about what I just said, that if your platform is the destruction of Israel, it means you're not a partner in peace. And we're interested in peace.[8]

Why not say this before the election? Why not at least make clear to the Palestinians that of course they are free to vote for whomever they prefer, but they should know that America and the world are also free to choose whom they will deal with and that those who reject peace will not be considered a partner? If we had said this in advance, no one could have accused the United States of having a double standard for pushing for the elections and then not being willing to accept what such elections produced.

What about the case of Lebanon? The story looks much the same. But in Lebanon, UN Security Council Resolution 1559 actually required both that Syrian troops leave Lebanon and that Hizbollah be disarmed. The Bush administration demanded the exit of Syria. Yet, given its fervent belief that elections are basically self-correcting mechanisms, the administration had no problem with Hizbollah's contesting elections, suggesting disarmament would come later.[9] Needless to say, this did not occur. Hizbollah kept its weapons—with the predictable results.

Theorists on where and how democracy is most likely to develop would have understood clearly the advantages that Islamist groups such as Hamas and Hizbollah (even apart from their possessing arms) have in circumstances where there is a premature push for elections. Jack Snyder and Edward Mansfield state, for example, that rapid democratic transitions in places where there is no consensus on identity tend to spawn backlashes, which they term "illiberal nationalist" strategies. Opposition groups seek to capitalize on governments of weak central authority and gain legitimacy by drawing on religious or nationalist roots, rather than espousing a liberal democratic future. This model has shown itself to be to the advantage of Islamist groups in countries where often the only forums for free expression outside of the regime are the mosque and Islamic associations.

The Bush administration, however, simply did not understand the context in which it was operating and sought to promote elections. Worse, as Tamara Cofman Wittes points out, the administration actually thought it could push elections precisely because of the weakness of the polities it chose—and that very weakness would make cases such as Lebanon and the PA more tractable than others:

> In attempting democratic change first in places where it was least likely to succeed, the Bush administration made a fundamental misjudgment. It did so because it failed to understand that weak states need functional governance if they are ever to have democratic governance, and it missed this crucial point precisely because it saw these weak places as riper targets, unable to resist American pressure for democracy and unable to retaliate against other American interests. In their desire to avoid confronting autocratic allies on human rights and democracy, Bush and his advisers turned their energies to the most dysfunctional places in the Middle East in the bizarre expectation of easier victory. Clearly, the outcome was a policy failure for Bush's effort at democracy promotion.[10]

Few have captured the essence of the Bush misreading more clearly than Wittes.

Third Mistake—Halting Efforts in Egypt

To be fair, at least for a period of time the Bush administration did not focus only on weak states or regimes as it emphasized democracy promotion. Secretary Rice made a strong speech in Cairo in 2005, explaining why it was in Egypt's interests to open up and embrace the development of democracy. At the time, Rice met with Egyptian dissidents and democracy advocates. And Egypt—as a stronger state—should have been a better test case for political reform than Lebanon or the West Bank and Gaza. However, scared off by the Hamas election in 2006, the Bush administration dropped the effort in Egypt. Had there been a serious commitment to democracy promotion, it needed to be sustained and nurtured.

One thing is certain: in a place like Egypt change was not going to come rapidly or easily. Egyptians are well known for saying that the strength of their state goes back to the times of the Pharaohs. Moreover, the Egyptian intelligence service is legendary for its dominance inside the country. Reform efforts require a serious commitment and a thought-out strategy. They must embody more than short-term pressures and rhetorical flourishes.

But such pressures and statements are what the Bush administration applied to Egypt, at least in 2005. And they had an effect, at least to the extent that Egypt held elections in 2005. The Egyptian parliament adopted rules that essentially permitted competition in the first election but imposed sharp limitations on the follow-up elections, and Egyptian president Hosni Mubarak refused to accept international monitors. Still, it was the first time that Mubarak had run in a contested election. Until that time, he ruled Egypt for twenty-four years thanks to a mere referendum. Yet as soon as the election ended, Mubarak's regime imprisoned his opponent, Ayman Nour, on contested charges.[11]

Once again, the problem in Egypt was not just about elections. The Egyptian government has been unwilling to allow dissidence. Although individual dissidents are treated harshly, the regime is most afraid of Islamist ideology. Do not get us wrong. The Egyptian regime has no problem arresting thousands of Islamist militants; but it never takes on the ideology they represent. In general, Arab regimes virtually never attack the animating ideas of the Islamist ideology, believing that the appearance of piety confers a patina of legitimacy on unelected leaders. The regime shows no such deference to Arab democrats, who lack a broad constituency of sympathizers. As Hala Mustafa states:

> The regime fears too confrontationalist of a stance towards the Islamist ideology. They know how to distinguish between specific Islamist troublemakers and the overall ideology that the Islamists espouse. In the 1950's, Nasser's pan-Arab nationalism actively undermined political Islamist ideology. Now Arab nationalism is dead and the regime was never able to develop a new rationale for its rule. What a stagnant regime today shares with the Islamists is that the political legitimacy of both of them derives from common roots, specifically, unity of the Arab/Muslim nation (*umma*) as part of defiance against the West instead of performance-based accountability. This collective orientation rejects political pluralism, diversity, and especially denies the dignity of the individual. Therefore, the regime and the Islamists are essentially on a collision course with Arab liberals, who put the dignity of the individual at the center.[12]

In other words, the Arab liberals are crowded out—the very ones who might help socialize attitudes on political participation, tolerance, compromise, and the rule of law. If the Egyptian regime cannot explain publicly, to its own people, that the Islamists undermine the progress of the country in the twenty-first century, this creates a false choice for the Egyptian people: either vote for those who are corrupt, or vote for the Islamists who put forward the alluring slogan "Islam is the answer."

It is clear that at a minimum, the United States needs to find a way to engage with the Egyptian authorities on how to foster the development of liberal institutions that could promote important elements of democracy, such as a free judiciary, more rights for women, and free media. These sorts of institutions create both mechanisms of accountability and stronger internal advocates for political reform. But this is bound to be a complex, at times frustrating effort that necessarily will be incremental and take time, and the Bush administration—preferring grand gestures to hard, sustained effort—never embraced such an approach.

Fourth Mistake—No Discerning Approach to Islamists and Political Reform

It is clear that the specter of Islamist ascendance has created confusion in the Bush administration about the desirability of Islamist participation in the political process. Fear of being accused of hypocrisy may have created a bizarre situation in which, as noted above, President Bush both praised the results of the Hamas victory in 2006 and then condemned it within virtually the same breath. Yet an American president should not be afraid to make distinctions between Islamist organizational militias that carry weapons and disrupt the ability of a nascent entity such as the PA or Lebanon to function, and other Islamist groups that have a track record of abjuring violence and are willing to be part of a broader political system. In other words, there is a lack of consistency among the Islamist parties themselves. So it is crucial that we not fall into the hypocrisy trap set by critics, namely, defending the right of inclusion of all Islamist groups when they themselves clearly fit into different categories.

We have made it abundantly clear that groups that demand the right to keep their own militias are not seeking to join any democratic process but rather to subvert it or retain a hedge over it. At the same time, there are Islamist parties that think differently. Whether it is the Islamists in secular Turkey or Morocco or perhaps the Muslim Brotherhood in Egypt, some have learned that they will be marginalized if they do not play within the rules of the system. The question remains—are these groups truly committed to the system, or are they going to try to use democratic means to subvert democracy? Here judgment calls are required.

While we, too, are skeptical of the intentions of many Islamist parties, we believe that when they cross the threshold and repudiate having a militia, they need to be accommodated, at least in terms of the right to participate in politics and compete in elections. And yet there are more fundamental issues that will have to be sorted out over time, both by those who seek to promote democracy and by the Islamic parties themselves. As analyst Martin Kramer has observed: "I think that the Islamists who most stand to profit from political openings have yet to fathom what democracy means. It is not merely about voting or parties. Democracy means a willingness to fight and die so that those who differ from you can enjoy the right to be different, and even criticize you." He added, "Islamists, with their dichotomization of believer and unbeliever, man and woman, Islam and West, do not share the values that underpin democracy. Islam itself, interpreted differently, can be rendered compatible with it. But that is not how it gets interpreted by most Islamists."[13] Therefore it is important to know that these parties accept the rules of the game and do not seek supremacy in order to overturn the democratic system.

WHAT SHOULD THE UNITED STATES DO?

We do not mean to suggest that the Bush administration did not undertake any favorable conceptual changes. Its concept of a Middle East Partnership Initiative to support Arab civic groups was good, yet in practice most of its early funding went to governments rather than to nongovernmental organizations.[14] This approach needs to be revisited, with greater funding for genuine Arab civic groups. The administration also secured a series of bilateral free trade agreements with Jordan, Morocco, Bahrain, and Oman. Hopefully, trade liberalization would improve economic conditions. It should encourage some form of property rights with a modicum of financial accountability that could create transparency, which is helpful both for economic progress and broader reform. In addition, one very useful program of the Bush administration was the Millennium Challenge grants, which gave extra aid to countries that met reform benchmarks and began to develop a pattern of good governance.

These are certainly programs and concepts that could be embraced and expanded and pursued far more vigorously in the Obama administration. But the mind-set of the new administration, and its point of departure, must be different. While the old adage that mature democracies do not fight one another may be true, it is also true that the path to democracy is fraught with turbulence. A new administration needs to understand this—needs to understand that progress will not be linear and that its central task in democracy promotion is to make the pathway less rocky, even if it means the pace is more deliberate.

Elections were disastrous in Lebanon and in the West Bank and Gaza, and they seemed to matter little in Egypt, which had only a 22 percent turnout, with Mubarak winning almost 90 percent of the vote. By not participating, the Egyptian people were making their own statement about the credibility of the elections and whether they would mean anything.

The Direction and Pace of Reform

All this should not be taken as an excuse for doing nothing. The guiding principle should be to pursue liberal means to obtaining liberal ends. We need to realize that, for a variety of reasons, democratization is about more than holding one election. This means focusing on both establishing and bolstering institutions that are crucial to reform, and also focusing on the reformers themselves. When it comes to the question of reformers, the issues are how we identify reformers, and how we support them so that they can pose a real challenge to the Islamists while still making sure that they are using that support appropriately.

Time is a key factor when it comes to developing institutions. Creating the foundation of meaningful civil institutions seems to us a worthy effort, as part of an effort to create the basis for sustainable reform. Creating sturdy foundations is required in Arab countries where civic life has been sharply restricted over decades. We see value in gradualism for another reason. The alternatives have their dangers. Go too quickly where the conditions are not ripe, and the outcome could be an Islamist takeover when such groups represent the most organized opposition. Go too slowly, and the Islamists could be poised to exploit the backlash against an authoritarian regime. Of course, calibrating change will not be easy and must differ in each country. What we do know is that those who say any radical alternative is always better than the status quo are typically wrong. As Barry Rubin writes, "There have been many such cases in history: those who said that anything was better than the czar and wound up with Stalin; the collapse of the weak, imperfect Weimar Republic of Germany; or the impetus to reform in Iran that turned into an Islamist revolution. Good intentions can become wishful thinking that, in turn, leads to a deadly outcome."[15]

Evolutionary political reform is key. It is important to encourage reform of media laws to widen the discourse on public policy. Such reforms are essential to avoiding governmental prosecution of journalists on the basis that any criticism of the head of state constitutes "defamation." Emphasizing free media and access to them will be essential. While much of the new media in the Middle East is populist in its appeal, there are outlets such as al-Arabiya that are trying hard to be responsible and create accountability among regimes that have traditionally controlled the press as government mouthpieces. There will be no democracy (or liberalization) in the Arab world without free media that can act as a watchdog, and we must continue to emphasize access as a central theme.

Pushing for reform of the judiciary laws to promote the development of an independent judiciary is fundamental. Such reforms must be genuine and not like the one passed in Egypt; in spite of that "reform," human rights activists indicate that judges are still paid partly by the justice ministry (if they rule against the state, their salary can be cut for many months at a time).

While the scope of specific reforms in law should reflect the different pace of change in individual countries, the general direction should be clear. In all countries, however, there are programmatic points for the United States that could be attainable if we sustain our focus. Those seeking an evolutionary pathway to democratization know where to put the effort: women's rights, free media, an independent judiciary, and education reform, alongside the greater transparency required for economic growth.

Focus on Reformers

Democratic institutions, if properly cultivated, are the foundations for a democratization process that should lead to progress over time. But the issue is not just investing in creating and bolstering more democratic institutions. It is about identifying credible reformers who have authenticity in their own societies. We have spoken at length about our natural partners, the non-Islamists in the Middle East. We think it is important to give a thumbnail sketch of three people whom we see as fitting in this category—and who demonstrate why they are our natural partners and how they seem determined to make a difference in their societies from the ground up.

Salam Fayyad. One example is Palestinian Authority prime minister Salam Fayyad. He has won respect at home and abroad for his desire to raise Palestinian living standards and introduce transparency in Palestinian spending. When he speaks of transparency, it is not only to prevent the kind of corruption that characterized and plagued the Palestinian Authority under Yasir Arafat, but also to foster political institutions that will be accountable and responsible for their actions.

Fayyad was born in the West Bank in 1952. He earned a doctorate in economics at the University of Texas and worked at the World Bank in Washington from 1987 to 1995. He then served as the International Monetary Fund's representative to the Palestinian Authority based in Jerusalem until 2001. Amid pressure from the international community, which was exasperated with Arafat and widespread corruption, Fayyad served as the finance minister of the PA from 2002 to 2005. He became prime minister of a Palestinian emergency government in 2007 and has consistently been praised for introducing genuine economic reforms. These include breaking up the gasoline and cement cartels and introducing a standardized monthly salary for Palestinian police. The international community has pledged (though not always delivered) billions of dollars to the PA based on its confidence that money directed to Fayyad will not be stolen or wasted.

Rola Dashti. Another prominent Arab reformer is Dr. Rola Dashti. A courageous and effective activist, she wants civil society to be a driving force in pursuing political and economic reform. She led an inspirational and unprecedented movement of Kuwaiti women, pressing the case of gender equality. Thanks to Dr. Dashti's effort, an official decree went out in May 2005 that gave women the right to vote for the Kuwaiti parliament for the first time. She has been named one of the Arab world's one hundred most influential people in 2007 and 2008.

Ali Salem. A third courageous reformer is Cairo playwright Ali Salem. He is known for his biting satire in a country that has not been tolerant of dissent. He has been eloquent in speaking out against Islamist suicide bombing, saying this "culture of death" will not succeed in building either a Palestinian state or human rights. The stabbing of his friend and Nobel Prize laureate Naguib Mahfouz by a militant has not deterred his railing against the Islamists. Salem also broke from Egyptian convention when he visited Israel. He subsequently wrote a book in Arabic about his visit. Salem has not been intimidated by the campaign against him in the Egyptian state-run media.

Reformers in the Arab world are doing their own soul-searching. They realize that they must also change and become less focused on offering an abstract message of reform. A few guidelines should shape U.S. policy toward democracy promotion in the Arab world:

- *Elections are part of the process, but should not come first.* Given the current environment, we should not be pushing for premature elections; we should focus instead on helping secular, moderate alternatives to organize and emphasize fighting corruption and developing the rule of law and good governance in the near term.
- *There should be eligibility requirements when elections are held.* Militias and their members should not be allowed to run as parties or to field candidates. It is either ballots or bullets but not both, and potential candidates must make a choice.
- *Reformers should help us frame our public message and posture in the area.* On a country-by-country basis, we should identify credible reformers and let them advise us on how to address Arab publics; our goal is to help and not hurt them, and they are better arbiters of what will resonate locally.
- *U.S. and donor aid should be geared toward helping reformers provide services and programs that actually foster development and employment.* We need to take a page from the Islamist playbook. They have used the provision of social services to build a following. Reformers should now do the same, and we could help fund such programs. For example, reformer-led after-school programs that teach English and computer skills would be a magnet for many Arab parents and kids and put reformers in a position of responding to real needs and offering hope.
- *Donor assistance must also be geared toward helping reforming governments become efficient.* Reforming governments in the region, like Jordan and Morocco, need to build models of success. They need to deliver, and we and others should target our assistance toward programs

that help them provide services in impoverished areas where Islamist recruiting in the mosques is greatest and the governments have been traditionally unresponsive.

- *Reformers must know they are not alone.* Too often reformers have been pressured and arrested by authoritarian regimes, including those that are friendly to the United States. Unfortunately, some Arab reformers have come forward and been jailed, believing the U.S. will not let them down. Jailed dissident Ayman Nour may feel that way in Egypt. We cannot be seen as urging reformers to take untoward risks and then dropping their cases once they are imprisoned.

Democracy can neither be imposed nor appear magically overnight in the Arab world. The same is true for secular, moderate alternatives to the autocratic regimes and their theocratic rivals. But working to promote democracy is the right course, and there are practical steps that we can take now to move us down the right path and help our natural partners in the region.

There will be a debate between those who insist that the focus should be on government-led, gradual liberalization versus those who believe—like Wittes—that only bottom-up insistence on political rights such as freedom of speech and assembly will create the needed internal pressure to sustain the domestic constituencies for reform. Still others say that economic reform will create those constituencies. We do not think there are hard-and-fast rules, and the choice of approaches may depend upon the unique circumstances of individual Middle East countries. Yet what is common to all schools of thought is a belief that what will sustain reform over time is giving expression to the demands from within. The United States can facilitate this process and use its considerable leverage with Arab regimes to make it clear that there is no other way, over the long haul, to sustain hopes for the future against domestic dissent—which for now is only temporarily repressed by intelligence services.

Ultimately, political reform represents the convergence of values and interests. We think the realists have once again failed to appreciate how the two fit together. If they had more understanding of regional realities, they would recognize that democratization is an issue of fundamental and enduring American interests. Regimes that the realists see as crucial for stability in the region and critical to the free flow of oil are likely to become focal points of instability if they do not address the domestic sources of anger and alienation—which sooner or later may well erupt to the point that they cannot be contained. So, for realist reasons, the issue of reform needs to be taken seriously.

Meanwhile, the neoconservatives—who insist that they are more animated by values than interests—should realize that pressure and attrition alone cannot achieve their objectives in dealing with Arab regimes. There must be a strategy; it must be rooted in the realities of the region; it must be nurtured over time; it must be guided by identifying and working with our natural partners in the region who, for their own reasons, see that reform and inclusion (economically and politically) over time are essential for their own salvation.

In short, we need to work with authoritarian Middle Eastern regimes even as we put pressure on them. It will not always be an easy balance to strike. But unlike the approaches of the realists or the neoconservatives, such an approach will allow us to balance our interests and values against each other and be true to them at the same time. It will not yield a quick turnaround, but it will offer a pathway without illusions and without myths—and it might even help produce a gradual transformation in the region.

Chapter Thirteen

A NEW REALISM FOR U.S. POLICY IN THE MIDDLE EAST

If there is one thing that the neoconservatives and the self-described realists have in common when it comes to the Middle East, it is that neither understands reality in the region. Neither pays sufficient attention to the context to understand the real factors or circumstances that shape what can be done in the Middle East. Both are guided far more by their sweeping belief systems about what ought to be than by looking at what actually exists.

Neoconservatives have believed that American power and basic goodness give us the right and the duty to spread our values and promote regime change and democracy—regardless of the context, the sources of resistance, the sectarian divides, the absence of a civic culture, or the dearth of institutions that provide the foundation for democracy. The realists—of course, realists only in name and theory—have defined American interests in a vacuum; oil mattered, linkage was a given, values were largely irrelevant, and the costs of dissociation from Israel were by definition small. Peace could be imposed because Israelis could not say no if the United States insisted, and the Arabs would then be drawn to us because we had responded to their interests—or so the realists have believed.

But context matters. Neither democracy nor peace can emerge in the Middle East without being nurtured. Each requires building from the ground up, and at times from the top down. Both are worth pursuing, just as changing the behaviors of rogue states and rogue nonstate actors is also a necessary objective. However, like trying to promote peace and democracy, the effort to change or affect the behaviors of rogue actors—and to counter the radical Islamists—requires a carefully thought-out strategy and an understanding of the context in which we are operating. There is little prospect of succeeding in changing Iran's behavior, for example, if we fail to understand who and what may influence Iran's behavior—and which particular set of circumstances are most likely to work in our favor. To this end, we must read the internal dynamics in Iran and at the same time understand Iran's vulnerabilities, the leverage that we have and that others like the Saudis may have, and what it will take to mobilize those who have greater leverage than we do and actually apply it. Lastly, we must know how to effectively engage the Iranians without illusions.

Whether trying to foster peace or liberalization in the Middle East or alter regime behaviors, we have to see the world as it is. The sad truth is that neither the neoconservatives nor the self-described realists have understood reality. Each might criticize us for being too willing to be constrained by reality. But we would respond by saying that one cannot change an unacceptable reality before one understands it—and then it becomes possible to shape a strategy that produces change in stages. In other words, our call to understand the region is not a call for us to pursue a foreign policy that is merely reactive. Rather, it is our view that if one puts forward an objective, both the objective and the strategy to reach the objective must be shaped by the complex reality inside the region.

We agree that change is needed in the Middle East. We acknowledge that there is an unacceptable reality in the Middle East and we must find a way to transform this region, particularly given the rising danger that radical Islamists pose. Where we part company with the neoconservatives and the realists is at the realization that their prescriptions are not just doomed to fail, but bound to make things worse.

To effect change in the region, a new realism is needed. We must start by seeing the region as it is. The principles that guide us must reflect this understanding of reality and provide us the basis to change it—that is what being realistic is all about.

So where do we begin? A good starting point is to understand that our interests in the region—and our abiding need to compete with the radical Islamists—will be served by promoting peacemaking between Arabs and Israelis.

We say this not because it is a panacea for all the ills or conflicts in the area. As we have outlined in the book, there is no linkage between solving this conflict and solving other conflicts in the Middle East. We do not believe the road to Baghdad or anywhere else runs through Jerusalem, or vice versa. Yet we do understand that this conflict is evocative in the region, and if it was possible to resolve it, it would remove one of the key sources of anger and grievance throughout the Middle East. The Palestinian cause is embedded in the DNA, in the psychic reality, of those in Arab and Muslim countries. There is a widespread conviction that the Palestinians have suffered a grievous injustice. They have lost a homeland and suffer under occupation. In the eyes of Arab publics, this injustice must be undone and the wrong must be righted. As long as it is not addressed and corrected, it is a constant reminder of an imposition that feeds an abiding sense of powerlessness. Radical Islamists prey on this sense of powerlessness and the anger it provokes.

The Islamists seek a revolutionary new order in the Middle East governed by sharia (Islamic law). They declare that all truth is revealed in the Koran and the Hadith (the sayings of the Prophet) and their exclusive interpretation of them; label their Muslim opponents apostates; employ terror as their principal tool; and see the United States as their main enemy. They exploit the Palestinian grievance, which is so basic, to build resentment against the United States and against the current regimes in the region.

It is in America's interest to take this "club" away from the Islamists if it is possible to do so. Yet the Palestinian issue is not the only source of anger and alienation—and these other sources of powerlessness and the frustration they breed must also be addressed if we are to succeed against the Islamists, who constitute the greatest threat to our interests in the Middle East and increasingly around the world.

The Islamists will not be discredited by outsiders. Whether we like it or not, they have a high degree of authenticity in the region. Only other Muslims can discredit them. The good news is that they often overplay their hand and produce a backlash. Al-Qaeda, which is made up of radical Sunni Muslims, has done this in Iraq by killing Sunni tribal leaders and trying to impose an austere, intolerant brand of Islamic rule. The Iranians, who are Shia and represent a different brand of Islamism, have helped to provoke a deeper awareness of the Sunni-Shia divide in Islam and therefore are not exactly a model for the majority Sunnis in the Arab and

Muslim worlds. And yet al-Qaeda and the Iranians, though in many respects competitors, remain formidable because there has been no consistent and credible counterpoint in the area that seeks to discredit them.

From an ideological and religious standpoint, these two groups too often seem to speak to the vast majority of those in Arab or Muslim countries who are jobless or underemployed, feel excluded, and have few prospects and no say over their lives or their children's lives. The Islamists often speak a language that connects with these elements more than do most of the current regimes—regimes that are perceived by their publics as corrupt and exclusionary, benefiting only a very select few at the expense of the many.

It is for this reason that the United States has a profound interest in liberalizing regimes and helping reformers throughout the Middle East. It is essential that the options in the Middle East not be reduced to a choice between corrupt regimes and Islamists. The United States will continue to lose if these are the only alternatives, and if the United States continues to be seen as backing the corrupt regimes and the status quo. America must work with those who want to open their political systems and must help them to become more effective.

Democracy promotion is important, but it is a process. While the Bush policies have discredited the term "democracy" in the Middle East, the Pew and Gallup polls indicate clearly that most of those in the Middle East crave not only a better life but also a greater say over their own destiny. So the United States must identify its natural partners, listen to them, work with them, and protect them from regimes that have little interest in opening up or becoming more inclusive. Inevitably, liberalization will be more evolutionary than revolutionary, but it must be a cornerstone of a new U.S. policy in the region.

No approach to peacemaking or reform promotion in the Middle East will work without a new emphasis on accountability. The political culture of the region has been geared more to entitlement than responsibility. U.S. policies must emphasize accountability. Our efforts at peacemaking cannot succeed unless all sides are accountable—in the first instance, to and for themselves. Reform cannot work unless the reformers are perceived as producing useful services or programs (especially relevant education and employment) and not just words.

Competition with radical Islamists requires that the governments

America helps must also be seen as being responsive to their publics, delivering basic necessities, creating level playing fields, offering social justice, and being generally accountable. Though few governments in the region meet this standard, polling indicates the increasing awareness of publics and their demands for greater responsiveness and effectiveness. Significantly, the al-Arabiya satellite network is contrasting itself with al-Jazeera by emphasizing that the news media need to play a watchdog role—no longer seeking to incite and mobilize publics behind regional struggles and regional causes (that often appear to mix Islamism and Arab nationalism) but instead seeking to make local authorities explain themselves and be accountable to their publics. This effort must also guide a new American approach to the region.

Peacemaking, promotion of reform, and a new focus on accountability should all be central premises (or core assumptions) of U.S. policy toward the Middle East. Security will necessarily continue to be a linchpin. The radical Islamists—whether in al-Qaeda or Iran—may have varying strategies but uniformly employ violence, terror, and intimidation as their central tactics. True, the Iranians back militias that are also political movements, such as Hizbollah, Hamas, and the Mahdi Army, but terror is an instrument these groups employ even as they offer social services and compete in elections. Al-Qaeda may reject political and social strategies and because of that may represent a less formidable challenge, at least insofar as the answer to their violence is violence. But with Iran and its various instrumentalities like Hizbollah or Hamas, the threat is more complex. These groups are not now and cannot be partners so long as they remain guided by their ideological credo. We need to see them as they are, not as others would like them to be. Our struggle with these forces requires a comprehensive strategy that uses political, social, economic, diplomatic, informational, and military tools and emphasizes cooperation with our regional partners in all these domains.

We must be credible in the eyes of those who feel threatened by the Islamists. We must have answers to the military or terror threats. We certainly believe that terrorism must be fought. But we must also develop answers to the more subtle threats, in arenas where America's image is part of the competition and affects the value or costs of being associated with us. Being credible on our engagement on the Arab-Israeli peace front is essential; the same is true for knowing how to deal with Iran or other threatening regimes in the region. The United States should not rule out direct talks. Too often with countries like Iran or Syria we have made "engaging" or talking a big issue. The problem with that is that our reluctance to talk has frequently made the United States the issue, instead of the behavior we seek to change in Iran or Syria. We should want the focus to be on them, not us.

If that means being prepared to talk to such regimes, so be it. But such a readiness to talk must not be accompanied by illusions about the purposes of those we are dealing with, nor should it be done without considering the possible effect on our friends or partners in the region. The last thing we should do is surprise those who depend on us. Certainly, we should consult with those who feel threatened by Iran or Syria (like the Saudis or Israelis or Lebanese) before engaging. We need not give our friends or partners a veto, but they should not feel that such engagement will come at their expense, or that their interests will not be considered, or that the agenda for such engagement is naïve or will be sending the Iranians or Syrians the wrong message. Reliability stems not only from being there when needed but also from being predictable and well grounded.

Surprising our friends is not the way to sustain our credibility. Whether dealing with threatening states or raising the issue of internal reform, it is essential not to surprise those who have been America's partners in the region.

Truth be told, credibility is a function of many facets of our behavior. Are we effective? Do we tend to preserve the moral high ground? Do we frame issues or objectives in a way that others internationally or regionally accept? Do we shape policies in which our objectives and our means are in sync, or is there always a wide gap between them? Do others believe that we will do what we say we will do, or are we likely to put those who join with us in an exposed position? Do we avoid surprises that raise questions about our purposes or judgment or both? Ultimately, credibility boils down to reliability and effectiveness. After the ineffective policies of the Bush administration, its successor must recognize the importance of being able to produce on the objectives it proclaims.

One final point on reliability and credibility is worth reiterating, particularly as it relates to what should be the core premises driving U.S. policy in the Middle East. America has a strong stake in its relationship with Israel. It is a democracy; it shares our basic values; it can be counted on to support America in good times and bad. Its military and intelligence assets have often been of direct and indirect benefit to us and our allies inside and outside the region. And Israel is threatened by the very same forces that threaten us.

America and Israel may not always see eye to eye; the fact is that the United States rarely agrees with any ally all of the time. Where the United States disagrees with Israeli policies, there is no reason to shy away from saying so—privately at first if our aim is to change that policy, and publicly when it is appropriate to do so. But disagreement is one thing; dissociation from Israel would be quite another. There can be little doubt about the damage it would do to U.S. credibility in the region. As we pointed out in chapter 11, there is no relationship in the Middle East that the United States has affirmed more fervently or consistently in public than its ties and commitment to Israel and its security. For the United States to walk away or leave Israel in the lurch would raise questions throughout the region—among our friends and our foes—about whether the United States would live up to any commitments it has made.

It is hard to imagine steps by the United States that would do more to embolden al-Qaeda or Iran. While each may seek to weaken and demoralize Israel, they do so because they believe it will weaken and undermine the U.S. position in the region—and, for perhaps different reasons, that is the fundamental aim of each. (Al-Qaeda because it believes that the United States props up the very Arab regimes—Egypt and Saudi Arabia—it seeks to subvert and overthrow, and Iran because it sees the United States as competing for regional dominance and determined to prevent Iran from achieving its rightful status in the area.)

To those who think that dissociation from Israel would help us in the region, it is worth saying again, simply and bluntly, that they are fundamentally wrong. It would not help us, it would hurt us. It would also surely convince al-Qaeda and the Iranians and their acolytes that they were succeeding and could not be stopped.

Not surprisingly, anything that is likely to embolden al-Qaeda or the Iranians is bound to be seen as alarming by most of the Arab governments that in one way or another have counted on the United States to preserve a certain order in the region. Ironically, many in the Arab world also count on a strong Israel, at least indirectly, to do much the same thing by countering the radical Islamists. A weak Israel is the last thing they want to see. Like it or not, a strong Israel is a bulwark against the radical Islamists. They may seize on its presence and seek to exploit anger against it, but Israel's power is also a constraint on what the Iranians, Hizbollah, and Hamas can do.

The fact is that many Arab regimes were shaken by the Israeli military performance against Hizbollah in the summer of 2006. They wanted Hizbollah to be defeated, not emerge stronger from that conflict. As we noted earlier, in September 2007, when Israel bombed the nuclear reactor that Syria was building (but never took credit publicly for this action), there was not a single word of condemnation from any Arab government. Here was an effective use of Israeli military power, and no Arab leadership was unhappy about it—other than the Syrians. Most Arab governments want Israel to be strong when it comes to Iran, Hizbollah, Hamas, and Syria.

Israel is certainly not loved in the region, and Israeli behaviors against the Palestinians often embarrass Arab leaders and put them on the defensive, particularly as the Iranians seek to exploit the anger these actions provoke among Arab publics. They will consistently complain about Israel, and consistently seek American pressure on Israel to change its behavior toward the Palestinians. However, U.S. dissociation or even distance from Israel would raise more questions than it answers for nearly every Arab government.

That is the reality in which the United States must develop and implement policy in a region that has become the pivot of our foreign policy. In this book, we have shown the fallacies of two schools of thought that have misguided America in the Middle East, and we have offered a centrist alternative to their mythologies and prescriptions. We have explained why America must restore its position as a mediator on peace and a security guarantor in conflict; why the United States must identify with reform and work to make reforming governments and reformers more capable of delivering; and why the United States must not give up its ideals, but must pursue them in a way that reflects the realities of the region and not wishful thinking.

Ours has been a call for a more grounded approach to the Middle East. No longer can America afford to operate at a high level of generality and offer sweeping slogans for the region that ignore the texture of real

322   MYTHS, ILLUSIONS, AND PEACE

life, real politics, real pressures, and the real forces that shape the decision making of Arab, Palestinian, Israeli, and Iranian leaders. Pseudorealism and grand theories have led American policymakers down a mistaken and costly path. It is time for a change in U.S. policy; it is time for a new realism in the Middle East.

Afterword

As of this writing in February 2010, the Obama administration is entering its second year. With an agenda that has been dominated by increasing troop levels in Afghanistan, a severe recession, high unemployment, major health-care legislation and prospects that the Republicans may make a major comeback in the mid-term elections later this year, it may seem that the Middle East has had to fight for attention.

The Israeli-Palestinian issue has not worked out as the Obama administration had hoped. The picture is mixed. The ground up developments in the West Bank have shown promise and hope. However, the top-down political negotiations have not only made little progress, they have regressed. This is due in no small part to an early miscalculation by Washington that triggered a series of events and expectations that would not be overcome during the administration's first year.

Iran's nuclear program has become another Middle East focal point for the administration. Unlike the Arab-Israel issue, the Iranian strategy seems to be proceeding along the course predicted by our book. We say in the book that we cannot guarantee that political engagement with Iran will work to persuade Iran to halt its nuclear program. We now know the course of isolation that dominated the decade also did not succeed and Iran is closer to a nuclear bomb than ever before. Moreover, we said if the effort of political engagement with Iran fails as a strategy, it could succeed as a tactic to frame our subsequent decisions and make them more legitimate and credible. This seems to be the current course of the administration, and it seems to be gaining support around the world. Many countries are supporting increased sanctions on Iran in a bid to ensure that Teheran stops its drive for nuclear weapons.

It is worth reviewing both these issues in greater depth.

On the Israeli-Palestinian front, the administration sought to demonstrate its commitment to being active on this issue by naming an envoy on its second day. The envoy, who gained acclaim for his work in brokering peace in Northern Ireland, was former Democratic Senate majority leader George Mitchell.

Yet, the administration embarked on a strategy that proved to be unattainable. The idea of a settlement freeze was introduced in a public fashion. As such, it became the measure of how the public on all sides judged President Obama's policy for the year. When Israel fell short on the objective, it enabled the Arab side to avoid obligations rather than fulfill them. The Obama administration wanted to set the bar high for what it asked from Israel, but did not think through the impact and implications of the move should the strategy fail after expectations had been raised. In other words, this miscalculation, in large measure, doomed peacemaking for 2009.

In short, as 2010 begins, U.S. peace strategy has alienated Israelis and Palestinians alike and the Arab states are not forthcoming. What went wrong?

The U.S. approach was predicated upon the idea of going beyond a focus on halting West Bank settlement land expansion. An approach based on the idea of no land expansion would be designed to avoid prejudging the final disposition of the West Bank in final territorial negotiations. Such an approach would be a legitimate sign to the Palestinians that the United States would not permit settlement encroachment during land negotiations.

Indeed, the bar was set high by the Obama administration. This would be no small matter as until now, a settlement freeze had never been a prerequisite to peace negotiations. The new approach created a backlash in Israel. When the administration subsequently sought to modify its approach during the summer of 2009, the net result was a backlash on the Palestinian side. Raising expectations ultimately proved not to be a recipe for progress but deadlock.

Specifically, the United States focused on a settlement freeze within the perimeter of existing settlements. In other words, the Obama administration chose a much higher standard than ensuring that settlements would not expand outward geographically that could potentially prejudge negotiations. The Israeli public did not understand why it was insufficient to refrain from territorially expanding settlements. They wondered how adding a second story inside a house inside a settlement would derail Middle East peace. While much of the world would oppose any form of settlement expansion, the Israelis had a differentiated view of settlements. It is widely assumed in Israel that most of the settlements adjacent to Israeli urban areas will be part of Israel in any final deal. This belief meant that most Israelis would view the idea of a freeze inside a settlement that was to be incorporated into Israel anyway as too blunt of a policy instrument. Moreover, some Israelis questioned the premise. Everyone knows when there is a commitment for withdrawal, Israel has destroyed settlements. It destroyed eight thousand homes in Gaza in 2005 and demolished thousands of homes in northern Sinai in compliance with the Egypt-Israel peace treaty of 1979.

The bottom line of this disparate thinking on settlements meant that nobody in the Israeli political system, including the head of Israel's liberal opposition, echoed the Obama call for a freeze. This problem was compounded by the fact that Obama did not communicate his approach to the Israeli public. While Obama would visit Egypt, Saudi Arabia, and Turkey during his first year, he did not visit Israel. It proved to be one country where support for the United States dropped precipitously. According to one poll, the support level was 4 percent, while another poll would say the percentage was in the low thirties.

In the tragic zero-sum philosophy of that conflict, one may think that any losses that the United States suffered in Israel would lead to greater popularity for the United States among the Palestinians and the Arab world. Indeed, this was the immediate reaction. When Obama gave his speech in Cairo in June 2009, he said he would not recognize the "legitimacy" of future settlement activity. There were other elements of the speech that won acclaim. In general, Arab reaction to the speech was very favorable.

However, the Palestinians drew their conclusions from the U.S. approach. They viewed it as a call to inaction. Mahmoud Abbas told American journalists that the Palestinians could be passive while the United

States presses Israel. The Palestinians also interpreted the United States approach as meaning that the demand for a settlement freeze would be a precondition for peace negotiations on the final disposition of the West Bank, which technically, was not the United States' formal position. This marked a change for Abbas, who as noted, had never made a settlement freeze a precondition for peace talks.

Seeing that its focus on a settlement freeze was not bearing fruit through midsummer of 2009, the Obama administration sought to change gears. It sought a deal with the Netanyahu government that amounted to less than a freeze for a ten-month period, which the United States would formally welcome. There would be an exception for 2,500 residential units that were already partially constructed and nonresidential structures like schools and synagogues. Moreover, East Jerusalem would not be included as Israel does not view that area as a settlement.

Israel has also backed off from several positions unfavorable to the resumption of talks. For example, Prime Minister Binyamin Netanyahu originally held that there should be no further talks until the United States found a way to halt the Iranian nuclear program. He also opposed the creation of a Palestinian state. Over the past several months, however, he has adjusted his stance, endorsing statehood, abandoning the Iranian requirement, and insisting to Washington that no Israeli leader has supported a settlement moratorium to the extent he has. He would win praise from Secretary of State Hillary Clinton for his ten-month moratorium. (Menachem Begin agreed to a three-month halt at the request of President Jimmy Carter at Camp David in 1978.) His aides pointed to the fact that Netanyahu took the step despite its unpopularity within his own coalition.

However, Abbas was boxed in by the administration, which thought it was helping him by setting the bar high at a full settlement freeze. He could not be less pro-Palestinian than the United States. Once he signed on to the settlement freeze approach of the Obama administration, he felt he had no ladder to climb down from the limb. In a December 22, 2009, interview with the London-based pan-Arab daily *al-Sharq al-Awsat*, Abbas blamed Washington for putting forward the freeze idea and then asking him to compromise. He recalled telling U.S. officials during a September meeting at the UN, "You put me on top of a tree, and now you ask me for a solution and to climb down." Abbas continued, "Obama laid down the condition of halting the settlements completely. What could I say to him? Should I say this is too much?"

So what are the lessons of 2009? As one learns from the book, foreign-policy "realists," including Brzezinski and Brent Scowcroft, want to impose peace. The problem with the realist approach is that it assumes the status quo can be instantly transformed. This is as flawed as the neo-conservative approach as advocated by Norman Podhoretz, which presumes the status quo can be sustained. Neither approach can be applied to a complex reality on the ground.

It is foolish to believe that Israel can continue to build settlements for decades without considering the impact it has on the lives of the Palestinians. It is also implausible that successive Israeli governments will view the settler population as mere bargaining chips in a final peace agreement. One cannot disregard the needs of either the Palestinians or of the Israelis. Israel has been unable to freeze settlement construction since the enterprise began in 1968, and it is difficult to see how it could do so now. How would the government justify the new policy to its voters?

Brzezinski never questions the initial objective of the Obama administration. Was a freeze the right goal? Was it not no expansion? Was there anyone in the administration who was thinking through the likelihood of a settlement freeze and the consequences for setting it as a bar and failing? What motivated the administration? It is hard to say. It is possible that a few factors came together to drive the administration's policy, and they should not be viewed as mutually exclusive.

First, new administrations often like to distance themselves from their predecessors. To the extent that the incoming administration viewed the Bush administration as too closely aligned with Israel, there would be some in the Obama administration who viewed settlements as exemplifying an attitude of indulgence toward Israel. Therefore, a settlement freeze was viewed as the polar opposite. It would be the embodiment of tough love and act as a sign to all that the United States will be an activist and assertive mediator that has increased its distance from Israel.

Second, the Obama administration entered office seeking to ameliorate some of the tensions with the Arab world that resulted from the war in Iraq and the war on terror being distorted by some in the Middle East as a war against Islam. In this context, an assault on settlements would bolster the perception that the United States has reoriented its policy. In other words, a tough position on Israel would assist in creating a wider perception shift throughout the Middle East. Yet this did not materialize. After a major speech in Cairo that accentuated U.S. ambitions for improved relations with the Arab world, Obama returned from Saudi Arabia empty-handed. Saudi officials publicly declared that they would refuse the U.S. approach of matching Israeli steps on settlements with Arab gestures toward Israel.

A third factor may be personal. In a 2001 report, Mitchell declared the need for a settlement freeze. It is likely that he did not want to be seen as stepping back his support for this idea.

A fourth factor cannot be dismissed either. Some of players in the Obama administration were active during the Clinton years of the '90s. During that earlier period, they felt that Netanyahu was not genuinely committed to peace as much as Yitzhak Rabin and Shimon Peres. Some may even have blamed Netanyahu for the atmosphere that permeated Israel and ultimately contributed to Rabin's death. Therefore, with Netanyahu's election following Obama's taking office in early 2009, it is likely that some of these officials viewed the settlement freeze as a signal that the United States will be hard-nosed in the future.

If there has been a miscalculation early in the administration, this is not to suggest that the other parties have not made mistakes as well. Abbas found himself cornered and has not been able to extricate himself.

Israel has also made its share of mistakes. Israelis have bemoaned the lack of trust between Obama and Netanyahu. Israel believes it was ambushed on the issue of a settlement freeze. On the one hand, Israel is correct in claiming that the Obama administration erred by denying the verbal understanding between the United States and Israel in 2003 on defining the geographic expansion of settlements. This undermines the prospect of future verbal understandings with the United States.

On the other hand, trust runs both ways. Israel does not emphasize the fact that it never implemented the West Bank understanding of 2003 that it now declares to be key. Moreover, the Obama administration resented comments made by Foreign Minister Avigdor Lieberman after the United States agreed to compromise with Israel over settlements. Obama was surprised by the announcement of new construction in the Jerusalem neighborhood of Gilo since it came just a week after a rare tête-à-tête with Netanyahu in November 2009. Netanyahu insists that he is transparent, but was also surprised by this Israeli bureaucratic move from below. The action provided fodder to Netanyahu's critics while undercutting those wishing to give him the benefit of the doubt.

Netanyahu aides are correct that the United States was not as stringent with Olmert as it is with this government. While this can be partially attributed to the change in the U.S. administration, one cannot rule out the possibility that the lack of internal U.S. debate in the past was due to the certainty of Olmert's direction. Netanyahu hopes his current move on settlements will put the issue of intentions to rest. He feels he has been unfairly singled out by this administration, given his support for a Palestinian state and for the dismantling of most West Bank checkpoints. Some in Washington may quietly say that Netanyahu's concessions are grudging and extended over many months and therefore can be discounted. Netanyahu's rejoinder will be that belated Israeli concessions are better than no concessions from the Arab side.

Yet there are lessons for the Palestinians and Arab states, too. The old paradigm as we pointed out in the book is that the Palestinians and Arabs usually want the United States to twist Israel's arm and therefore Palestine can be passive. Such an approach means the Palestinians do not have to compromise, since the United States will "deliver" Israel to accept Palestinian demands. Here, the United States pressed Israel, but the paradigm did not work. Despite Obama's speech in Cairo, which raised expectations, the long-standing Arab dream of the United States bending Israel to its will did not materialize. The Palestinians cannot be passive and expect the United States to do the work for them. There are no shortcuts to the give and take of negotiations.

In the Arab states' anger at not getting a 100 percent freeze from Israel, they want to give nothing for now. They fail to act on the fact that Israel went more than halfway. If Israel did not give 100 percent, the Arab states feel they are justified to give zero. As in the past, the Arab states believe in never making early moves that could provide political cover for the Palestinians to make progress, preferring instead, at best, to ride on the Palestinians' coattails. The Arab states need to contribute their share to ensure that Netanyahu's gesture is not lost. They need to provide Abbas with political cover and declare their unambiguous support for peace negotiations now between Israel and the Palestinians.

So 2010 began with no path for commencing peace negotiations. In short, all the squabbling had occurred in a proverbial hallway and the parties never were able to enter the main room of negotiations.

On March 3, 2010, Arab foreign ministers gave their long awaited support for Abbas to participate in proximity talks, whereby Senator Mitchell will shuttle between Israelis and Palestinians. In some ways, it is a step back from where the parties have been since a landmark conference in 1991 when the parties began meeting directly. Yet, Abbas would not agree to more given the snafu over settlements in 2009. Such proximity talks must be a transition to direct talks between the parties themselves. In contrast, if these talks become an alternative to direct talks, they will fail. It is impossible for any party or any country to make the most vital decisions possible without the confidence of dealing directly with the other side.

Let's assume peace talks will commence. The issue is where to focus the conversations. The prospect of the Israelis and Palestinians reaching a grand agreement on all the core or so-called final status issues is very unlikely at this time. The four core issues are: the rights of refugees, control of Jerusalem, security, and territory/borders. The first two issues seem unlikely to be resolved anytime soon.

Refugees and Jerusalem are narrative issues, and both are tied into the historic connection of the people to this conflict. Jerusalem has both religious and nationalistic dimensions for Israelis and Palestinians and for key constituencies in and outside the region. The refugee issue taps into the self-definition of Palestinians, including many Gazans. Yet, neither Israeli nor Palestinian leaders have conditioned their respective publics to deal with these third-rail issues. In the case of refugees, many of the descendents come from Gaza, which is not even under the control of the Palestinian Authority at this time, but rather is controlled by Hamas. This complicates the refugee issue even further. In short, whenever it is all or nothing in the Middle East, it is always nothing. We should not set ourselves or the parties up for failure. Too much is at stake. Hamas rejectionists are waiting in the wings for pragmatists like Abbas to fail. Furthermore, Israel will be facing demographic challenges, which will threaten its goal of ensuring its future as a democratic and Jewish state. With these increasingly high stakes, it is vital that we concentrate our efforts on areas that are amenable to progress.

Instead, we should focus on what is attainable. Ironically, the issue where the gaps between the parties are the most narrow is land. This might sound counterintuitive to some because many think the conflict is only about land, but this is not the case. This is why I have sought to advance the idea of "borders first" for the past year and was delighted to see that Senator Mitchell endorsed it in a press conference in November. He declared, "My personal and fervent wish is that we will during this process at some point have a resolution of the issue of borders so that there will no longer be any question about settlement construction, so that Israelis will be able to build what they want in Israel and Palestinians will be able to build what they want in Palestine."

In negotiations between Olmert and Abbas in 2008 and 2009, their differences were over only 4.5 percent of the land. Olmert suggested retaining 6.4 percent of the West Bank in return for equivalent land inside Israel. In a November 2009 interview Olmert stated, "It might be a fraction more, it might be a fraction less, but in total it would be about 6.4 percent." Abbas thought the figure should be 1.9 percent. Both said any land taken by Israel could be swapped for an equal amount of land inside Israel. The narrow percentage differences coupled with the fact that both parties agreed to the idea of land swaps suggests that the differences regarding land are bridgeable. For example, 80 percent of all Israeli settlers, which is approximately 240,000 people, live in less than 4.5 percent of the territory being negotiated, largely adjacent to the pre-1967 boundaries. The remaining 60,000 settlers live in the 95.5 percent remainder of the West Bank. As these statistics illustrate, the so-called insurmountable obstacle of settlements is actually relatively open to resolution.

The only way to deal with the settlement issue is to render it moot by widening it to peacemaking and heading straight into the final negotiations on territory. There are three distinct advantages to focusing the negotiations on territory now. First, it allows the Palestinian authority to tell its people that it has obtained the equivalent of 100 percent of the land to be part of a contiguous Palestinian state. As such, negotiations, not Hamas terrorism, will be vindicated. Second, Israelis will have something to gain and won't have to just give. Until now, no Israeli leader has succeeded in legally annexing a single settler, let alone a large majority of them. This approach would give many of the settlers who live in the major blocs a stake in being part of the solution rather than part of the problem. They would have their legal status normalized as part of Israel. Settlements and security would be decoupled. The Israeli army would not leave until the Palestinian security services demonstrated an ability to root out terror. Finally, after many decades, the settlement issue would no longer be a thorn in United States–Israel relations.

Needless to say, a focus on borders will have to be accompanied with a focus on security arrangements. These issues go together. At the Camp David II talks in 2000 led by President Clinton, this was the most straightforward issue that was technical in character. Much has happened subsequently. Security cooperation crashed in the second intifada between 2000 and 2004. Hamas came to power in Gaza, stand-alone rockets became a factor, and the idea of borders management after Israeli withdrawal has been undermined by the expansion of cross-border tunnels under Gaza for rocket smuggling. Many Israelis see the Gaza withdrawal in 2004 as triggering thousands of rockets which culminated in the Gaza war of 2008–2009. Therefore, as part of the growing cynicism of the public on both sides about the very enterprise of peacemaking, Israelis increasingly equate withdrawal with vulnerability and not security. (Palestinians and Israelis are equally jaded about the idea of grand peace conferences that do not yield results.) Therefore, the security dimension needs to be considered very carefully.

This approach alone will not guarantee successful resolution of the Jerusalem and refugee issues. Yet, after success on land, these issues will have to be addressed. Over time, Israel will need to make concessions on Jerusalem, and the Palestinians will need to concede that refugees can only return to the Palestinian state and not to Israel.

A proactive approach could shatter old myths and create a more positive and more permanent reality for both sides.

For all the problems of restarting peace talks during 2009, there was an important bright spot between Israelis and Palestinians. There were signs on the ground in the West Bank of economic progress, as well as a heightened security cooperation between Palestinians and Israelis. Of course, economic development is not a substitute for political progress, but it is a key component that could facilitate progress and moderation. Economic progress enables the public to gain faith that the future can be better when they see improvements, and it creates political space for the leadership to gain more political capital with success. The hope is that economic improvement facilitates political moderation as people develop a stake in success. Palestinian polls consistently show that Gazans living under Hamas and West Bankers alike prefer living in the West Bank where there is economic progress, rather than living under the repressive hand of Hamas in Gaza.

International Monetary Fund officials report that economic growth in the West Bank is making major strides despite a worldwide recession. They say that growth could reach as much as 7 percent in 2010 if Israel continues its current policy of relaxing security restrictions, most notably the removal of roadblocks. It is estimated that Israel has removed all but a dozen of the forty-five roadblocks that were in place to prevent suicide bombers. Among the benefits of the relaxation of restrictions is that it enables Israeli Arabs to enter the West Bank, engage in commerce, and generate jobs. Unemployment in the West Bank may be high by American standards, but it has been cut by a third in the last few years.

The following examples of growth provide a glimpse of the changes occurring in the West Bank. There have been approximately two thousand new Palestinian small businesses and other companies registered with the Palestine Authority since 2008. A second new cell phone company in the West Bank, Wataniya Palestine, was recently launched. The introduction of this second mobile phone company is expected to inject US$700 million investment into the Palestinian Territory and to generate $354 million in fiscal revenue for the PA. It will also create thousands of jobs. Another project underway is Rawabi, or "hills" in Arabic, which will be the first ever planned Palestinian city. Located about five miles north of the Palestinian provisional capital of Ramallah, it is expected to have forty thousand residents at its formation. In Bethlehem, the rise of tourism has already yielded six thousand new jobs, and tourists are filling up hotels in the city, marking a significant change. Previously, due to an uncertain security situation, tourists feared staying overnight in the West Bank but the security is indeed improving. Palestinian security forces have been trained with American and European money and guidance. It is estimated that 410 Israelis were killed in attacks emanating from the West Bank in 2002. In 2009, the figure was 3. This dramatic drop has allowed Israel to take more risks than it would have even two years ago. The improvement in security has not just facilitated economic progress, but has meant that chaos no longer reigns in the West Bank. In a sharp departure from the past, Palestinian polls show that most Palestinians feel safe in their towns.

For the first half of the decade, Israeli and Palestinian officials shot at each other, but now they are working together to prevent Hamas from expanding a foothold in the West Bank. Beyond the security establishments of both sides, there are other factors at play. Palestinian president Mahmoud Abbas and Palestinian prime minister Salaam Fayyad have a set an antiviolence tone. Fayyad has worked very closely with his commanders on the ground to ensure coordination with Israeli counterparts. Special mention should be given to U.S. Lieutenant General Keith Dayton, who has spearheaded the training of over two thousand Palestinian troops in a bid to professionalize the Palestinian security services. Netanyahu also deserves credit in prioritizing economic growth by lifting restrictions. Israeli military officials say that their cushion to lift such restrictions as West Bank roadblocks is a function of the Israeli security barrier, which limits the amount of suicide bombers who can penetrate Israel.

Perhaps the most exciting idea that emerged from the West Bank in 2009 is Fayyad's idea of state-building or creating institutions as a precursor to Palestinian statehood. Fayyad has won over the international community during the last few years with his focus on transparency and his opposition to corruption. As we point out in the book, he is someone who has a doctorate in economics and who excelled at the World Bank/ International Monetary Fund before becoming first Palestinian finance minister and then prime minister. The U.S. Congress, which was reluctant during the Arafat period to give any money to the Palestine Authority, no longer worries that its $200 million per annum in assistance will go to private coffers. This is a tribute to the stature of Fayyad.

Fayyad's idea of state-building is a departure from the approach favored by his predecessor Yasser Arafat. His approach is nothing short of a new paradigm for Palestinian nationalism. Arafat always defined Palestinian nationalism in revolutionary terms—physical defiance and armed resistance, while Fayyad seems to be defining institution building as the ticket to statehood.

There are profound implications to these very different approaches. Arafat viewed the Palestinian condition as guaranteeing a sense of victimhood and entitlement—Palestinians were responsible for nothing. The world owed them. In contrast, Fayyad seems to see institution building as creating a culture of accountability among Palestinians. In the Arafat era, airports, railroads, and sea ports seemed like adornments of a sovereign state, not central vehicles to achieving statehood. In contrast, Fayyad has said that building Palestine Authority institutions is important "to gain the international community respect and pass its unjust test of building these institutions under occupation." While Fayyad has yet to fully flesh out how state-building would be accomplished beyond using donor aid from around the world to assist the formation of legal, economic, and security institutions, he wants to maintain the momentum of his previous economic plans until a political breakthrough occurs. This way he can keep his security plans in place during a time of political void that might devolve into unpredictable violence.

It is said that after George Bush visited Israel for its sixtieth anniversary in May 2008, Fayyad told him that he should look to the example of the Zionists, meaning to point out that the Israelis built the institutions of their state for thirty years before they declared it. While Fayyad certainly would not accept the timetable, he accepts the principle that statehood should be earned. In general, these economic and security developments provide hope of a brighter future for both peoples in 2010.

While I have made abundantly clear that I have a very favorable view of Prime Minister Fayyad for the important new elements that he has introduced to the political equation, I would be remiss if I did not voice caution about two sets of relationships that will be important to focus on in the future. One is the Abbas-Fayyad relationship. On one hand, Abbas's veteran credentials in the Fatah party provide cover for Fayyad as he pursues his course. Yet, there have been clear differences between the two over appointment of personnel and even a sense that Abbas may be somewhat envious at times of the international attention showered on Fayyad.

The second set of relations that merits attention is Fayyad's relations with Israel, which have cooled somewhat of late. Specifically, Israel is unsure if Fayyad's focus on nonviolent protest will spill over in an unintended violent direction. Moreover, in a bid to cool episodic tensions on the ground, Fayyad has on several occasions in the last few months visited families of Palestinians whose sons have been involved in fatal violent actions against Israel. Israelis see this behavior as sending the wrong signal to the Palestinian people especially because it is coming from someone identified with nonviolence. At least in one of the two incidents Palestinians claim the violence was not premeditated. Finally, the third source of concern in the Fayyad-Israel relationship is his sense that institution building is a unilateral enterprise that is part of a two-year sprint toward statehood. Israelis suspect that this bottom up state-building is a unilateral move coming at their expense. The irony is that the only way for Fayyad to deliver on institution building is by working with Israel, given the security dimension of proposed projects and Israel's control over West Bank land. A good working relationship is key for the Fayyad plan to succeed. In short, there are no substitutes for negotiations.

This is precisely why the bottom up approach cannot substitute for top down negotiations. The two must go together. Without a top down approach, the bottom up approach will be unsustainable over time. Palestinian soldiers will think security cooperation is designed to make Israeli control more palatable, and Israelis will harbor doubts about Palestinian state-building intentions.

While there have been important signs of progress on the ground in the last few years, one must be careful not to extrapolate too much in looking ahead. Much is at stake. If moderates on the Palestinian and Israeli sides do not come together, it will not be surprising if the extremists discredit the moderates and exploit time for their own benefit.

Indeed, there should no doubts about the implications if extremists are strengthened. It is clear that if Iran develops a nuclear weapon, the prospects for the Middle East peace process are very bleak. Rejectionists will be emboldened and moderates will be intimidated. Alternatively, there is no doubt that if the Israelis and the Palestinian Authority did not think Iran was on its way to being a nuclear problem and a regional power in a manner that will boost Hamas, their evaluation of risk would certainly drop.

Indeed, the issue of Iran posed a different set of challenges for the Obama administration. The success of the Obama administration has been its ability to persuade the world that the Iranian regime and not the United States is the one blocking a rapprochement between the two countries. Today, the onus is widely seen as being on Iran and not on the United States. This was not apparent during the Bush administration, when many thought the problem was a lack of a good faith effort by Washington.

Needless to say, the Obama's administration's ability to isolate Iran more effectively was facilitated by the mass outpouring of the Iranian people into the streets against what was viewed as a fraudulent election on June 12, 2009. Those sham elections and the protest movement that ensued have been very consequential and are major changes since we first wrote this book. The Iranian regime proved incapable of quelling the protest. It is estimated that Iran has arrested four thousand political prisoners.[1] Meanwhile, the ruthless repression by Iranian Revolutionary Guards and others only served to narrow the base of the Islamic Republic of Iran. The authoritarianism of Ayatollah Khamenei and President Ahmadinejad was laid bare for all to see, and Iran therefore lost a lot of its legitimacy. The more violent the crackdown by the regime, the more its popularity with the public is sure to plummet further.

It is hard to know if the mass protest movement marks a prerevolutionary ferment to end the regime of the mullahs, but the chaos certainly calls into question the fundamental tenets of the regime. A few facts are worth noting. The protestors transcend geographic sectors, age, gender, and education—they come from all walks of life. It is also interesting that the refusal of the regime to make any concessions to the protestors has united them, even winning the sympathy of establishment figures such as former president Ali Akbar Rafsanjani. This has created fissures within the regime itself.

The mass beatings of the protestors by the Basij, members of the Iranian Revolutionary Guard Corps, along with the arrests of other loyalists, has galvanized the protest movement. Moreover, in the process, Supreme Leader Ayatollah Khameini has lost his luster as he unambiguously sided with Iranian President Ahmadinejad. This is a stunning change in an Islamic Republic that has been built on the on the "rule of the jurist"—which gives the supreme leader a virtual sense of divine right.

The net effect of all this is a visible radicalization of the protestors. At the start, they only wished to see the vote recast. Now protests increasingly include slogans that call into question the very idea of an Islamic republic. While the protest movement has no identifiable leaders now, it is bound to produce them as it continues. It is significant that the protest movement is somehow able to communicate nationally despite efforts of the regime to disrupt any network of communication.

The combination of the Obama administration's willingness to deal with Iran and Tehran's domestic turmoil have together created the context for tougher international sanctions against Iran's nuclear program. Iran is firmly on the defensive. It will be easier to isolate in the future, as the regime weakens.

The administration has been criticized, especially during the summer of 2009 for its support for the democracy movement—now called the Green movement—being too timid. Obama himself has admitted that it took him a while to find his voice on this issue, and his tone has become somewhat sharper with time. Some criticism seems to be valid. The line seems to be avoiding what George H. W. Bush did in 1991 after the Gulf War, when he urged the Shia Iraqis to rise up against Iraq's Saddam Hussein. When the Shia did rise up, the United States stood by as they were subsequently slaughtered. There is a moral responsibility when advocating such action that must be considered when calibrating an appropriate response.

At the same time, the United States approach toward the democracy movement could be similar to the U.S. policy regarding the Soviet Union in the 1970s and 1980s. At this time, the United States routinely negotiated arms control with the Soviet Union while at the same time focusing on Soviet human rights. The United States never saw a contradiction in that duality. In 1987, the same year as he concluded an arms control agreement with the Soviets, Ronald Reagan dramatically challenged them by going to West Berlin and saying "Mr. Gorbachev, tear down this wall." The U.S.S.R. dissolved a few years thereafter. By highlighting the shortcomings of how the Soviets dealt with dissidents as well as the Jewish emigration movement, the United States placed a spotlight on the legitimacy deficit of the Soviet regime. In other words, the United States did the right thing in focusing on human rights abuses; it also did well in questioning the very tenets of a regime that would collapse very shortly thereafter. So instead of the United States being forced to choose between its nuclear and human rights objectives when it came to the Soviet Union, the objectives proved to be complementary. This argues for the Obama administration finding ways to be more active in support of the Green movement, since this is the right side of history. This ranges from U.S. efforts to maintain Internet access to radio broadcasts, along with other ideas. Yet, given the stakes of a nuclear Iran, there are real questions about whether this makes sense for it to be the exclusive focus of American foreign policy in the short and intermediate term.

While political engagement with Iran seems less likely going forward, it will not be because the United States did not try. Indeed, it did. The United States turned to political engagement in the fall of 2009. Its argument that political engagement has a considerable upside for the United States is one of the pillars of our book and has been the primary approach of the administration. This approach was designed to ensure that if engagement did not succeed as a strategy, it would succeed as a tactic. The United States would come in good faith, but could not guarantee the result of engagement. The onus would lie on Iran. Therefore, if engagement did not achieve strategic results, it would be tactically beneficial since it would enable the United States to frame subsequent alternatives as more credible. In this manner, one could ensure for the first time that a major price would be exacted from Iran for its intransigence. Major sanctions would become possible because the other options had been tried and had failed. In other words, if engagement would not succeed as a strategy, it would succeed as a vehicle for pressuring the regime. It would be a vehicle for pressure not just because it set the stage for sanctions by showing American reasonableness. This approach was significant because it probably contributed to Iran's internal problems by showing there was an opportunity from the outside world and the Iranian leadership was incapable of giving up its hostility and taking advantage of it. (French diplomat David Cvach, who was posted in Tehran during the outbreak of violence, thinks the Obama administration's outreach played a favorable role in contributing to the domestic outpouring.[2])

As such, this inability on the part of the Iranian leadership would exact a terrible price on the Iranian regime. It was not just Obama's willingness to unconditionally negotiate with Iran that helped set the context. One should not disregard the importance of even symbolic gestures that may have won some public resonance, including Obama's greetings for the Iranian new year known as Nowruz. His comments at the inauguration should also not be forgotten, where he said U.S. relations with the Muslim world would be based on "mutual interest and mutual respect." He added, alluding to Iran and other difficult regimes, "we will extend a hand if you are willing to unclench your fist."[3] Taken together, the Obama messages were an unmistakable message to the people of Iran and to the rest of the world. Failure will be due to the obduracy of the Iranian regime. It is the Tehran government that will incur the cost of breakdown.

Ironically, during the Bush administration, Iran paid no such price. It seemed content with the United States's pursual of a strategy of non-negotiation. There were no major sanctions, since many in the world believed that the United States and not Iran was the obstacle to talks. Instead, Iran utilized the time to its fullest. According to the International Atomic Energy Agency (IAEA), Iran used its Natanz enrichment plant to generate approximately enough low-enriched uranium (LEU) to convert to high enriched uranium for weapons-grade fuel. By January 2010, senior U.S. officials said that Iran had 1,800 kilos of LEU. Approximately 1,500 kilos are needed to convert LEU into weapons-grade nuclear fuel. For this to occur, Iran would have to manufacture a political crisis and expel the IAEA inspectors and then convert the LEU to high-enriched uranium. A large majority of the 1,800 kilos of LEU was generated during the Bush administration.

As a result, the Obama administration's approach has mandated that if Iran does not stop its low-enriched uranium program through political engagement, a price will need to be exacted from Iran so that it can not go forward with impunity.

Some say the United States should put all its eggs in the basket of the "regime change" school. This will not be surprising to the readers of this book. After all, it was the neo-conservatives in this book who were the most vocal supporters of regime change, while realists were the ones who felt toppling regimes sounded good, but were hard to do in practice. Yet, the neo-conservatives have said this is the one approach that works given the efforts of the Iranian people. One would have to be heartless not to cheer nor assist those Iranian masses as they throw off the yoke of this authoritarian regime. The issue that may divide them from the rest is whether all of America's eggs should be put in this basket.

A militant Iran is clearly undesirable. The issue is whether the United States can be decisive in making a non-nuclear, less militant regime a realistic short-term or intermediate-term possibility. There is little doubt that the regime's collapse might be one of the greatest strategic windfalls that has accrued to the West, certainly since the end of the Cold War. As we have previously pointed out at length, Iran is fomenting radicalism and anti-Americanism throughout the Middle East. It does so not just by word, but also by deed. It has been financing Hizbollah, Hamas, and the Islamic Jihad terror groups. Hizbollah alone has stymied the effort for more pro-Western orientation in Lebanon. All three of the proxy groups have waged an unrelenting war against Israel and the prospects for a two-state solution to the conflict between Israel and the Palestinians. Additionally, many fear that if Iran obtains a nuclear bomb, it will trigger a regional arms race involving Egypt, Saudi Arabia, and Turkey. Therefore an Iran with nuclear weapons is a "game changer" in the Middle East, as Obama has maintained.

Can the United States be decisive in toppling Iran in a relatively short period? Time matters. Over time, the current regime cannot succeed without the support of its people. Yet in terms of the immediate future, losing the people and losing power are not synonymous. Losing a debilitating amount of power could take years, yet a nuclear capable Iran could still cause havoc within as little as ten years. As we have pointed out, many fear that Iran could spark a nuclear arms race in the Middle East and embolden rejectionists. But, does the new Iranian opposition share the views of the West about the Iranian nuclear program? Are these opponents certain allies? So far, the Iranian opposition has not crystallized a position on the nuclear issue, although there is a genuine hope that the opponents cannot be worse than the current Iranian government. What has primarily united them is their antagonism toward Ahmadinejad. They currently have no foreign policy manifesto, as their focus is purely domestic. Unfortunately, rivals for the presidency, Moussavi and Karoubbi, have used even the possibility that Iran may make concessions to the United States on its nuclear program as an instrument to attack the Iranian leader. In other words, people from Ahmadinejad's left are attacking him from the right.

Taken together, these issues have made the United States hesitant to put all its eggs in the basket of the regime change school.

In January 2010, Iran issued a formal response rejecting an international proposal that would have it ship abroad low-enriched nuclear fuel that could be used as part of a nuclear bomb. Generating nuclear fuel is the most difficult part of assembling such a bomb. A coalition consisting of most of the world's biggest countries—the United States, China, Russia,

Germany, France, and Britain—proposed that Tehran ship low-enriched uranium abroad for further enrichment so it could be used for peaceful purposes. In a landmark meeting with the world powers in Geneva in October 2009, Tehran agreed to ship out most, or 70 percent, of its stock of enriched uranium and then wait for up to one year for its return in the form of fuel rods for its Tehran research reactor. This would have denied Iran the ability to seize much of its existing uranium stockpile away from IAEA inspectors and convert it to the high-enriched uranium needed for a nuclear weapon. After Iran accepted the proposal in Geneva and then held a follow-up meeting to discuss its implementation with the United States, Russia, and France in Vienna, Iran reneged on its agreement. This has set the stage for a focus on enhanced sanctions against Iran.

Anger against Iran intensified. In addition to reneging on the offer put forth in Geneva, the Iranians hid a secret uranium enrichment facility from the United States near the holy city of Qom. (Curiously, Iran publicly stated that the facility was devoted to civilian nuclear energy. But if so, why was it in a secret military base of the Iranian Revolutionary Guards Corps [IRGC]?) While the facility had yet to produce any nuclear fuel, the mere existence of a concealed facility pointed to Iranian prevarication. Iran had been insisting for years to the IAEA that it had no such facility. Only when it became clear that the United States had found out about the facility did Iran disclose the truth.

Iran looks to be a central foreign policy and possibly domestic story. The primary question now is whether sanctions will effectively ensure Iran's responsivity and cooperation. While the United Nations Security Council has passed three rounds of sanctions in the past, they have not been sufficiently effective enough to halt Iran from installing centrifuges and producing enriched uranium.

The question is if further sanctions will be different than in the past. Will trade-offs be necessary in order to garner support from Russia and China, the two countries in the UN Security Council which will likely work to dilute the impact of sanctions, as they engage in substantial trade with Iran? Beijing is the second largest importer of Iranian oil, and has made commitments to revitalize the Iranian energy sector by building refineries, which Tehran is sorely lacking. The Obama administration has made concerted efforts to win the support of Russia and China for further sanctions. Obama has held multiple summit meetings with the leaders of both countries, along with other senior level encounters.

The United States has focused the renewed sanctions upon the IRGC, which has been at the forefront of repressing Iran's nascent democracy movement. The Obama administration is also working on a second tier of sanctions. Ideally, it would like to use the imprimatur of the UN Security Council as a means of enabling like-minded countries to ramp up sanctions on Iran. Minimally, the United States would like to use the second tier of sanctions as a means to signal to Russia and China that the United States has options apart from the UN Security Council. At the core of this strategy is the European Union. While Americans may have an image of Europe as always favoring accommodation to confrontation, in fact Europeans leaders are tired of futile negotiations with Iran. They have been involved in such outreach since 2003, but without result.

France's President Nicolas Sarkozy, for example, declared in January 2010 that strong measures are needed. "Despite all our efforts, and a new engagement by the United States, and despite our ambitious proposals for cooperation, the Iranian authorities are blocked in a one-way street of proliferation and radicalism," Sarkozy said. "Today, they have added to that the brutal repression of their own people," he added.

"France wants the [UN Security] Council to adopt strong measures and for the European Union as well to assume its responsibilities," he said.[4] Angela Merkel, the Chancellor of Germany, also declared in January 2010, "If Iran's reactions don't change, we will help work on comprehensive sanctions."[5] At a press conference shortly after she met her Chinese counterpart to discuss Iran, Secretary of State Hillary Clinton declared, "The Iran government has provided a continuous stream of threats to intensify its violations of international nuclear norms." She added, "Iran's approach leaves us with little choice but to work with our partners to apply greater pressure in the hopes that it will cause Iran to reconsider its rejection of diplomatic efforts with respect to its nuclear ambitions."[6]

Clinton explained that U.S. sanctions would be primarily geared toward the IRGC, which experts believe controls a third of the Iranian economy. She declared in an interview with CNN, "They have a lot of business interests, as we have discovered. And our assessment is that the sanctions will be tough and clearly aimed at the Iranian economy, but that the international community does not have a choice, that this is, unfortunately, a situation in which the behavior of the Iranian Government."

She added, "We think it's imperative to change the calculus of the leadership, and we think this is an appropriate way to proceed, so we are pursuing it."

She continued,

It's meant to change their behavior, and it's not meant as a target at any one person. It's meant to change the calculation of the leadership, whether that leadership is in the supreme leader's office or in the Revolutionary Guard or the president or anyone else. And I think that it's hard to sit here and predict exactly how Iran will respond, because we still are open to the diplomatic track, but we haven't seen much to really prove that they're willing to engage with us.

And I think the time has come for the international community to say, no, we cannot permit your continued pursuit of nuclear weapons. It is destabilizing, it is dangerous, and we're going to take a stand against you. . . . I think that the Iranian people are at a crossroads. They have the opportunity to demand more from their own leadership, which has, obviously, from the outside, appeared to have failed the Iranian people and failed the very principles that they claim to govern by. So the voices of protest, the voices of opposition, are going to continue to challenge this regime in Iran. But the outside world is not involved in that. This is an internal societal matter for Iranians to decide. What the outside world is concerned about is their nuclear program. Absent a nuclear program, we would still be expressing our regrets and our condemnation of their behavior toward their citizens, but we would not be looking for sanctions. We are looking for sanctions because their nuclear ambitions threaten the rest of the world."[7]

Clinton's remarks make it unmistakable that it is Iran's nuclear program that drives the sanction effort, not the protests. The question is what will happen if the sanctions effort falls short after a certain period of time. The likelihood, many believe, is that Israel will strike Iran. Of course, a military strike is only a final course of action. There is no guarantee of technical success nor any certainty regarding the scope of Iranian retaliation. Furthermore, it is unclear how much time a strike would buy before Iran rebuilds its program. For all these reasons, a military option is not an ideal choice. Yet, to Israel's credit, it has not sought to interfere with United States efforts for political engagement nor in the move toward sanctions. Israel has favored sanctions, but it has sought to stay out of the way of the international community has it debates this issue. A military strike should be seen only as a last resort, to be engaged only after other approaches have been tried and have failed. The specter of a military strike might, however, be used as a tactical lever by the international community on its road toward sanctions. Finally, all parties who wish to avoid the military option would do well to consider serious sanctions.

Will the United States ultimately strike Iran? This option needs to be seriously explored if indeed sanctions clearly fail to stop the Iranian nuclear program.

As our book makes clear, context is everything. The U.S. preference was for political engagement, but this approach has been spurned by Tehran. If persuasion does not succeed, the next step is dissuasion. This is where the United States finds itself as it presses for sanctions at the UN Security Council. However, if this strategy is not effective, it will probably be countered by other Iranian measures, such as Iran's withdrawal from the nuclear Non-Proliferation Treaty (NPT), which obligates them to be forthright about their nuclear activities, and the expulsion of the International Atomic Energy Agency inspectors. Ahmedinijad has already declared Iran to be a nuclear state. Iran should know that context changes circumstances. As much as the United States does not relish the idea of military intervention in Iran, it may have to act. Much is at stake for the United States in the Middle East, as we make clear in the book. If Iran develops a nuclear bomb, potential consequences include a nuclear arms race, the end of the Middle East peace process, and the emboldening of rejections.

The United States has already taken some quiet steps. It has reached bilateral agreements with Persian Gulf states for shared early warning systems, and it has dispatched missile defense systems to four Middle East countries: Bahrain, Kuwait, United Arab Emirates, and Qatar. The Saudis and the Israelis already have a missile defense system, and the Israelis have been given the advanced x-band radar system for tracking incoming attacks. In a speech in January, United States top Middle East commander General David Petreaus departed from the usual practice when he revealed that new missile defense agreements have been reached. He also stated that the United States has Aegis missile defense cruisers indefinitely entrenched in the Persian Gulf.

This strategy of military build-up creates options. It should remind Iran that it is playing with fire as the context changes, and that there are consequences for thumbing its nose at the world. If persuasion and dissuasion fail, it is possible that the last stop is coercion. There are serious questions regarding whether the United States will be viewed by others—whether correctly or incorrectly—as subcontracting a military strike to Israel. There is little doubt that an attack by the United States would be more militarily effective since the United States is the world's only superpower. The issue goes beyond technical capability; it also relates to regional resonance in an aftermath. It will also be understood by many in the region that the United States is enforcing a regional order after several rounds of UN Security Council resolutions will have been defied with impunity. It is not cost-free for the United States, but there is a cost to inaction, as well. Iran with a nuclear bomb changes the balance of power in the Middle East away from the United States. This is not a call for attack, as we all hope and pray that sanctions will persuade the Iranians to back off from their quest. Yet, we must be aware that this scenario may not succeed. Even a realist like Richard Haass, president of the Council on Foreign Relations, who has eschewed military steps in favor of engagement, now believes the United States must seriously consider the viability of American military action.

Whether the Iranian regime will be toppled or sanctions will be effective in halting Iran's nuclear program, the future of Iran will be a gripping story to follow in the months and years ahead.

David Makovsky
March 2010

Acknowledgments

We are indebted to the many people who made this book possible.

As we wrote this book, we benefited from the wise advice and helpful comments of those who read part or all of this manuscript. In particular, we are grateful to Kenneth Stein of Emory University and Steve Spiegel of UCLA, two leading Middle East diplomatic historians. We are also appreciative of the helpful suggestions of Rob Satloff and Alan Makovsky.

We both owe a great deal to the Washington Institute for Near East Policy for providing us extensive support for this project, supplying whatever we required throughout the writing process. Rob Satloff, the executive director, ensured that we were given the time and staff assistance that made it possible to write the book. Rob and deputy director for research Patrick Clawson have fostered a stimulating atmosphere for research, scholarship, and serious work. Our numerous conversations with other members of the senior staff were extremely beneficial. We are also obliged to the Institute's board under the leadership of Howard Berkowitz and Fred Lafer for showing tremendous interest in and supporting all our research endeavors.

We would like to acknowledge Zack Snyder, Lauren Cohen, and Margaret Weiss for their tireless dedication, key research, valuable suggestions, constructive criticism, and meticulous attention to detail. Zack, in particular, assumed the burden of integrating our collective efforts and ensuring that all comments were considered. Lauren worked long hours, and proved to be a steady hand as she helped spearhead our fact-checking to ensure that we avoided inaccuracies. Margaret was very helpful in the early stages of the book before she embarked on her graduate studies. Without the work of Zack, Lauren, and Margaret, this book would not have been possible. Research assistants Gerri Pozez and Curtis Cannon provided additional help in fact-checking. Nathan Cohen made many trips to the library on our behalf, and we are grateful. We also want to thank Fayre Makeig for her helpful editorial assistance.

We are also fortunate to have great editors, Wendy Wolf and Kevin Doughten of Viking/Penguin. Wendy gave us the encouragement to go forward. Kevin acted as the shepherd for this project. His editing improved the manuscript, ensuring that our assumptions were clear and that our writing was accessible to the initiated and uninitiated alike. We must also thank Esther Newberg of International Creative Management (ICM). She has no peer in her field. She believed in this book and put us on the road to writing it.

For the two of us engaged in this project, it has been a wonderful experience. We have known each other for nineteen years, and have worked closely together for nearly a decade. Yet there is nothing like writing a book. It forces two people to go beyond their normal conversations and explore their assumptions and attitudes in depth. It has been very stimulating to discuss our usual, and occasionally varying, perspectives. It has enabled us to work through myriad profound and complex issues as well as discuss implications that flow from our conclusions. We have been grateful for the opportunity.

Above all, we would like to thank our families. Dennis would like to thank his wife, Debbie, and children Gabe, Rachel, and Ilana for once again accepting with good humor and patience his preoccupations while writing. All share an interest and passion for policy, politics, and the Middle East—and he thanks them not just for their support but for their searching and challenging questions. He dedicates this book to them.

David would like to thank his wife, Varda, and his three children, Jonathan (Tani), Joshua, and Elliana for being joys in his life. His family sustained him and was patient throughout this project. There is no doubt that David could not have done it without their support. Varda always provides him with love, support, and encouragement and he could not be more grateful. Therefore, David dedicates this book to his family.

Notes

CHAPTER TWO

1. White House–published transcript of press conference, January 16, 2008.
2. Interview with George Stephanopoulos on the ABC News program *This Week*, November 26, 2006, http://abcnews.go.com/Video/playerIndex?id= 2679846/.
3. Brent Scowcroft, "Getting the Middle East Back on Our Side," *New York Times*, January 4, 2007.
4. Iraq Study Group Report, December 2006, pp. 43–44.
5. Marine Corps Historical Publication, "Lessons Learned: Iran-Iraq War," December 10, 1990. (U.S. Marine Corps: Washington, DC), http://www.fas.org/man/dod-101/ops/war/docs/3203/.
6. Dennis Ross, *The Missing Peace: The Inside Story of the Fight for Middle East Peace* (New York: Farrar, Straus and Giroux, 2004), pp. 44–45.
7. For the text of the 1996 fatwa, see "Bin Laden's Fatwa," Public Broadcasting Service (PBS), August 1996. Available at http://www.pbs.org/newshour/terrorism/international/fatwa_1996.html; for the text of the 1998 fatwa see "Al Qaeda's Fatwa," PBS, February 23, 1998. Available at http://www.pbs.org/newshour/terrorism/international/fatwa_1998.html.
8. Ibid.
9. Text of Osama bin Laden's statement, broadcast after U.S.-British strikes, *Guardian*, October 7, 2001. http://www.guardian.co.uk/world/2001/oct/07/afghanistan.terrorism15.
10. Sayyed Hassan Nasrallah, Hizbollah Secretary General, speech hosted by the Hizbollah Support Committee, September 5, 2008.
11. Hala Mustafa and David Makovsky, "Building Arab Democracy," *Washington Post*, November 18, 2003, p. A25.

12. Barry Rubin, *The Tragedy of the Middle East* (Cambridge: Cambridge University Press, 2002), p. 280.

13. Abdullah Larqoui, *The Crisis of the Arab Intellectual* (Berkeley: University of California Press, 1976), pp. 31–32.

14. Dennis Ross, *Statecraft: And How to Restore America's Standing in the World* (New York: Farrar, Straus and Giroux, 2007), p. 291.

15. *al-Wafd*, February 26, 2000. Translation in Middle East Media Research Institute (MEMRI) no. 91, May 5, 2000.

16. Ross, *Statecraft*, p. 291.

17. United Nations Development Program (UNDP) and Arab Fund for Economic and Social Development, *Arab Human Development Report 2002*, p. 2.

18. Interview, Middle East News Agency, January 24, 1989, in Foreign Broadcast Information Service (FBIS), January 25, 1989, p. 15.

19. Fouad Ajami, "The Sentry's Solitude," *Foreign Affairs* (November/December 2001), pp. 2–16.

20. www.presidency.gov.eg/html/8-October2000_press.html.

CHAPTER THREE

1. Foreign Relations of the United States (FRUS), *The Near East and Africa* 4 (1943): 775, letter of Ibn Saud to FDR on May 11, 1943, http://digicoll.library.wisc.edu/cgi-bin/FRUS/FRUS-idx?type=turn&entity=FRUS.FRUS1943v04.p0787&isize=M.

2. "Texts of Letters Exchanged by Ibn Saud and Roosevelt," *New York Times*, October 19, 1945.

3. FRUS 4 (1943): 773–74; letter of Ibn Saud to FDR, May 11, 1943.

4. FRUS 8 (1945): 687; telegram from William Eddy to the secretary of state.

5. Michael Oren, *Power, Faith and Fantasy: America in the Middle East, 1776 to the Present* (New York: W. W. Norton, 2007), p. 472.

6. Peter Grose, *Israel in the Mind of America* (New York: Knopf, 1983), p. 113.

7. Robert D. Kaplan, *The Arabists: The Romance of an American Elite* (New York: Free Press, 1993), p. 86.

8. Ibid.

9. Ibid., p. 7.

10. Ibid., p. 87.

11. Grose, p. 287, depicts a conversation between Secretary of State George Marshall, the famed U.S. general of World War II, who discusses the likely military scenario with Moshe Shertok, who held the foreign affairs portfolio for the Zionist state in waiting, the Jewish Agency, and years later would be the prime minister. In a conversation just a week before Israel declared independence, Marshall showed Shertok a map on the wall at his State Department office. Pointing to southern Israel, Marshall said, "Here you are surrounded

by Arabs." And then pointing to northern Israel, he says, "And here, in the Galilee, you are surrounded by other Arabs. You have Arab states all around you and your backs are to the sea." He added, "Believe me, I am talking about things which I know." Marshall continued, "You are sitting here in the coastal plains of Palestine while the Arabs hold the mountain ridges. I know you have some arms and your Haganah, but the Arabs have regular armies. They are well trained and they have heavy arms. How can you hope to hold out?"

12. Ibid., p. 372.

13. James Forrestal, *The Forrestal Diaries* (New York: Viking Press, 1951), p. 357.

14. Grose, p. 270.

15. Grose, p. 290.

16. It is possible that Truman made up his mind before the meeting, but did not want to tip his hand. Grose insists that Truman told confidants three weeks beforehand that his intention was to recognize Israel.

17. Margaret Truman, *Harry S. Truman* (New York: William Morrow, 1973), p. 420.

18. When Truman was introduced in New York as someone who helped establish the state of Israel, Truman responded, "What do you mean 'helped create'? I am Cyrus. I am Cyrus." See Oren, *Power, Faith and Fantasy*, p. 501. David McCullough, *Truman* (New York: Simon and Schuster, 1992), p. x.

19. This arms embargo would continue as part of the Tripartite Declaration of 1950 with Britain and France, which the three countries believed was necessary to avoid a Middle East arms race. The United States kept the embargo in place until defensive Hawk missiles were sold by the Kennedy administration in the early 1960s.

20. FRUS 5 (1950): 1190–91.

21. Daniel Yergin, *The Prize: The Epic Quest for Oil, Money and Power* (New York: Simon and Schuster, 1992), p. 412.

22. Ibid., p. 447.

23. Peter W. Rodman, *More Precious than Peace: The Cold War and the Struggle for the Third World* (New York: Scribner's, 1994), p. 75.

24. Ibid.

25. *The Papers of Dwight David Eisenhower*, vol. 16, *The Presidency: The Middle Way*, document no. 1784 (March 13, 1956).

26. Sir Anthony Eden, *Memoirs: Full Circle* (London: Cassell, 1960), p. 498.

27. Rodman, p. 80.

28. Stephen E. Ambrose, *Eisenhower: Soldier and President* (New York: Simon and Schuster, 1990), p. 427.

29. Rodman, p. 81.

30. Steven L. Spiegel, *The Other Arab-Israel Conflict: Making America's Middle East Policy, from Truman to Reagan* (Chicago: University of Chicago Press, 1985), p. 79.

31. Text of remarks made by President Eisenhower, February 20, 1957.

32. P. J. Vatikiiotis, *Nasser and His Generation* (New York: St. Martin's Press, 1978), p. 226.

33. Rodman, p. 85.

34. Ibid., p. 84.

35. Ambrose, p. 469.

36. Ibid.

37. Wilfrid L. Kohl, "The French Nuclear Deterrent," *Proceedings of the Academy of Political Science,* 29, no. 2 (November 1968), The Atlantic Community. In this piece is a paragraph that talks about the motivations for France's nuclear program. Furthermore, Kohl discusses how France intended to go nuclear in order to bolster its position within NATO and only in spring 1966 did it leave NATO.

38. Rodman, p. 86.

39. Ibid.

40. Raymond Aron, *De Gaulle, Israel and the Jews* (New York: Praeger Publishers, 1968), pp. 65–66.

41. Abba Eban, *Personal Witness: Israel Through My Eyes* (New York: G. P. Putnam's Sons, 1992), pp. 373–74.

42. Abba Eban, *An Autobiography* (New York: Random House, 1977), p. 343.

43. Ibid., p. 344.

44. Michael B. Oren, *Six Days of War* (New York: Oxford University Press, 2002), p. 112.

45. Lyndon B. Johnson, National Security File, Memoranda to the President (W. Rostow), Box 16: Minutes of Meeting (Saunders), May 16, 1967.

46. Oren, pp. 113–15.

47. Ibid., p. 125.

48. For a more detailed explanation, see Robert D. Kaplan, *The Arabists: The Romance of an American Elite* (New York: Free Press, 1993).

49. Kaplan. Oren, p. 143.

50. Oren, pp. 142–43.

51. Ibid., p. 143.

52. Ibid., p. 144.

53. Ibid. Kaplan, p. 143.

54. Oren, p. 140.

55. Ibid., p. 141.

56. http://news.bbc.co.uk/onthisday/hi/dates/stories/may/30/newsid_2493000/2493177.stm.

57. Kaplan. Oren, p. 147.

58. Lord Caradon, the British ambassador to the UN who drafted Resolution 242, explained the intent of the framers, stating, "We didn't say there should be a withdrawal to the '67 line; we did not put the 'the' in, we did not say 'all the

territories' deliberately. We all knew that the boundaries of '67 were not drawn as permanent frontiers, they were a cease-fire line of a couple of decades earlier." *MacNeil/Lehrer Report*, PBS, March 30, 1978.

59. Nixon, Richard, *RN: The Memoirs of Richard Nixon* (New York: Grosset and Dunlap, 1978), p. 346.

60. Ibid.

61. Ibid., p. 68.

62. Ibid., p. 479.

63. Ibid., p. 69.

64. Henry Kissinger, *Years of Upheaval—White House Years* (Boston: Little, Brown, 1979), p. 376.

65. Henry Kissinger, *Crisis: The Anatomy of Two Major Foreign Policy Crises* (New York: Simon and Schuster, 2003), p. 12.

66. Kenneth W. Stein, *Heroic Diplomacy: Sadat, Kissinger, Carter, Begin and the Quest for Arab-Israeli Peace* (New York: Routledge, 1999), pp. 66–67.

67. Remarks by Kissinger at a Washington Institute dinner in New York on October 6, 2008, http://washingtoninstitute.org/templateC05.php?CID=2937.

68. Kissinger, *Crisis*.

69. Ibid., p. 65.

70. Ibid., pp. 86–87.

71. Ibid., p. 86.

72. Ibid., p. 43.

73. Ibid., p. 143–45.

74. Ibid., p. 147.

75. Ibid., p. 173.

76. Ibid., p. 245.

77. Ismail Fahmy, *Negotiating for Peace in the Middle East* (Johns Hopkins University Press: Baltimore, 1983), p. 39.

78. William Quandt, *Decade of Decisions*: American Policy Toward the Arab-Israeli Conflict, 1967–1976 (Berkeley: University of California Press, 1977), p. 182.

79. Fahmy, p. 39.

80. Kissinger, *Crisis*, pp. 197–98.

81. Kissinger, *Crisis*, pp. 213–15.

82. Fahmy, pp. 26–27.

83. Kissinger, *Crisis*, p. 225.

84. Ibid., pp. 182–83.

85. Henry Kissinger, *Years of Upheaval*, p. 518.

86. Ibid., p. 532.

87. Kissinger, *Crisis*, p. 245.

88. Yergin, *Prize*, p. 607. Nixon told Saqqaf: "I can see that you are concerned about the fact that Henry Kissinger is a Jewish-American. A Jewish-American

can be a good American, and Kissinger is a good American. He will work with you."

89. Ibid., p. 608.
90. Ibid., p. 609.
91. Kissinger, *Years of Upheaval*, p. 859.
92. Ibid., p. 868.
93. Ibid.
94. Yergin, p. 597.
95. Ibid., p. 598.
96. Ibid.
97. U.S. Senate Subcommittee on Multinational Corporations hearings, *Multinational Corporations and United States Foreign Policy*, part 7 (February 20–21 and March 27–28, 1974), p. 517. See also Kissinger, *Years of Upheaval*, p. 1252.
98. Nixon would say in his State of the Union address in January 1974: "The first priority is energy. Let me begin by reporting a new development which I know will be welcome news to every American. As you know, we have committed ourselves to an active role in helping to achieve a just and durable peace in the Middle East, on the basis of full implementation of Security Council Resolutions 242 and 338. The first step in the process is the disengagement of Egyptian and Israeli forces which is now taking place. Because of this hopeful development, I can announce tonight that I have been assured, through my personal contacts with friendly leaders in the Middle Eastern area, that an urgent meeting will be called in the immediate future to discuss the lifting of the oil embargo. This is an encouraging sign. However, it should be clearly understood by our friends in the Middle East that the United States will not be coerced on this issue."
99. Due to different factors, the Golan Heights, East Jerusalem, the West Bank, and Gaza would largely be outside the Israel-Egyptian contractual treaty context.
100. Yergin, p. 614.
101. Ibid., p. 625.
102. Nadav Safran, *Saudi Arabia: The Ceaseless Quest for Security* (Ithaca, NY: Cornell University Press, 1985), p. 170.
103. Mohamed Heikal, *Secret Channels: The Inside Story of Arab-Israeli Peace Negotiations* (New York: HarperCollins, 1996), p. 243.
104. Anwar Sadat, *In Search of Identity* (New York: Harper and Row, 1977), p. 293. Sadat referred to the signing of the first disengagement with Israel in 1974 by writing the following: "The United States did not impose the first disengagement agreement: she intervened to achieve a breakthrough and overcome the apparent impasse. The heading of the first disengagement document reads: American Proposal. Hence my assertion that the United States holds 99 percent of the cards in this game. And I shall go on saying this, even if it angers the others, namely the Soviet agents and the Soviets themselves."

105. See previous note.

106. Stein, p. 218. See also Moshe Dayan, *Breakthrough* (New York: Alfred A. Knopf, 1981), p. 55. In his book, Dayan goes into great detail about how difficult it was to deal with Carter. Dayan described one meeting with Carter in 1977 as "most unpleasant" (p. 59), and he called his sessions at that time an "ugly environment" (p. 64).

107. William B. Quandt, *Peace Process: American Diplomacy and the Arab-Israeli Conflict* (Berkeley: University of California Press, 2005), p. 189

108. Stein, p. 217.

109. Sadat, p. 297.

110. Stein, p. 208. Also see Jimmy Carter, *The Blood of Abraham: Insights into the Middle East* (Boston: Houghton Mifflin, 1985), p. 166.

111. Dayan, p. 48.

112. Heikal, p. 262.

113. Stein, p. 208.

114. Ibid., p. 35.

115. Eilts made his remarks at the November 1997 symposium of the Washington Institute for Near East Policy, proceedings published as *Sadat and His Legacy, 1977–1997: On the Occasion of the Twentieth Anniversary of President Sadat's Journey to Jerusalem* (Washington, DC: Washington Institute for Near East Policy, 1998).

116. Author interview with Veliotes, June 25, 2008.

117. Heikal, p. 253.

118. Ibid., p. 254.

119. Ibid.

120. Ibid, pp. 254–55.

121. Author interview with Veliotes, June 26, 2008.

122. Stein, p. 232.

123. Heikal, p. 248.

124. "West Bank: The Cruelest Conflict," *Time*, June 19, 1978, http://www.time.com/time/printout/0,8816,919757,00.html.

125. http://www.un.org/News/Press/docs/2003/sc7666.doc.htm.

126. Alan Travis, "Casualty of War," *Guardian*, February 18, 2003.

127. Author conversation with senior Bush administration official, March 27, 2003.

128. www.whitehouse.gov/news/releases/2003/03/20030327-3.html.

129. Tom Baldwin, "Blair Wants Debt Repaid with Push for Mideast Peace," London *Times*, March 29, 2003.

130. Iraq Study Group Report (December 2006), pp. 43–44.

131. British prime minister Tony Blair's speech to the Los Angeles World Affairs Council (August 1, 2006), http://www.lawac.org/speech/2005-2006/Blair,%Tony%202006.pdf.

CHAPTER FOUR

1. Ron Suskind, "Without a Doubt," *New York Times Magazine*, October 17, 2004.
2. Ibid.
3. Ron Suskind, *The Price of Loyalty: George W. Bush, the White House, and the Education of Paul O'Neill* (New York: Simon and Schuster, 2004), p. 71.
4. Elizabeth Bumiller, "Bush Aide Attacks Clinton on Mideast, Then Retracts Remark," *New York Times*, March 1, 2002.
5. Tony Karon, "Did Bill Clinton Start the Intifada?" Time.com, March 6, 2002.
6. Ron Kampeas, "In the Mideast, Both Sides Doubt Bush's Detachment," Associated Press, February 10, 2001.
7. Elliott Abrams, "Israel and the 'Peace Process,'" in Robert Kagan and William Kristol, eds., *Present Dangers: Crisis and Opportunity in American Foreign Policy* (San Francisco: Encounter Books, 2000), p. 239.
8. Ibid.
9. Ibid., p. 223.
10. Norman Podhoretz, "Intifada II: Death of an Illusion," *Commentary* (December 2000), p. 37.
11. Ibid., p. 27.
12. Fouad Ajami, quoted in Abrams, pp. 232–33.
13. See for instance Prof. Shibley Telhami, "2008 Annual Arab Public Opinion Poll, Survey of the Anwar Sadat Chair for Peace and Development at the University of Maryland (with Zogby International) conducted March 2008. Available at http://www.brookings.edu/~/media/Files/events/2008/0414_middle _east/0414_middle_east_telhami.pdf.
14. For instance, even King Abdullah II of Jordan reacted to the May 2002 suicide bombing in Rishon Letzion, which killed sixteen and injured more than fifty by saying, "I think that there has been a tremendous negative reaction towards the suicide bombing that happened several days ago simply because it's been so counterproductive to moving people forward." Interview with King Abdullah, *The NewsHour with Jim Lehrer*, PBS, May 10, 2002. It must be noted that there are certainly exceptions like Dr. Sari Nusseibeh who view such attacks as morally unacceptable as well as politically counterproductive.
15. Quoted in Norman Podhoretz, "Another Statement on the Peace Process," *Commentary* (June 1993), p. 29.
16. Ibid.
17. Douglas Feith, "Assessing Risk in the Israel-PLO Deal," *Washington Times*, October 26, 1993.
18. Douglas Feith, "Land for No Peace," *Commentary* (June 1994), p. 35.
19. This scenario was repeatedly outlined by Podhoretz, but one can see it spelled out in his "Statement on the Peace Process," *Commentary* (April 1993), p. 23.

20. Adopted in Cairo on June 9, 1974, the PLO's "Ten-Point Program" or "Phased Plan" resolution called for armed struggle to liberate Palestinian territory under Israeli control, establish a national authority in those territories liberated from Israeli rule, and work with the other Arab "confrontation countries, with the aim of completing the liberation of all Palestinian territory." See "Political Program Adopted at the 12th Session of the Palestine National Council," Cairo, June 9, 1974. Available through Permanent Observer Mission of Palestine to the United Nations, New York, www.un.int/palestine/PLO/docone.html.

21. Feith, "Land for No Peace," p. 33.

22. Elliott Abrams, "Israel and the 'Peace Process,'" p. 222.

23. Norman Podhoretz, "The Peacemongers Return," *Commentary* (October 2001), p. 29.

24. Ibid.

25. One of the leading Palestinian negotiators said this to Dennis Ross before Dennis left to go to Geneva with President Clinton for a meeting with President al-Asad on March 26, 2000; the fear was that the Syrians would make a deal at the expense of the Palestinians since Israeli Prime Minister Ehud Barak, having made painful concessions as part of the expected Syrian peace deal, would not have the political capital or wherewithal to make the difficult compromises that would be necessary with the Palestinians, and the Arab states, led by the Saudis, would then do their own deals with Israel, leaving the Palestinian out in the cold.

26. Feith, "Land for No Peace," p. 35.

27. Norman Podhoretz, "Another Statement on the Peace Process," *Commentary*, (June 1993), p. 30.

28. Douglas Feith, "No Alternative to Peace," *Jerusalem Post*, March 25, 1996.

29. Douglas Feith, "Land for No Peace," *Commentary* (June 1994), pp. 35–36.

30. Norman Podhoretz, "Israel and the United States: A Complex History," *Commentary*, May 1998, quoted in Elliott Abrams, "Israel and the 'Peace Process,'" p. 225.

31. Abrams, "Israel and the 'Peace Process,'" p. 234.

32. Norman Podhoretz, "America and Israel: An Ominous Change," *Commentary* (January 1992), p. 23.

33. Ibid.

34. Dennis Ross, *The Missing Peace: The Inside Story of the Fight for Middle East Peace* (New York: Farrar, Straus and Giroux, 2004), p. 781.

35. James Wolfensohn, "Post-Palestinian Election Challenges," testimony, March 15, 2006, before the U.S. Senate Committee on Foreign Relations (Federal News Service), available on LexisNexis, accessed October 2, 2008.

36. Steven Lee Myers, "Bush Offers a Nudge to Start Mideast Talks," *New York Times*, November 27, 2007.

CHAPTER FIVE

1. Jerome Slater, "What Went Wrong? The Collapse of the Israeli-Palestinian Peace Process," *Political Science Quarterly*, vol. 116 (Summer 2001), p. 196.

2. Slater, p. 197.

3. Stephen Zunes, "The United States and the Breakdown of the Israeli-Palestinian Peace Process," *Middle East Policy*, vol. 3, no. 4 (December 2001), p. 70.

4. Zbigniew Brzezinski, "Moral Duty, National Interest," *New York Times*, April 7, 2002.

5. Ibid.

6. Aaron David Miller, "Israel's Lawyer," *Washington Post*, May 23, 2005. See also Aaron David Miller, *The Much Too Promised Land: America's Elusive Search for Middle East Peace* (New York: Bantam, 2008), pp. 75–124, 204–5.

7. John Mearsheimer and Stephen M. Walt, *The Israel Lobby and U.S. Foreign Policy* (New York: Farrar, Straus and Giroux, 2007), p. 75.

8. Quoted in Daniel Kurtzer and Scott Lasensky, *Negotiating Arab-Israeli Peace: American Leadership in the Middle East* (Washington, DC: United States Institute of Peace, 2008), p. 30.

9. Kurtzer and Lasensky, p. 16.

10. See "Letter from President Ford to Prime Minister Rabin, September 1, 1975," Jewish Virtual Library. Available at http://www.jewishvirtuallibrary.org/jsource/Peace/ford_rabin_letter.html.

11. Dennis Ross served as Secretary Baker's chief assistant on these issues and the head of his peace team. He has recounted in detail the Baker policy approach in his *The Missing Peace: The Inside Story of the Fight for Middle East Peace* (New York: Farrar, Straus and Giroux, 2004), pp. 53–57.

12. Zbigniew Brzezinski, "A Peaceful Intervention: The Israeli-Palestinian Conflict Will Never Be Resolved Without a US Blueprint," *Washington Post*, December 24, 2001.

13. Ibid.

14. Slater, pp. 198–99.

15. Mearsheimer and Walt, p. 226.

16. William Quandt, "Reluctant Peacemaker: Bush Brought Arabs and Israelis Together but Failed to Put Forth Proposals and Apply Pressure," *Newsday*, December 2, 2007.

17. Ibid.

18. Zbigniew Brzezinski and William Quandt, "From Bush, Middle East Words to Act On," *Washington Post*, June 17, 2005.

19. Slater, p. 199.

20. Mearsheimer and Walt, p. 226.

21. Ibid.

22. For instance, in the latest poll from the Palestinian Center for Policy and Survey Research, only 41 percent of respondents support a compromise on the refugee issue. Palestinian Public Opinion Poll No. 28, PCPSR, June 12, 2008, available at http://www.pcpsr.org/survey/polls/2008/p28e.html.

CHAPTER SIX

1. See for instance Dr. Sari Nusseibeh quoted in Akiva Eldar, "We Are Running Out of Time for a Two-State Solution," *Haaretz*, August 16, 2008. Palestinian negotiator Abu Ala has said, "If Israel continues to oppose making this a reality, then the Palestinian demand for the Palestinian people and its leadership [would be] one state, a binational state," in "PA: We May Demand Binational Israel-Palestinian State," Reuters, August 10, 2008.

2. For example, after four terror bombs in nine days in 1996, the Israeli government and the public were both shaken to their core and doubted the worth of the peace process. President Clinton produced Arab condemnations at a conference in which Arab leaders came to meet in Egypt with the Israeli prime minister and plan responses to terror, and pressed for and got Arafat to go after those responsible for the bombings.

3. Israeli prime minister Barak made it clear that his readiness to withdraw from the Golan Heights was tied to commitments he felt he needed from the United States to compensate Israel for what it would be giving up militarily by getting off the Heights—and while the shopping list of items was significant and related to preserving Israel's qualitative edge over time, President Clinton was prepared to provide it. With both Prime Ministers Netanyahu and Barak, President Clinton was prepared to offer a formal defense treaty with Israel as part of any peace agreement that would provide for a Palestinian state.

4. Dennis Ross, *The Missing Peace: The Inside Story of the Fight for Middle East Peace* (New York: Farrar, Straus and Giroux, 2004), pp. 319–22.

5. Kurtzer and Lasensky, p. 81.

6. Several officials in the Bush administration also recounted such conversations to us, even making the point that the secretary was counseled by several of her Arab counterparts that it might be better not to launch such an effort given the costs of dashing expectations again. They were not arguing against U.S. involvement, but worried that it was late in the day for the Bush administration and that it might be best to let the next administration launch something new.

7. Kevin Sullivan, "Rights Group Accuses Hezbollah of 'Indiscriminate' Killing," *Washington Post*, September 15, 2006.

8. "West Bank and Gaza: Economic Development in 2006—A First Assessment," International Monetary Fund—The World Bank, March 2007, p. 8.

9. President Abbas favored such an approach at one time, even challenging those who prefer to keep the refugee camps as symbols, asking where it says that Palestinians should live in misery.

10. "UAE to Build Town for Palestinians at Site of Gaza Settlements," *Haaretz*, July 24, 2005.

11. The point here is that publicly stated Arab concerns about the Palestinians provide us with some leverage if we are publicly calling on them to help meet these needs and they are doing nothing—and we are prepared to expose them as a result.

12. As Itamar Rabinovich told Dennis in the fall of 1994 after a meeting Dennis hosted at his suburban Washington home with Rabinovich and the then Syrian ambassador Walid Mualem, "The Syrians may be willing to go for an agreement with us but it is only to get peace with you [the United States] and all they think that will mean."

CHAPTER SEVEN

1. Zbigniew Brzezinski, "Do Not Attack Iran," *International Herald Tribune*, April 26, 2006.

2. See for instance Jung Chang and Jon Halliday, *Mao: The Unknown Story* (London: Jonathan Cape, 2005) pp. 457–58.

3. For discussion of Alsop and U.S. deliberations about military strikes to prevent China from developing a nuclear capability, see William Burr and Jeffrey T. Richelson, "Whether to 'Strangle the Baby in the Cradle': The United States and the Chinese Nuclear Program, 1960–64," *International Security*, vol. 25, no. 3 (Winter 2000), pp. 54–99.

4. Lyndon Baines Johnson, "Statement by the President on the First Chinese Nuclear Device," October 16, 1964. Available at www.presidency.ucsb.edu/ws/index.php?pid=26615.

5. Karim Sadjadpour, "Reading Khamenei: The World View of Iran's Most Powerful Leader," Carnegie Endowment for Peace, March 2008, p. 1.

6. Karim Sadjadpour, "Oil or the Atom? The Economic Underpinnings of Iranian Power," in Patrick Clawson and Michael Eisenstadt, eds., *Deterring the Ayatollahs*, Policy Focus no. 72, Washington Institute for Near East Policy, July 2007, p. 28.

7. Mehdi Khalaji, "Apocalyptic Visions and Iran's Security Policy," in Clawson and Eisenstadt, *Deterring the Ayatollahs*, p. 33.

8. Sadjadpour, "Reading Khamenei," p. 14.

9. Barry Posen, "A Nuclear-Armed Iran: A Difficult but Not Impossible Policy Problem," The Century Foundation, 2006, p. 15.

10. For more on classic deterrence strategy see Graham Allison, *Essence of Decision: Explaining the Cuban Missile Crisis* (Boston: Little, Brown, 1971); Alexander L. George and Richard Smoke, *Deterrence in American Foreign Policy: Theory and Practice* (New York: Columbia University Press, 1974); Robert Jervis, Janice Gross-Stein, and Richard Ned Lebow, *Psychology and Deterrence* (Baltimore: Johns Hopkins University Press, 1989); Herman Kahn, *Thinking About the Unthinkable* (New York: Horizon Press, 1962); Henry Kissinger, *Nuclear Weapons and Foreign Policy* (Garden City, NY: Doubleday, 1958); Keith Payne, *The Fallacies of Cold War Deterrence and a New Direction* (Lexington: University of Kentucky Press, 2001); and Thomas Schelling, *The Strategy of Conflict* (Cambridge, MA: Harvard University Press, 1960).

11. Brzezinski, "Do Not Attack Iran."

12. For example, Supreme Leader Ayatollah Ali Khamenei has declared, "Our enemies know very well that any aggression will have a response from all sides by Iranian people on their interests all over the world." Nazila Fathi, "Iran's Supreme Leader Lashes Out Against U.S.," *New York Times*, February 8, 2007.

13. These comments were made at a private dinner with one of the authors in March 2008.

14. "Iran Warns of Revenge over Israel," BBC News, October 20, 2006.

15. Judith Yaphe and Charles Lutes, "Reassessing the Implications of a Nuclear-Armed Iran," McNair Paper 69, National Defense University, August 2005, p. 13. Available at http://www.ndu.edu/inss/mcnair/mcnair69/McNairPDF .pdf.

16. Robert S. McNamara, "Forty Years After 13 Days," *Arms Control Today*, November 2002, pp. 4–8.

17. Keith Payne, "Deterring Iran: The Values at Stake and the Acceptable Risks," in Clawson and Eisenstadt, *Deterring the Ayatollahs*, pp. 2–3.

18. Yaphe and Lutes, p. 17.

19. Ibid., p. 13.

20. Gerald Steinberg, "Walking the Tightrope: Israeli Options in Response to Iranian Nuclear Developments," Appendix C, in Yaphe and Lutes, pp. 79–80.

21. Foreign Minister Tzipi Livni recently declared, "Iran must understand that the threat of military action exists, and it won't be taken off the table. . . . We've made it clear that D-Day isn't the day they procure the bomb or have the technology, but now." Amnon Meranda, "Livni: Military Option Against Iran—on the Table," *Yediot Aharanot Online*, June 3, 2008.

22. The International Atomic Energy Agency reported that Iran had, as of January 31, 2009, produced approximately 1,010 kg of low-enriched uranium. See International Atomic Energy Agency, "Report by the Director-General," GOV/2009/8, February 2009. Available at http://www.iaea.org/Publications/ Documents/Board/2009/gov2008-58.pdf.

23. President George W. Bush, "President Discusses Medicare, Iraq, Iran, and the Middle East," Office of the Press Secretary, June 18, 2003. Available at http://www.whitehouse.gov/news/releases/2003/06/20030618-6.html.

24. See for instance Secretary of State Condoleezza Rice, "Press Conference on Iran," May 31, 2006. Available at http://www.state.gov/secretary/rm/2006/67103.htm.

25. Vice President Richard Cheney, "Vice President Cheney: Address to the Washington Institute's Weinberg Founders Conference," Washington Institute, October 21, 2007. Available at http://washingtoninstitute.org/templateC07.php?CID=361.

26. For a time line of Iranian nuclear advances, see the Nuclear Threat Initiative Web site, "Iran Country Profile: Nuclear Chronology," available at http://www.nti.org/e_research/profiles/Iran/Nuclear/.

27. Ray Takeyh, *Hidden Iran: Paradox and Power in the Islamic Republic* (New York: Times Books, 2006), p. 34.

28. Gregory Giles, "Command-and-Control Challenges of an Iranian Nuclear Force," in Clawson and Eisenstadt, *Deterring the Ayatollahs*, p. 13.

29. Author interview with David B. Crist, History Office, Office of the Chairman, Joint Chiefs of Staff, June 2008. Crist recounted specific episodes in which the U.S. intercepted conversations between IRGC local commanders and the government in which they received instructions, acknowledged them, and then ignored them.

30. Kenneth Katzman, *The Warriors of Islam: Iran's Revolutionary Guards* (Boulder, CO: Westview Press, 1993), pp. 132–34, 175.

31. Colin Gray and Keith Payne, "Victory Is Possible," *Foreign Policy*, no. 39 (Summer 1980), 14–27, p. 22.

32. "Qods Day Speech (Jerusalem Day), Chairman of the Expediency Council Akbar Hashemi-Rafsanjani," Voice of the Islamic Republic of Iran, translated by BBC Worldwide Monitoring, December 14, 2001.

33. Bernard Lewis, quoted in Norman Podhoretz, *World War IV: The Long Struggle Against Islamofascism* (New York: Doubleday, 2007), pp. 3–4.

34. Aftab News, November 16, 2005, quoted in Hossein Bastani, "Ahmadinejad's Belief in the Shiite Messiah?" *Rooz Online*, March 3, 2008. Available at http://www.roozonline.com/english/archives/2008/03/ahmadinejads_belief_in_the_shi.html.

35. Michael Ledeen, *The Iranian Time Bomb: The Mullah Zealots' Quest for Destruction* (New York: St. Martin's Press, 2007), p. 201.

36. Fars News Agency, November 11, 2007, quoted in Bastani, "Ahmadinejad's Belief in the Shiite Messiah?"

37. Mahmoud Ahmadinejad, speech at Mashhad, May 5, 2008, quoted in "Iranian President Says US President's Life 'Empty,'" BBC Monitoring Worldwide, May 6, 2008.

38. Ibid.
39. Raja News, November 12, 2007, quoted in Bastani, "Ahmadinejad's Belief in the Shiite Messiah?"
40. Fars News Agency, November 11, 2007, quoted in Bastani, "Ahmadinejad's Belief in the Shiite Messiah?"
41. Frances Harrison, "Row over Ahmadinejad Imam Beliefs," BBC News, February 19, 2008.
42. Iranian Students News Agency (ISNA), February 19, 2008, quoted in Bastani, "Ahmadinejad's Belief in the Shiite Messiah?"
43. Khalaji, "Apocalyptic Visions," in Clawson and Eisenstadt, *Deterring the Ayatollahs*, p. 32.
44. Ibid., p. 31.
45. Mahmoud Ahmadinejad, June 26, 2007, quoted in Mehdi Khalaji, "Apocalyptic Politics: On the Rationality of Iranian Policy," Policy Focus no. 79, Washington Institute for Near East Policy, January 2008, p. 24.
46. Mahmoud Ahmadinejad, speech in Gorgan, northern Iran, Press TV and Aftab, May 14, 2008. Translation via MEMRI, Inquiry and Analysis no. 447, June 6, 2008. Available at http://memri.org/bin/articles.cgi?Page=archives& Area=ia&ID=IA44708#_edn9.
47. See for instance, on Hizbollah involvement, "Khobar Towers Indictment Returned," CNN.com, June 22, 2001; and Michael Gordon and Dexter Filkins, "Hezbollah Said to Help Shiite Army in Iraq," *New York Times*, November 27, 2006.
48. Barry Posen, "A Nuclear-Armed Iran," p. 14.
49. Golnaz Esfandiari, "Iran: President Says Israel Should Be 'Wiped Off Map,'" Radio Free Europe / Radio Liberty, October 27, 2005.
50. Kenneth Katzman, "Iran: U.S. Concerns and Policy Responses," *Congressional Research Service Report*, May 6, 2008. See also Raid Qusti, "GCC to Develop Civilian Nuclear Energy," *Arab News*, December 11, 2006.
51. Author interview in the fall of 2007 with senior Egyptian official.
52. Richard Haass, "Living with a Nuclear Iran," in *Iran: Assessing U.S. Strategic Options*, James Miller, Christine Parthemore, and Kurt Campbell, eds., Center for New American Security, September 2008, pp. 109–118. Available at: http://www.cnas.org/files/documents/publications/MillerParthemore-Campbell_Iran%20Assessing%20US%20Strategy_Sept08.pdf, p. 117.

CHAPTER EIGHT

1. Michael Ledeen, *The Iranian Time Bomb: The Mullah Zealots' Quest for Destruction* (New York: St. Martin's Press, 2007), p. 1.
2. Ibid., p. 24.

3. Ibid., p. 17.

4. Ibid., p. 24. "The World Towards Illumination," Islamic Republic of Iran Broadcasting Web site, translated in "Waiting for the Mahdi: Official Iranian Eschatology Outlined in Public Broadcasting Program in Iran," MEMRI, Special Dispatch series no. 1436, January 25, 2007. Available at: htttp://www.memri.org/bin/articles.cgi?Page=archives&Area=SD&ID=SP143607.

5. Letter of President Ahmadinejad to President Bush, May 8, 2006, quoted in Richard Perle, "Why Did Bush Blink on Iran? (Ask Condi)," *Washington Post*, June 25, 2006.

6. Warren Hoge, "Diatribes and Dialogues in Mideast for Annan," *New York Times*, September 11, 2006, p. A9.

7. Robin Wright, "U.S. and Europe Gird for Hard Line from Iran's New President," *Washington Post*, June 26, 2005.

8. Karim Sadjadpour, "Reading Khamenei: The World View of Iran's Most Powerful Leader," Carnegie Endowment for Peace, March 2008, p. 15. http://www.carnegieendowment.org/files/sadjadpour_iran_final2.pdf.

9. Ledeen, p. 136.

10. Ibid., p. 203.

11. The Bush administration did send Undersecretary of State for Political Affairs William J. Burns to join the UN Permanent 5 plus Germany at one meeting in Geneva with Iranian negotiator Saeed Jalili on July 19, 2008. The United States made it clear that his participation in the talks would be a one-time deal.

12. Quoted in Norman Podhoretz, *World War IV: The Long Struggle Against Islamofascism* (New York: Doubleday, 2007), p. 189.

13. William Kristol, "It's Our War: Bush Should Go to Jerusalem—and the U.S. Should Confront Iran," *Weekly Standard*, vol. 11, no. 42 (July 24, 2006).

14. Ledeen, *Time Bomb*, p. 178.

15. Perle, "Why Did Bush Blink on Iran?"

16. Ledeen, *Time Bomb*, p. 216.

17. Ibid., p. 221.

18. Ibid., p. 223.

19. See for instance Jesse Nunes, "Iran Detains Two on Accusations of Plotting 'Velvet Revolution,'" *Christian Science Monitor*, May 23, 2007.

20. Sadjadpour, "Reading Khamenei," p. 18.

21. Patrick Clawson in an address to the Washington Institute's Soref Symposium, May 29, 2008.

22. Sadjadpour, "Reading Khamenei," p. 18.

23. A copy of the Tim Guldimann fax can be found at http://media.washingtonpost.com/wp-srv/world/documents/us_iran_roadmap.pdf. For more, see Gregory Beals, "A Missed Opportunity with Iran," *Newsday*, February 19,

2006; Glenn Kessler, "In 2003, US Spurned Iran's Offer of Dialogue," *Washington Post*, June 18, 2006; Nicholas Kristof, "Diplomacy at Its Worst," *New York Times*, April 29, 2007; Gareth Porter, "How a Secret 2003 Overture from Tehran Might Have Led to a Deal on Iran's Nuclear Capability," *American Prospect*, May 21, 2006.

24. Tim Guldimann fax.

25. Among the most prominent officials who doubted that the proposal was in fact authoritative was Richard Armitage—the deputy secretary of state at the time—who said, in an interview with *Newsweek*, "We couldn't determine what [in the proposal] was the Iranians' and what was the Swiss ambassador's." Michael Hirsh and Maziar Bahari, "Rumors of War," *Newsweek*, February 19, 2007.

26. Beals, "A Missed Opportunity with Iran."

27. PBS *Frontline*, "Interview with Richard Armitage," http://www.pbs.org/wgbh/pages/frontline/showdown/interviews/armitage.html.

28. Kessler, "In 2003, US Spurned Iran's Offer."

29. Ibid.

30. Ibid.

31. Former United Nations weapons inspector David Albright quoted in Daniel Dombey and James Blitz, "Iran Could Reach Nuclear Goal 'in a Year,'" *Financial Times*, November 16, 2007.

32. On April 16, 2007, Hizbollah Deputy Secretary General Sheikh Naim Qassem, in an interview on al-Kawthar TV, declared, "Hizbullah, when it comes to matters of jurisprudence pertaining to its general direction, as well as to its jihad direction, based itself on the decisions of the Jurisprudent [Iranian Supreme Leader]. It is the Jurisprudent who permits, and it is the Jurisprudent who forbids. When the resistance of Hizbullah was launched in 1982, it was based on the Jurisprudent position and decision of Imam Khomeini." See MEMRI, Special Dispatch 1549, April 19, 2007, available at http://memri.org/bin/articles.cgi?Page=archives&Area=sd&ID=SP154907.

33. See for instance Iranian secretary general of the "Intifada conference" Mohtashami Pur quoted in "Iran: We Supplied Zelzal-2 to Hizbullah," *Jerusalem Post*, August 4, 2006.

34. "Defence Officials: Hezbollah Rockets Can Now Reach Almost All of Israel," *Haaretz*, March 27, 2008.

35. Ledeen, *Time Bomb*, p. 156.

36. Ray Takeyh, *Hidden Iran: Paradox and Power in the Islamic Republic* (New York: Times Books, 2006), p. 225.

37. Raja News, February 20, 2007.

38. Reuters, April 19, 2003.

39. Takeyh, *Hidden Iran*, p. 217.

40. Anoush Ehteshami, "The Rise and Impact of Iran's Neo-Cons," *Policy Analysis Brief*, the Stanley Foundation, April 2008, p. 1. Available at: www.stanleyfoundation.org/publications/pab/RiseandImpactEhtesham08PAB.pdf.

41. Quoted in Fariba Sarraf, "Ahmadinejad Advisor Calls for 'Change' of Zionist Regime," *Rooz Online*, June 26, 2007. Available at: www.roozonline.com/English/archives/2007/06/ahmadinejad_advisor_calls_for.html.

42. *Jomhouri Eslami*, May 26, 2004, quoted in Takeyh, *Hidden Iran*, p. 145.

43. *Jame'eh*, April 27, 1998, quoted in Takeyh, p. 157.

44. Quoted in Parisa Hafezi, "Iranian President Prefers Slogans to Policy—Cleric," Reuters, February 27, 2008.

45. Quoted in Steven Lee Myers and Nazila Fathi, "Europeans Back Bush on Iran Nuclear Curbs," *New York Times*, June 11, 2008.

46. Sadjadpour, "Reading Khamenei, p. 9.

47. Ibid., p. 16.

48. Address to students at Shahid Beheshti University, May 28, 2003, quoted in Sadjadpour, "Reading Khamenei," p. 16.

49. Elpais.com, September 18, 2001, quoted in Ehteshami, "The Rise and Impact of Iran's Neo-Cons," p. 7.

50. Address to students in Yazd, January 3, 2008, quoted in Sadjadpour, "Reading Khamenei," p. 17.

CHAPTER NINE

1. Dan Williams, "Israel Attack on Iran 'Unavoidable'—Olmert Deputy," Reuters, June 6, 2008.

2. David Sanger and Eric Schmitt, "Cheney's Power No Longer Goes Unquestioned," *New York Times*, September 10, 2006.

3. Not only was the U.S. offer to negotiate—which after all offered only direct talks, no other inducements—rejected, but so too was a Russian proposal to do enrichment for Iran in Russia, supply its nuclear fuel needs, and, for face-saving purposes, still permit Iran to have a small research facility for enrichment. See Karl Vick, "Iran Rejects Russia's Proposal on Uranium," *Washington Post*, March 13, 2006. While the administration supported the EU offer, it did not support the Russian proposal.

4. UN Security Council, 5612th Meeting, "Resolution 1737(2006)," December 23, 2006.

5. *Jomhouri Eslami*, quoted in *Akhbar Rooz*, Tehran, vol. 27, no. 229 (January 9, 2007), p. 4.

6. UN Security Council, 5647th Meeting, "Resolution 1747(2007)," March 24, 2007.

7. Elaine Sciolino, "On Nuclear Seesaw, the Balance Seems to Shift to Iran," *New York Times*, November 30, 2007.

8. Ibid. Also, this proposal was slightly refined and presented again in June 2008. In the revised proposal, there was a time line for the initial freeze of six weeks and also a readiness to talk at some point about a broad array of cooperative approaches, including on regional security. See Steven Erlanger and Elaine Sciolino, "Bush Says Iran Spurns New Offer on Uranium," *New York Times*, June 15, 2008.

9. International Atomic Energy Agency, "Communication dated 27 August 2007 from the Permanent Mission of the Islamic Republic of Iran to the Agency concerning the text of the 'Understandings of the Islamic Republic of Iran and the IAEA on the Modalities of Resolution of the Outstanding Issues,'" Information Circular 711, August 27, 2007. Available at http://www.iaea.org/Publications/Documents/Infcircs/2007/infcirc711.pdf.

10. Helene Cooper, "Split in Group Delays Vote on Sanctions Against Iran," *New York Times*, September 29, 2007.

11. John F. Burns, "As Talks with Europe End, Iran Gives No Sign of Concession on Nuclear Program," *New York Times*, December 1, 2007.

12. Ibid.

13. Elaine Sciolino, "Iranian Pushes Nuclear Talks Back to Square 1," *New York Times*, December 2, 2007.

14. Ibid.

15. National Intelligence Council, "Iran: Nuclear Intentions and Capabilities," November 2007. Available at http://www.dni.gov/press_releases/20071203_release.pdf.

16. UN Security Council, 5848th Meeting, "Resolution 1803(2008)," March 3, 2008.

17. Roula Khalaf, "Saudis Urge Iran to Join Gulf Plan for Nuclear Plant," *Financial Times*, November 2, 2007.

18. Ibid.

19. Ahmad Maher, "President Bush: Post-Tour Reflections," *Asharq al-Awsat*, January 19, 2008.

20. "Iran Says U.S. Report a 'Declaration of Surrender,'" Reuters, December 16, 2007.

21. "President: Iran's Nuclear Issue, Heaviest Contemporary Political Struggle," Presidency of the Islamic Republic of Iran News Service, December 5, 2007. Available at http://www.President.ir/en/?ArtID=7624.

22. Patrick Clawson and Michael Eisenstadt, "The Last Resort: Consequences of Preventive Military Action Against Iran," Policy Focus no. 84, Washington Institute for Near East Policy, p. 2.

23. "Iran Leader Hails Ahmadinejad for 'Nuclear Success,'" Agence France Presse, February 26, 2008.

24. See note 21 above.

25. Parisa Hafezi, "ElBaradei to Press Iran Leaders on Atom Cooperation," *Washington Post*, January 12, 2008.

26. Iraqi officials offered us an interesting view of Iranian behavior prior to and after the release of the NIE. According to two senior Iraqi officials that we met with—who were focused primarily on Iranian behavior vis-à-vis Iraq—the Iranians were nervous prior to the release of the NIE about what the United States might do, and it gave them a reason to be somewhat more cautious about Iraq. After the release of the NIE, they said, the Iranian demeanor changed; the Iranians became much more confident and far more assertive in terms of pressing their interests in Iraq.

27. Clawson and Eisenstadt, "The Last Resort," p. 7.

28. Bhushan Bahree, "How Iran Is Vulnerable to a Decline in Oil Exports," *Wall Street Journal*, February 20, 2007.

29. "Middle East and Africa Oil and Gas Insight," *Business Monitor International*, no. 7 (November 2006).

30. Roger Stern, "The Iranian Petroleum Crisis and the United States National Security," *Proceedings of the National Academy of Sciences of the United States of America*, vol. 104, no. 1 (January 2, 2007), p. 377. Available at http://www.pnas.org/cgi/reprint/0603903104v1.

31. Jad Mouawad, "West Adds to Strains on Iran's Lifeline," *New York Times*, February 13, 2007.

32. See Najmeh Bozorgmehr, "Malaysia Signs $16bn Gas Deal with Iran," *Financial Times*, December 26, 2007; "Iran, China Finalise Two Billion Dollar Oil Contract," Agence France Presse, December 9, 2007; Parisa Hafezi, "Iran, Italy's Edison Sign $107 mln Oil Deal," Reuters, January 9, 2008.

33. Mouawad, "West Adds to Strains."

34. U.S. Department of State, "Remarks with Secretary of the Treasury Henry M. Paulson," October 25, 2007. Available at http://www.state.gov/secretary/rm/2007/10/94133.htm.

35. Borzou Daragahi and Ramin Mostaghim, "Iran Sanctions Ripple Past Those in Power," *Los Angeles Times*, January 20, 2008.

36. Ibid. It is worth noting that on October 25, 2006, the U.S. adopted additional unilateral sanctions on Banks Melli and Mellat, for their involvement in proliferation activities, and on Bank Saderat, for its involvement in terrorist financing; the Islamic Revolutionary Guard Corps and its al-Quds force were similarly designated.

37. Ibid.

38. Nazila Fathi, "Tax Delay Fails to Quell Iranian Protest," *New York Times*, October 13, 2008.

39. Ray Takeyh, *Hidden Iran: Paradox and Power in the Islamic Republic* (New York: Times Books, 2006), p. 151.

40. Steven R. Weisman, "Europe Resists U.S. Push to Curb Iran Ties," *New York Times*, January 30, 2007.

41. Mouawad, "West Adds to Strains."

42. Michael Jacobson, "Pressure Gauges," *Guardian Online*, January 16, 2008.

43. See note 21 above.

44. See Flynt Leverett and Hillary Mann Leverett, "How to Defuse Iran," *New York Times*, December 11, 2007; Ray Takeyh, "Time to Start Talking to Tehran," *Newsweek*, January 2008; and Vali Nasr and Ray Takeyh, "Get Tehran Inside the Tent: Sizing Up Iran," *International Herald Tribune*, December 7, 2007.

45. Mark Brzezinski and Ray Takeyh, "Forging Ties with Iran," *Boston Globe*, January 11, 2008.

46. Ibid.

47. See Leverett and Leverett, "How to Defuse Iran"; Takeyh, "Time to Start Talking to Tehran"; and Vali Nasr and Ray Takeyh, "The Costs of Containing Iran: Washington's Misguided New Middle East Policy," *Foreign Affairs* (January/February 2008).

48. Brzezinski and Takeyh, "Forging Ties with Iran."

49. Glenn Kessler, "Iran's Conflicting Signals to the West," *Washington Post*, July 11, 2008.

50. Farhad Pouladi, "Top Iran Cleric Makes Rare Criticism of Government," Agence France-Presse, August 16, 2007.

51. We have had several conversations with the lead EU negotiators who, even when the "double freeze" proposal was being presented, felt it could not succeed without the United States coming directly to the table.

52. We are indebted to Robert Einhorn for drawing our attention to this point.

53. In 1989, Dennis Ross, then head of the Policy Planning Staff in the State Department, actually conducted such secret back-channel negotiations with the Syrian minister of state for foreign affairs to determine if an agenda meeting mutual U.S.-Syrian interests could be developed prior to more formal negotiations.

54. Richard Haass, "Living with a Nuclear Iran," Center for New American Security, May 2008, p. 7.

CHAPTER TEN

1. Issued in November 2007, preceding the Middle East peace conference in Annapolis, Maryland, the statement was a joint initiative of the U.S. / Middle East Project, the International Crisis Group, and the New America Foundation / America Strategy Program. It recommended that the engagement be done by the United Nations or a European envoy, but in other remarks, Brzezinski and Scowcroft do not specify whether the engagement would be done by the United States or others.

2. From a speech given in 1918 at Munich University, later published as "Politics as a Vocation."

3. "The Arab Center: The Promise of Moderation," a talk given at the Brookings

Institution Saban Center for Middle East Policy, June 16, 2008. Available at http://www.brookings.edu/~/media/Files/events/2008/0616_arab_center/20080616_moderation.pdf.

4. Tha'ir Abbas, "Lebanese Interior Minister on Hizbollah's 'Deterrence Theory,' UN Troops," *Asharq al-Awsat*, September 2, 2006.

5. Interview on al-Arabiya Television, May 8, 2008.

6. Ibid.

7. Cable News Network (CNN), May 14, 2008. Nada Husseini, "Lebanon Officials Reverse Decisions that Set Off Violence, http://www.cnn.com/2008/WORLD/meast/05/14/lebanon.crisis/.

8. Dean Godson, "Why Hizbollah Should Be Condemned," http://www.timesonline.co.uk/tol/comment/columnists/guest_contributors/article3926959.ece.

9. General Intelligence and Security Services (Ministry of the Interior), the Netherlands, 2004 Annual Report, p. 19.

10. James Kitfield, "The Hezbollah Model," *National Journal*, May 17, 2002.

11. Lally Weymouth, "The Safest Way," *Washington Post*, September 11, 2005.

12. Zbigniew Brzezinski, "Confronting Anti-American Grievances," *New York Times*, September 1, 2002.

13. Ali Abunima, reading the words of Ahmed Yousef at the Middle East Policy Council on April 11, 2008.

14. John J. Mearsheimer and Stephen W. Walt, *The Israel Lobby and U.S. Foreign Policy* (New York: Farrar, Straus and Giroux, 2007), p. 223.

15. August 4, 2008, http://newsweek.washingtonpost.com/postglobal/rami_g_khouri/.

16. Interview of Brzezinski on PBS *Charlie Rose* show, June 15, 2007.

17. One exception was in 2006, when Arab states condemned Hizbollah for crossing an international line into northern Israel. This was a unique instance when Arab states saw the group as an Iranian proxy that could also undermine the stability of their own regimes.

18. http://www.publications.parliament.uk/pa/cm199394/cmhansrd/1993-12-15/Debate-1.html#prof.

19. George Mitchell, *Making Peace* (London: William Heinemann, 1999), p. 24.

20. Ibid., p. 25.

21. Ibid., p. 32.

22. Ibid., pp. 35–36.

23. Frank Millar, *David Trimble: The Price of Peace* (Dublin: Liffey Press, 2008), p. 51.

24. Steven Simon and Jonathan Stevenson, "Confronting Hamas," *The National Interest*, Winter 2003–2004, p. 68.

25. How does Hamas define a cease-fire? The group leaders openly state that a cease-fire is an opportunity to rearm. So long as Hamas is preaching hatred in

its educational system and insisting that Israel is an illegitimate entity, Israel will view any long-term cease-fire as a respite that enables Hamas to win broader Palestinian public support while retaining the ideological tools necessary for future conflict. As such, a cease-fire provides Hamas with the benefits of quiet without incurring any risks, since Israel's hands are tied. Hamas would never accept coexistence with Israel no matter what demands Israel were to meet. With that mind-set, how can a cease-fire hold over time? Moreover, if the international bar is lowered and an Israeli-Hamas armistice becomes a sufficient substitute for peace, this will create pressure in Egypt and Jordan to repudiate their respective peace treaties with Israel in favor of a mere armistice.

26. Rory McCarthy, "Hamas Accepts Two-State Idea, Says Carter," *Guardian*, April 22, 2008.

27. Hamas-run al-Aqsa satellite TV carried the news conference, and this address was recorded by the BBC World Monitoring Middle East Service on April 22, 2008.

28. Similar suspicions existed when it came to dealing with the PLO during the period 1974–88, when the group was widely accused of having staged a plan for Israel's destruction. In 1988 the PLO clarified that it accepts a two-state solution, although neoconservatives such as Norman Podhoretz and others believe that the PLO's commitment to destroying Israel remains. It is up to Hamas to convince the world that it has changed.

29. It is also logistically impossible to arrange such a referendum all over the globe. Imagine if Israel did not ratify its peace agreements in the Israeli parliament, or Knesset, but insisted that these be approved by the millions of Jews living all over the world.

30. "Carter-Hamas Meeting Achieved Nothing: Palestinian Foreign Minister," Agence France-Presse, April 23, 2008. Available at http://afp.google.com/article/ALeqM5gwXa15X1KlCjYANxHCjgySSAYlYw.

31. Associated Press, May 26, 2000.

32. He exhorted Palestinians to choose the path of violence over negotiation in dealing with Israel. He declared, "[I]n order to liberate your land, you don't need tanks and planes. With the example of the martyrs, you can impose your demands on the Zionist aggressors."

33. Al-Manar Television, May 23, 2006.

34. Associated Press, April 28, 2008.

35. Interview with Washington Institute fellow Mehdi Khalaji.

36. *Al-Siyassa* (Kuwait), December 14, 2006. It is true that Al-Tufeili has some resentment that Nasrallah replaced him, but it would seem too contrived to suggest that therefore his statement is not factual.

37. Interview with Egyptian Television, June 2, 2000.

38. *Washington Post*, July 16, 2000.

39. *Al-Ahram Al-Arabi*, October 28, 2000. The clerics who glorify suicide bombers are not limited to Palestinians. A favorite Arab preacher who appears frequently on the popular Arab satellite channel al-Jazeera is Sheikh Yousef al-Qaradhawi. It may be noted that he is also a favorite of top Hamas official Khaled Mashal. The sheikh has declared:

"Our brothers in Palestine have sacrificed many lives as well as much efforts and blood. The Palestinian people proved, in the first Intifada and in the second Intifada, that we spare nothing for our cause. We have seen this among the old and the young, men and women. . . . We have seen these martyrdom operations, in which these young people took their lives in their hands and cared not whether they took death or whether death took them. [We also have seen] mothers receiving their martyred sons . . . with cries of joy and celebration. Similarly, the man [the martyr's father] refuses to accept condolences on the death of his son, saying "Congratulate me, do not comfort me."

40. At the start of the war, the Shiites threw rice at Israeli soldiers out of gratitude for Israel ending the Palestinians' "state within a state" in southern Lebanon. When Israel stayed too long, however, Hizbollah used suicide car bombs against the Israeli military and fired rockets into northern Israeli towns, thereby claiming credit for Israel's unilateral exit in 2000.

41. Jimmy Carter, "Don't Punish the Palestinians," *Washington Post*, February 19, 2006.

42. Palestinian Center for Policy Survey and Research, http://www.pcpsr.org; An-Najah National University Opinion Polls and Survey Studies Center, http://www.najah.edu/nnu_portal/index.php?page=137&lang=en.

43. Fouad Ajami, "Lebanon's Soldiers of Virtue," *Wall Street Journal*, July 23, 2008.

44. Ibid.

CHAPTER ELEVEN

1. John J. Mearsheimer and Stephen M. Walt, *The Israel Lobby and U.S. Foreign Policy* (New York: Farrar, Straus and Giroux, 2007), p. 50.

2. Ibid., p. 49.

3. David Sanger, "Bush Administration Releases Images to Bolster Its Claims About Syrian Reactor," *New York Times*, April 25, 2008.

4. Khaled Abu Toameh, "Arab World Fed Up with Hizbollah," *Jerusalem Post*, July 18, 2006.

5. http://www.spa.gov.sa/English/details.php?id=375423.

6. http://memri.org/bin/articles.cgi?Page=countries&Area=lebanon&ID=IA43708.

7. Ibid.

8. August 4, 2008, column in the liberal Arab e-journal *Elaph*.

9. In 1995 Egypt did make a diplomatic effort to curb Israel's reputed nuclear arsenal, but this failed; the abandoned effort underscores the idea that Egypt does not feel an existential threat from Israel.

10. A senior Israeli official who had met Putin told us this.

11. Mubarak press conference on October 8, 2000, http://www.presidency.gov .eg/html/8October2000_press.html.

12. Thomas Friedman, "Syria's Tactical Leap into the Peace Process," *New York Times*, July 21, 1991.

13. Mearsheimer and Walt, p. 50.

14. Ibid.

15. *New York Times*, March 9, 1986. Retired U.S. Air Force general George Keegan compared the intelligence contribution of Israel to "more than five CIAs." He said, "The ability of the U.S. Air Force in particular, and the Army in general, to defend whatever position it has in NATO owes more to the Israeli intelligence input than it does to any single source of intelligence, be it satellite reconnaissance, be it technology intercept, or what have you."

16. Perhaps the most famous act of intelligence sharing occurred in 1956, when an Israeli spy in the Eastern Bloc obtained Nikita Khrushchev's famed secret speech denouncing the crimes of his predecessor, Joseph Stalin.

17. Dore Gold, *Understanding the US-Israel Alliance*, Jerusalem Center for Public Affairs, September 2007.

18. Mearsheimer and Walt, p. 52.

19. Michael Oren, *Power, Faith and Fantasy: America in the Middle East 1776 to the Present* (New York: W.W. Norton, 2007), p. 13.

20. Steven Spiegel, *The Other Arab-Israeli Conflict: Making America's Middle East Policy from Truman to Reagan* (Chicago: University of Chicago Press, 1985), p. 11.

21. Moshe Davis, *With Eyes Toward Zion: Scholars Colloquium on America–Holy Land Studies* (Manchester, NH: Ayer Publishing, 1977), p. 25.

CHAPTER TWELVE

1. John J. Mearsheimer, "Hans Morgenthau and the Iraq war: Realism Versus Neo-conservatism," http://mearsheimer.uchicago.edu/pdfs/A0037.pdf.

2. http://people-press.org/questions/?qid=1684663&pid=51&ccid=50#top.

3. Condoleezza Rice, "Rethinking the National Interest," *Foreign Affairs* (July/August 2008).

4. Joshua Muravchik, "Bringing Democracy to the Arab World," *Journal of Current History* (January 1, 2004).

5. Ibid.

6. Thomas Carothers, "The Fallacy of Sequencing," *Journal of Democracy* (January 2007).

7. Rice, "Rethinking."

8. Bush press conference at White House, January 26, 2006. Available at http://www.whitehouse.gov/news/releases/2006/01/20060126.html.

9. At a press conference at the White House on March 10, 2005, White House spokesman Scott McClellan was asked about the U.S. view on the participation of Hizbollah in the upcoming elections. He replied,

> "We want to see free and fair elections, without outside intimidation and outside interference. And we want all Lebanese people, from all walks of life, to participate in those elections. And I think that experience shows that when people are able to choose their leaders, they choose people who are committed to improving their lives, not terrorists. And I think experience has shown that.

> "But our view on Hezbollah has not changed. Our focus remains on working with the international community to make sure that Syria gets out of Lebanon, so that the parliamentary elections in May can proceed forward in a free and fair way."

After the follow-up question, McClellan suggested that the United States has not given up on disarmament as a principle, but made it clear that this was not going to be something that the United States would push now:

> "Well, again, this is not about Hezbollah, this is about ensuring that the Lebanese people have free and fair elections. And in terms of 1559, it also calls for the disarming of militias. I mean, that's spelled out in 1559. But that's why free and fair elections are so important, because when you have free and fair elections, you see the power of democracy. People will step forward and choose leaders committed to improving their lives. And experience shows us that. We see that in elections all across the world. http://www.whitehouse.gov/news/releases/2005/03/20050310-2.html.

10. Tamara Cofman Wittes, *Freedom's Unsteady March: America's Role in Building Arab Democracy* (Washington, DC: Brookings Institution, 2008), p. 85.

11. Nour was still in prison in the fall of 2008; Mubarak contends that the matter rests in the courts, which are paid in no small measure by the regime.

12. Author interview with Hala Mustafa on September 1, 2008.

13. Speech by Martin Kramer on September 19, 2005, at the Center for Strategic and International Studies, in Washington, DC. http://sandbox.blog-city.com/islamists_of_all_kinds_and_alastair_crooke.htm.

14. Wittes, p. 90, writes that 70 percent of early funding went to government agencies: "Programs that actually supported either the capacities or the actual activities of Arab civic groups always represented a small portion of its overall funding."

15. Barry Rubin, *The Long War for Freedom: The Arab Struggle for Democracy in the Middle East* (New York: John Wiley and Sons, 2006).

AFTERWORD

1. Speech by Iran expert Mehdi Khalaji at the Washington Institute for Near East Policy, February 5, 2010.
2. Cvach speech at the Washington Institute for Near East Policy, February 5, 2010.
3. Obama Inauguration Speech, January 20, 2009.
4. "France says U.N. Must Take Tough Action Against Iran," Reuters, January 22, 2010.
5. "Merkel Backs More Sanctions Against Iran," Associated Press, January 18, 2010.
6. Press conference of Secretary of State Hillary Rodham Clinton, January 29, 2010, http://www.state.gov/secretary/rm/2010/01/136159.htm.
7. CNN's Jill Dougherty's interview with Secretary of State Clinton on January 28, 2010.

Index